D1826552

Ecocritical Theory

Under the Sign of Nature: Explorations in Ecocriticism

Ecocritical Theory

NEW EUROPEAN APPROACHES

Edited by Axel Goodbody and Kate Rigby

UNIVERSITY OF VIRGINIA PRESS   CHARLOTTESVILLE AND LONDON

University of Virginia Press
© 2011 by the Rector and Visitors of the University of Virginia
All rights reserved
Printed in the United States of America on acid-free paper

First published 2011

9 8 7 6 5 4 3 2 1

LIBRARY OF CONGRESS CATALOGING-IN-PUBLICATION DATA

Ecocritical theory : new European approaches / edited by Axel Goodbody
and Kate Rigby.
    p. cm. — (Under the sign of nature: explorations in ecocriticism)
Includes bibliographical references and index.
ISBN 978-0-8139-3135-7 (cloth : alk. paper) — ISBN 978-0-8139-3148-7 (pbk. : alk.
paper) — ISBN 978-0-8139-3163-0 (ebk.)
    1. Ecocriticism—Europe. I. Goodbody, Axel, 1950– II. Rigby, Catherine E.
PN98.E36E36 2011
809'.9336—dc22

                                              2011011294

Contents

Acknowledgements

The initial impetus for this essay collection came from Patrick Murphy, and so it is to him that our first thanks are due. We are also very grateful to Boyd Zenner of the University of Virginia Press for her faith in the volume; our anonymous readers for their encouraging comments and helpful recommendations; Susan Murray for her scrupulous editorial work; and all members of the production team at UVA Press for their collaboration in realizing the finished product. The Australian Research Council and the School of English, Communications and Performance Studies at Monash University provided welcome financial support for further editorial assistance, which was ably carried out by Elyse Rider, David Lane, and Gene Flenady. Last, but by no means least, we would like to thank all the contributors for their patience and cooperation in the finalization of the volume.

The original French version of Luce Irigaray's essay was first published as "La democratie ne peu se passer d'une culture de la difference" in *Illusio* 4 (Autumn 2007): 9–20; and the translation was commissioned specifically for this volume. Some parts of Anne Elvey's essay have appeared previously in chapter 2 of her monograph *The Matter of the Text: Material Engagements between Luke and the Five Senses* (Sheffield: Sheffield Phoenix, 2011) and are reproduced with permission of the author and Sheffield Phoenix.

Ecocritical Theory

Introduction

"From its inception ecocriticism adopted a belligerent attitude towards critical theory."[1] This is the opening gambit of John Parham's article entitled "The Poverty of Ecocritical Theory" in the ecocritical special issue of *New Formations*, a major British journal of culture, theory, and politics. Edited by Wendy Wheeler and Hugh Dunkerley, "Earthographies" joins a number of other recent publications, including Catrin Gersdorf and Sylvia Mayer's collection *Nature in Literary and Cultural Studies* and several new monographs, such as those of Kevin Hutchings, Dana Phillips, and Timothy Morton (and, we might add immodestly, Axel Goodbody and Kate Rigby), which signal that the alleged ecocritical antipathy to theory is on the wane. This is in our view a welcome development, and one to which this volume seeks to contribute.

Yet there is a sense in which the oft-repeated allegation that, until recently, ecocriticism has been universally atheoretical is misleading. For one thing, it overlooks some valuable early forays into ecocritical theorization, such as those of Patrick Murphy, who effectively harnessed Bakhtinian dialogics to the practice of ecofeminist criticism, and SueEllen Campbell, who was among the first to discern some significant points of confluence between poststructuralist critique and the kind of deep ecological thinking that informs much contemporary American nature writing. More generally, though, the charge of ecocritical theory-phobia fails to recognize the theoretical moment that is implicit in the admittedly widespread rejection of the then dominant mode of critical or cultural theory by most first-wave ecocritics. As Terry Eagleton avers in *After Theory*—a work that is itself eminently theoretical—theory "comes about when we are forced into a new self-consciousness about what we are doing. It is a symptom of the fact that we can no longer take those practices for granted."[2] If this is so, then Cheryll Glotfelty's insistence in the introduction to the first ecocriticism reader that, at a time when "earth's life support systems were under stress," it was simply unconscionable to continue with literary critical "business as usual" must be seen to mark a crucial point of departure for ecocritical theory.[3]

In the hip world of North American literary and cultural studies where ecocriticism was to enjoy its first efflorescence, "business as usual" was dominated by a set of theoretical approaches drawn largely from French poststructuralist and postmodernist thought, which purported to be subversive (as they certainly once were), but which had come to represent, as Eagleton observes, "a rather stifling orthodoxy" that seemed to offer no point of entry for ecological concerns.[4] In this context, it is hardly surprising that the theoretical space opened up by ecocriticism was, in the first place, largely antipathetical to theory in its then prevalent modality. Thus, for example, in his first work of ecocriticism, Jonathan Bate expressed his exasperation with the doctrinaire linguistic constructivism of New Historicist Romanticism studies by proclaiming that it was "profoundly unhelpful to say 'There is no nature' at a time when our most urgent need is to address and redress the consequences of human civilization's insatiable desire to consume the products of the earth."[5]

And yet, as Laurence Coupe succinctly puts it in the introduction to his *Green Studies Reader*, "in order to defend nature," as most ecocritics seek to do, they also need to "debate 'Nature.'"[6] In other words, the ecocritical objective of lending salience to what David Abram helpfully termed the "more-than-human world" within literary and cultural studies necessitates, among other things, a critique of inherited notions of "nature," and thereby also "culture," to which said "nature" is always implicitly opposed. In its very resistance to "theory," then, ecocriticism cannot avoid assuming the burden of theoretical reflection that this resistance itself entails. The pressing question then becomes not how to escape from theory, but which path of theoretical reflection to pursue. Coupe offers some possibilities by including in his *Reader* texts by a number of European philosophers and cultural theorists, including Kate Soper, Raymond Williams, Theodor Adorno, Max Horkheimer, and Martin Heidegger (to whom Bate himself turned in seeking to offer a more theoretically reflected model of ecocritical practice in *The Song of the Earth*). By and large, however, it is true to say that the "ecocritical insurgency," as Lawrence Buell terms it,[7] has so far failed to take advantage of the powerful and varied means of critique supplied by European philosophy, such as are presented in this volume.

If there is such a thing as European ecocriticism, its distinctive features might be sought in a number of dimensions. First, geographically, in that it is likely to be primarily concerned with cultural landscapes, with the pastoral rather than wilderness, given the shaping impact of relatively dense popula-tions on the land over the centuries, and hence with a largely domesticated and, in places such as the Low Countries, even "artificial" nature depen-dent for its survival on human agency. This may make European thinkers more open to perspectives departing from traditional ecocritical assump-tions about the dichotomy of nature and culture, and to conceiving of nature as a cultural responsibility and project. Second, European thinking about the natural environment is characterized by a historical rupture in the associa-tion of nature with national identity which still plays such an important role in the United States. The discrediting of local belonging, which is commonly regarded as one of the principal foundations of environmental conscious-ness in America, by its appropriation in the Nazi ideology of Blood and Soil was of course felt most strongly in Germany after the Second World War. But in France and Britain too, committed environmentalists have had to dis-tance themselves from problematic traditions associated with notions such as that of the organic community. Some consequences of this are arguably regrettable; others have been enriching: reluctance of academic critics to engage positively with texts with overt political implications on the one hand, but enhanced critical self-reflection on the other. And third, European ecocriticism takes inspiration from the proximity of the Continent's diverse languages, societies, and cultures. Its many sociopolitical structures, images, and narratives have prompted awareness of the relativity of cultural values and understandings of human interaction with the natural environment.

The contributions to this volume draw on traditions of thinking about nature and culture and about the role of literature and the arts in shaping and reshaping this thinking which arose in European Romanticism, but their primary focus is on thinkers of the twentieth century. They explore approaches ranging from Russian structuralism to German phenomenology, from British Marxism to French feminism, from poststructuralism and re-ception theory to chaos theory and biosemiotics. In some cases (for example, the essays on Heidegger and Bakhtin), they present new aspects of bodies of thought whose relevance for ecocritical practice has already begun to be explored elsewhere. In others, they introduce emerging fields and develop-ments in ecotheory in continental Europe which have so far gained limited exposure in the English-speaking world.

Selection is unavoidable in undertakings of this kind, but we hope that the volume succeeds in providing a general orientation for nonspecialists without sacrificing the detailed examination of individual thinkers neces-sary to inform future ecocritical analysis. To cover all areas of European thinking relevant to ecocritical theory and practice was not our aim; rather, we sought to present those theories and approaches which appeared to us and to our contributors to offer the greatest potential for innovative readings of literature and, by extension, other forms of cultural production. Our contributors were given the task of providing an introduction to a thinker, theory, or approach, explaining key concepts, and demonstrating their significance through practical application to a text or texts. However, the subject matter has been allowed to determine the balance between theory and practice in the individual essays. We are delighted to be able to include an original contribution by one of the leading voices in contemporary feminist theory, Luce Irigaray: her essay is followed by a commentary setting it in the context of her work in general and of ecofeminist theory.

The essays are grouped under five headings which reflect focuses of critical concern: Memory and Politics; Culture, Society, and Anthropology; Phenomenology; Ethics and Otherness; Models from Physics and Biology. Each essay stands alone, but the order in which they are presented works broadly from early ideas to more recent ones, and from foundational to increasingly complex systems of thought. A number of themes cut across these groupings, linking the essays in different sections of the volume: eco-aesthetics is for instance discussed by Müller as well as Rigby; intertextuality by Goodbody, Murphy, and Elvey; the language of nature by Müller, Westling, and Rigby; and metaphor by Müller and Westling. Shared concern with nostalgia, the body, and image, myth, and narrative, and engagement with thinkers including Darwin, von Uexküll, Benjamin, Curtius, and Prigogine can be traced through the index. The authors of the literary works discussed are also listed in the index, so that they can be readily identified and accessed.

The essays in the first section of the book are devoted to memory and the politics of memory. Kate Soper's opening call for a reappraisal of Romantic thinking and a practice of "avant-garde nostalgia" as a politically progressive cultural strategy is followed by Catriona Sandilands's discussion of Walter Benjamin's relevance for ecocriticism. Martin Ryle reflects on underlying tensions between the quest for political justice and tendentially backward-looking care for the rural in Raymond Williams's landmark study *The Country and the City*, while Axel Goodbody argues that ecocriticism can benefit from adopting perspectives on place developed in cultural memory studies.

Romanticism's particular achievement is, according to Kate Soper, the expression it gives to the otherness of nature while reminding us of the cultural mediation of all means of access to it. The fusion of yearning for immersion in the natural world with awareness of its unreachable otherness which we find in Keats or Wordsworth finds a philosophical equivalent in Adorno's aesthetics, in which natural beauty is both a projection of our desire for reconciliation onto nature and a utopian gesture toward a world in which humanity would enjoy a harmonious egalitarian existence. Soper defends progressive, "avant-garde" nostalgia as a Romantic remembering and mourning of what is irretrievable, but one directed toward an emancipatory future. It reflects on past experience in ways which highlight what we are deprived of in the present, and stimulate desire for a better future. She also advocates the discursive and visual representation in literature and art of an alternative hedonism, avoiding excessive material consumption.

A rather different way of relating to the past, and specifically to the past (and potential future) that inheres in the present, is explored by Catriona Sandilands in relation to Walter Benjamin's *Arcades Project*. This extraordinary and (perhaps necessarily) incomplete text is composed out of the detritus of commodity capitalism in the form of fragments of experience gleaned from the nineteenth-century arcades of Paris during the time of their decline in the 1920s and brought together in surprising new constellations in the guise of the "dialectical image," within which the possibility of a different kind of future might be glimpsed. Sandilands indicates how this model of cultural criticism might be deployed to illuminate the cultural politics of current environmental conditions, and in particular, the place of nature in contemporary forms of commodity fetishism (with which nature writing and ecocriticism are in some ways complicit). Her contribution concludes with a discussion of how Benjamin himself prefigures such a materialist ecocritical project in his recollections of his own urban nature experiences in *Berlin Childhood around 1900*.

Martin Ryle shows how the British Marxist critic Raymond Williams accommodated rural and urban values in a complex dialectical perspective in his theoretical writing. *The Country and the City* displays no interest in the nonhuman, and opens with a powerful critique of texts mixing realistic observation with myths concealing structures of oppression and exploitation. However, the later chapters of the book give an appreciative account of the depiction of the displacement and ruptures of history in the countryside by major British novelists such as Thomas Hardy and D. H. Lawrence. Ryle comments on the significance of border country as a theme in Williams's writing. It is depicted as a privileged site of a structure of feeling with radical potential resulting from the impact of modernity on popular traditional forms of life. Ryle also discusses shorter pieces written by Williams in the early 1980s, in which he traces Williams's growing recognition of the potential of "retrospective radicalism" as a form of rural resistance to socialism's self-understanding as completing the capitalist project of mode through ever-greater mastery of nature.

Axel Goodbody notes that while memory studies would apȷ concerned with politics rather than nature, and with time rather ᵗ it shares with ecocriticism a central concern with place and belonging. "Places/sites of memory" form the focus of many texts interweaving identity construction with interrogation of our interaction with nature. In both fiction and nonfiction, symbolic "figurations of memory" also provide nodes of intertextual reference, which often possess ecosocial significance. The memory studies focus on the adaptation of existing tropes and *topoi* in a context of collective value negotiation, and identity construction can yield new insights into the meaning of literary representations of nature. Two texts are examined, an autobiographical novel by the Austrian writer Peter Handke, and a short work of poetic prose by the East German Volker Braun. While the first describes a mythical Slovenian rural community living in utopian harmony with nature as an antidote to the repressive world of the author's childhood, the second presents East Germany's opencast coal mines as a dystopian place of memory.

The second section of the volume contains three contributions relating to one of the most influential approaches in contemporary German literary studies, cultural anthropology. Timo Müller compares two theoretical approaches building on the ecocritical dimension of Wolfgang Iser's reception theory, Hartmut Böhme's eco-aesthetic, and Hubert Zapf's conception of literature as a medium for cultural ecology. There follow essays by Linda Williams on how the theorist of civilization Norbert Elias sees the development of our relationship with the nonhuman world, and by Laura Dassow Walls on the application of Bruno Latour's thinking on modernity and post-modernity for ecocritical textual analysis.

Timo Müller argues that Wolfgang Iser's groundbreaking work in reception theory and cultural anthropology in the 1970s and 1980s provided the basis for Germany's principal contributions to ecocritical theory to date. The cultural theorist Hartmut Böhme calls for a reexamination of the archive of literary images of human beings in their interaction with nature, for this constitutes a vital resource for our renaturalization. Müller shows how Edgar Allan Poe's tale "The Fall of the House of Usher" articulates the language of nature by interweaving linguistic elements that address us bodily and immediately. The second approach examined here, Hubert Zapf's fusion of cultural ecology (rooted in Gregory Bateson) with textual criticism, offers a poststructuralist variant of literary anthropology: literature revitalizes the cultural system by condensing, undermining, and transforming elements of public discourse in symbols and metaphors. In further readings from Poe's story, Müller demonstrates the usefulness of both models, which accord literature a crucial mediating function between the cultural system and its imaginary alternatives.

Linda Williams asks whether the conception of modern human subjectivity in Norbert Elias's theory of civilization as unaware of its substantive
connectedness with others includes a lack of awareness of our dependence
on the nonhuman world. For Elias, the civilization process is based on self-
control and self-restraint. The former balance between instrumental approaches to the natural world and forms of knowledge recognizing our
interdependency is being lost. Writing in his late work of the need for a new
epistemology that accepts nature's materiality and extradiscursivity, Elias
suggests that forms of secondary involvement have the potential to act as a
counterbalance to instrumentalism. This leads Williams to consider the
relationship between human beings and companion animals. Empathy with
companion species may be crucial to our responses to other nonhuman
species. Examining a recording of a dressage event on YouTube, she notes
the commentator's and spectators' belief that the horse is "dancing," that is,
that it is an agent consciously contributing to and even enjoying the performance. This might be wishful thinking. Yet the scenario is a valuable
vignette of the human envisaging itself in partnership with animal alterity.

In the concluding essay in the section, Laura Dassow Walls extends
Bruno Latour's theorizing of modernity into literary territory. Modernity
may be powered by a metaphysics of command and control, and assumes a
radical separation between nature and culture, science and literature, but we
have never, in this sense, been modern. In practice, Latour has shown, the
empirical sciences have woven together nature, discourse, society, and politics. Dassow Walls's Latourian reading of Emerson's *Nature* (1836) and Thoreau's *Walden* (1854) shows that while Emerson created a conception of
"Nature" as limitless resource, and of science as a "cudgel of eternal truth"
objectively settling all disputes, Thoreau already began imagining the limits of this modern constitution and outlining alternatives. Throughout the
1850s, his writings weave the human and the nonhuman together, naturalizing the social and socializing the natural, in an actor-network of humans and
nonhumans. It is the task of literary criticism to investigate how works like
Walden register the fact that we have always been involved in the managing,
combination, and negotiation of human and nonhuman agencies.

The third section of the book, which is devoted to phenomenology, consists
of essays reexamining the significance for ecocritical work of the philosophies of Martin Heidegger and Maurice Merleau-Ponty, and introducing the
ecophenomenology of Gernot Böhme, brother of the cultural theorist Hartmut Böhme discussed earlier by Timo Müller. Trevor Norris opens with
Heidegger's challenge to reconceive being-in-the-world as an alternative to
the instrumental approach to nature which has led to the environmental

crisis. Whereas previous ecocritics such as Jonathan Bate have been primarily concerned with late writings of Heidegger's such as "The Question Concerning Technology," Norris focuses on the earlier, interwar essay "The Origin of the Work of Art," and his poetic quest for truth as unconcealment, via a mode of being as "care," that is, involvement in a project alongside and engaged with other beings. The artwork is here envisaged as a field of being which allows us to gain insight into relations between things, people, and environment which we fail to note in everyday life. Norris finds similar thoughts on art and poetry in the novels of D. H. Lawrence. Passages in *Women in Love* are shown to correspond to Heidegger's conception of the language of poetry as a dense, opaque, and enigmatic form of revelation. Like Heidegger, Lawrence subscribes to a view of poetry as a presencing-by-absencing, and a call to contemplative attention to embodiment.

Louise Westling begins by noting how phenomenology broke with Cartesian mind/matter dualism and redefined the place of humans in the natural world by turning from abstract idealism to lived human experience. However, she argues, Merleau-Ponty differs from Husserl and Heidegger, who continued to assume human superiority to other life forms, in stressing human immersion in the natural world. He develops a unique notion of coevolution of all living beings and an ontology of "wild being." Westling shows how Merleau-Ponty is also concerned with the extent to which our experience of the natural world is mediated by human perception and culture, and with the participation of language, because of its physical properties, in the flesh of the world. Building on Merleau-Ponty's conception of philosophy and literature as authentic uses of language articulating the bond between materiality and the world of ideas, Westling finds in poetry and fiction (exemplified by a short story of Eudora Welty's and a poem by W. H. Auden) passages relating to embodiment and the intertwining of human and animal which constitute ecophenomenological descriptions of the world.

Kate Rigby's contribution is concerned with the ecological aesthetics developed by Gernot Böhme since the 1980s, which builds on both Adorno's critical theory and the New Phenomenology of Hermann Schmitz. Böhme's central tenet is that nature must be envisaged as an undertaking that lies before us, a cultural project directed toward transforming our industrially degraded environment into a humane living space. This transformation can draw on a knowing of nature through shared physicality and relationality. Art and literature have a key role to play in discovering other-than-human nature and recovering our own naturality. Böhme's theorizing is focused on "atmospheres," or moods evoked by places and experienced corporeally, and how they can be cultivated and developed. The arts, he writes, can serve as a field for public training in the experience, articulation, and production of atmospheres. By translating inchoate impressions into articulate speech, literature in particular can raise bodily experience of atmosphere into a transformative social practice. Poetry depicts and produces atmospheres, evoking bodily responses, as Rigby demonstrates with reference to a poem by the nineteenth-century Australian author Charles Harpur.

The fourth section, which is devoted to ethics and otherness, opens with essays by Patrick Murphy, Timothy Morton, and Anne Elvey on the Russian philosopher, literary critic, and semiotician Mikhail Bakhtin, the Lithuanian-born Jew and French philosopher and religious thinker Emmanuel Levinas, and the Bulgarian-French philosopher, critic, psychoanalyst, and feminist Julia Kristeva. These are followed by an original piece by the Belgian feminist, philosopher, and cultural theorist Luce Irigaray, and an essay on the ecological dimension of her thinking by Christopher Cohoon.

The focus of Patrick Murphy's essay is on "anothering" and its ethical implications. Murphy, who has explored the relevance of Bakhtin's dialogics for the study of nature-oriented literature in *Literature, Nature, and Other*, takes as his starting point the emphasis in Bakhtin's early writing on the responsibility of the speaker/writer for the impact of their words on (human and nonhuman) others. Bakhtin asserts that writers must be willing to identify their observational point of view as one perspective among others. The ecological crisis is due in part, Murphy argues, to societies and individuals not allowing nonhuman others to participate in generating our perceptions of ourselves as actors. Seeing oneself through the eyes of animals, plants, or inanimate objects is a prerequisite for ethical interaction with the rest of the world. Different styles and genres of literature and techniques such as sincerity, internal persuasiveness, comic structure, and chronotopes all have a role to play in shaping the response to nature of diverse groups of readers.

Tim Morton's quest for a way of grounding ecological concern and our intervention in nature that is more reliable than popular sentiment leads him to Levinas, at the heart of whose philosophy lies personal ethical responsibility toward the other. For Levinas, the self is only possible by means of a recognition of the other that implies respect for and carries responsibility toward what is irreducibly different. Morton finds Levinas's conception of the epiphanic encounter with the other mirrored in the appearance of the albatross to the sailors in Coleridge's "Rime of the Ancient Mariner." He explores the possibility of employing Levinasian terms such as the "thereness" of nature and "exteriority" as a way to read the poem as an allegory of the fact that our existence is always coexistence with other life forms, a fact that should profoundly disturb us and awaken us to ecological responsibility.

What leaves the wedding guest "of sense forlorn" at the end of the poem is the traumatic intimacy with the other. The albatross is an unnerving reminder of our unbearable dependence on a "nature" which at bottom is nothing other than life forms themselves.

Ecocritical approaches to biblical interpretation have so far tended to focus on the principle of ecological justice, the question of nature's intrinsic worth, or the retrieval of an earth perspective from the text. Anne Elvey uses the conception of intertextuality in Julia Kristeva's *Revolution in Poetic Language* as a framework for engaging ecocritically with Bibles as material artifacts. On the one hand, Bibles are sites of interconnectedness between plants, minerals, bodies, and languages. On the other, biblical language is full of traces of the maternal body from which all reading subjects have emerged. It is rich in the language of desire, rhythm, and imitation celebrated by Kristeva as the "semiotic." The various layers of intertextuality she describes, ranging from explicit allusions to sources to what has been repressed in it, are identified in a discussion of the parable of the Sower from St. Luke's Gospel. Elvey ends by suggesting ways in which a scriptural world increasingly bereft of its material context can be enriched again by reading practices embedding the text in its very materiality in the more-than-human earth community.

The issue of gender which is present in Kristeva moves center stage in Luce Irigaray's essay "There Can Be No Democracy without a Culture of Difference," which appeared in French in 2006 and has been translated for this volume. Irigaray argues that the erasure of gender which has gone hand in hand with the suppression of the body has contributed toward the emergence of totalitarian politics and the destruction of the planet. The invention of the category of the "neuter" and its substitution for the masculine have permitted a focus on quantity at the expense of qualitative difference, and created a universe in which human identity is defined by domination and material appropriation. Calling for the cultivation of a "coexistence in difference" with nature, rooted in recognition of our separate sexuate identities, she suggests at the end of her essay that the study of myth and literature can contribute to this project. Antigone, guardian of spiritual principles including bodily existence and the matriarchal tradition of returning the body to nature in death, invites us to learn to coexist and respect difference relative to our natural belonging and the values it represents.

Christopher Cohoon demonstrates the presence of environmental thought in Irigaray's wider work, and confirms her importance for ecophilosophy and ecocritics. Though gender and social issues stand center stage in her writing, she often addresses them by appealing to nature. Cohoon pursues three

dimensions of ecological attunement in works such as *Sexes and Genealogies,
Thinking the Difference,* and *I Love to You* as well as "There Can Be No
Democracy." The first is an ecofeminist appreciation of the historical oppression of women as bound up with the degradation of the earth. The second is
her sustained engagement with Sophocles' *Antigone* and its interlinked representations of women and nature. Finally, he argues, Irigaray's vision of a
"positive becoming" of femininity is inseparable from her understanding of
nature and its relation to human culture. Her proposed "return to nature,"
which has puzzled many feminists, is explained in the context of her insistence on sexual difference: her hope is that this return to a reinterpreted
nature will enable women to discover a way to cultivate a "natural belonging"
that has yet to find adequate expression.

The five contributions in the final section of the volume present approaches
united by their erosion of the nature-culture dualism. Two derive from
systems and chaos theory: Hannes Bergthaller and Heather Sullivan discuss
Niklas Luhmann and Ilya Prigogine respectively. A further two stem from
postmodern scientific theory: Serpil Oppermann writes on the new paradigm which has emerged from quantum physics, postmodern theory, and
deep ecology, while Mark Lussier explores parallels between William Blake's
poems and the thinking of Deleuze and Guattari. In the last essay, Wendy
Wheeler demonstrates how biosemiotic investigations into the communicative processes that are inherent in all biological systems enable a new understanding of human cultural creativity.

    Hannes Bergthaller begins by pointing out an unacknowledged contra-
diction in Aldo Leopold's thinking in the *Sand County Almanac.* The land
community is assumed to work because each creature's blindness comple-
ments that of the others. But human beings, who have perceptual limitations
like other animals, are being asked to act differently, namely to subordinate
the interests of their species to those of the whole. This undermines the idea
of nature as a self-regulating system. After tracing the emergence of cybernetics, which sought to solve this very problem in the natural sciences, in the
first part of his essay, Bergthaller examines Luhmann's writing as the most
sustained, provocative, and philosophically ambitious attempt to develop
second-order systems theory into a theory of social systems. While acknowledging an ecological crisis, Luhmann rejected what he saw as the environmental movement's simplistic moralizing. Modern society is characterized
by a functional differentiation which effectively precludes its realignment
toward ecological imperatives. Rather than expecting literature to raise environmental consciousness and change society, ecocritics should examine

how environmental thinkers observe, critique their distinctions, and note their blind spots.

Serpil Oppermann argues that ecocentric postmodern theory not only provides the best way out of the epistemological crisis responsible for today's environmental situation, but also offers a theoretical model of relevance to literary critics. The most rigorous postmodern formulations of our relationship with nature are to be found in the new physics of quantum theory. Drawing on David Bohm and others, Oppermann observes that nature responds in accordance with the theory with which we approach it. We therefore need a new, less fragmented "way of doing science," and "a new kind of consciousness" freeing our discursive formulations from the misleading dichotomies of anthropocentrism and instrumentalism. Reconstructive postmodern theory acknowledges the inseparability of the world "out there" from the observing subject, and the fact that reality in its quantum states exhibits itself as an undivided whole. Ecological postmodern fiction combines literary realism with metafictional narrative strategies, thereby presenting the natural world as both object of experience and discursive construct. Jeanette Winterson's novel *Gut Symmetries* projects a holistic vision of reality while citing multiple scientific and other discourses problematizing binary thought.

Ecocriticism is, according to Heather Sullivan, part of a general shift away from describing our interactions with the world in terms of dichotomies, whose exemplary theorization may be found in Ilya Prigogine's open-system, nonequilibrium thermodynamics, with its conception of open flows of matter, systems of exchange, and reciprocal shaping. Postmodern science has come to regard nature and culture as hybrid forms with permeable boundaries, and to dissolve subjects into embodiments, situations and affinities, and human agency into an entanglement of cultural and physical pulses. The body and nonhuman nature are enabling conditions: we construct, but are simultaneously constructed by the world. This approach informs Sullivan's reading of Goethe's *Faust*, not as the tragedy of masculine power-seeking and instrumental exploitation of the environment, but as a complex work undermining such interpretation through its framing of the protagonist's choices in cosmic situations, its focus on Mephistophelean influence, and the fluidity of its water imagery. It is no accident that Goethe inspired pioneers of chaos theory such as Prigogine and Gleick: his great play portrays the provocative in-between of hybridity as affinity.

The "experiential assemblage" which Deleuze and Guattari describe as characterizing all encounters with reality in the tenth chapter of *A Thousand*

Plateaus is equated by Mark Lussier with an ecological mode of consciousness involving giving up traditional notions of a discrete self. Fibers spanning the boundaries of self and alterity are among the many tropes from chaos theory, high-energy physics, and quantum cosmology in Deleuze's writing. Mentality and materiality merge, dissolving selfhood in a multiplicity of varying relations. "Becoming-animal" through unselfing facilitates ecological inhabitation. How, Lussier asks, can this mutual determination of subject and object be articulated so as to foster ecological consciousness? William Blake's rhythmic poetry, and his composite of word and image, provide a model. Blake, who recognized the deadening effects of Enlightenment rationalism on the more-than-human, and the role played by self-consciousness in this alienated rationalism, anticipated the interconnectedness, nonlocalizability, and indeterminacy that Deleuze sees as the ontological basis for transcendental empiricism. The final plates of *Jerusalem* show the awakening of awareness at the position of the other, through a sequence of acts of becoming-animal, -woman, and -other.

The field of biosemiotics has a double genesis, having emerged around the same time independently in both Europe and North America. In her contribution, Wendy Wheeler expands the geographical bounds of the volume by examining the thought of the major American originator of the biosemiotic approach, Charles Sanders Pierce, alongside that of his European counterpart, Jacob von Uexküll. In particular, Wheeler focuses on Pierce's notion of "abduction" (the process whereby signs we have read and interpreted below the level of consciousness give rise to those odd hunches or sudden intuitions that enable new understandings to be formulated) as a key to understanding human cultural creativity and its continuity with the evolutionary processes evident in biophysical systems. With reference also to Heidegger's reworking of von Uexküll's concept of *Umwelt* in relation to human *poiesis* or artistic making, Wheeler argues that the peculiar value of art lies in its ability to cause us to reflect on the complexities of human meaning-making itself. Her contribution concludes with a consideration of how this is accomplished in two recent British novels, A. S. Byatt's *Angels and Insects* and Ian McEwan's *Black Dogs*.

This is by no means an exhaustive survey of European thinkers whose work is capable of providing new insights into literary texts—Derrida, Virilio, Nancy, and Agamben are among those whom we would have liked to include, had space permitted. Our purpose will, however, have been served if the volume attracts new readers to ecocritical theory and stimulates further exploration of fresh approaches.

NOTES

1. Parham, "Poverty of Ecocritical Theory," 25.
2. Eagleton, *After Theory,* 27.
3. Glotfelty and Fromm, *Ecocriticism Reader,* xvi.
4. Eagleton, *After Theory,* 222.
5. Bate, *Romantic Ecology,* 56.
6. Coupe, *Green Studies,* 5.
7. Buell, "The Ecocritical Insurgency."

MEMORY & POLITICS

Passing Glories and Romantic Retrievals: Avant-garde Nostalgia and Hedonist Renewal

This essay offers a rather more general argument than do many others in this collection. It arose out of a paper delivered to a conference entitled "Romanticism, Environment, Crisis" organized by the Centre for Romantic Studies at the University of Wales, Aberystwyth, in 2006, and its main aim is to consider the nature and extent of the relevance of Romantic thinking about nature, particularly that associated with the English Romantic poets, to our contemporary ecological "crisis." In pursuing this theme, it takes issue with simplistic interpretations of the nature philosophy attributed to Romanticism by some environmentalists. But it also resists the suggestion that Romantic understanding has nothing to offer in our current predicament, and claims instead that there are aspects of it that could be harnessed to the development of a new politics of consumption organized around more sensually rewarding and ecologically progressive conceptions of pleasure and fulfillment.

In developing these arguments, the essay draws on the dialectical approach to the ontology and aesthetic of nature developed in the philosophy of the Frankfurt school critical theorist Theodor Adorno. In that sense, although it does not offer a full or contextualized exposition and discussion of his more environmentally relevant writings (such as is to be found in the treatments given to other theorists in this collection), it does give some sense of Adorno's contribution to ecocriticism. It should be noted, too, that this is an essentially English- rather than American-oriented discussion, although its argument on the possible resources of Romantic forms of self-consciousness and imagination for rethinking the commitment to the "work and spend" economy and its consumerist dynamic applies to all affluent societies, and those aspiring to emulate them, in the era of globalization.

War, Poetry, and Commemoration

The bicentenary of the naval victory at Trafalgar that checked Bonaparte's invasion of England in 1805 was the occasion of commemorations lasting over several months, beginning with Queen Elizabeth's review of the fleet in June and mounting to their culmination with the beacon lighting on Trafalgar Day (21 October). Very feeble in contrast have been the memorials to the great flowering of Romantic poetry two hundred years ago. Preferring military to poetic glory, the nation has celebrated the immortal Nelson rather than the Immortality Ode, the feats of war rather than those of literature.

Our finest writers—and maybe particularly those of the Romantic period—are, it is true, still held in great esteem. What is more, literary and artistic work generally, some of that of the Romantics included, has been the vehicle for patriotic celebration itself or has been harnessed to that end. Romanticism has also of late become an adjunct in various ways of the British heritage industry, for example, in the millennium spectacles of the Greenwich Dome and the London Eye big wheel. As Mark Dorrian has pointed out, if Coleridge was the Romantic figure implicit in "the pleasure dome," Wordsworth is the one explicit in the London Eye, where an engraving of his poem "Composed upon Westminster Bridge, Sept. 3, 1802" faces visitors as they queue for their "flight."[1] But such qualifications apart, I am speaking here of a rather more general cultural tilt toward finding the primary sources of national pride and rejoicing in military rather than artistic achievement.[2]

This constant privileging of a bellicose patriotism over other sources of national pride is, however, but one aspect of a larger set of post-Trafalgar afflictions. For we are also, of course, now living with all the consequences of two hundred years of industrial capitalism and its progressive globalization. Our economic, social, and cultural life remains shaped throughout by the uncurbed commitment to economic growth and hence to a dynamic of production and consumption, work and spend, that is exploitative of poorer regions, and has proved hugely damaging to the environment. The forms of consumption this has encouraged are both unsustainable, and in many respects dystopian, yet despite all this, mainstream politics remains committed to technical-fix responses to everything from climate change to childhood obesity. Put the package together and one might be forgiven for claiming that Romanticism—construed in the broadest sense as a countering impulse to instrumental rationality, the dominance of the cash nexus, and the constant recourse to what Raymond Williams in *Towards 2000* has called "Plan X" (short-term, technological solutions to social problems)—has failed abjectly. For if Romanticism remains relevant today, it might seem as if it does so only as supplying the epithet for a naïvely idealist aspiration to what can never be; or else in the invocation of catastrophic sublimities and the aesthetic of the ruin: only in that sense of a world where, as Keats put it, "but to think is to be full of sorrow / And leaden-eyed despairs";[3] or else (to invoke the image of Shelley's poem on Ozymandias) in the apocalyptic contemplation of the "colossal wreck, boundless and bare" that our children's children may have to look upon and despair.[4]

Romanticism and Dialectics

Perhaps what *seems* is indeed the case, and the gloomy and elegiac cultural role is all that remains to Romanticism. I want to suggest otherwise here, and to sketch a more complex and somewhat less negative picture of its resources for us today. Thus I shall present Romantic poetry as an abidingly important dialectical asset of critical thought in our times because of the powerful expression it gives to the "otherness" and preconceptuality of "nature" even as it reminds us of the cultural mediation of all ideas about or supposed means of access to that "otherness." I shall also argue that there are elements of Romanticism understood in a broader sense that could play a role in the revisions of thinking about pleasure and the good life that I see as crucial to the furtherance of a green political agenda.

I am not implying, however, that one can trace some continuous movement of Romanticism through to its supposed *telos* in a green renaissance today, but only that there is a past of Romanticism available in a present for which it may provide some resources or inspiration.[5] Nor do I want to give the impression that I feel greatly optimistic that any more constructive Romantic revival will come to our aid. Nor, finally, do I want to endorse the rather simplistic "back to nature" responses within the environmental movement that have sometimes been associated with the Romantic critique. I refer here to the unqualified celebration of "nature" conceived as an independent site of truth, authenticity, and intrinsic value that should everywhere be preserved against the intrusion of the human and to whose superior wisdom we should now attend as a condition of any redemption.

For the Romantic influence on the ecological movement is by no means exhausted in this problematic mysticism or "back to nature" ethic, and there are less simplified and more authentically Romantic aspects of cognition and aesthetic response that are of greater relevance to our time. Indeed, the approach of much of the poetry of the period is altogether more complex, since even as it summons the otherness of nature and celebrates its independence, it also recalls us to the culturally mediating role of the summons, and to the extent of the dependence of the aesthetic response to nature on its human representation. It is a characteristic of much Romantic poetry, nota-

bly that of Wordsworth, in poems such as "Animal Tranquility and Decay,"
"Resolution and Independence," "Michael," and "Old Man Travelling," that
it reflects the pull of what I have elsewhere termed the "envy of immanence." It reflects, that is, the yearning for an immersion within the natural
world, or closeness to it, that is associated either with animality or a peasant
existence. Such poetry is also often written in a heightened awareness of the
unreachable otherness of nature and the "betrayal" involved in giving voice
to its "dumbness" and preconceptuality. Its inspiration can thus prompt a
certain intellectual self-deprecation whereby the poet expresses regret for
the self-distancing and alienation of expression itself. In "Animal Tranquility
and Decay," the old laborer is so unintrusive in his progress that "The little
hedgerow birds, / That peck along the road, regard him not"; his peace is so
perfect that "the young behold / With envy, what the Old Man hardly feels."[6]
In "Resolution and Independence," the leech gatherer is compared, on first
encounter, to a huge stone "endued with sense" and to a "sea-beast" that has
crawled out to sun itself. His silence or inarticulacy "was like a stream /
Scarce heard: nor word from word could I divide," and it is presented in
idealized contrast to the voluble angst of the poet: "I could have laughed
myself to scorn to find / In that decrepit Man so firm a mind."[7] Yet the
essential point is that poetry is being written, the alienated writer "envies"
immanence, but cannot give voice to the envy.[8]

The dialectic involved in this has received sophisticated philosophical
exposition (as opposed to poetic expression) in Theodor Adorno's work.
Adorno always presents nature as compelling for us precisely as a counter to
commodification and the dominance of our own constructions;[9] but even as
he recognizes the summons of the spontaneously given and preconceptual in
nature, he also acknowledges the extent to which what is discoverable as
beautiful or worthy in virtue of its naturalness owes its reception as such to
culture. He is as cautious about the appeal to nature as he is about the appeal
to what is cultural or historical, and he constantly uses the one to correct the
confident pronouncements of the other and vice versa. Hence his resistance
both to false and fetishizing forms of naturalization of history and to the
"enchantment of history," that is, to any view of history as a form of mastery
of or escape from nature.[10]

Of particular relevance to the understanding of the nature-culture dialectic of the Romantic text are the passages in *Aesthetic Theory* where Adorno
expands on his claim that the disinclination to talk about natural beauty "is
strongest where love of it survives." The "How beautiful!" at the sight of a
landscape, he tells us, "insults its mute language and reduces its beauty."[11]
But landscape in reality can sense no insults, and it is, of course, we who
observe and admire it and who experience any diminishment there might be

of its beauty. Speech or writing mediates, either deliberately or as an effect, that which is immediate and preconceptual, and thus renders conceptual— and in the process in some sense "betrays"—that which is as it is, and is experienced as it is, only because it cannot be spoken.[12] On the other hand, even as nature transcends expression, anyone capable of experiencing its beauty feels compelled, Adorno tells us, to speak as a way of signaling the momentary liberation it affords from the confines of the enclosure within the perceiving and representing self. One might note in this context the detachment or erasure of self-consciousness that critics have associated with Keats's "negative capability" and his aspiration to an "art of sensations rather than an art of thought."[13] Comparable, too, is Wordsworth's famous conclud- ing sentiment in the "Intimations of Immortality": "To me the meanest flower that blows can give / Thoughts that do often lie too deep for tears." What nature prompts at times is a grief beyond emotion or an understanding that transcends articulation. Speech cannot fathom it, nor in the spirit of acceptance of the unfathomable associated with "negative capability," does it even want to.[14] Yet the poetic reminder of this natural power that can reside in the "meanest flower" helps to keep alive that potency by rendering us more sensible of it.

The paradox is that one talks in order to register the beyond of nature to conceptualization; one represents it in order to capture its independence of representation. Natural beauty demands to be conceptualized, but to be conceptually determined as something that is not conceptual. It also acts as a kind of reminder of, or utopian gesture toward, a world in which humanity would enjoy a harmonious and egalitarian existence. Adorno argues, for example, that aesthetic appreciation of natural beauty recollects a world without domination. But this romance, too, is paradoxical. Not only is this a world that almost certainly never existed (so that any recollection of it could only be a fantasy), there is the further consideration that it is "through this recollection that experience dissolves back into that amorphousness out of which genius arose and for the first time became conscious of the idea of freedom that could be realised in the world free of domination."[15] A similar idea is to be found in Keats's "Ode to Autumn" in which, as Jerome McGann has put it, Keats asks us to believe in a universal "season of mists and mellow fruitfulness" because he knows that it is not true, and that so perfect an autumn is purely an "autumn of the mind."[16] According to Keats, it is only the poetic imagination that can create the image of beauty that we, who are caught up in temporality and historical contradictions, project on nature as a mirror of our desire for unity and reconciliation. Harmonious immersion in nature, Adorno suggests, is incompatible with the human consciousness that comes to an understanding of freedom and desires the release from domination. There cannot, in the end, be any "envy of immanence" because the envy itself is in contradiction to its own desire. In all this, the dialectical position on nature that is intimated by the Romantic poets and theorized by Adorno is altogether more complex and politically perceptive than that of the many nature lovers and environmentalists who have more recently emphasized the dumb-striking and ineffable qualities of natural beauty (especially wilderness) but who fail to acknowledge its dependency on subjective representation and articulation and the always aesthetically mediated quality of what we value or find beautiful in landscape.[17] They thus underestimate the contribution that human beings and their ideas make—not least, through their art, music, and literature—to the realization of the joys, and pains, occasioned by nature.

It is, moreover, only a dialectic that registers both the objective otherness and the dependency on human representation that does theoretical justice to the connection between Romantic writing and green ideals: that can fully respect the role of, for example, Romantic poetry in keeping alive a sensibility and love affair with the natural world without which our concern for its conservation is inevitably diminished. The Romantic text so conceived is not simply a pleasurable addition to or reflection of our existing ecological concerns, but is in an important sense constitutive of them. Of course, it will be objected that only a tiny minority are readers of the classic Romantic texts. This is regrettably true. The dearth of readers does not in itself invalidate claims about the role of literature in sustaining—at least for some—an environmental appreciation and concern. But it does point to the political limitations of any ecocritical project that thinks too exclusively in terms of the actual Romantic text and its readership.

Some ecocritics will accept these limits or qualifications of ecocriticism's political reach. Others seem more equivocal. In *The Song of the Earth*, for example, Jonathan Bate recognizes that there is no immediate transition from poetic text to green politics. But he also follows Heidegger in presenting what he terms "eco-poetics" as phenomenologically revelatory of a seemingly originary and ecologically redemptive "dwelling" or way of being in, or with, nature—a dwelling that is prepolitical and has nothing, so he asserts, to do with ownership or property relations, but is nonetheless not merely mythic or fantastical. Indeed, the revelation of dwelling as the harmony between nature and humanity is the basis in his work for the very large and comprehensive claims he makes (echoing Heidegger) about poetry as "saving the earth."[18]

This, however, arguably evades the question about the restrictions imposed by a limited readership of poetry because of the way it slides from an understanding of poetry as a set of texts, to an understanding of it as the

Heideggerian "saving spirit" (whereupon, of course, this "eco-poetics" defi-
nitionally becomes the name, or philosophical category, of whatever con-
trives the "saving," if there is to be a "saving," and the role of any actual
poetic texts is left obscure). In the process, too, there is a rather curious
opposition set up between "green politics" and the nonpolitical redemption
of "saving the earth."

I would argue, more modestly, that poetry in the sense of literary text
can probably do rather little in itself by way of "saving the earth" and that we
should in any case recognize that anything it can do is always conditional on
its finding readers. Accepting that truth, however, does not mean that we
should hold back from considering the possible summons for our time of
some broader aspects of the Romantic cultural outlook. It may mean only
that we have to accept that they will not always, or even generally, be
associated with a literary register or experienced in a textually anchored
form. (Or, even if it is objected that what it more accurately means is that it
is indeed, as Adorno suggested, only in art that the image of a better world is
conserved, there is still a kind of onus on the critic to continue to invoke and
rework that image.) So it is to some of the resources that Romanticism offers
in this conception to which I now turn.

Romanticism and Nostalgia

One such is the Romantic reflection on vanished or vanishing times and
spaces, and the importance of promoting this kind of retrospection in the
current context: of reconnecting with a tradition of acknowledged and la-
mented, if also always cognitively self-realizing, forms of loss. I speak in my
title of an avant-garde nostalgia, and this is obviously a provocatively contradictory notion. But I invoke it in order to capture a movement of thought
that remembers, and mourns, that which is irretrievable, but also attains to a
more complex political wisdom and energy in the memorializing process
itself. I suppose one model might indeed be found in the Immortality Ode,
with its sense that even with advanced years and the shifts of sensibility and
loss of immediacy in the response to the world, something is still retained—
some life in the embers, to use Wordsworth's image—that points to the
possibility of personal transcendence over death and destruction. Can we
think today of the poem, in this sense, as offering a kind of metaphor or
analogue of a social and collective process of transition in which a green
renaissance or transcendence is energized through the heightened sense of
what has now gone missing, but might possibly be restored in a transmuted,
less politically divisive, and more sustainable form? I am not sure. Perhaps
this is too fanciful. But certainly I would claim a Romantic dialectic in the
perspective of those theorists—Adorno again, but also Raymond Williams—

who have insisted on the links between emancipatory futures and the scrupulous remembrance of things past, both in their negative and their more
positive aspects. As Adorno has said, in explanation, if not justification,
of nostalgia:

> So long as progress, deformed by utilitarianism, does violence to the surface
> of the earth, it will be impossible—in spite of all proof to the contrary—
> completely to counter the perception that what antedates the trend is in
> its backwardness better and more humane. . . . Rationalization is not yet
> rational; the universality of mediation has yet to be transformed into living
> life; and this endows the traces of immediacy, however dubious and anti-
> quated, with the element of corrective justice. . . . If today the aesthetic
> relation to the past is poisoned by a reactionary tendency with which this
> relation is in league, an ahistorical aesthetic consciousness that sweeps aside
> the dimension of the past as rubbish is no better. Without historical remem-
> brance there would be no beauty.[19]

This emphasizes the importance of the "backward" look even as it acknowledges its fantastical dimension and the impossibility—and undesirability—
of an unmediated return to past experience. Raymond Williams, too, as
Martin Ryle points out in his essay on Williams in this volume, has warned
us against both the "simple backward look" with its patrician (and patriarchal) forms of nostalgia and the "simple progressive thrust" with its
unthinking adulation of industrial progress.[20] And both theorists would have
us see what is truly progressive as lying beyond these antitheses. For
Williams, the importance of transcending the modernizing thrust was seen
as increasingly urgent in his later writings, notably *Towards 2000*, where he
comes implicitly to acknowledge that socialism, engendered from within the
dynamic of modernity, seemed incapable of framing an adequate critique of
"progress."[21]

What I am terming an "avant-garde nostalgia" could here make a contribution by reflecting on past experience in ways that highlight what is preempted by contemporary forms of consumption, and thereby stimulate desire for a future that will be at once less environmentally destructive and
more sensually gratifying. In this connection, it is worth noting how utopian
what is remembered even from the relatively recent past can now seem. Here
is my father, aged ninety-eight, reflecting on the joys of his early cycling days
in the 1920s as a member of the Birmingham Speedwell Cycling Club:

> An annual event was the ride to the then remote and little known village of
> Llanarmon Dyfryn Ceiriog in the Berwyn hills south of Llangollen, 76 miles
> from Birmingham centre. We followed the Holyhead road, the A5 through

Shrewsbury, arriving at The Hand at Llanarmon in time for the substantial dinner essential to replace all the calories converted to pedal power. The following morning, Sunday, we responded to the challenge of the enticing network of lanes and farm tracks flanking the Berwyns: rough and unsurfaced they were then, with few bridges for crossing streams. We climbed the steep 1 in 7 gradient track above Glyn Ceiriog, crossed the ridge and at breakneck speed went down the other equally steep side into Llangollen for lunch. Around four o'clock our leader reminded us that tomorrow was a working day. Some of us took the more scenic route via Wenlock and Bridgenorth, not arriving home until well after midnight. Work that Monday seemed very restful after so strenuous a weekend.

Elsewhere in this memoir, he notes wistfully: " 'In Sommer Time on Bredon' had its own significance for us. Within two and a half hours from home we could be quenching thirst at one of the delightful inns around the periphery of the hill with rough cider at sixpence halfpenny [old pence] a pint. We ate our lunch in some shady area half way up the slopes. The world then seemed very nearly perfect."[22] "Very nearly perfect" it was not, of course. Yet in certain respects contemporary consumer culture can seem, by comparison with earlier ages, less joyous and sensually rewarding. This is true particularly of the amount of time we spend at work, and the stress occasioned by it. But anyone who has spent time trapped in traffic, or who regularly commutes, or who lives in deprived areas of the city or close to industrial zones will be well aware of the dystopian aspects of modern life. And as I have argued in various writings around the concept of "alternative hedonism," there are many now who are beginning to question the benefits of the work-and-spend economy and to regret what has been sacrificed in the pursuit of the dominant model of the "good life."[23] Implicit in the diverse range of contemporary laments over lost spaces and communities, the commercialization of children, the shifts toward vocational education, the ravages of "development," the "cloning" of our cities, and so forth, is a Romantically accented hankering for a society less subordinate to the imperatives of the growth economy and consumerist expansion. Diffuse and politically unfocussed though this may be, it speaks to a now quite widely felt sense of the opportunities that have been squandered in recent decades for acceding to a fairer, less harassed, less environmentally destructive, and more enjoyable existence. To defend the progressive dimension of this kind of nostalgia against our subsumption to consumerist "progress" and its pressures is not to recommend a more ascetic or less sensually enriching existence. On the contrary, it is to highlight the more brutalizing, disquieting, and irrational aspects of contemporary consumer culture. It is to represent the forms of sensual enhancement and complex fulfillments that people might be able to enjoy were they to opt for a more sustainable economy.[24]

Romanticism and Hedonism

In contrast to these kinds of argument, Colin Campbell, in his influential work, has claimed to discover the roots of modern hedonism in the Romantic ethic. Campbell sees Romantic dreaming and dissatisfaction at work, not in nostalgia for lost gratifications, but in the insatiability that typifies modern consumerism. Thus he writes, "the romantic ideal of character, together with its associated theory of moral renewal through art, functioned to stimulate and legitimate that form of autonomous, self-illusory hedonism, which underlines modern consumer behaviour." Self-illusory hedonism, he goes on to explain,

> is characterized by a longing which results in the ceaseless consumption of novelty. Such an outlook, with its characteristic dissatisfaction with real life and an eagerness for new experiences, lies at the heart of much conduct that is most typical of modern life, and underpins such central institutions as fashion and romantic love. The romantic ethic can be seen to possess a basic congruence, or "elective affinity" with this spirit, and to have given rise to a character type and ethical conduct highly conducive to the adoption of such attitudes. In particular, romantic teachings concerning the good, the true and the beautiful, provide both the legitimation and the motivation necessary for modern consumer behaviour to become prevalent throughout the industrial world.[25]

Campbell argues that the Romantic movement not only assisted crucially at the birth of modern consumerism, but has continued over the last two centuries to work against the forces of traditionalism and to provide a renewed impetus to the dynamic of consumerism.

It is true that the Romantic ethic challenges restrictive "puritanism" and the reining in of carnal pleasure. But little illumination seems shed on the homogenizing pressures of modern consumerism by viewing this as a legacy of the self-expressive "Bohemian" hedonism Campbell has described as being of the essence of Romanticism. And Campbell is in fact obliged to acknowledge that the contemporary consumerist outcome of the Romantic ethic is "ironic," in other words never intended by the Romantics themselves, who abhorred commercialism.[26] Today, however, consumerism is indeed almost exclusively associated with an aggressively materialist consumption, for which novelty means not so much nonconformist self-expression but the acquisition of the latest cell phone or iPod or Nike trainers. It is associated with the car culture, constant flying, and continuous shopping in increasingly standardized environments. And even where it is pursuing some concern for nature or interest in the sublime, it is rife with contradiction. The first and last step in almost all ecotourist itineraries is an international flight. The very air flights that enable ecotourists to observe wild tigers or polar bears contribute to the climate change that is eroding the animals' habitat.[27]

All this today seems so incongruous with the original impulse and intention of Romanticism that it is the betrayal rather than the continuity of its hedonist ethic that is most striking today. I would therefore argue that the yearning of Romanticism has today rather more "elective affinity" with the interest in moving to a postconsumerist culture and its forms of pleasure.

But this, of course, is the interest of a minority at present rather than a motivation of the public at large. For "alternative hedonism" to acquire the more general appeal that could eventually lead on to social and economic changes, it would need more extensive representation, both discursively and visually, of its new political imaginary. This will not prove easy. But there is much that art and literature could contribute to the needed revisions of response to contemporary life and its material culture, and they might well exercise a more important "ecocritical" influence in this role than in more traditional "Romantic" engagements with the philosophy and aesthetics of nature.

Shelley insisted in his *Defence of Poetry* that the "great instrument of the moral good is the imagination."[28] More recently, the artist Joseph Beuys has emphasized the significance of imaginative cultural production in any reconfiguration of the world of materiality, arguing that "only from art can a new concept of economics be formed, in terms of human need, not in the sense of use and consumption, politics and property, but above all in terms of the production of spiritual goods."[29] Some such application of the imagination certainly seems needed today, not only as an altruistic source of identification with the experiences of others, but as a capacity for dramatizing the dreariness of consumerist pleasure and for envisaging seductive alternatives to it.

Given the recent forecasts on climate change and resource exhaustion, a cultural revolution in our thinking about consumption and the "good life" is now widely accepted as a condition of warding off the worst consequences of global warming regardless of any other attractions it may have. But it takes a different kind of imagination, and shift of moral and aesthetic focus, to see that even were it ecologically possible to sustain consumerism forever, and to extend the Coca-Cola and car culture to all parts of the planet (and maybe beyond), that would be not a relief but a curse, a blight upon the human spirit rather than a blessing. By prompting "avant-garde nostalgia" and intimating the pleasures and fulfillments preempted by the consumerist lifestyle, the legacy of Romanticism can help to keep alive that needed imagination.

NOTES

1. Cf. Dorrian, "The Way the World Sees London," 54.

2. Albeit the nostalgia has now been tempered, as Paul Gilroy has pointed out, by a certain "post-colonial melancholy" (see his "Melancholia or Conviviality," 35–36).

3. John Keats, "Ode to a Nightingale," in Bloom and Trilling, *Romantic Poetry*, 539.

4. Percy Bysshe Shelley, "Ozymandias," in Bloom and Trilling, *Romantic Poetry*, 414.

5. Cf. McGann, *Beauty of Inflections*, 1–13.

6. Wordsworth, *Selected Poems*, 42–43.

7. Ibid., 87, 89–90.

8. Soper, *What Is Nature?* 236–43; Soper, "Nature and Culture," 69.

9. In his *Aesthetic Theory*, Adorno presents himself as salvaging an aesthetic of nature from the influence exercised by Kant's emphasis on human freedom and autonomy on subsequent idealist aesthetics, whose upshot was that nothing came to be treated as worthy of respect that did not owe its existence to the human subject (see esp. 92).

10. Adorno, *History and Freedom*.

11. Adorno, *Aesthetic Theory*, 69.

12. This would conform with his argument elsewhere in the same chapter that natural beauty cannot be copied, a point he links with his claim that the taboo on images in the Old Testament has an aesthetic as well as a theological dimension: the prohibition on imagery is itself an expression of the impossibility of creating it.

13. As Keats himself put it, in his letter of 22 December 1817 to his brothers, George and Thomas Keats, "when a man is capable of being in uncertainties, mysteries, doubts, without any irritable reaching after fact and reason" (quoted in Bloom and Trilling, *Romantic Poetry*, 495; cf. Hartman, *Fate of Reading*, 124–46; and McGann, *Beauty of Inflections*, 59, 60).

14. A spirit also associated with Heidegger's concept of *Gelassenheit*, or "letting be" (see his "Conversation" in *Discourse on Thinking*). Cf. Nathan Scott, *Negative Capability*.

15. Adorno, *Aesthetic Theory*, 66.

16. McGann, *Beauty of Inflections*, 57–58.

17. Nicholsen, *Love of Nature*, 7–33; Snyder, *Practice of the Wild*, 21.

18. Bate, *Song of the Earth*.

19. Adorno, *Aesthetic Theory*, 64–65.

20. Williams, *Country and City*, 184; 36–37.

21. "In every kind of radicalism the moment comes when any critique of the present must choose its bearings, between past and future" (Williams, *Towards 2000*, 36). Cf. Ryle, "The Past, the Future and the Golden Age"; and, in this volume, "Raymond Williams, 43–54.

22. Private communication with the author.

23. Cf. Soper, "Re-thinking the 'Good Life'"; "Other Pleasures of Post-Consumerism";

"Alternative Hedonism, Cultural Theory"; and "Fulfillments of Post-Consumerism." For details of the research project entitled "Alternative Hedonism and the Theory and Politics of a new Anti-Consumerism," in the ESRC/AHRC "Cultures of Consumption Programme," see www.consume.bbk.ac.uk.

24. For some recent and diverse perspectives on this theme, see Soper, Ryle, and Thomas, *Politics and Pleasures.*

25. Campbell, *Romantic Ethic,* 200–201, 205–6.

26. Ibid.; Campbell, "Traditional and Modern Patterns," 40–57; Campbell, *Romantic Ethic,* 209–11.

27. The rapidly expanding ecotourist industry companies cannot but abstract from the contradictions of encouraging more influx, usually by air flight, into areas hitherto "untouched" by the tourist trade.

28. Bloom and Trilling, *Romantic Poetry and Prose,* 780.

29. Schellmann, *Joseph Beuys,* 28.

Green Things in the Garbage: Ecocritical Gleaning in Walter Benjamin's Arcades

In his beautiful, terrible image of the angel of history drawn from the Klee painting *Angelus Novus*, Walter Benjamin offers a glimpse of his view of the relationship between garbage and history:

> Where we perceive a chain of events, [the angel] sees one single catastrophe which keeps piling wreckage upon wreckage and hurls it in front of his feet. The angel would like to stay, awaken the dead, and make whole what has been smashed. But a storm is blowing in from Paradise; it has got caught in his wings with such violence that the angel can no longer close them. This storm irresistibly propels him into the future to which his back is turned, while the pile of debris before him grows skyward. This storm is what we call progress.[1]

For Benjamin, garbage is not only a metaphor. Clearly, the debris piling up as the angel is blown backward represents the ruins of the past in the largest sense: it is the sum total of the barbarism that is an inevitable part of that "document of civilization" that is our triumphalist bourgeois history, "in which the present rulers step over those who are lying prostrate."[2] For Benjamin, the unquestioned, progressivist universalism by which history appears to justify the barbarism of the present is a cornerstone of capitalism's continued existence; therefore, "brush[ing] history against the grain" is a key task for the historical materialist, who must "seize the past . . . as an image which flashes up at the instant when it can be recognized and is never seen again."[3] The past is thus something ephemeral that the materialist must, in order for it to appear, blow explosively out of its encrustation in the magma of universal, bourgeois happening.

Later in the same essay, Benjamin goes out of his way to point out the nature in this pile of historical garbage.[4] He argues that a belief in technological "advancement" has been part of the process by which workers have been caught up in this forceful current of corrupting self-congratulation, and that this belief "recognizes only the progress in the mastery of nature, not the retrogression of society. . . . The new conception of labor amounts to the exploitation of nature." Exploitative technological development is, here, part of a naturalization of capitalist progress, a "stream" with which the working class "thought it was moving." In these conditions of human exploitation, nature "exists gratis" and is also exploited; a genuinely human history of co-operation with nature can only begin in conditions in which, along the lines of Charles Fourier's early-nineteenth-century socialist utopia, "labor . . . far from exploiting nature, is capable of delivering her of the creations which lie dormant in her womb [!] as potentials."[5]

In capitalism, then, history is garbage. And nature is garbage. But *garbage* is also garbage, and, for Benjamin, it is in the careful examination of the detritus of "progress" that the historical materialist might find the past beyond its apparent assumption of the present. By violently wrenching salvaged objects out of their comfortable places in the mythic history of the commodity, by gleaning them from their place in the trash can of bourgeois utility, Benjamin reconfigures and arrests them as monads, shocking "cessations of happening" that forcibly insert into the present "a revolutionary chance in the fight for the oppressed past."[6]

In his extraordinary *Passagen-Werk* (*Arcades Project*), Benjamin demonstrates a critical practice of montage that seeks to transform the obsolescent fragments of commodity capitalism into "dialectical images," groupings of things that reveal elements of the experience of capitalist modernity obscured in everyday existence. By removing objects from their places as relics littering the path of progress and placing them in new, proximate "constellations," Benjamin seeks to reveal each object's particularity in light of a newly configured relationship. Similar to and influenced by surrealism— and also, as Terry Eagleton indicates, by Kabbalism[7]—Benjamin's constellatory method seeks, through the juxtaposition of fragments, to redraw the relationship between the part and the whole: to destroy the assumed and habitual place of the thing in the historical logic of commodity fetishism, and to show the arrested object as the embodiment of history itself: "dialectics at a standstill."

Benjamin understands this work as a necessary awakening from the dream-state of commodity capitalism.[8] Each montage, each reconstellated fetish-object blasted from the phantasmagoria of spectacular consumer display, offers a shock, a "profane illumination" that holds out the possibility of transformative meaning. Constellations are, here, meticulous redeployments of things, including but not limited to textual ones, so that they are freed to speak in the service of a radical politics of consciousness. As Benjamin describes his own method in a fragment from one of the "Konvoluts" around which the *Passagen-Werk* is organized (the word translates literally to "mixed lots" or "bundles [of papers]"): "Method of this project: literary montage. I needn't *say* anything. Merely show. I shall purloin no valuables, appropriate no ingenious formulations. But the rags, the refuse—these I will not inventory but allow, in the only way possible, to come into their own: by making use of them."[9]

Devoted to the presentation of these profane illuminations, the *Passagen-Werk* is full of garbage in at least two senses. In the first, the work is a massive, unfinished collection of nineteenth-century literary litter, interspersed with commentary from Benjamin: fragmentary quotations on topics located in and related to the Paris Arcades (more on these below). In the beginning of Konvolut B, "Fashion," for example, we have a comment from Benjamin in which "boredom is the grating before which the courtesan teases death," a second on the strange seductiveness of nineteenth-century women's cycling costumes, a quotation from a 1925 German style magazine describing changes in women's dresses from 1882 to 1885, a further insertion from Benjamin that begins "here fashion has opened the business of dialectical exchange between women and ware—between carnal pleasure and the corpse," and then a quote from Rilke.[10] The experience of reading the *Passagen-Werk* can be, as a result, decidedly like that of looking around a large and idiosyncratically organized junk store:[11] each item on display, removed from its original context of utility, takes on a shine that is as much the result of its particular placement, its aesthetic qualities, and/or its relationship to other items as it is the actual or potential use or exchange value of the thing in question (later on in "Fashion," for example, there is a truly luminous image: "the eternal is in any case far more the ruffle on the dress than some idea").[12] Benjamin himself writes on the experience of collection in Konvolut H: "What is decisive in collecting is that the object is detached from all its original functions in order to enter into the closest conceivable relation to things of the same kind. . . . And for the true collector, every single thing in this system becomes an encyclopedia of knowledge of the epoch, the landscape, the industry, and the owner from which it comes."[13] Reading the *Passagen-Werk* is, in this light, an experience of witness to a collection in which the items, having been collected, are transformed (alchemically, in Hannah Arendt's interpretation) from rags to riches.[14]

In a second and equally important sense, the fragments Benjamin offers are frequently *about* garbage. In Konvolut B, the junk-store contents are literally as well as metaphorically displayed: not only outmoded women's cycling clothes but also "nip-waisted frockcoat[s . . . and] dainty fabric boots," "a knit scarf—a brightly striped muffler—worn also, in muted colors, by men" and, for the hair, "fruit braided in graceful little branches."[15] Benjamin's illuminations are not only profane but mundane: "his goal," writes Susan Buck-Morss, "was to take materialism so seriously that the historical phenomena themselves were brought to speech. . . . Corsets, feather dusters, red and green-colored combs, old photographs, souvenir replicas of the Venus de Milo, collar buttons to shirts long since discarded—these battered historical survivors from the dawn of industrial culture that appeared together in the dying *were* the philosophical ideas."[16] The form of the text as a collection of scraps amplifies the broken-down content, the remnants of the nineteenth century; it also *makes* garbage of many more "serious" fragments, including Konvoluts on Baudelaire and Marx, both of whom are, for Benjamin, key interlocutors. In this trashing, Benjamin thus emphasizes that materialist theory must be immanent to the phenomena it theorizes: garbage in, garbage out.

Arcades

As part of her description of Benjamin as "the most peculiar Marxist ever produced by this movement," Arendt emphasizes Benjamin's almost animistic (and fairly un-Marxist) belief in the ability of things to shine by themselves, to speak their own essences when brought to a "standstill" in the right company of other things.[17] Although it is important to emphasize that Benjamin does not *simply* juxtapose things (without, as he was accused by Adorno, the dialectically necessary intervention of mediating theory),[18] it is equally important to note that he understands his pieces of detritus as their own source of truth: commentary might enrich, but does not replace, the particularity of fragment against fragment, as in modernity, historical facts are "congealed in the form of things."[19] This overtly kaleidoscopic understanding is, for Benjamin, not only the content of the past, but also an embodiment of its form. Each fragment takes on the fullness of history, and the arrangement of fragments into bundles takes a structure that closely approximates both the technology of the kaleidoscope itself (from the nineteenth century) and also the phantasmagorical commodity circus from which the fragments were blasted, embodied in the arcades themselves. The Paris Arcades offer both the content and the form of the project, both the content and the ur-form of the nineteenth century.

Benjamin begins the first Konvolut of the *Passagen-Werk* with a quote from the 1852 *Illustrated Guide to Paris*: "These arcades, a recent invention of industrial luxury, are glass-roofed, marble-paneled corridors extending through whole blocks of buildings. . . . Lining both sides of these corridors, which get their light from above, are the most elegant shops, so that the arcade is a city, a world in miniature."[20] The arcades, like their sibling-sites,

world exhibitions (about which Benjamin wrote in Konvolut G), were historically specific utopian spaces that sought to create and transform urban
experience through technological innovations such as the then-revolutionary
use of iron construction and gas lighting, as well as new arrangements of
sociality such as the blurring of the distinction between bourgeois interior
(on which the spaces were modeled) and exterior. They are thus, for Benjamin, exemplary spaces of the nineteenth century's movement into modern,
urban capitalism: the phantasmagoria of the arcades offers a living miniature,
a "fairyland," of the century itself, what he calls its wish-image.

In a 1939 essay entitled "Paris, Capital of the Nineteenth Century,"
Benjamin writes:

> Our investigation proposes to show how . . . the new forms of behavior and
> the new economically and technologically based creations that we owe to the
> nineteenth century enter the universe of a phantasmagoria. These creations
> undergo this "illumination" not only in a theoretical manner, by an ideologi-
> cal transposition, but also in the immediacy of their perceptible presence.
> *They are manifest as phantasmagorias.* Thus appear the arcades—first entry in
> the field of iron construction; thus appear the world exhibitions, whose link
> to the entertainment industry is significant. Also included in this order of
> phenomena is the experience of the flâneur, who abandons himself to the
> phantasmagorias of the marketplace.[21]

As manifestations of the phantasmagoria, the arcades are historically specific
assemblages of emerging urban capitalist technologies and relations. They
are both icons of commodity fetishism and concrete sites through which the
spectacular practices of commodity exchange are announced and developed:
as icons, they crystallize the utopian desires of the new, emerging city, but as
spaces of/for capital, they cannot help but fail.

In the arcades, people are commodities. Crowds circulate between
inward-facing rows of display windows, and in the interior/exterior arcade
world of merchandising, sign, fashion, and spectacle, the boundary between
consumable and consumer becomes indistinct. People are reflected in the
windows and see themselves among the goods; people are reflected in other
people as fashions ripple through the crowds and mark faces and bodies with
the repetition enabled by mass production; people sell things, sell themselves, sell themselves to sell things. The crowd becomes an embodiment of
spectacular exchange, and the vertiginous, mass quality of urban conflagra-
tion is exacerbated by the reconstitution of objects and bodies alike as items
on display. We become, in the arcade, part of the phantasmagoria itself. In
particular, we come to embody modes of consciousness that result from the

experience of being in a crowd, what Benjamin describes as the shock experiences of knocked-together passersby in the crowd.

Into this crowd, of course, wanders the flâneur. As described by Charles Baudelaire, on whose evocative poetry Benjamin relies heavily for his formulations of nineteenth-century Paris, the flâneur is a man[22] who strolls idly through the streets of Paris in search of interesting things to see and (reputedly) has the turtles he is walking set his pace. He is intoxicated by the mass of people in the arcades, physically jostled and agitated by them, but he is also a marginal dandy who pushes the limits of good taste, "in" rather than "of" the crowd. Indeed, "the flâneur is someone abandoned in the crowd. In this he shares the situation of the commodity."[23]

For Benjamin, the arcade-dwelling flâneur is actually a privileged commentator on the experience of the arcades and of commodity capitalism itself. As an individual who must eventually sell his literary perceptions of the phantasmagoria for a price, he is uniquely *conscious* of his status as a commodity in a world of commodities. But even by the time Benjamin is writing, this habitat is in decline as the arcades became relics of a past capitalist era. Although some have argued that the flâneur simply adapted and went elsewhere (to the mall and to the Internet), "explode[d] into a myriad of forms,"[24] Benjamin is also interested in the flâneur precisely because he is, like the nip-waisted frockcoat he might have worn, a relic who, once blasted from evolutionary narratives of urban social development, refuses to condone them. For a historical materialist analysis, the Paris Arcades are both metonym and site: the flâneur plays a similarly dual role. His was a specific position in the historic city and crowd, but he also stands in for the larger possibility of criticism—perhaps especially Benjamin's own form of criticism—to turn the everyday shocks of urban experience in the phantasmagoria into a self-aware lyric poetry of and for capitalist modernity.

Ecocritical Gleaning

We have in the *Passagen-Werk*, then, an extraordinary model of cultural criticism. It is composed of refuse and seeks to deliver from these dregs of an era enduring truth, in so doing exposing the ways in which the myth-structure of that era disguises its fundamentally exploitative nature; it is organized to describe the exemplary spaces of that era in a way that is faithful to their contents and also reproduces key elements of their form and arrangement; it gives privilege to modes of perception and subjectivity organic to these spaces; and it attempts to deliver, beginning with a self-awareness on the critic's part of her/his own implication in the commodity world, a shock-experience to blast the things in which the truth is congealed away from their absorption in the triumphalism in which exploitation is historically cloaked. It is a great work of philosophy, combining a precise (if iconoclastic) historical materialism with a messianic understanding of time and redemption; it is an overtly political work, a direct and awakening intervention into the somnambulance of mid-twentieth-century commodity capitalism; it is a brilliant work of literature, considered variously as modernist novel, epic poem, and urban memoir.

But, beginning with a broad definition of "the study of the relationship between literature and the environment,"[25] what can we glean from the *Passagen-Werk* that might explicitly animate a practice of *ecocriticism*? Short of demanding a full-scale environmental Arcades Project (which wouldn't be a bad idea, even if it might be—as it was for Benjamin—impossible), what does Benjamin's understanding of the relationships among truth, history, things, nature, garbage, commodity, and perception suggest as tools for environmental literary understanding?

First, Benjamin clearly reminds us to pay attention to the cultural politics of our current environmental condition. There is no question that we live in a phantasmagoria, if not exactly the ironworked Parisian arcades, then somewhere disconcertingly similar. Begun in the nineteenth century and well-metastasized by the early twenty-first, commodity fetishism has managed, quite thoroughly, to transform cultural life into that kaleidoscopic display that is both a metaphor for and the condition of experience, including environmental experience, in late capitalism. And the natural world has become part of the phantasmagoria, not only in that its exploitation provides the material for the generation of commodities, but also in that its experience and perception *as commodity* is no longer really separable (if it ever was) from the dominant conditions of kaleidoscopic display. Indeed, the contemporary, full-color, digitized proliferation of natures-as-commodities acts as a screen covering the exploitation of the natural world that is a central condition of capitalist production; this incorporation of the natural world into the bourgeois narrative of progress via green technologies and nature documentaries serves only to continue the barbarism of the present.

This incorporation is obvious in, for example, advertisements for "green" sports utility vehicles: nature is for sale, along with the SUV, and unquestioned belief in the inevitability of technological progress under capital (in this case, via green technology) fuels both purchases in its position that capitalism can indeed be "good for nature."[26] But according to Benjamin, we should also look for nature elsewhere in the phantasmagoria, including, I think, in the literatures we call nature writing (which I define very broadly). To what extent, he might insist, is the natural world of nature writing, however brilliantly or ecologically manifest, still a commodity that circulates among other commodities, including SUV ads? To what extent does the commodity-quality of literary nature-work not only shape its content but also, more insidiously, cover the tracks of its own involvement in a profoundly anti-environmental capitalism by proclaiming the continued possibility of a nature outside commodity relations even as it extends the reach of the commodity further into our experiences of the natural world?

These are disturbing questions that lie at the heart of any discussion of the role of environmental literature and criticism in (and against) capitalist cultural formations. Benjamin, however, has a particular answer that is of great relevance for ecocriticism: remember the garbage. Thus second, in developing a mode of cultural critique based on the discernment of the truth of the whole when it is blown, in the fragment, out of the progressivist narrative of bourgeois history, Benjamin suggests that we begin an ecocritical project not with the natures that capitalism currently celebrates and markets, but with those it has discarded along the way. What once-precious nature-commodities might, when thrust up against one another, reveal history? How can we glean, in the ecological refuse of the decaying dream-worlds of earlier modes of nature-consumption, a collection of objects to *profanely* illuminate that ur-nature that is its fleeting truth?

Susan Buck-Morss offers an explicitly ecocritical image for interpreting Benjamin's garbage-gleaning expeditions: that the fetish-objects we excavate from the "natural history" of capitalism are *fossils* of the prehistory from which we have yet to emerge. "The *Passagen-Werk*," she writes, "treats the historical *origins* of the present: Natural history becomes ur-history. Its goal is not only to polemicize against the still-barbaric level of the modern age, but . . . to disclose the essence of the 'new nature" as even more transient, more fleeting than the old.' "[27] For Buck-Morss, Benjamin is making explicit his claim that the utopian possibility of technological modernity to bring about this new nature can be glimpsed only in the dialectical cessations of time that are fragmentary objects wrested from their historical incorporations. The nature that we see within this (pre)history—or rather, the nature that appears *as such* in the progression of commodity history— needs to be perceived differently, as a fossilized remnant of *prehistory*. What we now know as nature is really a set of petrified objects, and only a reconstellated, dialectical image will allow it to appear in its potential to become new nature.

Bourgeois nature, here, becomes a junk store, and the individual objects within it obtain new potential for brilliance once blasted from their roles as alibis for capitalism and given space to appear differently.[28] Think about what nature might appear, for example, when arrested in a montage assembled from a 1972 Nova Scotia travel poster, a pulp western or two by a now-forgotten author, an old copy of *National Geographic* from the doctor's waiting room, last year's treatise on the "right" kind of diet for optimal cardiovascular health (found right beside the dusty Stairmaster), *The Bell Curve* (garbage even before it was published), one of George W. Bush's televised speeches on oil exploration in the Arctic National Wildlife Refuge, and just about any policy document that speaks earnestly about the merits of sustainable "development."

Finally, Benjamin offers the ecocritic a figure with whom to walk through the eco-arcades and glean their trash: the flâneur.[29] The flâneur is not simply an archaic character who strolls slowly through the palimpsest of merchandise and people in the arcades of commodity capitalism; s/he is also a writer of her surroundings and (shocking) experiences, aware of her marginality and of her involvement, as a commodity, in the world of commodities. She is thus a self-reflective character to take to a critical practice of montage in the environmental phantasmagoria. For our purposes, she is an allegorical, out-of-step, out-of-time, probably disgruntled ecocritical interpreter of the dreamworld of nature commodities. Tasked (in my version) to re/collect the fragments of nature experience in late capitalism and write them into something like the constellatory modernist novel/epic poetry/urban memoir that is the *Passagen-Werk*, she must also come to terms with her own relationship to commodity capitalism. As Benjamin writes, "as flâneurs, the intelligentsia came into the marketplace. As they thought, to observe it—but in reality it was already to find a buyer."[30] Simply put, she asks us: to what extent do our own ecocritical texts participate in the phantasmagoria?

If we understand the flâneur more as a historical figure and less as a metaphor for the ecocritical intelligentsia (although s/he is both at once), other possibilities emerge. The historical flâneur's activities and modes of perception were, historically, organized and enabled by the physical and social space of the arcades: he was a pedestrian, idler, and his mode of critical reflection emerged from specific spatial and perceptual relations. What modes of knowing, one might ask, are generated in the *eco*-arcades that are the iconic/historic sites of late capitalism? I have argued elsewhere that flânerie is an appropriate epistemic activity to take to the specific passages that are parks (not least because some parks are decaying nineteenth-century configurations of spectacular visual exchange that, like arcades, center on pedestrian activity and spectacle),[31] but perhaps Benjamin would ask us to be more materialist: what kind of marginal-critical figure is enabled, not by the metonym/site of nineteenth-century arcade/exhibition, but by that of twenty-first-century Facebook/ecotour? Critical narration of relations between literature and environment would, from this position, take on a different charge.

Green Things in the Garbage

The question remains, though: Within this urban, modern imaginary, what of Benjamin's own thinking on the place of the natural world in capitalism and, by extension, in literary critical practice? Beatrice Hanssen writes that "Benjamin stayed at a distance from the mountains and the green pastures, evoking nature only in its auratic capacity, as he wandered through the streets of urban Europe, developing a method of cultural analysis that was honed on the activity . . . of the flâneur."[32] But I am not so sure. Although Benjamin avoided the pastoral in his dialectical bringing-to-light of the wish-images and ruins of urban modernity, he was clear that he considered the explosive technological exploitation of nature as a key part of the commodity capitalism that emerged in the mid-nineteenth century.[33] In addition, although they did not contain mountains and pastures, he also had something to say more directly about the natural worlds that were part of his urban experience.

Specifically, in his *Berlin Childhood around 1900*, Benjamin's remembered montage of the city-spaces of his past includes several that were designated as "nature" in that era, including Berlin's Tiergarten and Zoological Garden; it also "makes" nature out of others from the perspective of a (past) child. *Berlin Childhood* is both a palimpsest echoing what might be understood as the montage character of memory itself and a richly poetic text illustrating the particular ability of the child—an exemplary collector, in Benjamin's view—to create constellations of things that speak animatedly to one another outside their intended, bourgeois uses and identities. As Howard Eiland writes: "The child is collector, flâneur and allegorist in one. He [*sic*] lives in an antiquity of the everyday; for him everything is natural and therefore endowed with chthonic force."[34] In *Berlin Childhood*, then, we have a glimpse of the arcades as they might be remembered, and also of the ability of the phenomenal world of the past, reconstellated and animate, to illuminate the present; that world most certainly includes the more-than-human.

Although *Berlin Childhood* deserves a fuller ecocritical reading in itself, let me end with a fragmentary image from a text that might (by way of Benjamin reading Benjamin) offer a final illumination of the oddly materialist ecocritical project I have argued he suggests. In "Butterfly Hunt," Benjamin begins with a childhood collection: butterflies "whose oldest specimens had been captured in the garden of the Brauhausberg." This is a montage of dead objects arrested from life and splayed out in decorative rows, but in its character as an assemblage it has the ability to summon a past beyond, for example, taxonomic or economic order. For Benjamin, it "vividly brought back the ardors of the hunt, which so often had lured me away from the well-kept garden paths into a wilderness, where I stood powerless before the conspiring elements." This memory of butterfly hunting is, too, emblematic: the butterfly becomes the occasion for Benjamin's own slippage into animality: "When in this way a vanessa or a sphinx moth (which I should have been able to overtake easily) made a fool of me through its hesitations, vacillations, and delays, I would gladly have been dissolved into light and air, merely in order to approach my prey unnoticed and be able to subdue it." Indeed, he and the animal change positions: "the more butterfly-like I became in my heart and soul—the more this butterfly itself, in every-thing it did, took on the color of human volition; and in the end, it was as if its capture was the price I had to pay to regain my human existence."[35]

One can read this movement from (dead) collection to vivid memory of becoming-butterfly as a metonym for Benjamin's understanding of the place of nature in human history: the remembered animality of the butterfly-Benjamin reveals the place of this memory-fossil in a natural history of a present that has not yet achieved conditions for human/nature collabora-tion. The collection is thus a wish-image for a future of butterfly-human mutuality, but also a ruin in which the trashed insects show their character as exploited objects. Indeed, as Benjamin exclaims after a reminder of the technologies of his collection ("ether, cotton wadding, pins with colored heads, and tweezers"), "what a state the hunting ground was in when I left! Grass was flattened, flowers trampled underfoot; the hunter himself, hold-ing his own body cheap, had flung it heedlessly after his butterfly net." One is tempted to read, here, an environmentalist metaphor as well as a com-ment about the role of labor in the bourgeois capture and transformation of nature into inert, consumable matter. Certainly, however, Benjamin is creat-ing in this fragment a dialectical image in which the utopian possibility of a new nature is revealed in the same activity as its ruin, in capitalist consump-tion, is laid out: "And borne aloft—over so much destruction, clumsiness, and violence—in a fold of this net, trembling and yet full of charm, was the terrified butterfly. On that laborious way back, the spirit of the doomed creature entered into the hunter. From the foreign language in which the butterfly and the flowers had come to an understanding before his eyes, he now derived some precepts. His lust for blood had diminished; his confi-dence was grown all the greater."[36]

A fragment in fragments, Benjamin's butterfly is deeply instructive for ecocriticism. To take this image seriously, we are compelled to consider modes of writing in which possibilities for the new are blasted from the decaying ruins of the present. Such a task requires us to look seriously at the green things in the garbage as garbage themselves, for in illuminating them we might find a nature that is not an apology for its own exploitation.

NOTES

1. Benjamin, "Theses," 257–58.

2. Ibid., 256.

3. Ibid., 255.

4. He is referring specifically to a "vulgar-Marxist" dialectical materialism (Josef Dietzgen), which he then contrasts with Fourier, proclaiming the latter "surprisingly sound."

5. Benjamin, "Theses," 259, 263.

6. Ibid., 263.

7. Eagleton, "Marxist Rabbi," 329.

8. Rolf Tiedemann notes that Benjamin's insistence that "the nineteenth century is the dream we must wake up from" distinguishes his political desires for montage from those of the early surrealists ("Dialectics at a Standstill," 935).

9. Benjamin, *Passagen-Werk* [N1a, 8], 460, original emphasis. The numbers in square brackets are Benjamin's filing system.

10. Ibid. [B1, 1], [B1, 2], [B1, 3], [B1, 4], and [B1, 5], 62–63.

11. I say "can be": I have read Benjamin, and have also gone to junk stores, looking for specific things (such as Benjamin's thoughts on flânerie or the old mason jars with the glass lids); I have also wandered less purposefully through quotes and things and allowed proximity, rather than utility, to guide my perception.

12. Ibid. [B3,7], 69. The passage is repeated at [N3, 2].

13. Ibid. [H1a, 2], 204–5. For a further discussion of collecting, see Benjamin, "Unpacking My Library."

14. Arendt, "Introduction," 5.

15. Benjamin, *Passagen-Werk* [B1a, 4], [B2a, 4], and [B3, 5], 64, 67, 69.

16. Buck-Morss, *Dialectics of Seeing,* 4, original emphasis.

17. Arendt, "Introduction," 11.

18. Buck-Morss, *Dialectics of Seeing,* 73–75.

19. Benjamin, *Passagen-Werk,* 14.

20. Ibid. [A1, 1], 31.

21. This essay is the second of two compact "exposés" laying out ideas about the final presentation of his work on the arcades. Benjamin wrote two versions of "Paris, Capital," the first in 1935 to explain his project to his colleagues at the Institute for Social Research in New York, the second in 1939 to entice a potential sponsor (both in *Passagen-Werk,* 3–13, 14–26). Benjamin, *Passagen-Werk,* 14, emphasis added.

22. There are, of course, many important things to say about the sex and sexuality of the flâneur, but space limitations restrict their discussion here. For such a discussion, and also for an example of scholarship that takes Benjamin's criticism to brilliant insights on contemporary urban experience, see Chisholm, *Queer Constellations.*

23. Benjamin, *Charles Baudelaire,* 55.

24. Buck-Morss, "The Flâneur," 38.

25. Glotfelty, "Introduction," xviii.

26. For an excellent discussion of nature and SUV advertising, see Gunster, "You Belong Outside."

27. Buck-Morss, *Dialectics of Seeing,* 64.

28. There is not space here to explore fully the ecocritical implications of the fact that Benjamin's universe is animate: objects themselves reveal their essences, and nature thus has a language. Mick Smith's writings on Benjamin include consideration of this important possibility (see Smith, "Lost for Words?").

29. One might choose different marginal characters as models for ecocritical movement through the landscape: for Buck-Morss, there are, in addition to the flâneur, the sandwichman and the prostitute; for Chisholm, there is (among others) the lesbian bohème; for Wohlfarth, there is the *chiffonier* (ragpicker). All emphasize the critical, but nevertheless *implicated,* subjective possibilities of urban marginality.

30. Benjamin, *Charles Baudelaire,* 170–71.

31. See Sandilands, "A Flâneur in the Forest?"

32. Hanssen, *Walter Benjamin and the Arcades,* 1.

33. Benjamin was not averse to technology; he believed, following Fourier, in the utopian possibility of technology as a tool to bring about cooperative relations between human beings and the natural world for their mutual benefit. "One of the most remarkable features of the Fourierist utopia is that it never advocated the exploitation of nature by man, an idea that became widespread in the following period. Instead, in Fourier, technology appears as the spark that ignites the powder of nature" (*Passagen-Werk,* 17). This possibility is part of capitalism's utopian possibility, which coexists with its ruinous history.

34. Eiland, "Translator's Foreword," xiv. It is important to note that the figure of the child in *Berlin Childhood* is not nostalgic. The act of revealing an animate past from the point of its future gives the elements their particular luminosity. Again, on the chthonic qualities of nature and objects-as-nature, see Smith, "Lost for Words?"

35. Benjamin, *Berlin Childhood,* 50, 51. The Brauhausberg (Brewery Hill) was the site of the Benjamin summer home.

36. Ibid., 51–52, 52.

Raymond Williams:
Materialism and Ecocriticism

Raymond Williams was born in 1921 and died in 1988. Many would regard him as the single-most important critic of literature and culture at work in postwar Britain. He was a major figure on the British intellectual left: "by far the most commanding figure," in Terry Eagleton's assessment.[1] Working initially in university adult education, at the age of forty he was appointed a Lecturer, and subsequently became Professor of Drama, at Cambridge. He made the ancient university a new base for his continued extramural commitments: to the critical public discussion of ideas, to the political Left, to his native Wales and its historical and renascent cultures. He was the author or coauthor of some thirty books, which include plays and novels as well as major works of criticism, and he wrote scores of articles, chapters, pamphlets, and reviews (his complete publications are listed in the invaluable forty-seven-page bibliography in Alan O'Connor's *Raymond Williams: Writing, Culture, Politics*). His writing was translated during his lifetime into several European languages and into Japanese, and was published and reviewed extensively in North America from the early 1960s onward, though he visited the United States and Canada only once, in the spring of 1973.

Williams's work as a whole drew continually on his socialist convictions and his working-class background. His late political writings also engaged with the destructive impact of industrialized societies on the natural environment; the editors of the papers from a 1997 symposium on his intellectual legacy argue that "it is possible to locate as far back as the late 1950s an intrinsic commitment to the principles of ecological critique."[2] This commitment made Williams unusual among British literary academics (very few of whom have shared it until quite recently), and it set him apart from the main currents of Laborism, social democracy, and Marxism. His scholarly and critical work on culture and the natural environment included reviews, talks, and essays. His deepening engagement with the theme can be traced in O'Connor's bibliography, where one notes, for example, that he wrote an article entitled "Ideas of Nature" in the *Times Literary Supplement* in late 1970, gave a lecture with the same title at London's Institute of Contemporary Arts the following year, and in 1972 contributed the chapter "Ideas of Nature" to J. Benthall's collection *Ecology: The Shaping Inquiry*. This dimension of his thinking came to the fore in a major work of his maturity, *The Country and the City*, which is among the earliest British books that might be described—albeit contentiously—as a work of ecocriticism: it deals at length, and centrally, with representations of the rural world, and although it expresses an orthodox socialist suspicion of ruralist cultural politics, it is also skeptical about metropolitan ideas of "progress." Greg Garrard, a leading contemporary British ecocritic, notes that the book "profoundly influenced both Marxist readings of pastoral and the ecocritical responses that arrived later to qualify or contradict them."[3]

Williams's distinctive contribution to ecocritical thinking is not a matter of a discrete paradigm, elaborated in theoretical mode. Rather, we can learn from his practice of politically engaged criticism, attentive to environment and ecology and committed to reading cultural works in social and historical contexts. Here, I consider *The Country and the City* after reviewing his directly political interventions of the early 1980s, made in the context of the self-reappraisal of the British Left that followed Margaret Thatcher's decisive Conservative election victory of 1979.[4] Williams published essays, mostly based on earlier journal articles, in four contributed volumes on the future of the Left and on antinuclear politics. A speech he gave in London to the Socialist Environment and Resources Association (SERA), then quite recently founded, was published by SERA as a pamphlet, *Socialism and Ecology*, in 1982. Other occasional writings included reviews of Rudolf Bahro's *The Alternative in Eastern Europe* and *Socialism and Survival*, which were key books in the development of red/green thinking in Europe; and of Alva Myrdal's *The Dynamics of European Nuclear Disarmament*.[5] Taken together, these interventions over a five-year period reflect Williams's conviction that the crisis demanded a fundamental rethinking of the socialist idea, in which the question of ecological limits—"the newly realized and decisive fact: that we cannot *materially* go on in the old ways"—would have to be made central.[6] Ecological and antimilitarist perspectives, linked to a critique of the limited horizons of the trades union and labor movement, are at the heart of the agenda proposed in his last major political reflection, *Towards 2000*. These interventions, their background and their context, provide our first focus.

The present discussion is largely confined to the writings already noted, and makes no pretence at giving an account of Williams's entire oeuvre or of the secondary literature on it. It reviews some key themes and aspects of his ecocritical and ecological-political thought in themselves, rather than in polemical contrast to the work of other critics. I must, however, underline at the outset the European context and formation of Williams's views, and note that this places him at an angle to—perhaps at odds with—the political perspectives that have tended to predominate in ecocritical writing from the United States. Williams, indeed, appears to have had rather little influence on U.S. ecocriticism: to a British reader, it is striking that his work is barely cited even in a recent anthology (Armbruster and Wallace's *Beyond Nature Writing*) which aims explicitly to expand the frontiers of the ecocritical project. Here, the sole contributor referring to Williams is Michael Bennett, in a forceful critique of the irrelevance and impertinence to African American readers of dominant ecocritical assumptions about the uses and enjoyment of "pastoral space and wilderness." Bennett's conclusion is one that Williams would certainly have endorsed: "the wilderness of the world cannot be preserved unless and until we have broken down some of the racial, class and gender barriers that distance wilderness and pastoral space from those outside the upper echelons of our society."[7]

Insofar as his characteristically European linking of social and ecological perspectives may stimulate fresh lines of inquiry in American and international ecocritical research and thinking, Williams, for all that he died twenty years ago, still speaks with a new voice.

Politics, 1980–1985: Red and Green

During the early 1980s, Williams, speaking and writing as a well-known and well-regarded socialist intellectual, addressed both the organizations and groupings of left social democracy in Britain and Europe, and the ecological or green movement that was emerging as an autonomous cultural and political force. To the former audience, he criticizes the familiar priorities of Labor (essentially, the defense and promotion of the interests of particular groups of organized workers, within a strategy of expanding capitalist production in general): inadequate in themselves, these old priorities also fail to take account of impending ecological scarcity.[8] At an international conference of socialists, he suggests that the new social movements (ecological, and also feminist and antinuclear) may prove to be key components of "the most active and effective" opposition to contemporary capitalism.[9]

When speaking to ecologists, he insists that it is only through an eventual alliance with the organizations of labor that they might ever implement, democratically, the changes to the structure of production that a sustainable economy would require. In pursuing that alliance, green activists must acknowledge and understand the experiences that have formed the industrial working class: "It is no use simply saying to South Wales miners that all around them is an ecological disaster. They already know. They live in it. They have lived in it for generations. They carry it in their lungs. . . . But you cannot just say to people who have committed their lives and their communities to certain kinds of production that this has all got to be changed. You can't just say: 'come out of the harmful industries.' . . . Everything will have to be done by negotiation, by equitable negotiation."[10]

That negotiation has never happened, and that alliance was never forged: I reflect below on some consequences of that failure. Here, I want to consider two contexts—one immediately personal, the other continental and generational—for Williams's interventions in red/green politics.

Williams wrote about the personal background of his work in his first, frankly autobiographical novel, *Border Country*. He refers to it in many asides and reflections—for example, the recollection of traveling by bus from Hereford into the mountains which opens his essay "Culture Is Ordinary," or the contrast drawn between Cambridgeshire and Wales in the opening chapter of *The Country and the City*. We have also the retrospection and self-assessment of *Politics and Letters*, based on searching interviews with members of the *New Left Review* editorial team.[11] The directness of voice in the passage just quoted ("It's no use simply saying," "You can't just say") reflects its source in experience: the mountain-girt rural village of Pandy in the Welsh borders, where Williams grew up, was not far from the very different, heavily industrialized landscapes of the South Wales coalfield. The railway ran through Pandy, connecting it to the wider world and offering unionized industrial employment to a handful of workers. *Border Country* records how the British General Strike of 1926 forged a temporary but powerful unity between miners and the local railwaymen (who included Williams's father). The rural and the urban were experienced as contrasting but closely connected worlds in topography, culture, and politics.

Rhetorically, Williams's modes of address strike a note rather different from the more impersonal discourses gaining ascendancy among literary academics during his career. This might be taken to signify a preference for "situated knowledge" over "pseudo-objectivity" (the opposed terms are Donna Haraway's),[12] a preference with some affinity to ecocritical values. Williams chose to acknowledge, and often to emphasize, the connections between his life and his varied kinds of work as an educator, as a cultural critic, and as a political activist; and he wrote mostly in a fairly informal—if sometimes convoluted—idiom that allowed ready cross-reference between these dimensions. (It must be added, for clarification, that he was in no sense hostile to abstract theoretical terms and positions, as elements in the process of cultural analysis: see, for example, and especially, his *Marxism and Literature.* In a cause célèbre of 1980, he supported the young Colin MacCabe, very much a "theorist" in the eyes of the traditionally minded, when MacCabe was trying, and failing, to have his Cambridge lectureship confirmed.)[13]

In its insistence on the need for "equitable negotiation," the passage suggests how the experiences of his youth informed Williams's approach to questions not only of red and green politics, but of nature, culture, and history. His search for respectful accommodation between the different traditions deriving from the country and from the city had an intimate biographical basis. The landscapes of the Border were the theme also of his last, unfinished novel, *People of the Black Mountain,* which offers a broad imaginative narrative of human habitation there since the Neolithic era. (The two completed volumes of this projected three-volume work appeared posthumously, with an outline of the intended conclusion by Williams's widow, Joy Williams.)[14] Place for Williams is, above all, place lived in and worked on by people. He knew the rural village too well to imagine it as a pseudo-Eden, all the better if "unspoiled" by progress, as was common in the once-dominant vein of English cultural criticism associated with F. R. Leavis's advocacy of "organic community."[15] The village was a place of poverty and limitation, as well as of warmth and intimacy. The scholarship Williams won to Cambridge offered him the opportunity (unprecedented for a working-class child before his own lifetime) to realize a potential that could only have been stifled in Pandy, and perhaps in Wales. The marginal place of the country childhood was bound, not just inevitably but also for the better, to the world at large—the coalfield, the university, the metropolis. This sense of necessary connection underlies Williams's insistence that the question of ecology is not a question of nature as a world apart, of how we might preserve and enjoy remote and wild places, but of the whole mode of production which frames and determines humanity's dealings with the earth.

This complex, dialectical perspective was brought to bear both in *The Country and the City* and in the political interventions of the early 1980s. Those years did not only bring the victory of neoliberalism in Britain; across Europe, they saw the beginning of the end of the cold war, the apogee of a pan-European peace and antinuclear movement (capable of bringing hundreds of thousands of demonstrators into the streets in Germany, Holland, Italy, and Britain), and the concomitant rise of other oppositional new social movements. Among the latter, the green and ecological parties, quite newly founded for the most part, held an important place, especially Die Grünen (Green Party) in the then Federal Republic of Germany; and their relationship with other, already established left-of-center parties and organizations was a matter of debate and contention, especially in Germany.[16] Despite these tensions between historic and emerging formations, it was widely believed among progressive groups in Europe that there were significant convergences, and that there might be an active political alliance between different anticapitalist perspectives. (One notes that the contemporary account of this political moment given by the North American writers Fritjof Capra and Charlene Spretnak offered a different and more skeptical assessment of the pertinence of socialist analysis to ecological politics.) In this context, the fact that Williams felt and expressed an affinity with "old" Left traditions rooted in organized labor and reaching back before the General Strike, while he was also sympathetic to the ecopolitics of the rising generation, made him an important advocate of dialogue and common purpose.

The failure of such advocacy is well known. Neither the rethinking to which Williams and others called the Left, nor the realignment of European progressive forces to which it might have contributed, has taken place. The green movement has remained near the political margins, the Marxist Left has gone on dwindling, while the mainstream parties of the Center-Left have almost without exception become unequivocal advocates and protectors of globalized neoliberalism. The antiglobalization movement, in my judgment, is constituted, and self-constituted, as a "protest," and an ineffectual one, largely because it cannot forge the kinds of alliance of which Williams spoke, and is therefore in a weak position to develop alternative strategies or institutions. Against this background, the moments of guarded optimism that Williams occasionally allowed himself ("I think we are at the beginning of constructing . . . a new kind of politics," to quote the concluding sentence of his pamphlet *Socialism and Ecology*) can make one wince, though a sigh would be a truer response. What we hoped was an emergent vision has become a lost possibility.

Nonetheless, if ecocriticism aspires to be a political rather than just a personal and academic project, then the questions Williams insisted on, in a critical practice informed by both social and ecological concerns, must continue to inform its agenda. I return to this point in my concluding remarks.

Progress and the "Border": *The Country and the City*

The title's reference is topographical, but the distinctive excellence of *The Country and the City* lies in its illumination of temporal and historical process. The textual readings take their place in, and their force from, a broad survey of changing cultural and economic relations within the countryside and between the metropolis and the marginal territories that metropolitan power exploits: rural communities within the English and British nation and also, in the book's final chapters, the exploited "periphery" of empire and neo-empire. Williams frequently emphasizes, especially in his later readings, the destructive impact of what is called progress—not least in discussing how writers such as Chinua Achebe, James Ngugi (as Williams calls him; he later became known as Ngugi wa Thiong'o), and Han Suyin represent the "uncomprehending and often brutal alien system" of colonial rule, as it "invaded and transformed" rural societies overseas.[17] However, neither in its overall tenor nor in its particular analyses does the book endorse a simple retrospective idealization of earlier days or of country life.

Indeed, the early chapters, in particular, are markedly deconstructive and demythologizing. Here (as Greg Garrard puts it) Williams sets out to demonstrate that the dominant pastoral tradition, in its classical origins and its English Renaissance avatar, offers a "vision of rural life so removed from the processes of labor and natural growth that [the literary works] constitute a persistent mystification of human ecology."[18] Country writing inscribes an ideological mirage, concealing real historical processes behind a nostalgic cultural fiction. Established in a sequence of close readings, the critical point is stated in general terms in the fourth chapter, "Golden Ages," where Williams writes that the "idea of an ordered and happier past set against the disturbance and disorder of the present [is an] idealisation . . . [which] served to cover and evade the actual and bitter contradictions of the time."[19] Those contradictions are epitomized in Sidney's *Arcadia:* the work which "gives a continuing title to English neo-pastoral" was written, Williams reminds us, "in a park which had been made by enclosing a whole village and evicting the tenants."[20]

This deconstructive edge continues to come through in a persistent vigilance vis-à-vis any literary representation in which images of the rural and natural are offered as emblematic of the good life, especially when the perspective is backward-looking. Much closer to our own times, Williams dismisses the bulk of twentieth-century writing about the country as an "elegiac, neo-pastoral mode" in which "the real land and its people were falsified."[21] He distinguishes, in his discussion of the poet Edward Thomas, between decadent tropes and conventions and the more distinctive and responsive sensibility that may push through them to utter something new; but his conclusion is unequivocal: "Very few country writers, in the twentieth century, have wholly escaped this strange formation in which observation, myth, record and half-history are so deeply entwined."[22] Williams is referring here to writers about rural England. Critics working on other national literatures may well reflect on the similar or analogous compound formations to be found there.

Less ideologically fraught modes of country writing, focussed on the nonhuman, are of limited interest to Williams. In the chapter "Three around Farnham," for example, he acknowledges the importance of Gilbert White's newly precise and detailed kind of nature description: but the fact that White isolates and attends closely to "nature in a sense that could now be separated from man" is not for Williams[23]—as surely it would be for most ecocritics—a particular recommendation of his work. To the contrary: White gets less than a page of discussion, while his neighbors on the Surrey-Hampshire border, William Cobbett and Jane Austen, for whom the rural setting is a background for socially oriented reportage or fiction, are treated at some length.

Contemporary ecocritics may well find unsympathetic both Williams's a priori skepticism about country writing, and his lack of interest in the non-human; for some, *The Country and the City* will hardly count as ecocriticism. Certainly Williams will be convicted of "speciesism," by those who like to use the term—often with a hardy disregard for the underlying metaphysical complexities (of which there is much relevant discussion in Kate Soper's *What Is Nature?* one of many British works on nature and culture in which the fruitful influence of Williams is evident). In reply, one can suggest that the celebration of wild nature and the other-than-human, which gives the keynote of much writing favoured by ecocritics, does not necessarily encourage reflection on the forces and processes that threaten nature and humanity alike, or on our own participation in these. Subjectively, many of us know we need material and symbolic access to "nature . . . separated from man"—that is, to a green space not "smeared with toil" (in Gerard Manley Hopkins's phrase); Williams himself felt this, and in middle age bought a cottage at the foot of his native Black Mountains to which he often retreated. But Williams characteristically insists on turning his readers' thought back from delight in such consoling spaces to the "actual and bitter contradictions" of the whole history we partake in. As uncompromising in his way as the deep ecologists are in theirs, he reminds us that the cultural taste for "nature" arose and flourished in societies that have systematically and ruthlessly exploited natural resources (including human labor-power). We think in Williams's spirit if we reflect on what it means that today, protected wilderness areas and nature parks abound in most of the overdeveloped societies, still hell-bent on "growth," whose citizens' per-capita consumption of energy and raw materials contributes most notably to global eco-destruction.

Williams thus brings a salutary negativity to bear on some conventions of country writing, and on habits and assumptions that have framed our readings of it. In more positive terms, he offers an appreciative account of some major British novelists whose representations of country and city are important in their depiction of the displacements and ruptures of history. His discussions of Thomas Hardy and D. H. Lawrence, in particular,[24] draw on his own experience of the journey that takes the writer away, geographically and culturally, from the loved place of childhood. What engages him most deeply about these novelists is their tenacity in sustaining, against the historical current that has caught them up in its flow, a critical perspective on metropolitan modernity: on its commercial and industrial priorities, and their consequence in human relationships. His chapter on Hardy, in particular ("Wessex and the Border"—the only chapter devoted exclusively to a single writer), is memorable for the breadth and sureness of its judgments. Williams's subtle assessment here suggests the conceptual frame in which it will be profitable to consider other and later examples: the oeuvre of the Irish novelist John McGahern (1934–2006), for example, whose work, like Hardy's, focuses on a vulnerable, peripheral landscape, dominated economically by the culturally distant metropolis.[25] The frame serves not just to evaluate literary work, but to prompt critical thought about the shapes and claims of historical progress in general—the thematic nexus at which Williams's cultural readings in The Country and the City intersect most significantly with his engagement a few years later with red/green politics.

We can capture the shape of this conceptual frame by reflecting on the idea of the "border," a term that appears in the titles of two chapters of The Country and the City and of Williams's first novel, Border Country (Williams's colleagues John McIlroy and Sallie Westwood aptly used this again for the posthumous edition they made of his writings about and for the adult-education movement).

In all these contexts and uses, the "border" denotes a place or space whose exposure and vulnerability is the condition of a certain form of knowledge. To be remote from the metropolis while subject to the economic dynamics unleashed there is radically to lack agency in the face of history; to be shut out (like Hardy's Jude) from the citadels of formal learning is to suffer an exclusion. Far from being insulated from history, those in marginal and so to speak belated positions are sharply exposed to its progressive-destructive impact. But Williams identifies a particular "structure of feeling,"[26] with radical potential, that derives from the impact of modernity on the border's customary, popular, and subaltern forms of life. Noting at the start of his discussion that, a few years before Hardy's birth, a group of agricultural laborers in his native Dorset (the "Tolpuddle martyrs") had been sentenced to deportation for forming a trade union, Williams comments: "This fact alone should remind us that Hardy was born into a changing and struggling rural society, rather than the timeless backwater to which he is so often deported [by critics]."[27]

The subsequent readings stress the concrete, material particularity of Hardy's delineation of change and struggle: "the . . . pressures [toward change] within rural society itself are accurately seen"; "we miss almost all of what Hardy has to show us if we impose on the actual relationships he describes a neo-pastoral convention"; Hardy represents "the specific forms of this modern rural world. . . . This was Hardy's actual society, and we cannot suppress it in favour of a seamless abstracted 'country way of life.' "[28] The form of realist fiction makes possible, and Hardy's historical insight brings to realization, an image of "border country" in which the relations between progress and retrospect, between the price modernity exacts of old solidarities and customs and the rewards it offers to the educated and newly mobile individual, are dramatized as a matter, precisely, of struggle, and so related ultimately to the world of politics.

There is thus a marked shift, in some later chapters of *The Country and the City*, away from the deconstructive and skeptical engagement with earlier country writing. This is partly an effect of the generic move from pastoral poetry to the novel, Williams's sympathies and powers being as a rule most effectively engaged when he discusses realist genres. Rereading the book now, thirty-five years after its appearance, one senses more strongly that the shift in tone also reflects the movement toward the threatening present, the newly liberating but newly destructive powers of twentieth-century modernity, and the need for a less deathly alternative: Williams had fought, had killed, and had faced an early death in Normandy at the end of the Second World War, and was growing ever more certain that "we cannot *materially* go on in the old ways." In that perspective, Hardy (as Williams reads him) has taken the measure of a world where, while it remains futile to dream of golden ages and "timeless pasts," it has become impossible to believe the dream of progress either.

The (Im)possibility of "Retrospective Radicalism"

Early in *The Country and the City*, as if to clear the ground for the subsequent critical and historical argument, Williams offers a brief abstract discussion of the political potential of "retrospective radicalism," and I conclude with a comment on this discussion and the reflections it prompts.[29]

As in his "red/green" interventions of a few years later, Williams can here be heard to address both the Labor movement and a subculture of "ruralist" dissent. He criticizes sharply the tendency of many socialists to accept as "progressive" the technical and social modes of industrial production developed under capitalism, along with their ideological talk of "productive efficiency" and their "unreflecting celebration of mastery—power, yield, production, man's mastery of nature." Williams is especially scornful of the notion that, capitalism having now lost its "progressive" character, socialism will "offer to complete the capitalist enterprise" through "still more telling mastery." In these same few paragraphs, he deals quite sympathetically with the subculture of English ruralist dissidence, acknowledging that along with reactionary and perhaps proto-fascist elements, it includes "a precarious but persistent rural-intellectual radicalism [which is] genuinely and actively hostile to industrialism and capitalism." However, he concludes that although this "old, sad, retrospective radicalism seems to bear and to embody a human concern," it cannot in the end offer an adequate, historically rooted basis for an oppositional politics.

This rhetorical antithesis between "retrospective radicalism" and the destructive technologies, social relations and ideologies of "progress" (engendered by capitalism but embraced by many who call themselves socialists) prompts diverse thoughts and readings. It recalls the opposition between delusively attractive pastoral and the exposed "actual society" Hardy depicted, in which Williams finds a real (though subaltern) resource for struggle and opposition—but which will not survive the impact of "progress." It half-mirrors the opposition of the 1980s, between the as-yet-ineffectual "human concern" of the green movement and the all-too-narrow pragmatism of conventional Labor politics. Psychically, it recalls the tension between the impulse to seek an escape in wild or rural landscape, and the impulse to turn back and confront the knowledge of "bitter contradiction" in the historical mainstream. It may put us in mind of the fraught (dis)connections between culture and not-culture, between scholarship and political engagement, between the congenial work of writing or criticism and the uncongenial world that is traced there. Finally, holding these different tensions together, we may think of Theodor Adorno, a critic less different from Williams than he seems, and his well-known metaphor of the two torn halves that do not add up to a whole. Although it was consistently affirmative in tone and spirit, the voice of Raymond Williams, as it returns to haunt the present, now speaks clearly of negation and contradiction.

NOTES

1. Eagleton, *Raymond Williams*, vi.

2. Wallace, Jones, and Nield, *Raymond Williams Now*, 1–2.

3. Garrard, *Ecocriticism*, 37.

4. For the context, see Inglis, *Raymond Williams*, 264–77.

5. The reviews of Bahro were published in 1980 and 1983 and of Myrdal in 1981. Publication details of these and of all works by Williams referred to in the text are given in the bibliography.

6. Williams, "Response to the Debate," 148–49.

7. Bennett, "Anti-Pastoralism," 196, 207.

8. Williams insists on this point especially in "Response to the Debate."

9. Williams, "Towards Many Socialisms," 306.

10. Williams, *Socialism and Ecology*, 13–14.

11. Inglis discusses the unsettling personal impact of the interview process (see Inglis, *Raymond Williams,* 259–64).

12. Haraway, *Modest Witness,* 142.

13. See Inglis, *Raymond Williams,* 278–82.

14. See ibid., 319 n. 50.

15. For a brief survey of this formation, see Ryle, *Journeys in Ireland,* 95–98.

16. For contemporary comment, see Ryle, *Ecology and Socialism,* 89–93; and Castellina, "Why Red Must Be Green Too."

17. Williams, *Country and City,* 285f.

18. Garrard, *Ecocriticism,* 38.

19. Williams, *Country and City,* 45.

20. Ibid., 22.

21. Ibid., 256, 258.

22. Ibid., 261; for the discussion of Thomas, 257–61.

23. Ibid., 119.

24. See Williams, *Country and City,* 197–214 (on Hardy); and 264–68 (on Lawrence).

25. The bibliography lists two of McGahern's most important novels. For critical discussion, see Ryle, "Place, Time and Perspective."

26. For the term "structure of feeling," see Williams, *Marxism and Literature,* 128, and subsequent discussion.

27. Williams, *Country and City,* 197.

28. Ibid., 208–9.

29. See Williams, *Country and City,* 35–37 (all quotations in the relevant paragraphs of the text are from these pages). For fuller discussion, see Soper, *What Is Nature?* 205–6; and Ryle, "The Past, the Future and the Golden Age."

Sense of Place and Lieu de Mémoire: A Cultural Memory Approach to Environmental Texts

It is striking how often literary representations of nature appear within recollections of childhood, or more broadly in the context of acts of remembering. At the same time, memories of the past, in literature as in life, are commonly anchored in places, landscapes, or buildings. As approaches to the study of culture, ecocriticism and cultural memory studies differ in their principal concerns: while the former relates to nature and space, and examines cultural constructions of the natural environment, the latter is oriented toward history and time, and principally preoccupied with representations and understandings of the social, in formulations relating the present and future to the past. However, both are concerned with how writers critique contemporary Western sociopolitical structures and cultural values, how they envision alternatives, and how their work facilitates cultural renewal. They share interests in the interaction between personal experience and imagining on the one hand and collective values and identity on the other, and in textual mechanisms and techniques involving the adaptation and reinterpretation of received narratives and images. And their interests converge in place. In this essay, I argue that a cultural memory approach affords insights into the cultural and textual construction of places from which ecocritics can profit.

Among the foremost convictions of the environmental movement since the 1960s has been that in order to reduce environmental damage, we need to strengthen individuals' ties to the local area, which have been increasingly eroded in modern society. Aldo Leopold's land ethic, E. F. Schumacher's "small is beautiful" economic program, bioregionalism, and food miles are all variants of the philosophy of localism. The Kentucky farmer, poet, and essayist Wendell Berry, the Native American writer Leslie Marmon Silko, and the author, naturalist, and environmental activist Terry Tempest Williams are among the most frequently cited literary proponents of sense of place. In his essay "The Regional Motive," Berry writes: "Without a complex knowledge of one's place, and without the faithfulness to one's place on which such knowledge depends, it is inevitable that the place will be used carelessly, and eventually destroyed."[1] At the same time, philosophers as different as Hans Jonas, Arne Naess, and Zygmunt Bauman have developed an ethics of spatial proximity, and argued for physical immersion as a way for individuals to reintegrate in the biotic community. Since the emergence of literary ecocriticism in the early 1990s, advocates including Lawrence Buell, Glen Love, and Scott Slovic have therefore been centrally concerned with the role of literature in fostering a sense of locality and place.

However, the assumption underlying much ecocriticism that environmental consciousness is necessarily grounded in sense of place, and that sustainable behavior can be fostered by reconnecting individuals with place, has recently been challenged by Ursula Heise in her book *Sense of Place and Sense of Planet*. Not all premodern societies were rooted in place, Heise reminds us, and those that were have by no means always been models of ecologically sensitive inhabitation. In the mobile world of the twenty-first century, moreover, there can be no simple return to local belonging and the caring which allegedly follows from it: sense of place must be complemented by "sense of planet," and local belonging subordinated to global identification.

Heise attributes the "persistent utopian reinvestment in the local" which she identifies to a fundamental ambivalence in public attitudes toward the notion of global connectedness dating back to the 1960s, and to the weakening of utopian impulses over the last four decades. There are, she suggests, also particular reasons why American environmentalists and ecocritics have committed themselves to localism and the ethics of proximity: rootedness in place has acquired a special value as counterweight to the restless mobility perceived as paradigmatic of American society and American character. However, Heise argues, "eco-cosmopolitanism" is a more appropriate goal today, when identity is more commonly defined by relations to a multiplicity of places than a singular place. Traditional place-attachment has become an anachronism. Restoring individuals' sense of place may remain a useful tool in environmentalist practice, but it is a "dead end if it is understood as a founding ideological principle or a principal didactic means of guiding individuals and communities back to nature."[2]

However desirable, even necessary, it is to develop the sense of planet outlined by Heise, this does not mean ecocritics can afford to ignore place as a cultural phenomenon. The main target of Heise's critique is the conviction that an ethic of responsibility and care for the natural environment is rooted in either sensual experience gained through physical proximity or cognitive knowledge of the surrounding ecosystems.[3] Quite rightly, she challenges this assumption and points out that environmental consciousness is also grounded in other ways which have nothing to do with place, or which derive from awareness of the connections between places rather than attachment to a particular place. However, Heise underestimates the affective ties with place which arise out of identification, as part of processes of individual and collective identity-construction. The cultural memory approach developed by Maurice Halbwachs, Pierre Nora, and Jan and Aleida Assmann which I examine in this essay is concerned with places less as geographical realities than as symbolic entities, remembered and imagined, which play a central role in subject constitution, and serve crucial political, social, and cultural functions. Places in this sense are under constant reconstruction, as the founding myths of communities are adapted to changing political circumstances. Providing a more precise understanding of the imaginative strategies and devices, cultural practices, and institutions that allow individuals and communities to form attachments to places and to maintain them over time as an integral part of their identities, cultural memory studies draws attention to dimensions of the affective investment in place and of place-belonging whose implications have hitherto been largely ignored by ecocritics.[4]

Cultural Memory Studies

Memory studies began to gain wider recognition as a theoretical approach in the 1980s, with the "memory turn" in the study of history inaugurated by the French historian Pierre Nora. In Germany, where the collapse of the Soviet Union, political reunification, and the emergence of Holocaust memory into new prominence triggered a surge of new interest in the nation's past, Jan and Aleida Assmann gave memory studies a distinctive direction through their elaboration of the concept of "cultural memory" (see especially Jan Assmann's *Das kulturelle Gedächtnis* and Aleida Assmann's *Erinnerungsräume*).[5] Both Nora and the Assmanns drew on the ideas of the French sociologist Maurice Halbwachs. Writing between the 1920s and the 1940s, Halbwachs sought to provide a corrective to Henri Bergson's and Sigmund Freud's understanding of memory as a purely subjective and individual phenomenon.[6] He shifted his focus from the individual realm to the domain of the "social frames" of collective experience, and saw acts of remembering as always related to the repository of images and ideals that constitute our sociocultural relations. Halbwachs introduced the term "collective memory" for articulations of the relationship with the past of social groups and cultural communities in rituals and customs, verbal communication, the media, and institutions. He saw the construction of identity as a central function of relating to the past: we recall those events which are relevant to the self-understanding and present interests of the group.

The Assmanns' conception of "cultural memory" corresponds to this broad understanding of culture, subsuming media practices and myth, monuments and ritual rememberings alongside written texts including letters, diaries, and autobiographies as well as prose fiction, drama, and poetry. However, they distinguish cultural memory from "communicative/social memory," the product of everyday interaction of living people, comprising events going back a maximum of about eighty years. Social memory is the subject of oral history and research into family and generation memory, and its contents are open to constantly shifting interpretation. Cultural memory, by contrast, possesses greater stability and longevity due to its inscription in collective practices and physical objects. The common denominator of its configurations of cultural knowledge lies in patterns of thought, narratives, and images giving meaning to the past, and converting past experiences into a basis for individual and collective identity in the present.

In the human brain, remembering depends on invention as much as retrieval. Though there is as yet no universally accepted model for how memory works, it is generally held that memories are not stores of complete sets of sense data, but consist rather of fragments of experience encoded in engrams, or patterns of neuronal excitement, which must be reactivated in processes linking them up into coherent patterns of information. This process of "re-membering" the raw experiential data explains why memories are subjective and context-dependent, and why they often tell us as much about the present needs and desires of the remembering subject as they do about the past. The reliving of memory can be compared with theatrical or musical rehearsals, which entail making reality of something which exists only in abstract notation, and creating as much as repeating. (For a detailed account of the functioning of memory, see Daniel Schacter, *Searching for Memory*.)

Literary remembering, which has attracted increasing attention in the last fifteen years, can also be understood as a *performance* of the past, an active production of "lived reality," through the selection and arrangement, synthesis, and dramatic intensification of past events. The free embrace of imaginary elements is one of the distinguishing features of literature and feature films. The "depragmatization" which alleviates them from the burden of telling the historical truth enables them to try out interpretations of the past. Historical facts can be readily invested with new meanings. This linking of the real with the imagined facilitates the generation of new structures of cultural perception. Literary works typically seek to respond to a crisis or problem in the existing memory culture by focusing on forgotten aspects of the past, articulating as yet unformed memories, and making stories out of them.

While authors participate in the omnipresent competition between different rememberings, they also frequently reflect on the process, either by commenting explicitly on the shortcomings of a specific memory culture, or by directing attention to their own authorial strategies of representation and construction. In these and other ways, writers prompt critical reflection on the functioning and problems of collective memory, and help their communities adapt to changing circumstances.[7] Literary texts also possess distinctive formal properties: the process of condensation present in all remembering is intensified. Uniting and overlaying different semantic spheres in allegory and metaphor, works of literature are characteristically structured by symbolic figurations of memory. The term "figurations of memory" was introduced by the Assmanns to denote a constantly evolving archive of narratives and images deriving from the Bible, Greek myth, fairy tales, history, world literature, etc. These structures, which crystallize meaning around events, people, and places, blend factual and textual recall with imagination. They evoke established memory patterns and interpretations of the past, and actualize them. This process of intertextual revisiting and reconfiguring of tropes, narratives, and images plays a central role in the constant reshaping of public perceptions of nature and the environment. Figurations of memory focusing on places serve as particularly important vehicles for the communication and redefinition of understandings of our relationship with the natural environment.

Places of Memory

Places of memory and the relationship between place and memory have been key areas of memory research. Jan Assmann has written of the role played by sacred places in premodern cultures, originally as physical habitations of the divine, later as locations embodying the memory of the experience of divine presence, and finally as the sites of past events leading to the founding of the nation. Visiting such places of memory was a refreshing of these memories, and was practiced ritually as a rededication to the nation and the values for which it stood. Places associated with the ruling family thus served to confirm the stability and continuity of the community. Aleida Assmann and others have since shown how places associated with traumatic events such as military defeat and the Holocaust have played an equally important role in fixing and mediating individuals' identification with the nation in recent times.

In *Erinnerungsräume*, Aleida Assmann identifies texts, images, the body, and places as the four principal media through which memories and identity are anchored in cultural memory. The lingering material traces which constitute physical links mediating between present and past make places of memory auratic sites of immediate encounter with a forgotten past. Places are special symbols of events and associated values, because they possess an indexical relationship with their meaning. Not only do they bridge the gap between mental constructs and reality with a unique degree of physical validity and longevity, they are also typically sites where individual and collective memories reinforce each other. Ecological configuration of the symbolic meaning of places does not necessarily entail a restoration of spiritual significance or reenchantment. However, Aleida Assmann notes a basic human need for "holy places," from which miracles, reconciliation, healing or spiritual renewal can be derived. She writes of the combination of philological learning/historical knowledge and intuition/imagination in place-based encounters with the past since the Renaissance, and shows how poetic imagination gained in importance in the Romantic period. The Romantic cult of ruins, historical places, and picturesque or sublime landscapes was a gesture of resistance to Enlightenment modernity's rational exploitation of space, which at the same time facilitated the new interest in autobiographical self-reflection. Places came to be associated with forgetting and the eruptive return of the repressed.

However, the importance of place for memory goes beyond such "real" places of memory, which are typically defined by their collective investment with overlapping, often conflicting significances, and open to constant reinterpretation and reappropriation. Spatializing ideas and events is an inherent feature of human memory, as illustrated by the ancient mnemonic technique *ars memoriae*, which linked arguments with places in order to recall them. Cicero, in *De oratore*, recommended that orators attach *loci et imagines* (places and images) to the things to be remembered in their speeches. The images helped recall the facts and ideas, while the places helped order them. The speaker could then walk round in his imagination and collect them. In *The Art of Memory*, Frances Yates showed that this once widely practiced technique is not merely one of the main origins of the system of conventional symbols whose iconographic presence may be found in art and literature down to the end of the eighteenth century, but also exercised a powerful influence over the cultural organization of knowledge in Europe.

It was Yates's book from which Pierre Nora took the notion of "lieu de mémoire" in his monumental, seven-volume *Les lieux de mémoire* (1984– 92). Besides signifying "places of memory," *lieux de mémoire* refers more broadly to "realms" or "sites" "where [cultural] memory crystallizes and secretes itself."[8] The lieux de mémoire discussed by Nora and his colleagues include places such as Reims, Paris, the prehistoric caves of Lascaux, buildings, and museums; rituals, festivals, and calendars; objects such as monuments, flags, and texts (Marcel Proust's *Remembrance of Things Past*); real people (René Descartes and Joan of Arc); mythical ones (the Good Soldier, Nicolas Chauvin); events (the Battle of Verdun, the Tour de France); and concepts, mottos, and symbols. Whether they constitute physical locations of memory, or just its place in the social imagination, these are all approached as the result of an imaginary process that codifies and represents the historical consciousness of France.

Nora's distinction of memory (the totality of forms through which cultural communities imagine themselves in diverse representational modes), from history (an intellectual practice rooted in the evidence derived from the study of empirical reality), and his work in general have been major influences on younger researchers. However, international interest in places of memory has been frequently associated with Holocaust scholarship, and researchers have been keener to embrace localized, diffuse, polysemic memories than to reconstruct hegemonic national identities. They have sought to preserve or salvage the memories of individuals and small communities as antidotes to the narrative of dominant groups and oppressive states. Nora's pessimistic conception of the replacement of the unitary framework of French collective memory by smaller configurations or identities, resulting in a regrettable fragmentation and politicization of memory, and of memory functioning in our era of commemoration as a mere simulation of the past,[9] has also been discarded. Vagueness over the definition of lieux de mémoire led the Assmanns to distinguish between figurations of memory (*lieux* in the broader sense) and the actual physical spaces which memory focuses upon, real places in which vestiges evoke the past in a particularly intense way.

In *Landscape and Memory* (1996), Simon Schama has written eloquently about the interplay between individual imaginings of place and cultural templates, and about the political functions which individuals' nostalgic responses have served over the centuries. However, Schama's interest in ecological issues is only marginal, and the same has been true for most other studies of place and memory. In the final part of this essay, I wish to show how places of memory form the focus of two works from the 1980s which combine collective identity construction with interrogation of our interaction with nature: an autobiographical novel by the Austrian Peter Handke and a short work of poetic prose by the East German Volker Braun. Handke's novel, *Repetition*, published in 1986, is a fictionalized account of the author's discovery of his ancestral homeland in Slovenia, written at a time when western Europeans had largely "forgotten" their eastern and southeastern neighbours. Volker Braun's *Bodenloser Satz* (Groundless Sentence) was written in 1988, and published in the autumn of 1989. It presented a critical review of forty years of socialism in the German Democratic Republic (GDR) on the eve of the state's collapse and absorption into the Federal Republic of Germany (FRG).

The weakening of the economies of countries in eastern Europe, the decline of Soviet power, and the growing disillusionment with socialist ideology prompted major changes in cultures of memory in both Austria and the German Democratic Republic in the years leading up to the collapse of the Soviet Union and the end of the cold war. Handke and Braun contributed to processes whereby national and personal identities were being reconfigured, by revisiting and reinterpreting their own past and that of the collective. At the same time, *Repetition* and *Groundless Sentence* sought to promote ecological principles. The utopian and dystopian places they present respectively mobilized individual and collective memories in order to construct new collective identities in which ecological sustainability played a central role.

Peter Handke's *Repetition*

Handke's mother belonged to a Slovenian-speaking minority that was discriminated against in Carinthia, the southeastern province of Austria where he grew up. From the late 1970s on, his writing reflects growing interest in his Slovenian heritage. Looking back from the time of writing in the mid-1980s, Filip Kobal, the fictional protagonist of *Repetition*, remembers the summer of 1960, when he left school at age eighteen and set off, alone and on foot, on a journey to discover the home of his ancestors. Getting to know Slovenia, its people, and language is described as reestablishing contact with the family's past and with a dimension of the nation whose memory had been suppressed. This past is linked with emancipatory political activism through the story of a Kobal who was executed for leading a failed Peasants' Rising in 1713. Filip's itinerary is determined by the search for traces of a lost older brother. Twenty-one years his elder, Gregor Kobal had studied horticulture in Maribor before the Second World War. When he was drafted into the Wehrmacht and sent to fight former classmates, he deserted. It is rumored that he joined a group of partisans who declared a "Free Republic of Kobarid."

Filip's journey ends where his brother disappeared, on the barren karst plateau in the hinterland of the city of Trieste. The rural community he finds there, living in utopian harmony with the environment in fertile dolinas (sinkholes, or large circular depressions in the limestone pavement),[10] contrasts with contemporary Austrian materialism, affluence, and distrust of foreigners. The same holds true for a second place of memory in *Repetition*, an orchard which Filip's older brother had planted back home in Austria after his return from Maribor.[11] Both are presented as models of productive human interaction with the natural environment. A rich diversity of crops is grown by patient grafting and selective cultivation. Gregor Kobal's and the Slovenian small farmers' methodical stewardship serves as a model, not only for Filip's life, but also for his writing, in which he seeks to erect a permanent memorial to his brother's values.

Slovenia is for Handke less a political or geographical entity than a bucolic dreamland, a mythical ancestral nation, and the projection of a longing for a better world. His descriptions of the sinkholes in the Slovenian karst contain biblical echoes of the Garden of Eden and Noah's Ark, and he refers to them as the "Ninth Country," a term derived from a Slovenian folktale which alludes to an Arcadian land of plenty that will one day return. A passage describing Filip Kobal reading his older brother's handwritten manual for fruit-growing reflects Handke's own reading of Virgil's *Georgics*. Other passages echo Ernst Bloch's conception of *Heimat* in *The Principle of Hope*, and the Heideggerian concepts of dwelling and belonging resonate in allusions to homelessness, home, and Filip's attachment to the farming community toward the end of the novel. Alongside these intertextual references, which are confirmed by entries in his diaries, Handke constructs new figurations of memory of his own, which recur throughout the novel as enigmatic leitmotifs. The titles of the first two sections of the three into which the book is divided, "Blind Windows" and "Empty Cowpaths," are complex symbols of loss and the degradation of the present, hinting at the possible return of a better life which is fleetingly associated with the old Austro-Hungarian Empire.

Volker Braun's *Groundless Sentence*

In *Groundless Sentence*, Braun asks what has become of the ideals and principles on which the GDR was founded. The narrative, in which a first-person protagonist revisits a village standing in the path of an opencast mining project where he had worked thirty years before, incorporates elements of the author's own experience as a civil engineering laborer in the late 1950s. The narrator recalls the actions of his work brigade, clearing the ground of vegetation so that the topsoil could be removed and the underlying coal extracted. As the houses are evacuated, ancient trees are felled, and orchards bulldozed, he becomes painfully aware of the losses incurred.

By evoking a "bottomless" pit, the title alludes literally to the brown coal mining which was a central plank in the GDR economy, providing the main source of energy for its heavy industry, but also a major source of atmospheric and water pollution because of the high sulphur content of the extracted coal. The "groundless sentence," taken metaphorically, also reflects the author's sense of the ideological ground disappearing under his feet, and anxieties about losing the territory, community, and home for which he had written over the last three decades. Third, understood as a "monstrous" sentence, it expresses his fear that human invention and striving may ultimately be indistinguishable from the impulse to destroy, and that an instrumental relationship with nature may yet be our undoing. And finally, it refers to the form of the piece, whose thirty-two pages are written in one continuous sentence, albeit a highly complex one, juxtaposing heterogeneous elements in a stream of consciousness, and involving alternation between fact and fiction, narrated events and dreams, and different time frames.

The narrative of *Groundless Sentence* is one of self-incurred expropriation. Since the 1970s, Braun had expressed doubts about the practical realization of Marx's vision of humanity's self-realization through "metabolic" interaction with the natural environment. These come to a head in the text, which rejects the idea of man's Promethean struggle with the elements, culminating in the subjugation of nature to rational exploitation. The bleakness of Braun's perception of socialism, and of modernity in general, by the late 1980s is partially alleviated by a utopian vision at the end of the piece, in which the slender trees struggling to reestablish themselves on a recultivated part of the site offer encouragement to confused bystanders, as if remembering men as friends and carers.

The text provides a historical explanation for the corruption of the original ideals of socialism. Disinterring human remains from the village cemetery, the workers come upon a mass grave of wartime Russian slave laborers. We learn that the villagers failed to intervene while these unfortunate people were kept in cattle trucks in a siding, without food or water, or to protest when the SS shot the survivors after forcing them to bury their dead.[12] The founding myth of the GDR, the assumption that East Germans had been antifascists, is exposed as a lie which has condemned them to self-alienation. This has led in turn to the suppression of legitimate individual aspirations and needs in the name of the collective, and ruthless exploitation of the natural environment.

Ecological Belonging as Part of a Wider Redefinition of the Relationship with Place

Groundless Sentence redefined East German collective identity by reinterpreting the people's relationship with the coal mine as a lieu de mémoire. Stripping it of its significance as a site of collective self-realization and the construction of a socialist society, Braun endowed it with new meaning as one of self-deception and quasi-military destruction. The GDR's self-image as a nation of coal miners heroically battling with the land is rejected, and the villagers' loss of their homes is presented as just punishment for their suppression of the past and estrangement from nature and the *Heimat*. Like Handke's places of memory, the opencast coal mine in which Braun sets his narrative is as much an ideological, literary, and mythical place as a real one: its name, Hardt, is an ironic echo of a classical poem by Friedrich Hölderlin, "Der Winkel von Hardt," which celebrated a natural shelter of rock in the Black Forest as the epitome of *Heimat*.

Braun met with harsh criticism after 1990 for his illusory hopes of retaining an independent, reformed communist state in East Germany. However, what *Groundless Sentence* actually was pleading for was a form of society to supersede both existing socialism and Western capitalism, in which mechanisms of domination in relations between men, between the sexes, and between nature and culture are radically restructured. Handke's text exemplifies by contrast the ambivalence of the ethical and political consequences of attachment to place. Traces of nostalgia for the old Austro-Hungarian Empire, as an enlightened, multiethnic democracy maintaining peace, justice, and religious tolerance, are present in *Repetition*,[13] and the book resonates with the idea of "Mitteleuropa." (This conception of a loose confederation of independent states in central Europe experienced a revival in the mid-1980s as a way of overcoming East-West divisions, military confrontation, and the economic stagnation of the Communist bloc.) Handke's karst sinkhole was partly inspired by Vilenica, a limestone cave which has served as a spiritual home for the Slovenians and stood at the same time for political opening to other central European countries and the memory of a shared transnational cultural heritage. The personal myth of Slovenia and the old Yugoslavia as places of freedom and the good life which Handke wove into his writing was to lead him into problematic territory in the 1990s, when he spoke out against the Slovenians' wish for independence and accession to the European Union, and later, when he defended the Serbs and their president Milošović during the Bosnian and Kosovo wars. Handke's alternative to mindless mainstream consumerism is also impracticable as a model for thinking and living in an environmental way because of the poverty and hardship whose acceptance it presupposed. He can thus be said to have fallen victim to his own attachment to place, by losing sight of the essentially fictional, symbolic, and mythical nature of the karst dolina in *Repetition* and confusing it with the Slovenian (and Yugoslavian) state.

With this cautionary proviso, though, literary *lieux de mémoire* can clearly serve an important function as localizations for a utopian vision of human reconciliation with nature which would otherwise lack concrete embodiment. When Ursula Heise writes that the increasing connectedness of societies today demands the emergence of new forms of culture which are no longer anchored in place, and calls for us to "envision how ecologically based advocacy on behalf of the non-human world as well as on behalf of greater socio-environmental justice might be formulated in terms that are *premised no longer on ties to local places,*"[14] this ignores quasi-universal mechanisms of collective memory as well as individual psychology. In Germany, sense of place has not enjoyed the same prominence in recent literary criticism as in the United States since conceptions of local belonging having been discredited through association with the "Blood and Soil" ideology of the Third Reich. However, there has been a gradual revival of interest in the concept of *Heimat* as a marker of affective ties with towns and cities, landscapes, and regions as places of habitation (if not necessarily of origin), in sociological and cultural debates since the 1970s.[15] It may be unwise to dismiss place-identity, and even the nostalgic idealization of places, as factors contributing to a caring attitude toward the environment.

NOTES

1. Berry, "The Regional Motive," 69.

2. Heise, *Sense of Place,* 28, 48–49, 21.

3. Ibid., 33.

4. Heise acknowledges this when she writes that "developing a 'sense of place' cannot mean a return to the natural in and of itself, but at best an approach to the natural from within a different cultural framework," and cites with approval the view that "the assumption that place possesses inherent physical as well as spiritual qualities to which human beings respond when they inhabit them must be replaced by an analysis of how such qualities are either 'socially produced' or 'culturally constructed'" (45). Yet the broad thrust of her argument is to deny place-attachment as a significant environmental factor, rather than to call for a more nuanced understanding of it: "The challenge for environmentalist thinking, then, is to shift the core of its cultural imagination from a sense of place to a less territorial and more systemic sense of planet" (56).

5. Works by the distinguished Egyptologist and cultural theorist Jan Assmann published in English translation include a selection of essays under the title *Religion and Cultural Memory* (2006). Aleida Assmann is principally known for her work on theories of memory and the history of memory in Germany since the Second World War. To date, her more important writings have not appeared in English, though individual books have been published in French and Swedish, and her principal work, *Erinnerungsräume,* has appeared in Italian and Japanese editions. An English translation is currently in preparation. Drawing on Egyptian culture and Greek, Roman, medieval, and Renaissance thinkers, on philosophers from Plato to Locke and Nietzsche, and on examples from English literature ranging from Shakespeare, Spencer, and Wordsworth to Hawthorne and Kurt Vonnegut, as well as on contemporary painting and sculpture, *Erinnerungsräume* presents

a panorama of Western cultural memory and has stimulated much subsequent research with its categorization of types, functions, and media of memory.

6. Halbwachs, *On Collective Memory*, contains extracts from three foundational texts.

7. Astrid Erll's *Kollektives Gedächtnis und Erinnerungskulturen* (Collective Memory and Memory Cultures) provides a helpful overview of research into memory studies in the disciplines of history, sociology, literature, and psychology; discusses the media of social memory; and presents an integrative semiotic model of collective memory. I am indebted here to the last two chapters of that work, which survey recent research on literature as a medium of cultural memory. Publications accessible to English readers include Erll and Nünning, "Where Literature and Memory Meet"; Rigney, "Plenitude, Scarcity"; and the collection of essays edited by Erll and Nünning, *Cultural Memory Studies*.

8. Nora, "Between Memory and History," 7. See also Nora, "From *Lieux de mémoire* to *Realms of Memory*," xvii: "If the expression *lieu de mémoire* must have an official definition, it should be this: a *lieu de mémoire* is any significant entity, whether material or nonmaterial in nature, which by dint of human will or the work of time has become a symbolic element of the memorial heritage of any community."

9. "There are *lieux de mémoire*, sites of memory, because there are no longer *milieux de mémoire*, real environments of memory" (Nora, "Between Memory and History," 7).

10. See Handke, *Repetition*, 196–215.

11. The orchard is described ibid., 120–27.

12. Braun's coal mine possesses characteristics of the traumatic places described by Aleida Assmann (*Erinnerungsräume*, 328–39), whose history is felt to be untellable for reasons of guilt or shame. His depiction of the place's association with past crimes against humanity may have been inspired by one of a number of historical incidents in late 1944 and early 1945, when many prisoners evacuated from concentration camps because of the advancing Allied armies died in transport, as well as on the notorious death marches. There is also a parallel with the exposure of the "Topography of Terror" in 1985, when West German archaeologists and historians discovered a surviving basement section of the Gestapo headquarters in Berlin, whose memory had been suppressed for decades.

13. Filip is prompted, for instance, by the sight of an ornamental footscraper in an old station building to sense "the breath of a gentle spirit, the spirit of those who long ago, in the days of the Empire, had designed it and made use of it" (171).

14. *Sense of Place*, 10, emphasis added.

15. See Gebhard, Geisler, and Schröter, *Heimat*.

2

CULTURE, SOCIETY, & ANTHROPOLOGY

From Literary Anthropology to Cultural Ecology: German Ecocritical Theory since Wolfgang Iser

While ecocriticism first emerged in the Anglophone world, the last decade or so has witnessed its rapid spread throughout other countries and academic communities. In many of these communities, new ecocritical theory has drawn on locally predominant traditions of thought, thus diversifying and enriching the ecological approach through specific cultural influences but also transforming these influences with regard to an ecological worldview. In Germany, ecocritical theory, and especially literary theory, has been shaped decisively by the anthropological approach, which reached the peak of its popularity around 1990. In the following, I compare two exemplary ecocritical models that are influenced by literary anthropology but develop it in different directions. Hartmut Böhme's "aesthetics of nature" is grounded in a traditional subjectivist humanism enriched by the ideal of a "sensibility," or sensual delicacy, that would allow humans to reconnect to nature in several ways. Literature, in his view, is both a means of attaining this sensibility and a particularly effective locus of communication between body, mind, and environment. Hubert Zapf's fusion of cultural ecology and textual criticism, on the other hand, offers a poststructuralist variant of literary anthropology, as it assumes that literary texts revitalize the cultural system by condensing, undermining, and transforming elements of public discourse in nodal constructs such as symbols and metaphors. After a short discussion of Wolfgang Iser's foundational role, I outline both approaches with a focus on the anthropological function they ascribe to literature. In order to clarify and validate these theoretical findings, each outline is followed by an application to a well-known but elusive literary text: Edgar Allan Poe's "The Fall of the House of Usher."

Iser popularized the anthropological approach to literature in German academic circles. Building on his reader-response theory as well as on his studies of anthropologists like Clifford Geertz and Eric Gans, Iser sought to explain the cultural function of fiction in terms of its formal and structural properties. "Since literature as a medium has been with us more or less since the beginning of recorded time," he observes in his 1989 essay "Towards a Literary Anthropology," "its presence must presumably meet certain anthropological needs." Fictional texts must be explained pragmatically—as "a mode of exercising an impact"—without, however, reducing them to one specific function, such as the incorporation of the inaccessible into everyday reality.[1] It is this distinction between the specifically shaped cultural manifestations of fiction and the vast, undefined reservoir of imaginary resources on which they draw that reappears in the title of Iser's influential 1991 study *The Fictive and the Imaginary*. Dissatisfied with the traditional opposition of "reality" and "fiction," Iser proposes a triadic model of fictional texts in their interaction with the cultural environment. While fictional texts do contain elements of the "real" (the extratextual world), these elements are embedded in and transformed by strategies of fictionalization in such a way that they adumbrate the intangible potentialities of the "imaginary": "Thus if the fictional text refers to reality without being reducible to it, this reproduction is an act of fictionalization which brings to light purposes that are *not* part of the reality reproduced. When the act of fictionalizing cannot be deduced from the reality repeated in the text, it stages an imaginary quality that is conjoined with this textually reproduced reality."[2] In this view, the cultural function of literary texts lies in their potential to contrast everyday experiences with possible alternatives. Iser conceives of them as spheres of "play" that allow human beings to "extend" themselves, that is, to develop and modify their self-image in a continual process of imaginative boundary-crossing.

Literary anthropology soon found itself caught in the struggle between classical humanism and poststructuralism—a struggle in which it usually has been aligned with the humanist tradition. In a 1994 volume entitled *Aesthetics and Contemporary Discourse*, Iser's work is promoted as an alternative to the "dehumanizing discourse-theory of poststructuralism" and enlisted in a deliberately anthropocentric project of exploring "the human potential."[3] On the opposite side of the theoretical spectrum, literary anthropology has met with less goodwill. It has been criticized for falling behind the theoretical premises of earlier culturalist approaches. With a view to Geertz's "culture as text" and Foucault's radical historicization of man, the call here is for a literary anthropology that does not accord literature epistemological superiority or any other unique position but analyzes it as one component of the system of signs which is culture. In this perspective, Iser's theory is suspected of containing "ahistorical premises" such as the definition of literature as an overstepping of cultural boundaries.[4] In its systematic conception of literature as a mediating force between the human being and its (cultural) environment, however, Iserian literary anthropology has exerted a strong influence in German ecocriticism—an influence already traceable in the very first major German contribution to ecocritical theory, Böhme's "aesthetics of nature."

In order to establish new, nonhierarchical relations with nature, Böhme argues, we need to recognize its irreducibility not only to the artificial structures of science and technology, but to rational thought in general. To reverse the anthropocentric ontology of the industrial age, we need to return to premodern, symbiotic concepts of the human being in its natural environment. As an example, Böhme cites the microcosm theory of Paracelsus, which regards the human body as a sort of miniature reproduction of its natural environment—a microcosm constituted and nourished by the surrounding macrocosm. Here, there is no distinction between scientific and hermeneutic methods, nor between a chemical and a semiological interpretation of nature. For Paracelsus, the entire process of life—what we might call the global ecosystem—is structured by a chemical as well as by a textual system; nature is thus one great web of signs: "nothing is without a sign; that is, nature gives nothing of herself away without giving a sign to that which is in it. . . . He who wants to describe the natural things must take on the signs, and gain knowledge of these things from the signs."[5] Out of the traditional Christian notion that God's creation originated from his word and could be read and interpreted like scripture, Paracelsus developed the first coherent concept of a natural science. While his notion of an inherent "language of nature" was soon replaced by the new science of physics and its revolutionary epistemological implications, it has remained a productive force in the history of ideas and has contributed to aesthetic concepts in both literature (in Novalis) and philosophy (in Kant, Benjamin, and Adorno). It is precisely the fact that Böhme draws on both the literary and the philosophical traditions, I believe, that makes his approach fruitful for ecocriticism.

Drawing on Kant in particular, Böhme defines the aesthetics of nature as "the practical shaping and culturally differentiated perception of nature with regard to a lust beneficial to life, to the intense experience of dissonance (the sublime), the beautiful order of the multifold in its unity, and purposiveness without purpose."[6] The very phrasing points to an underlying philosophy of the subject that reached its peak with Kant and has been in steady decline ever since. Far from endorsing an antiquated conservatism, however, Böhme insists on the importance of thinking outside the dominant

patterns of modern philosophy. Against the "spastic formation" of an econo-
mized, industrialized *ratio*—"cramped in efforts of holding itself together,
indicating a fear of that which is centrifugal, of that which it cannot itself be
or which it has excluded as its Other"[7]—he sets a new subjectivism: the
subject-in-nature as the only entity that can possibly reunite the vastly different rhythms of nature and culture. The "double alienation of the Modern
Age," Böhme argues, was brought about by the exclusion of aesthetics from
knowledge: "barred by the modern sciences from a direct, bodily experience
of nature, man was alienated both from nature and from his body."[8] This
critique of rationalism, as well as its resolution in a return to the subject and
its bodily experience, is reminiscent of Foucault; in fact, it might be helpful
to define Böhme's aesthetics of nature functionally, with Foucault, as a
discursive configuration that relies on (and tries to reinforce) a premodern
episteme marked by the nonalienation of nature and culture.

One of the key influences of this project is Walter Benjamin's theology of
language. Benjamin thinks of human language as the translation of an "un-
broken stream" of "communication, which flows through all of nature."[9] We
perceive nature not through language but within it. Drawing on this idea,
Böhme stresses the role of the body: it is through our bodily feelings and
reactions to the environment that we enter into communication with the
objective world. The communicative function of the body, he argues, can be
traced in everyday language, which contains manifestations of natural elements, phenomena, and objects in certain linguistic expressions. When we
speak of "burning sensations" or "seething pain," for instance, this is not a
mere metaphor; rather, nature makes itself felt within the Benjaminian
stream of communication in which we partake through our body: "Nature
reveals itself to the body and lays its trace in language."[10]

It is in poetic language, Böhme claims, that this trace is most palpable;
consequently, literature assumes an anthropological function as it offers the
rare—if not unique—opportunity to reconnect to nature by retranslating its
language.[11] Like much of Böhme's project, and avowedly so, this assumption is grounded in an existential metaphysics rather than in a rationalist
method; it is, however, supported by the observation that literature has
always been aware of the impact of the natural environment on humans *via*
the body.[12] In an age of environmental destruction and postbiological utopia,
Böhme argues, the cultural "archive" of literary texts is one of the few
sources still available of strategies of renaturalization. If we are to extract
this existential information, however, we need to develop strategies of analysis that take into account both the textual and the cultural aspects of literature. Böhme has a clear notion of what these strategies might look like:

> In this situation, "literary anthropology" is not just one area of literary stud-
> ies. We must realize that literature (the arts) is an irreplaceable archive of
> stored experience, perhaps the most important one . . . in which the histori-
> cal physiognomies of human beings are conserved. If, today, the importance
> of human beings seems to be in decline along with the formative force of
> history . . . literary studies are called to remind us of the images of the hu-
> man that are fading out both in their beauty and in their horror.[13]

Literature, in this view, is a perfected tool of anthropology. It records and
stores information about culture, "the historical form by which societies
position themselves within nature," but it does so with a more refined
methodology than traditional anthropological research: thanks to its inherent sensitivity to nature, it evades the pitfalls of the basic scientific distinction between ratio and nature, subject and object.[14] It is thus able to perceive
and give a voice to those aspects of human culture that anthropology has
tended to exclude or relegate to muteness in various periods of its history:
"women, 'uncivilized' peoples, the physical world, objects."[15]

On a broader scale, Böhme argues that the survival of the human race
depends on the institution of "sensibility—not as a moral, but as an aesthetic
capability—as a high-priority goal of development,"[16] and suggests that literature can contribute to this goal. He uses the term "sensibility" in a sense
reminiscent of T. S. Eliot, who described poetry as the exchange of images
and ideas between persons endowed with the sensuality necessary to experience the emotional potential of poetic structures. In Böhme's theory, this
conception of sensibility might provide a link between the two interrelated
anthropological functions he ascribes to literature: its expression of the
"language of nature" and its contribution to the development of an aesthetics of nature that alone can prevent humankind from self-extinction.

As an example, let us turn to a well-known tale from the early stages of
the Industrial Revolution, whose first sentence is among the most famous in
literature: "During the whole of a dull, dark, and soundless day in the
autumn of the year, when the clouds hung oppressively low in the heavens, I
had been passing alone, on horseback, through a singularly dreary tract of
country, and at length found myself, as the shades of the evening drew on,
within view of the melancholy House of Usher."[17] The first sentence of "The
Fall of the House of Usher" (1839) foreshadows the story's central themes and
plotlines, and it provides a first intimation of the narrator's state of mind as
he is descending into the underworld of his destabilized psyche. For many
critics, the narrator represents modern man or modern civilization: Darrel
Abel calls him "Anthropos," and Michael Hoffman reads him as a typical

intellectual of the nineteenth century.[18] Uneasy with the harmonious, rationalized Enlightenment belief in an isomorphic relationship between the order of the mind and the order of nature, he needs to reconcile this dominant discourse with his actual experiences of disorder, doubt, and repression.

Indeed, the story seems to express an anthropological dilemma that amounts to the following question: How can we return to a harmonious, balanced relationship with our environment from our present state of alienation? In many ways, "The Fall of the House of Usher" is an apocalyptic vision of civilization gone wrong. In a house built to look grand and now decaying, two siblings lead an isolated life. Sterile, indifferent to others, and the last of their race, they appear as a distorted caricature of Adam and Eve in biblical paradise; oblivious to their surroundings and incapable of harmonious sensual experience, they embody human civilization in a terminally regressive state. Roderick Usher's allegorical poem "The Haunted Palace" indicates that he and his house have indeed gone through a process of degeneration from "the greenest of our valleys," or harmony with nature, to the dreary landscape and chaotic disorder of the present day.[19]

But how did, to quote from the poem, "evil things" enter the scene and assail Usher's mind? Neither the poem nor the story offers a convincing explanation. It seems as if Usher feared nothing but fear itself, which would make his malady a self-fulfilling prophecy of sorts. The aesthetics of nature approach yields an illuminative variation of this reading. Usher, we learn, suffers from a "morbid acuteness of the senses" that limits decisively his range of communication with his environment. He can endure only certain kinds of optical, acoustic, haptic, olfactory, and gustatory sensations, which has forced him to retreat to a dark, isolated room of his fortresslike house.[20] Presumably, he has entered a vicious circle of hypersensitivity: while he ascribes the ailment to his constitution and his ancestry, it may well be his obsessive dread of and retreat from the natural world that has aggravated his condition. After many years of confinement to the house, he takes another turn in the circle by adopting a belief in "the sentience of all vegetable things"—in other words, he imagines nature to be encroaching upon him through the walls of his fortress, which are attacked by fungi, disintegrated by the "still waters of the tarn," and penetrated by the special "atmosphere" of their surroundings.[21] The fear that has engendered this vicious circle is a fear of the organic, which stands for the unpredictable, the unorganized, and the ungovernable. Unable to deal with these forces, Usher is barred from establishing a harmonious relationship with his environment. His aesthetics of nature is one of dread, mania, and repression.

To some extent, Usher's aesthetics is supported by the very language Poe employs. The narrator, who is introduced as a rational, scientific observer and has only scorn for Usher's sentience theory, nevertheless feels the special atmosphere of the place from the beginning. His very first sentence already blurs the boundaries between subject and object, the organic and the inorganic: even though he tries to describe his impressions with scientific distance and exactness, his language suggests an active influence of the objective world on his perception. The "dreary tract of country" and the "melancholy house" suggest a Benjaminian stream of communication in nature which comprises not only the organic world but also man-made elements like the house. The beginning of the story thus forms a sensual totality in which the subject is neither the center nor the constitutive force; quite the reverse, the narrator appears affected against his (rational) will by the "oppressively low" sky and the atmosphere of loneliness and unease. It is telling that of some forty adjectives in the first paragraph, all but two appear in an attributive construction. Attributive adjectives serve to convey direct impressions largely unmediated by the analytic distance of an interposed verb or qualification; they suggest an active influence of the object on the speaking subject rather than a scientific distance between observer and observed. This works within the story as well as in the reading process: we, too, are drawn into the surreal, uncanny atmosphere and come to share the narrator's impressions. The text skillfully conveys the communicative process between the animate and the inanimate. It gives a voice to the language of nature by interweaving linguistic elements that address us bodily and immediately, and it calls for a perceptive mutuality between the human and the natural spheres.

For Böhme's aesthetics of nature, literature holds an interest on both these levels. On a linguistic-semiotic level, it reveals the "language of nature" in a Benjaminian sense and sensitizes the reader to a more viable, nature-oriented way of communicating. On the anthropological macrolevel, literature contributes to the survival of the human race by criticizing, through the indirect but particularly effective structures of the fictive, perilous cultural developments and by giving "expression or language to that which has been excluded from culture, muted, or articulated in a distorted, stammering way."[22] On one level, Böhme's aesthetics of nature might be read as an attempt to develop a nonanthropocentric, yet still subjectivist approach to literature, which allows us to historicize "man" in a Foucauldian sense while at the same time emphasizing his irreducible connectedness with nature as the overarching frame of cultural reference.

While Böhme's fusion of subjectivism and ecology is a highly original answer to the problem of anthropocentrism, most proponents of literary anthropology within ecocritical theory have preferred systemic approaches to nature-culture relations. Some of them have rallied under the label of "cultural ecology," which was introduced by Julian Steward in the 1930s and is now taken to comprise all those approaches that analyze culture as an ecological system.

Zapf's model of literature as a medium of cultural ecology starts from the assumption that "literature acts as an ecological principle or an ecological force within the larger system of its culture."[23] He distinguishes three discursive functions of literature, which he calls the culture-critical, the imaginative, and the reintegrative: literature criticizes oppressive structures of the cultural system, gives a voice to what these structures suppress, and provides a testing-ground for alternative forms of cultural organization that integrate suppressed elements within the existing cultural system. This triadic structure, Zapf argues, is inscribed into every work of (narrative) literature, though it may take different shapes: the three functions are differentiated more clearly in some genres than in others; one of them might be predominant in a certain epoch, another in the next. For literary critics, the attraction of this approach lies in its proximity to critical practice. In fact, the larger part of Zapf's study is devoted to a methodically consistent application of his triadic model to six major American novels. These analyses locate the main point of connection between textual structures and their cultural impact in the symbolic and metaphorical condensation of public discourse. In *The Scarlet Letter,* for instance, Zapf reads the prison and the scaffold as culture-critical symbols of Puritan mechanisms of exclusion and surveillance; the scarlet letter itself acquires a wide range of imaginative connotations (nature, femininity, emotion, creativity) which subvert the Puritan system; and the reintegrative figure of Pearl "becomes an exemplary figuration of the novelistic process as a whole" as she embodies the power structures of her cultural environment while retaining an attitude of resistant spontaneity.[24]

This suggests that a systemic approach is not altogether incompatible with the tradition of literary anthropology. The Paracelsian conception of nature as a web of signs, for instance, already contains two of the central premises of Zapf's approach. For one thing, it foreshadows the "first law of ecology" as defined by Barry Commoner ("everything is connected to everything else"), which is at the heart of much of cultural ecology;[25] besides, it establishes the structural analogy between ecosystems and literary texts on which the triadic model is based. Zapf explicitly points to the anthropological influence when he names Iser among his theoretical sources.[26] Indeed, both these models accord literature a mediating function between the cultural system and its imaginary alternatives. However, Zapf shifts the focus from the subjective to the systemic aspect. Against Iser's notion of fiction as a self-extension of the subject, he emphasizes the role of fiction in shaping and improving the concrete systemic relations in which the subject is—and needs to be—embedded. In his model, literature holds a cultural rather than an individual potential.

A contrastive reading of "The Fall of the House of Usher" reveals some differences between the interpretive strategies of literary anthropology and cultural ecology. In the first sentence of the story, for instance, the latter approach would focus not so much on the subject's sensual experience but rather on symbols and metaphors that establish a relation between culture and its suppressed Other. As indicated above, critics have developed the motifs of the initial landscape description in many different directions; however, most of these readings embrace their specific interpretation to the extent that they consciously discard other aspects and readings.[27] A systemic approach like Zapf's, in contrast, attempts to include all the elements in the text that work toward its discursive contribution.

As for the culture-critical aspect of the story, the beginning indicates its concern with the intangible realm of the subconscious. Visualized as a *descensus ad inferos,* the narrator's venturing into the surreal area of the House of Usher and into the equally surreal consciousness of its last representative acquires connotations of insecurity and danger. Roderick Usher has failed to establish viable relations with his environment. Torn between the extreme states of hypersensitivity and total retreat, he must either repress the subconscious or completely submit to it. While the narrator remembers this tension between "excessive and habitual" reserve and "a peculiar sensitivity of temperament" from an early age,[28] Usher's allegorical poem "The Haunted Palace" indicates a development, in his mind, from a controlled harmony of these forces to the sheer chaos of the present day. In other words, Usher has gradually lost the ability to enter into a harmonious, mutual relation with his environment. When, in his first conversation with the narrator, he claims that his spiritual or "moral" decay has been brought about by the "physical" decay of the family mansion, he betrays an egocentric perspective that is at the root of his condition. Since the upkeep of the house lies in his own hands, its decay is likely to have resulted from his lack of motivation rather than the other way round. Usher expects his environment to sustain him, but refuses to enter into a mutually advantageous, symbiotic relation with it; his self-fulfilling prophecies engender a destructive dynamic that encompasses his entire environment. It is telling that the "severe and long-continued illness" of his twin sister, Madeline, is mentioned right after his revealing complaint.[29] By logical extension, it is safe to assume that Madeline, like the house, is suffering from neglect: isolated from the outside world and unable to communicate meaningfully with her increasingly self-contained brother, she is effectively barred from human life and turns into a ghost even before her death. Significantly, when she glides through the room during the conversation, Usher does not even try to reach out to her but buries his face in his hands so as to hide his emotional reaction. The narrator soon perceives that Usher's is "a mind from which darkness, as if an inherent positive quality, poured forth upon all objects of the moral and physical universe in one unceasing radiation of gloom."[30]

In his interaction with and description of Usher, the narrator develops into a contrastive figure. In many ways, he comes to embody a more viable alternative to Usher's self-centered attitude. From the very beginning, his perception of his environment is both sensitive and acute, which enables him to notice most of the things that perturb Usher while at the same time reflecting them more objectively than his host. At first sight of the house, he proves receptive to the "sense of insufferable gloom" that emanates from the desolate scenery;[31] instead of giving in to this feeling, however, he begins to analyze it with a remarkable propensity for experiment. Upon the assumption that a change of position relative to the house might change his impression, he rides up to the tarn and finds his assumption is confirmed. The rewarding increase in knowledge, however, goes far beyond this simple experiment: seeing his reflection in the tarn mingle with that of Usher's skull-like house, he is drawn into the nexus that enables him to enter the subconscious underworld of the House of Usher not only physically but, through its inhabitants, spiritually as well.

Once arrived, his main occupation is to work against Usher's self-destructive retreat from the outside world. In long conversations about Usher and his world, the narrator attempts to revive his host's ability to communicate himself to others. He quickly recognizes artistic expression as a particularly effective means of communication and starts to involve his patient in performances of music, painting, and poetry. It is through these media that Usher can best reflect his spiritual condition; his performances seem to open up a sphere as inaccessible as it is fascinating:

> Among other things, I hold painfully in my mind a certain singular perversion and amplification of the wild air of the last waltz of Von Weber. From the paintings over which his elaborate fancy brooded, and which grew, touch by touch, into vaguenesses at which I shuddered the more thrillingly, because I shuddered knowing not why—from these paintings . . . I would in vain endeavor to educe more than a small portion which should lie within the compass of merely written words. By the utter simplicity, by the nakedness of his designs, he arrested and overawed attention. If ever mortal painted an idea, that mortal was Roderick Usher.[32]

Usher's art takes conventional themes and images to their extreme. Driven by his own liminality—caught somewhere between life and death, reason and madness—he tries in his art to rid himself from all the elements that pertain to the real world and to achieve a purely imaginary vision. As a structure mediating between the real and the imaginary, art is a uniquely appropriate vehicle for Usher's self-conceptualization and self-expression. Thanks to its adaptability and scope, it is one of very few means of communication that still function in an environment of physical and spiritual decay.

While this potential of art as an imaginative counterforce is an important aspect on the diegetic level, it is taken beyond that level and developed into a reintegrative force in the act of narration that constitutes the story itself. The narrator of "The Fall of the House of Usher" is a gifted storyteller. We have already noted his remarkable sensitivity to his surroundings on his arrival at the house; the effectiveness of his communicative efforts is underscored when his reading of the *Mad Trist* propels Usher to full consciousness of his sister's horrifying fate and thus brings about the decisive turning-point of the plot. The narrator is thus developed into a mediating instance both on the diegetic level and beyond: in his continual effort to understand his new surroundings in all their facets, he is able not only to manipulate Usher's relation to the external world—his house, music, natural phenomena—but also, through his skillful management of language, to establish a relation between the events he narrates and the reader. Always eager to include and weigh fairly all aspects of his story, however incredible they may be, he comes to embody the reintegrative potential of storytelling.

In his conception of literature as a cultural corrective, Zapf is close to Iser, and in particular to Iser's attempts to reintegrate literary anthropology with a wider cultural perspective.[33] However, this also means that Zapf's model is open to the same criticism from culturalists, namely that he privileges literature as a unique medium of human or cultural expression. A proponent of a strictly systemic cultural ecology, Peter Finke, has taken issue with the very title of Zapf's study, *Literatur als kulturelle Ökologie*, arguing that literature in itself is neither an ecology nor a medium of ecology, but "just one field of cultural action that, among many others, [the discipline of cultural ecology] can thematize."[34] Given that Zapf's main focus is on literary studies, however, it appears more fruitful to engage with his theory on its own terms, that is, on the premise that fictional texts do fulfill a special function within their cultural environment. In critical practice, I suspect, the main challenge of Zapf's model is its enormous scope. Its claim to grasp all the different forms of text-culture interaction can hardly be fulfilled within the boundaries of a book-length study, much less in a short essay like this. It forces critics to limit themselves to one particular aspect of a text. While Zapf's own interpretations of American novels focus on symbols and metaphors, his model can be applied to other structural aspects of the text as well; I have argued elsewhere that a narratological approach yields particularly instructive results.[35] More generally, this vast range of possible applications illustrates once more the age-old problem of functional approaches to literature, namely, the complicated task of establishing a stringent, convincing relation between the formal specificities of fictional texts and their cultural impact.

In the larger context of contemporary German ecocritical theory, the work of Böhme and Zapf illustrates both the foundational role of the anthropological paradigm and the recent efforts to overcome its inherent limitations. While both theories are based on the assumption that "everything is connected to everything else," they develop the ecological approach in different directions. Böhme's emphasis is on the subject in its concrete relations to the natural environment, whereas Zapf's more abstract model focuses on the internal organization of the cultural system. Both, however, are guided by the vision of a human civilization reorganized on the model of the global ecosystem, and both regard literature as a mediating and integrative force that may contribute to realizing this vision.

NOTES

1. Iser, "Towards a Literary Anthropology," 210, 213.

2. Iser, The Fictive and the Imaginary, 2, translation modified.

3. Schlaeger, "Cultural Poetics," 77.

4. Cf. Neumeyer, "Historische und literarische Anthropologie," 118f., my translation.

5. Paracelsus, "Von den natürlichen Dingen," 297f., my translation.

6. Böhme, "Aussichten," 36, my translation.

7. Böhme, Natur und Subjekt, 10, my translation.

8. Böhme, "Aussichten," 37, my translation.

9. Benjamin, "Über Sprache überhaupt," 157, my translation.

10. Böhme, "Aussichten," 52, my translation.

11. Here, too, Böhme draws on Benjamin, who reads the fall from paradise as the turn of man from communicative unity with things and vaguely suggests that artistic language might help reestablish these sacred bonds: "There is a language of sculpture, of painting, of poetry. As the language of poetry is founded, albeit not exclusively, in the name-language of man, the language of sculpture or painting might be founded in certain kinds of thing-languages; they might constitute a translation of the language of things into a far higher sphere. . . . These are nameless, non-acoustic languages, languages made from material" (Benjamin, "Über Sprache überhaupt," 156, my translation).

12. Cf. Böhme, "Aussichten," 48.

13. Böhme, "Germanistik," 74–75, my translation.

14. Ibid., 66, my translation.

15. Ibid., 75, my translation.

16. Böhme, "Aussichten," 38, my translation.

17. Poe, "Fall of the House of Usher," 76.

18. Abel, "Key to the House of Usher," 176–85; Hoffman, "House of Usher," 158–68.

19. Poe, "Fall of the House of Usher," 85–86.

20. Ibid., 81.

21. Ibid., 86–87.

22. Böhme, "Germanistik," 75, my translation.

23. Zapf, *Literatur als kulturelle Ökologie*, 3, my translation.

24. Ibid., 77, my translation.

25. Cf. Commoner, *Closing Circle*, 33–39.

26. Zapf, *Literatur als kulturelle Ökologie*, 59.

27. Not surprisingly, the story has incited a number of fierce critical debates. See, for example, the discussion of its tragic aspects stretching from Cleanth Brooks and Robert Penn Warren (*Understanding Fiction* [New York: Appleton, 1943], 204) and Henning Cohen ("Roderick Usher's Tragic Struggle," *Nineteenth-Century Fiction* 14 [1959]: 270–72) to K. L. Goodwin ("Roderick Usher's Overrated Knowledge," *Nineteenth-Century Fiction* 16 [1961]: 173–75); or, with two ripostes, G. R. Thompson and Patrick F. Quinn on the narrator's reliability, in *Ruined Eden of the Present: Hawthorne, Melville, and Poe* (edited by G. R. Thompson and Virgil L. Lokke [West Lafayette: Purdue University Press, 1981], 303–54).

28. Poe, "Fall of the House of Usher," 77.

29. Ibid., 82.

30. Ibid.

31. Ibid., 76.

32. Ibid., 83–84.

33. Iser, "Towards a Literary Anthropology," 228.

34. Finke, "Die Evolutionäre Kulturökologie," 208 n. 36, my translation.

35. Müller, "Formen kulturökologischen Erzählens," 59–74; Müller, "The Poet's Voice," 503–19.

The Social Theory of Norbert Elias and the Question of the Nonhuman World

The ecological damage that has led to an emerging sixth world extinction event may not be derived entirely from Western modernity. It could, however, be argued that in spite of more general causal factors such as the exponential growth in human populations, the androgenic causes of this environmental crisis have many of their sociogenetic roots in the emergence of modernity in Europe. It was, after all, European modernity that gave rise to the Industrial Revolution, and to the heightened instrumentalization of nature that serves the vast engines of a Western capitalist system now global in its reach. Hence, in the contemporary context of global environmental damage and a loss of species diversity unprecedented in human history, it seems appropriate to begin this account of Elias's concept of the nonhuman world with his consistent focus on what he calls the "civilizing process" in Western modernity.

Though Elias's thinking on our relationship with the nonhuman world is always grounded in the complex contingencies of history, his response to the dominant Western approaches to nature might be best understood with reference to three key theoretical models within his historical sociology. These models devised by Elias pertain to Western modernity, combining dual and dialectically related social processes.

The first model is based on Elias's emphasis on the necessary condition of social interdependence. This is, however, contrasted dialectically with a condition he referred to as *homo clausus*, which is, in effect, a kind of modern false consciousness intent on ignoring the fundamental necessity of social interdependence.

The second is Elias's model of the dual societal processes of involvement and detachment. These dialectically related social forces developed and gained new momentum with the advent of modernity. At times, the dialectical process has produced effects of *secondary*, or *reflective* involvement.

Though Elias's concept of secondary involvement has not received much critical attention, it seems to me to offer a very useful model for ecological critique. Before turning to a discussion of secondary involvement, however, it is important to contextualize Elias's emphasis on the fundamental processes of interdependence in social relations, and the curious development of a way of thinking that refutes the necessity of social interdependence, in short a denial fundamental to the development of *homo clausus*. The uncertainty of the ontological borders between the social constructivist models of nature and the material realist recognition of a nonhuman world beyond human discursivity underpins this discussion, though its focus is on where Elias situates the nonhuman world.

A third key model, Elias's notion of social and cultural *figurations,* is also important to this account of his view of our relations with the nonhuman world. As Elias's studies of the civilizing process and the advent of modernity have shown so clearly, cultural figurations are a particularly effective means of gauging the development of the broad social processes of involvement and detachment. Dance, music, and theater, for example, have very long social histories, and my discussion of Elias concludes with a contemporary example of how these cultural forms are adapted in the popular global medium of YouTube. Certain cultural formations appearing on YouTube are selected as examples of nascent reconfigurations of the nonhuman world imbued with a sense of the potential recognition of the global biosphere as an effectively sufficient condition of human survival. Further to currents in European Romanticism that represented accelerations in the dialectical processes of involvement and detachment, such contemporary figurations indicate a renewed development of secondary, or reflective involvement and subsequent weakening of *homo clausus*. They suggest a significant shift in the civilizing process of Western modernity likely to gain momentum with advancing social awareness of the ecological crisis.

Homo clausus

Literally the "closed personality" of modern human subjectivity, *homo clausus* represents a model of the modern self "closed off" from, or essentially unaware of its necessary, substantive connectedness to others. This is an individual who is typically even less conscious of the long histories of human interdependency that are constitutive of modern subjectivity. How far Elias's concept extends to an individual unwittingly "closed off" from recognition of its historical dependence on the nonhuman world is, however, something I want to discuss here with reference to a number of key works by Elias.

Elias first identified *homo clausus* as an essentially modern self-image in the book for which he is best known, *The Civilising Process,* written in 1939 and first published in English in 1982. In this work, and in *The Court Society* (1983), Elias traced the complex social changes in the transitions from feudal society to the monarchy and court society of the *ancien régime*, and hence to the modern nation-state. By focusing on historical figurations of social decorum and manners in everyday life, Elias was able to demonstrate how the civilizing process required increasing levels of human detachment and self-restraint, a general raising of the threshold of people's personal sense of shame and a more nuanced experience of self-consciousness, along with a heightened revulsion for the direct experience of violence.

As this process unfolded, overt displays of violence were gradually transferred from their regular enactment by a brutal warrior class or from official spectacles of corporal punishment to a more abstracted monopoly of violence by the nation-state. Accordingly, acts of violence in everyday life were either hidden or became increasingly stylized. Elias regarded sport as an activity in which the violence in everyday life was subjected to stylized sublimation, and an example of the social figurations that have facilitated the gradual development of the civilizing process. Nonhuman animals were also subjected to the civilizing process, as is evident in the gradual diminution of blood sports and the exclusion of animal slaughter from public view—factors in a broader social process in which open displays of violence became less socially acceptable.

Elias's model of the civilizing process, however, by no means implied a unilinear progress toward enlightened modernity. As a German Jew whose mother was murdered in Auschwitz, he was surely as conscious as most of his generation of the countervailing de-civilizing processes of history. Nonetheless, he maintained that though the civilizing process moved unevenly, either in spurts of progression, or regressing in de-civilizing turns, at least in part, to previous stages of social development, there was a gradual civilizing process and transformation of the individual at the level of affects. Hence in distinction to the authoritarian structures of feudal society, modernity imbued the individual with a capacity for the kind of self-restraint or self-control that was conducive to the development of *homo clausus*.

The self-image of the individual in relation to society was also addressed in another work of 1939, the first part of *The Society of Individuals*.[1] In this work, Elias addressed the question of how the individual develops knowledge of society, or the world itself, as problems with their origins in particular historical circumstances, rather than being universal a priori conditions of human consciousness. As such, Elias's notion of *homo clausus* is a product of what he describes as "a peculiar form of self-consciousness and the image of man . . . [which] usually presents itself to the person concerned as something natural and universally human, as *the* form of human self-consciousness, the image that people have of themselves at all times."[2]

Though it is primarily associated with the present, Elias saw the origin of *homo clausus* in what he calls the "so-called renaissance in occidental societies."[3] This led to an advance in the early-modern human self-image that by the seventeenth century became particularly pronounced in Descartes' meditations. For Elias, Descartes' famous resolution of the problem of self-knowledge (the prioritization of the condition of doubt as proof of self) has less to do with sublime philosophical abstraction than with observation shaped by a broad social transition toward secularization. As a result of this transition, the human self-image lost its bearings in a world no longer contained by divine teleology and providence.

While the loss of a self bound securely to a world protected by religious certainty is a commonplace observation today, according to Elias the contemporary human self-image that has largely replaced it cannot be taken for granted as something which exists a priori. It should rather be seen as a particular *habitus* that had evolved, as he put it, "as a symptom of and a factor in a specific transformation, which, like all such changes, simultaneously affected all the three basic coordinates of human life: the shaping and the position of the individual within the social structure, the social structure itself, and the relation of social human beings to events in the non-human world."[4]

The early-modern European economy and urbanization had ensured a certain general relaxation of concerns about preserving human interests against the vicissitudes of nature. Cartesian dualism, along with the emphasis on the objectification of the nonhuman world in seventeenth-century science, now reinforced the rise of the notion that people were somehow separate from their dependency on nature. One of the manifestations of this massive social shift was the kind of overpowering need for individual self-restraint in society that Elias described so persuasively in *The Civilising Process*. However, he also observed that this shift has now become a *habitus* problem of the contemporary personality structure, of which he remarked: "One can see more clearly in retrospect how closely this new form of self-consciousness was linked to the growing commercialization and the formation of states, to the rise of rich court and urban classes and, not least, to the noticeably increasing power of human beings over non-human natural events."[5]

In *The Society of Individuals* (1991) Elias reflected on the process of globalization and the civilizing process, including the possibility that the civilizing process may still be annihilated by nuclear warfare. Elias's sense of the dangers inherent in the denial of the social processes of interdependencies and human dependence are analogous with those evident in the kind of human self-image that the ecophilosopher Mary Mellor has described succinctly as one caught in a web of "parasitical transcendence."[6] This is a phrase that could also be applied to *homo clausus,* insofar as the individual is sustained by a vast range of human interdependencies across time and space, yet remains at best only dimly aware that without them, or without structures developed by them, such as language or preexisting knowledge, the modern subject as such would no longer exist.

In recognition of Elias's focus on the *longue durée,*[7] it seems to me that a reflective ontology and historiography that acknowledges our social interdependence with the materiality of the nonhuman world requires long genealogies or archaeological approaches to the foundations of contemporary subjectivity. Yet the general consensus in contemporary accounts is more closely aligned to a concept of time based on a model of individual subjectivity, in which the generations in their relations with the nonhuman world have become effectively invisible. Hence in the canonical accounts of postmodernity, the nonhuman world disappears in a dazzling spectacle of simulacra, and the most enduring of all human stories, the human mastery of nature, is said to be subject to the same incredulity we bring to all our metanarratives.

Elias regarded as dangerous theories or practices of sociology that did not acknowledge a history of the *longue durée.* Such approaches, which he saw as the dominant trend in sociology from the Second World War, represented a slippage away from realism. He made this view clear in a journal article of 1987, "The Retreat of Sociology into the Present," in which he compared the political biases of the present with the need for more scientific scrutiny of the past. A theory of society based on the short-term historical view was for Elias "prompted by different political ideals of twentieth-century industrial societies and presented as a universal theory of human societies," and could thus have "only very limited cognitive value."[8]

The interest in paleological sociogenesis became a major focus of Elias's final, unfinished book, *The Symbol Theory.*[9] In his introduction, the editor, Richard Kilminster, observes that Elias sought here to steer a new course between sociobiologists and the philosophical or religious view that humans are separate from the animal world.

Perhaps unsurprisingly, Elias saw the transference of knowledge through language as the engine of social change that differentiates human from animal, as opposed to the emergence of change (rather than social development as such) in animals, that he saw as driven almost exclusively by genetic evolution. On the other hand, Elias recognized the animal origins of the human, and the long struggle to overcome its natural competitors, observing:

"Humanity has gained the ascendancy over most of its potential rivals and enemies in the animal kingdom, though at the level of viruses and bacilli the struggle goes on. On other levels humans are largely in control. They have killed, imprisoned or confined to reserves other animal species and are just beginning to notice that rule over others entails some responsibility for them."[10] The emergence of a new responsibility toward the nonhuman world is also foregrounded in Elias's contrast between some species where it may be possible for evolution to continue, and the vast majority of species subject to regimes of human dominance, where change will be a question of planned evolution with unintended consequences.

In the context of what the paleoanthropologist Richard Leakey called the "sixth extinction" (*The Sixth Extinction* was published in 1995, less than five years after Elias's *The Symbol Theory*),[11] it seems there is little in any social theory that might offer a redemptive means of dealing with problems of such scale. It is perhaps more relevant to raise questions of adaptation and relative damage control, or of how to evaluate the usefulness of the theoretical means of approaching problems that are essentially without human historical precedent. It is a question that requires a massive detachment from short-term human interests. Fortunately, if our scientific and cultural histories reveal a dominantly instrumentalist approach to the nonhuman world, these histories also produced nascent forms of detachment that respect the alterity of the nonhuman world on which we depend. While a complete refutation of anthropocentric perspectives may not be possible, detachment from short-term human self-interest is conceivable, and vital in the contemporary context. As Tim Newton put it in his recent study *Nature and Sociology*, "Unless we adopt an epistemology which accepts the materiality of nature, its otherness and extradiscursivity, we will limit our ability to challenge environmental degradation."[12]

Involvement and Detachment

The problem of detachment from primary emotions that characterize human involvement was the focus of an earlier work which I now discuss, before turning to contemporary social figurations of the nonhuman world. As has been rightly acknowledged,[13] in *Involvement and Detachment*, published in 1987, Elias developed his most extensive theory of knowledge, identifying the dialectically related processes of human involvement and detachment as a social dynamic driving the development of modernity.

He identified the two broad social processes of involvement and detachment as the essentially dialectical key indices of social development and the advance of human knowledge of the nonhuman world. He emphasized the importance of viewing involvement and detachment as comparative and *interdependent* points in historical processes rather than as opposing or static distinctions. "Involvement and detachment," he wrote, "whatever their other functions, serve as complementary indicators of the direction of knowledge processes."[14] They are never absolute states of human experience, but sociological conditions that are always relative to each other, so that one can refer to more, or less, detached or involved knowledge processes manifesting in various stages of human history. Elias saw involvement and detachment as universal conditions of all human societies, and was entirely consistent in his view that these universal conditions could never be reduced to metaphysical or philosophical abstractions, but must always be seen as grounded in the contingencies of history. In short, he proposed a sociological theory of knowledge, and one, as we have seen, that could not be limited to a "retreat to the present" but extended to a much broader sociology of history.[15]

For Elias, the modern ascendancy of the regime of scientific *detachment* is not a simple linear progression, but a dynamic process in relation to regimes of primary involvement. It is "circular and spiral,"[16] a *process* relationship which, like the civilizing process itself, can change direction at different points. Thus all observations about involvement and detachment are comparative. Notwithstanding this emphasis on dialectical processes, however, the two directions Elias defines as crucial to the acquisition of knowledge, involvement and detachment, are always linked to an even more fundamental process of the human mastery of nonhuman nature:

> The awareness of humanity's supremacy on earth demands reflection about the manner and aims of its rule. As yet, the awareness is dim. The prevalence of unending competitive struggles between human groups themselves has induced a chaotic and self-defeating utilization of human power over non-human nature, an employment of power which is dictated entirely by the short-term and sectional aims of the competitive struggles between human groups, regardless of the conditions of non-human nature on which, in the long run, human survival depends. In this vital field, people's involvement of thought and action clearly outweighs detachment. From the relative pacification of non-human nature stands out all the more starkly the untamed ferocity of the struggles between human groups themselves.[17]

It is clear from this that Elias's key concept of social *interdependence* applies not only to human societies, but also to our interdependence with *nature itself* upon which all social figurations ultimately rely.

Elias refers to this more explicitly in his discussion of interdependence in the second part of *Involvement and Detachment*, following his evocative account of Edgar Allen Poe's *The Fishermen in the Maelstrom:*

Ontological dualism, the notion of a world split into "subjects" and "objects," is misleading. It gives the impression that "subjects" can exist without "objects." It induces people to ask which of the two functions is cause and which is effect. Where units stand in a relationship of functional interdependence, as in the case of the stomach and the brain, economic and political institutions, or, for that matter, human beings and non-human nature, one encounters connections of a type no longer adequately covered by a cause-and-effect model.[18]

Elias's concept of the *principle of increasing facilitation,* or in his more succinct phrase, the "double-bind," represents social processes that gather momentum and reach a kind of "tipping point," which then rapidly accelerates, or *increases* and *facilitates* the process further. The increasing facilitation, or double-bind of interdependency with primarily emotional, *involved* forms of knowledge, from the Paleolithic era, was sustained through most of human history as a way of interpreting the incomprehensible forces of nature through magic and mythologies, which, in turn, were resistant to the development of more detached, "reality-congruent" knowledge.

According to Elias, social processes of detachment were first consolidated in early modernity with the gradual acknowledgment of the heliocentric model of cosmological space. This required a significant shift away from previously reassuring patterns of primary involvement evinced by the geocentric model of the universe, with man at the center of all things. Thus in the knowledge process, increasing facilitation in less emotionally gratifying, if more objective and *detached* ways of understanding the world can be applied to the period from the onset of modernity, when the mastery of nature was effected with exponential developments in technology. Processes of *detachment,* however, like processes within regimes characterized by patterns of primary involvement, may also be intensified by patterns of increasing facilitation, to the point where they extend to a range of unintended consequences. Hence, in Eliasian terms, a double-bind in the knowledge economy of our own time is manifest in escalating patterns of detachment. Thus, as the long struggle to gain control over nature eventually produced reliable levels of mastery, in turn this process enabled more exacting, and often less benign methods of control more easily facilitated by what had gone before.

Moreover, in this context, advances in essentially noninstrumentalist scientific detachment, evident, for example, in Darwinism, actually conflict with general regimes of more instrumentalist paradigms of detachment in everyday life. Thus, we find ourselves disconnected from what are frequently regarded as the redundant links between the human and other forms of animal life in ways that conceal advances in scientific knowledge. The long history of the human control and mastery of nature, and its implications for human society, are at the core of Elias's *Involvement and Detachment*. His model is useful in a number of ways, not least in his acknowledgment that while the processes of human detachment moving away from our vulnerability before the natural world were essential for the formation of human society, detached knowledge processes were always a question of degree rather than complete because they necessarily retained important components of involvement. The mutual spiraling development of technological progress and human detachment from nature notwithstanding, Elias maintained that a final state of pure detachment would never be humanly possible. "Pure detachment," as Kilminster was surely correct to observe,[19] would be for Elias a highly "involved" teleological assumption of a preconceived model or ideal. Moreover, recent speculation that an increasingly detached technological determinism will result in a virtual "posthuman" consciousness—as opposed to consciousness necessarily interdependent with the animal qualities of human corporeality—seems to me to fall into such a category.[20] Particularly since stories of redemption from the human condition—and from human mortality in particular—appear to be as old as human society itself, and certainly correspond with regimes of emotional involvement in traditional theological teleology.

The identification and acknowledgment of *involvement* in the primarily *detached* processes of scientific knowledge is important in relation to the question of our final supremacy over nature. Not only because it is important to acknowledge that at the level of affects there is always a certain measure of *primary involvement* even in the kind of detached knowledge required by a scientific objectification of nature; but also because more reflective forms of involvement entail a recognition of the long history of our relations of involvement with the nonhuman world, which along with the processes of detachment has effectively made us who we are. That is to say, acknowledgment of the dual historical processes of involvement and detachment is conducive to recognition of the necessary condition of our ontological *interdependence* with the nonhuman world.

The immediate crisis in the deterioration of the nonhuman world is a direct consequence of instrumentalist techniques within regimes of detachment. And I propose that it is the emergence of new forms of what Elias called *secondary involvement*, the more reflective and progressive forms of involvement arising in the modern period, that have provided a significant countervailing effect to the social primacy of regimes of detachment. It may be argued that this does not acknowledge the capacity for reflection evident in premodern or tribal forms of knowledge. Yet the advances of detachment that have produced late-modern economies and technology are required for this kind of secondary, or reflective involvement. In our world dominated by the processes of modernity, it is crucial that figurations of reflective involvement prevail, rather than the kind of primary involvement driven by instrumentalist models of detachment. The notion that the dominant global system today might adapt to tribal or premodern models of the nonhuman world, whatever wisdom such models may offer, is wholly impractical, given the rapidly diminishing time we have left to address mass extinctions.

To view all involvement as processes of *primary involvement* (and as such, processes not conducive to what Elias called *reality-congruent knowledge*), is essentially to deny the importance and influence of social figurations of secondary, or *reflective* involvement that may be crucial to our capacity to understand the extent of our interdependence with nature. A looser model, so to speak, of "detached involvement" may be worth considering, not only with reference to ecological problems wrought by excessive cycles of expedient detachment, but more essentially in recognition of how we can never entirely separate ourselves from relations of involvement with the nonhuman world, or from our bodily status as animals, and what it might mean if we try.

It seems to me that Elias's notion of *secondary involvement* is one of his most useful concepts in relation to emerging ecological crises. For one thing, it provides a valuable conceptual foil to essentially redundant fantasies of involvement advocating a low-tech return to a prelapsarian world, where to be human means a completely dependent connectedness with the animalic nature of the self. Moreover, secondary involvement is a product of modernity that has developed as a result of the social and historical processes of detachment, and a process that conveys a tacit acknowledgment of the immense human achievement and sheer difficulty of detachment and its resistance to less challenging patterns of primary involvement. Secondary involvement is a reflective process that acknowledges that the knowledge processes of modernity cannot simply be reversed. It is, as it were, a "knowing" type of involvement at the level of affects, which is particularly susceptible to the kind of changes in the nonhuman world that cannot remain ignored.

It is significant that the main examples Elias gives of secondary involvement in *Involvement and Detachment* are derived from his discussions of the aesthetic qualities of self-imaging in the "heightened detachment" of fifteenth- or seventeenth-century painting. In the contemporary context, Elias's trope of the mirror in art as a figuration of social self-imaging can, in my view, also be held up to nature, and in the current discussion particularly to human-animal relations, as a *figuration* of the civilizing process. That is to say, it can be held up to domesticated and companion animals, and the way they reflect back to us the human self-image. This is not to suggest that the ontological status of domesticated animals may be reduced to a mere reflection of the human social process, but rather that critical reflection should be focused on our interdependence with nonhuman animals.

Clearly the animal has played a crucial role in human history, and human interdependency with the nonhuman world. So to understand that much-marginalized history is to grasp a crucial dimension of human identity. Moreover, from the first domestication of animals to their contradictory status in late modernity, it is also the case that certain species have developed an interdependent relationship with humans. Most of these relationships are part of a global economy of cruelty and pain that usually remains unquestioned as a mode of production necessitated by human needs, though the civilizing process has meant its violence must remain out of sight. Some relationships, however, such as those with species we have chosen as companions, represent more progressive turns in the civilizing process. To what extent these relations might be included in Elias's model of figurations of secondary, or reflective involvement is the question with which I now want to conclude. It is also a question that pertains to the nonhuman world in general, since it is likely that any empathy we have gained for companion species will be pivotal to our responses to other nonhuman species.

Elias's concept of social figurations was first defined in his introduction to the second edition of *The Civilising Process* as a foil to the prevailing self-image of *homo clausus*. The term "figuration" was intended to convey a cluster of important insights, as Goudsblom and Mennell put it:

> First, that human beings are interdependent, and can only be understood as such: their lives develop in and are significantly shaped by, the social figurations they form with each other. Second, that these figurations are continually in flux, undergoing changes of different orders—some quick and ephemeral, others slower but more profound. Third, that the processes occurring in such figurations have dynamics of their own—dynamics in which individual motives and intentions play a part but which cannot possibly be reduced to those motives and intentions alone.[21]

Figurations

Elias used the analogy of social dances such as the folk dance or the courtly minuet to further explain his model of figurations as a foil for traditional distinctions between the individual and society, of which he observed:

> The image of the mobile figurations of interdependent people on a dance floor perhaps makes it easier to imagine states, cities, families, and also capitalist, communist, and feudal systems as figuration. . . . One can certainly

speak of a dance in general, but no one will imagine a dance as structure outside the individual or as a mere abstraction. The same dance figurations can certainly be danced by different people; but without a plurality of reciprocally oriented and dependent individuals, there is no dance. Like every other social figuration, a dance figuration is relatively independent of the specific individuals forming it here and now, but not of individuals as such.[22]

With reference to Elias's analogy of the dance, I would like to discuss the horse as an agent in social figurations. Archaeozoological evidence suggests that social transformations brought about by horses occurred relatively late in Europe, in the second millennium BC. An animal that was unrivaled in its capacity to enhance human bodily strength and military capacity, the horse was both ruthlessly exploited and prized as an emblem of status. Though the history of human-equine relations is long and complex, this is not self-evident in the use of horses today, because just as the military status of the horse concluded after the First World War, its other uses in transport and labor in everyday life also became largely redundant with the advent of motor power. Today the horse is mainly used in sport, including sports that are imbued with the social status that accrued to the transformation in the civilizing process when military horsemanship was refined into the aristocratic practice of equestrian dressage.

A contemporary figuration of the human-horse relationship can be seen in a six-minute video of an event at the World Equestrian Games in Aachen in 2006 featuring a nine-year-old gray mare, Blu Hors Matiné, and her rider, the Danish equestrian competitor Andreas Helgstrand.[23] Their performance won over the crowd of forty thousand, along with the English commentators, one of whom remarks at one stage: "This horse just gives everything and just seems to love every minute of it." This is, without doubt, a speculation that constitutes an important part of the audience response, as is the question of whether nonhuman animals are capable of detachment from the more immediate impulses of primary involvement. In Eliasian terms, the entire event is a social figuration, in which *primary involvement* is evident in the crowd's excitement with the spectacle, while processes of detachment are also clear in the self-control and training required of both horse and rider. Yet, notwithstanding the unequivocal authority of the rider, or the rigorous discipline that clearly underpins the performance, the crowd and commentators convey a palpable sense of respect for the horse, and this seems to me to be a response worthy of scrutiny.

The human responses suggest a desire to believe that the horse is not only a conscious agent in the dance, but also actually takes pleasure in it. In one sense, this could be seen simply as yet another instance of what is perhaps the ineluctable human capacity for anthropocentrism. Yet on the other hand, it is a collective desire that also clearly represents a civilizational advance. It is important to remember that dressage developed as a stylized refinement of the military advantages of the use of horses in fierce and bloody combat, and it is precisely this sublimation of violence through refined stylization that appeals to the crowd. This is a twenty-first-century audience, not an early-modern audience excited by the anticipation of watching an animal torn apart for its edification. Nor is this even an audience essentially gratified by how well the horse obeys her master. On the contrary, the audience is engaged by the possibility that not only the rider, but also the horse is enjoying herself in a mutually engaged performance. In short, the human self-image suggested by the performance and audience response is a vignette of the human envisaging itself in partnership with alterity. As such, this equestrian performance seems to me to be an interesting example of a shift away from *primary involvement* toward what Elias called *secondary involvement*.

In relation to what I propose here in terms of the nonhuman companion animal as a mirror of the human self-image, such forms of reflective, or secondary involvement are nascent figurations of the ability to begin to sense the importance of alterity in species other than human companions. The ecological imperatives we now face have become so urgent that it is clear how important shifts in popular culture will be if we are to have any chance of effecting change in our relations with the nonhuman world. Accordingly, I want to conclude with another site chosen from YouTube, a nine-minute American video focusing on the current mass extinction event.[24] This is a broadly populist call for reconnection with other species, and the acknowledgment of our biological interdependence with the nonhuman world. Toward the end of the video, the biologist Paul Ehrlich reminds the viewer about cultural evolution, which he says can take place with great rapidity when the time is ripe.

The age of mass species extinction and ecological degradation we have now entered will no doubt provide the momentum for such rapid cultural change, yet the crucial question is one of timing. There is certainly a significant gulf between the desire for a dancing horse to take pleasure in a performance, and the acknowledgment that the loss of other species leads to incalculable human impoverishment. They both represent processes of involvement in response to the nonhuman world, and as such are self-images necessarily linked to human self-interest. Yet it is a reflective form of involvement, tempered with enough detachment to gauge the alterity of the nonhuman world. If the question of reflective human self-interest may seem disconnected from the economy of affects surrounding the spectacle of a dancing horse, it is one of many cultural figurations that represent accelerations in the civilizing process crucial to adaptation, and perhaps even in some measure, of reparation in the current ecological crisis.

Elias is acknowledged as one of the most significant social theorists of the last century. He produced a substantial body of theory and developed a historically grounded methodology for the analysis of cultural and social practices, both contemporary and historical. I have suggested here that his model of reflective, or secondary involvement is particularly useful in relation to ecocritique, though this is but one of many potential lines of inquiry enabled by the remarkable depth and range of Elias's work.

NOTES

1. A work Elias did not complete until 1987 shortly before his death in 1990 at the age of ninety-three, which was first published in English in 1991.

2. Elias, *Society of Individuals*, 92.

3. Ibid., 92.

4. Ibid., 97.

5. Ibid., 97–98.

6. Mellor, *Feminism and Ecology*, 191.

7. *La longue durée* is a term used by the historians of the Annales school to refer to serial social changes over a long period of time. Rather than focusing on specific historical events, or specific individuals, historians of the *longue durée* examined long-term social processes.

8. Goudsblom and Mennell, *Norbert Elias*, 178.

9. Published in English in 1991, the year after Elias's death. Elias was almost completely blind by the time he came to this study, which was transcribed and edited by Kilminster.

10. Elias, *The Symbol Theory*, 101.

11. Leakey, *The Sixth Extinction*.

12. Newton, *Nature and Sociology*, 22.

13. Mennell, *Norbert Elias*; Kilminster, "From Distance to Detachment."

14. Elias, *Involvement and Detachment*, xxi.

15. Ibid., xvi.

16. Ibid., xxvii.

17. Ibid., xxviii–xxix.

18. Ibid., 49.

19. Kilminster, "From Distance to Detachment."

20. I discuss this in some detail in Williams, "Modernity and the Other Body," 221–39.

21. Goudsblom and Mennell, *Norbert Elias*, 131.

22. Ibid., 131.

23. YouTube, www.youtube.com/watch?v=zKQgTiqhPbw.

24. YouTube, www.youtube.com/watch?v=csqJ_ULmQL8.

From the Modern to the Ecological: Latour on Walden Pond

So long as ecocritics are trapped in the "two cultures" ideology that polarizes literature from science and human society from nonhuman nature, we will find it difficult to define a middle ground from which literature and science can be seen as partners, and humans and nonhumans as agents, all cooperating to form the world we share. To locate this middle ground we need to think not of a monolithic "Science" but of the various practices and disciplines of the sciences, and in this quest our natural allies will be our colleagues in science studies. Bruno Latour has spent a lifetime tracing the way natures, politics, and discourses weave together a common world. By asking how the texts of science are loaded with the real, Latour opens up the relational middle ground *between* subject and object, "subjective" literature and the "objective" sciences, and calls for a new, cosmopolitan, and interdisciplinary vision of "political ecology" to which the various disciplines all contribute their unique skills. For Cartesian metaphysics—the founding move of modern philosophy that split mind from nature—has collapsed in the face of today's interpenetration of humans and nature in a global ecology. Instead of struggling to imagine a new and alternative metaphysics, Latour suggests, simply but radically, that "we have *never been* modern." That is, what has collapsed is not a way of doing, but rather a way of thinking about our doing that has now reached its limits. In its place, the sciences and the humanities— instead of facing off across a no-man's-land, shaking in each other's faces the essentialist and reductive weapons of objectivity and subjectivity—will discover that we all along have been standing side by side, building a world in common. It's time we put down our weapons, shook hands, and set about the task of composing a world in common—a *cosmos*—in earnest.

What Latour calls the "modern settlement," by which literature inherited the labyrinths of subjectivity while science inherited the world, has done particular damage to Ralph Waldo Emerson and Henry David Thoreau, the canonical originators of American nature writing. A Latourian reading of these two authors suggests ways one might open up an ecocritical discourse by allowing the literary critic to trace not only how they are fictive, but also how they are "fact"-ive, masters at loading their prose with the real, by interweaving the networks of nature, culture, and discourse. Their stories themselves are tightly interwoven: Emerson, the elder, catalyzed and shaped Thoreau's literary ambitions; in turn, Thoreau refashioned his mentor's revolutionary ideas to mount a counter-revolution of his own. While Emerson helped negotiate the "modern constitution" for America, creating nature as a bottomless resource for the human imagination, Thoreau turned his attention to the middle ground of Walden Pond, where he found not objects apart from subjects but networks, agents, and a succession of temporal frames. Even as Emerson's modern constitution was crystalizing into modern politics, professions, and technologies, Thoreau was imagining the limits of modernism and outlining an alternative.

At the center of Latour's work is his analysis of modernism, which he sees as a double movement by two distinct but cooperative practices, "purification" and "translation": modernism must purify nature from culture, science from literature; then, having created a yawning abyss between the two, it must fill that abyss with hybrids or mixtures, the "translations"— sciences, arts, technologies, neighborhoods, institutions—that constitute our lived environment. The trick is that since modernism demands purity, the hybrid nature of these entities must be denied, and so modernism evacuates the conceptual center, emptying it of all the mixed entities by sending them back to the opposed domains of "natural" and "human." The work all this requires must be invisible, the mediators themselves transparent, for "they merely transport, convey, transfer the power of the only two beings that are real, Nature and Society."[1] Latourian modernism may be said to have started with Francis Bacon's injunction that we command nature only by obedience to her laws: while in practice, Baconian empirical sciences work like delicate shuttles to weave together nature, discourse, society, and politics, in ideology, Bacon's sciences became "Science," the monolithic arbiter of the timeless Laws of Nature invoked to silence the passions and quarrels of a humanity in permanent exile to Plato's Cave. To say that "we have never been modern" is to locate modernism as a Western cultural formation, diagnostic rather than universal, and to remind ourselves that while modernism has built and powered our contemporary metaphysics of command and control, now that the hybrids proliferate and boundaries between humans and natures are everywhere confused and interlaced, we can see what has always been visible: modernism is not a universal essence but a historical and political practice.

Latour suggests that the modern inserts itself into the arrow of time by positing a rupture with an old, archaic, primitive, and "premodern" past. Emerson's career can be arrayed across such a rift: one might say he became "modern" while visiting Paris, in 1833, when at the Muséum de Histoire Naturelle he for the first time saw the aggregate of all the world's minerals, fossils, bones, shells, plants, insects, birds, and mammals not as fixed objects arranged according to a static taxonomy but "mobilized," as Latour says, as ideas, unfixed and disposed around the axis of the human imagination: "Nature," *natura naturans*, the quick cause, the surging Idea that connected all natural objects as versions of itself. In this vision, Emerson was reborn: "I will be a naturalist," he rapturously declared.[2] As soon as he returned to the United States, he made good on that vow by delivering a series of lectures on natural science, which he worked up into his first book, the epochal *Nature* (1836). To "be a naturalist" did not mean, for Emerson, collecting plants or insects or tinkering in a laboratory, but making the Kantian/Copernican shift by which the mind can illuminate and dominate the world, can see "the *metaphysics* of conchology, of botany," rather than the empirical details of individual shells and plants.[3] Thus Emerson made his primer not a handbook of identification but a manifesto of modernism.

Emerson opens *Nature* with what Latour calls the founding gesture of the modernist, the purification of the world into the polar opposites of nature and human, object and subject—or, as Emerson says, "Nature and the Soul," the "NOT ME" and the "ME." Following this purification he repopulates the philosophical abyss he has just created with "Art," namely, "the mixture of his will" with the things of nature; as Latour posits, the mixtures or "hybrid entities" proliferate and threaten to create an "imbroglio" that would irreparably confuse the very terms Emerson is striving to separate. So Emerson hastens to purify them by declaring that despite filling the world with mixtures of nature and human will, "his operations taken together are so insignificant" that "they do not vary the result."[4] In a single paragraph, laid like a cornerstone at the onset of his career, Emerson has accomplished a miracle. All Nature lies ready to hand, a resource so infinite that all our arts and technologies will leave her, essentially, untouched and pure.

Latour posits that modernism connects these purified polar essences of Man and Nature by the equally pure self, which is emptied out of all subjectivity to act as the intermediary that, "void in itself," "simply transports, transfers, transmits energy from one of the poles of the Constitution."[5] Accordingly, Emerson's prose is filled with images of transparency, as when he becomes a "transparent eyeball" through which course the currents of Universal Being, or when the commanding eye of the poet/scientist turns "the world to glass" so that the light of "higher laws" shines through it.[6] That a transparent eyeball cannot see, nor a transparent universe be seen, forms the haunting corollary of Kant's modernist Copernican turn: nature, paradoxically, is always tragically just out of reach. Emerson recognizes this problem when he first entertains, then dismisses, Idealism (which asserts nature does not outwardly exist) to restore a warm and motherly nature in which he can "expand and live in the warm day like corn and melons."[7] Yet if Idealism denies us a livable planet, its opposite, empiricism, is also dangerous, for the risky allurements of nature's beautiful objects threaten to mix their nature with our own; we must resist nature's siren song "with a supernatural eye" that sees through nature to the cause of nature, turning the poet/scientist into a priest who is penetrated and dissolved into ecstasy, "a sort of bright casualty" whose will is surrendered "to the Universal power."[8]

This may sound exotic, but it owes much to Emerson's careful reading in Francis Bacon, from whom he learned how power is gained by surrender to nature's laws. Latour's many case studies detail how science works to socialize nonhuman entities "through the channels of laboratories, expeditions, institutions," an insight Emerson pursues through a literary analogy: the scientist "republishes" the natural into the "finer" sphere of the social.[9] Yet Latour's humble and quotidian process becomes, in Emerson, an unbearable, Promethean epic, as Man is pulled across the two poles of Man and Nature, Freedom and Fate until, as Emerson theorizes, "the whole world is the flux of matter over the wires of thought to the poles or points where it would build." Man, at the epicenter, becomes "a stupendous antagonism, a dragging together of the poles of the universe."[10] The sciences, Latour's delicate shuttle, have become Science, the monolith that chastens all human feeling and settles all earthly disputes with the cudgel of eternal Truth.

Thoreau, too, moved to the middle ground, not as a "stupendous antagonism" between Freedom and Fate but as a neighborhood reality between Concord and the wilderness: a small glacial lake on the outskirts of Concord, Massachusetts, now universally famous as Walden Pond. On the nonrandom date of 4 July 1845, Thoreau moved into the small and well-built house he had constructed that spring on Emerson's land, to begin his own small, nonmodern counter-revolution. It was no hermit's cabin: the neighborhood included scattered shacks housing the town's marginal residents—impoverished Irish laborers, freed slaves—and he made the short walk into town every day or two. Nor was it wilderness: the land had been tended and farmed for untold centuries by Indians, then by Europeans, and was in Thoreau's day being clear-cut for fuel and railroad ties. In this novel border-life, in this cutover and abused landscape, a new awareness dawned on Thoreau of the lives being

lived parallel to his own: mice, loons, ants, pines, owls, the pond itself. But
what those lives meant became clear only after he had traveled to a much
different landscape.

In 1846, Thoreau journeyed to the Maine wilderness, where on the
slopes of Mt. Katadhin (spelled "Ktaadn" in his work), he encountered a
nature "not bound to be kind to man," "no man's garden," a nature that,
unlike Walden, had never been socialized. The moment was as powerful for
Thoreau as the revelation at the Paris Muséum had been for Emerson—and
its exact antithesis: "What is it to be admitted to a museum, to see a myriad
of particular things, compared with being shown some star's surface, some
hard matter in its home!"[11] Instead of a universe mobilized and reduced to
its generative divine Idea, here was an irreducible universe, "matter, vast,
terrific," "vast, titanic, inhuman Nature" utterly indifferent to human design, not merely inaccessible but a threat.[12] Nowhere else in his writing did
Thoreau allow himself to reach such a pitch: "Talk of mysteries!—Think of
our life in nature,—daily to be shown matter, to come in contact with it,—
rocks, trees, wind on our cheeks! the *solid* earth! the *actual* world! the
common sense! Contact! Contact! Who are we? *where* are we?"[13]

Thoreau did not linger. He was relieved to return to civilization's
"smooth, but still varied landscape," leaving the wilderness behind as spiritual resource rather than as actual residence.[14] He lived for another year at
Walden before returning to town, where he helped his family move to a fine,
large house on Main Street. It was in this deeply socialized landscape that he
forged his solution to the problem of *"Contact!"*: if transcendent nature was
inaccessible, inhuman, like some star's surface, then bring nature down to
earth. Here, too, the gods are present, says Latour: here, too, even on the
streets of town, we walk on some star's surface. Thoreau addressed the big,
existential questions—*"Who* are we? *where* are we?"—by asking the small,
seemingly inconsequential questions: Who made this track? Where does
that flower grow? When does it bloom?

In his eulogy for his friend, Emerson expressed disappointment at Thoreau's unaccountable refusal to "engineer for America," leading, instead,
huckleberry parties—like the one Thoreau joined the instant he was let
out of jail for refusing to pay his poll tax. Twentieth-century readers found
it hard to connect Thoreau's nature writing with his rampant abolitionism
and the political critique of "Civil Disobedience." The more his journal
filled with details of animal tracks, fish scales, plant bloomings, and stream
depths, the more dry and tedious it seemed. Instead of revolving the world
around the axis of his thought, it seemed Thoreau had become the slave of
empiricism, a poet silenced by science. This misreading was itself a product
and symptom of modernism. In Latour's terms, Thoreau had found his

solution to the problem of contact by turning away from the modern settle-ment, following instead the nonmodern path of small, local, daily contacts, leading "a Copernican counter-revolution." At the center of Thoreau's world were not heaps of randomly observed natural objects but the collectives they formed: pond, forest, meadow, river, village. What he traced in his actions and his writing was the generation of nature *and* society out of the middle ground, the borderland where, having built his world, he allowed that world to rebuild him.

Another way to put this is to say that, starting at Walden Pond and with increasing skill through the 1850s, Thoreau followed the practice, not of Science, but of the sciences, weaving humans and nonhumans together by naturalizing the social and socializing the natural. He disciplined his daily rambles in Concord's woods and fields into deliberate field transepts, along which he collected specimens and observed behaviors. Using the pencils he himself had engineered and manufactured in the Thoreau family pencil factory, he jotted notes outdoors that he elaborated at home into journal entries that were, in turn, distilled and amplified into lectures and essays. In this sense, Thoreau did mobilize the world after all, gathering and preserv-ing plants, birds' nests, insects and turtles, arrowheads and thousands of pages of records, all of which he amplified into published works. His pro-cedure resembles the series of transformations traced by Latour in "Circulat-ing Reference": rather than erect a stark correspondence between the op-posed edifices of Word and World, Latour's botanists and soil scientists instead generate a linked sequence of transformations, from the Brazilian savannah to the published scientific article. "I can never verify the resem-blance between my mind and the world," Latour writes, "but I can, if I pay the price, extend the chain of transformations wherever verified reference circulates through constant substitutions."[15]

Through just such a chain of transformations, Thoreau loaded his prose with the real. His most practical success was his most "scientific" essay, "The Succession of Forest Trees," in which he resolved the puzzle of why, "when a pine wood was cut down an oak one commonly sprang up, and *vice versa*."[16] The first step was to establish that oaks and pines were the product, not of mind or of spontaneous generation, but of *seeds*, small material objects that must be transported from where they grow to where they are planted by such material agents as wind, water, and animals. Once Thoreau has identi-fied his agents—or in Latour's terms, "actors" or "actants"—he can put them into circulation: "in a word . . . while the wind is conveying the seeds of pines into hard woods and open lands, the squirrels and other animals are conveying the seeds of oaks and walnuts into the pine woods, and thus a rotation of crops is kept up."[17] This actor-network connects nonhumans with the humans who observe (who are in turn themselves observed—or more accurately, scolded—by jays and squirrels), who own the land, who log the forests, and who stupidly graze cattle on the newly opened land, destroying the infant forest nature had so providently prepared. The next step, then, is to appoint "forest wardens," managers of the land who oversee the actions of its owners to the end of creating healthier forests—the index of a healthy and fruitful collective.

Thoreau's engagement with the sciences was not limited to his private excursions and journals. He put himself on the network of international science long enough to understand its workings and to contribute to what Latour calls "centres of calculation," in Boston. When Louis Agassiz put out the call for specimens to stock his nascent Museum of Comparative Zoology at Harvard's Lawrence Scientific School, Thoreau responded by collecting, packing, and shipping to him fish, turtles, mice, and even a live fox. While he turned down an invitation to join the American Association for the Advancement of Science, he did join the Boston Society of Natural History, whose library and resident experts he visited frequently. But he kept himself aside from the mainstream—close enough to observe (and to argue with Agassiz), but distant enough to preserve his independence. From this tangential position, Thoreau developed his own network, turning his attic room on Main Street into his own, local "centre of calculation."

Embedded as he was in such networks, Thoreau could not accept the polarizing ideology of objectivity, which was just then hardening into scientific orthodoxy. In 1854, he observed, "There is no such thing as pure *objective* observation—Your observation to be interesting i.e. to be significant must be *subjective*." All any writer, poet, or scientist, could report "is simply some human experience," and by that standard, "The man of most science is the man most alive—whose life is the greatest event."[18] Three years later, Thoreau struggled for words to define that middle ground vacated by modernism as neither objective nor subjective but "somewhere *between*" himself and "the objects," which meant describing the object not as if it were "independent" but "as it is related to you. The important fact is its effect on me."[19] Planting himself on the point "*between*," that relational middle ground, meant foregoing "objectivity," transparency, one of Romanticism's most cherished ideals—or rather, transforming it into a nonmodern version. Early on in his engagement with science, Thoreau wished he could be "the scribe of all nature . . . the corn & the grass & the atmosphere writing."[20] But no ecstatic immersion in nature would send his pen across the page. Since he could not be nature's transparent scribe, he had to craft an alternative whereby authority would be exchanged and that elusive, relational middle ground opened up.

In his analysis of Pasteur's innovative science, Latour suggests that Pasteur "*authorizes the yeast to authorize him to speak in its name.*"[21] Similarly, Thoreau's intensive labor, walking and working those daily transepts, authorized a nature that won't write *for* him, but that will authorize him to speak *in its name*—"to speak a word for Nature," as he writes in "Walking."[22] As a result of this authorization, nature becomes not something one can walk *to*, as if one could travel from civil society to the wild, but something one walks *in*, wherever one might be. Nature is produced by a certain sort of living: "He would be a poet who could impress the winds and streams into his service, to speak for him; who nailed words to their primitive senses, as farmers drive down stakes in the spring, which the frost has heaved; who . . . transplanted them to his page with earth adhering to their roots."[23] This describes the project of *Walden*, carefully constructed not to lead from pure society to pure nature, but toward a mode of living "somewhere *between*," a mode that mixes nature and society in order to register more sensitively the interpenetration of words and earth.

Thoreau's vantage on nature is widely recognized; ironically, given the heavily socialized nature of the landscape, his house at Walden Pond has become an icon of the poet's escape to "pure" nature. This view leaves no room for the railroad except as a violent intruder, the counter-icon of modernism's despoliation of nature. Yet there it is, cutting through the cove across from Thoreau's house, a stone's throw away; according to railroad schedules, in 1847 eighteen passenger trains and at least two freight trains ran past Walden daily. How, then, does Thoreau weave this alleged intruder into his walks and observations? Much in the fashion of Latour, who uses the railroad as a model for "all the technological networks that we encounter daily." "Is a railroad local or global?" Latour asks. "Neither. It is local at all points since you always find sleepers and railroad workers" and stations scattered along the way. "Yet it is global," too, as Thoreau knew: he took it from Concord to Boston, to Quebec, to Minnesota, and Emerson took it all the way to California, where he met John Muir.[24] This telescoping of scale, local to global, fascinates Thoreau, who watches the train pass so many times a day and who walks to town along its tracks: "The men on the freight trains, who go over the whole length of the road, bow to me as to an old acquaintance, they pass me so often, and apparently they take me for an employee; and so I am. I too would fain be a track-repairer somewhere in the orbit of the earth."[25] At every step he keeps local and global in view, remembering, even as he nods to the railroad workers, the sleepers over which they run: "We do not ride on the railroad; it rides upon us. Did you even think what those sleepers are that underlie the railroad? Each one is a man, an Irishman, or a Yankee man. The rails are laid on them, and they are covered with sand, and the cars run smoothly over them. They are sound sleepers, I assure you." Thus the railroad becomes "a fate, an *Atropos*," that overruns us all; yet when the cars run past, instead of mourning the coming apocalypse, Thoreau feels "refreshed and expanded," and he relishes the odors that are wafted "from Long Wharf to Lake Champlain, reminding me of foreign parts, of coral reefs, and Indian oceans, and tropical climes, and the extent of the globe. I feel more like a citizen of the world."[26] Thus he walks the tracks and rides the cars, both worker and passenger; but he also steps over the tracks "like a cart-path in the woods," leaving the *Atropos* of modern technological networks behind to smoke and hiss and steam without him. As Latour observes, the tracks of technology run round the world, but they are not global enough to reach everywhere. While they reach Walden, they reach Thoreau only when he chooses. In a step, he can leave them behind. Latour notes that technological networks connect the world—local to global, circumstantial to universal, contingent to necessary—but "only so long as the branch lines are paid for."[27] We can extend the chains of translation only so long as we agree to pay the price. As Thoreau understood, technology fails without maintenance: the earth's track repairers must walk the lines daily.

Thoreau sought to be "the man most alive, whose life makes the greatest event."[28] If objectivity renders events into essences, history renders those essences back into *events*.[29] Thoreau's demonstration project was his survey of Walden, in which he engaged in a science that would yield essence as "event" by bringing together, through measurement, the poles of man and nature, local and global. This novel approach came easily to him, since he made his living as a surveyor; yet however natural to Thoreau, his surveys have been off-putting for literary critics who assume that instruments of measurement must be alienating. From a Latourian perspective we might ask instead how mensuration establishes relationship, "constructs a commensurability that did not exist before their own calibration."[30] Thoreau's act of measuring the pond calibrates the temporal and the spatial: on the spatial axis, a topographical description of a landscape; on the temporal axis, a historical intervention that turns space into narrative, an event that loops together place and time. More than one hundred times he drilled a hole in the ice and lowered the sounding line, always along transepts, locating the pond's precise point of greatest depth (102 feet), and mapping the pond to an accuracy confirmed by modern instruments. His narrative of commensuration takes several pages, as he labors to establish that the pond— rumored to be bottomless—in fact did have a solid bottom, one that would hold an anchor to brace the chain of translations that would amplify ever-outward.

Ultimately Thoreau sought to translate the physical pond into a moral significance that would circulate forever, even were the pond to disappear. He concludes his survey with a universal truth, that the pond measures the height, breadth, and depth of human character; but it is, in Latour's terms, a relative universal, a statement of relationship earned one sounding at a time. Thoreau makes a point of not covering his tracks, of letting them show, in order to model the laborious work of mediation. "Each stage is matter for what follows and form for what precedes it," says Latour. That is, the immense gap between word and thing is crossed one small step at a time: sounding with compass and chains and sounding line; marking the results on a rough map; laying the ruler across the map to derive the relationship between length, breadth, and depth; applying the physical relationship to the moral world. As Thoreau works, things get increasingly wordy; retrace his steps in reverse, and words get increasingly thingy. For the marvel of Latour's double movement of reference is that it goes in both directions: "To know is not simply to explore, but rather is to be able to make your way back over your own footsteps, following the path you have just marked out."[31] Readers of *Walden* are invited, then, to follow this model in their own lives, not to move to Walden Pond themselves but to anchor their own search for meaning in the circumstances of their own backyard. Via the book in our hand, Thoreau walks out of the pond, to take us by the hand and lead us back to earth, to our own Walden: in following Thoreau's footsteps, we are to locate, anchor, and make commensurate our own relative universals.

Today the pond has a paradoxical status: it is a popular swimming hole for Greater Boston, convenient and utterly banal. It is also a sacred site for pilgrims from across the globe. While radios blare and swimmers thrash their own transepts across the pond, here and there solitary souls in street clothes gaze out at it with tears in their eyes. The paradox of Walden can be integrated by thinking of it as a Latourian "quasi-object." It is a thing, a real lake belonging to nature, which no man made; it has a geological history in the glaciations of North America, a hydrology, an ecology. It is also a narrative, "historical, passionate, and peopled with actants of autonomous forms."[32] This narrative does not begin with Thoreau, as he himself makes clear, but, in Latour's word, it does "swerve" with Thoreau. After Thoreau happened to Walden, the pond was changed, made into a narrative—into many narratives—that circulate around the globe. Walden has become a social bond, attaching people into societies: visitors for whom the pond is a social experience; readers who constitute a literary audience; state park employees whose lives center on its daily management; Thoreau Society members for whom the pond is ground zero in an international educational enterprise. In this sense, Walden Pond is a "collective," attaching humans and nonhumans to one another, circulating in their hands and defining their social bond by that very circulation.[33] As a quasi-object, Walden Pond simultaneously socializes natural fact and naturalizes the human, tracing a network that loops nature and society together and creates each as a resource for the other, a common home for nonmodernism.

Latour writes that "a substance is more like the thread that holds the pearls of a necklace together than the rock bed that remains the same no matter what is built on it."[34] Thoreau sought an anchor point in a shifting world, an eternal lake that would be ever unchanged, "perennially young," the same as ever even after its shores had been logged off, unchanging not as the bedrock but as the waterfall, a perpetual renewal. But the term "Walden" came to refer not just to a place or a thing but to a circulation: in Latour's terms, what the substance of Walden Pond designates is "the stability of an assemblage" that Thoreau found and, finding, made.[35] To preserve Walden, the pond—and *Walden*, the text—is to preserve the double anchor that relates and associates this perpetual renewal.

The foregoing extension of Latour's theorizing into literary territory suggests that ecocritics interested in altering the canon will find useful a model that looks not at "text" and "context" but at the way a text acts as the beating heart that holds together a circulatory system of social/natural networks. Science texts will necessarily remain marginal, alien, even extraterrestrial, so long as literary scholars still believe that science exists outside of culture. This makes science un-landed, dis-placed, all space and no place, all time and no history. But as Thoreau insists, nature never wrote a single text that was legible, without translation, to human eyes. Thus whenever a literary text embraces nature—and which, pray tell, do not?—science, the imaginary by which nature is woven into society, is woven into that text's every page.

Could, then, all texts be read in a Latourian manner? It would be an experiment worth trying. Latour suggests that if literary scholars were to set down their "iconoclast's hammer"—the one with which they repetitively shatter the illusion of reality to reveal it yet again as a social construction—they might see "that we have always been involved in cosmopolitics . . . the management, diplomacy, combination, and negotiation of human and nonhuman agencies." This is the political order in which we actually live, that "brings together stars, prions, cows, heavens, and people, the task being to turn this collective into a 'cosmos' instead of an 'unruly shambles.'"[36] In his manifesto of political ecology, *The Politics of Nature*, Latour outlines a plan of procedure with the proviso that nothing in it is changed—all his steps are happening as we speak—but everything in it is changed: in his perspectival counter-revolution, we must become neither ecocentric nor anthropocentric but instead earthcentric. If we are to build a "cosmos" together, every discipline must bring its own gifts to the assembly, and literature brings the gift of articulation. Latour worries that as the new political settlement goes forward, some voices are missing from the roll call. This worry points to the crucial role of literature and literary scholarship: it is we who can help complete the roll call.

Ecocritics who study the way literature mixes itself with nonhumans—ponds and forests, mountains and oceans, woodchucks, loons, and wolves, polar bears and melting polar ice—bring unique and vital skills. Was it not literary theorists who opened the collective by making an appeal on behalf of the excluded, alienated, and voiceless—Indians, slaves, and the racially othered; all those silenced by gender; laborers silenced by poverty—who not long ago were not counted as human? Today, in our professional work, we daily celebrate our facility at reading all texts in terms of race, class, and gender. Not long ago, we remind our students, "man" was an unmarked universal used to silence women, until feminists taught us how all gender is marked. Now "Nature" is the last unmarked categorical universal, used to silence all those who cannot speak in human language. Ecocritics need to teach how nature, too, is marked and various and voluble, and that no literary reading is complete until it hears the multiple voices of races, classes, genders—*and natures*. Then we, too, will have joined our colleagues in the task of weaving nature, culture, politics, and discourse into the new cosmos, where we seek the common good together.

NOTES

1. Latour, *We Have Never Been Modern*, 80.
2. Emerson, *Essays* 545–46; *Early Lectures* 1:10.
3. Emerson, *Essays*, 43.
4. Ibid., 8.
5. Latour, *We Have Never Been Modern*, 77–78.
6. Emerson, *Essays*, 10, 456.
7. Ibid., 38.
8. Ibid., 126.
9. Latour, *Pandora's Hope* 259; Emerson, *Essays*, 126.
10. Emerson, *Essays*, 965, 953.
11. Thoreau, *Maine Woods*, 71.
12. Ibid., 70, 64.
13. Ibid., 71.
14. Ibid., 155.
15. Latour, *Pandora's Hope*, 79; Walls, "Technologies."
16. Thoreau, *Excursions*, 166.

17. Ibid., 170.

18. Henry David Thoreau, *The Writings of Henry David Thoreau: Journal*, edited by John C. Broderick et al., 7 vols. to date (Princeton: Princeton University Press, 1981–), 8:98. Citations of Thoreau's *Journal* are to this edition unless otherwise specified.

19. Henry David Thoreau, *The Journal of Henry David Thoreau*, 14 vols., ed. Bradford Torrey and Francis Allen (Boston: Houghton Mifflin, 1906), 10:164–65.

20. Thoreau, *Journal*, 4:28.

21. Latour, *Pandora's Hope*, 132.

22. Thoreau, *Excursions*, 185.

23. Ibid., 208.

24. Latour, *We Have Never Been Modern*, 117.

25. Thoreau, *Walden*, 115.

26. Ibid., 92, 118–19.

27. Latour, *We Have Never Been Modern*, 117.

28. Thoreau, *Journal*, 8:98.

29. Latour, *We Have Never Been Modern*, 82.

30. Ibid., 113.

31. Latour, *Pandora's Hope*, 74.

32. Latour, *We Have Never Been Modern*, 89.

33. Ibid.

34. Latour, *Pandora's Hope*, 151.

35. Thoreau, *Walden*, 193; Latour, *Pandora's Hope*, 151.

36. Latour, *Pandora's Hope*, 290, 261.

3

PHENOMENOLOGY

Martin Heidegger, D. H. Lawrence, and Poetic Attention to Being

> Of course, not everyone needs to explicitly hold in view what is already seen in all experience, but only those who make a claim to deciding, or even to asking, about nature, history, art, human beings, or beings as a whole.—Heidegger, *Pathmarks*

The thought of the German philosopher Martin Heidegger (1889–1976) is a challenge to thinking because it asks us to imagine being differently. His works are not straightforward and do not set out an explicit program for social change but rather invite a shift in attention and conception of self in relation to world, time, and the nature of knowledge. This shift involves refusing a major aspect of our late modernity, that is, the ubiquity and dominance of forms of abstract and theoretical knowledge. Heidegger wishes to return this knowledge to its proper place, grounded in pragmatic relationships that respond thoughtfully and ethically to the dynamism and changeability of nature, of which our sense of self and being in the world is necessarily a part.

Heidegger's later works suggest that we are living through a crisis in our relation to the environment, in which we treat the natural world, ourselves included, as a reserve of energy that can be turned perpetually and ceaselessly toward technological ends. Under this technological conception, nature is transformed into what Heidegger terms a *standing-reserve*. This idea is central to his argument in "The Question Concerning Technology" in which careless instrumentality leads us to misrecognize the true nature of technology and of our being.[1] His term for our mode of being, useful to hold onto when thinking along with Heidegger, is *Dasein*, or *being-there*, or more explicitly in English, *being-in-the-world*. This reminds us of the dynamic environmental relatedness that grounds our identity and that is, for Heidegger, the origin of our ability to discern truth.

What truth is, the various forms in which we encounter truth or think of its coming to be in the world, is an essential part of Heidegger's work, and we will return to this at various points throughout the argument that follows. Another important aspect of his work is his treatment of our tendency to misconstrue our sense of self, our relationship to others and to the environment around us. In response to our misconceptions, he introduces many new words and plays with the etymology and connotation of existing words in order to prevent the overfamiliar diversion of thinking toward the metaphysical errors that make up traditional philosophical and popular arguments. This gives rise to an aspect of his style for which he is often criticized, even dismissed, notably by Theodor Adorno in *The Jargon of Authenticity*, and which gives an additional density to English translations of his work.

While it is true that the works insist on finding new words for common aspects of our experience and depend on poetic associations that we might not consider part of legitimate philosophical argument, it is also useful to consider how we would best convey a counterintuitive and unfamiliar approach to the nature of thinking itself if not through such a distancing use of language. The complex thought of Heidegger is complex for good reason. He wants us not to forget that we are undertaking a new path, and that familiar meanings and tropes that no longer demand thought must give way to a new vocabulary and rhetoric. Old linguistic habits establish as the ground for thinking a series of assumptions that Heidegger believes are wrong and that he wishes to revise. Some critics find his style obscurely hieratic and unnecessarily mystifying, but there is also a great body of interpretation that acknowledges him as one of the twentieth century's major thinkers.

Heidegger's work is related to the late-nineteenth- and early-twentieth-century movement of phenomenology as formulated by Brentano and Husserl, but is opposed to the claim that an objective, detached, and theoretical self-knowledge can be foundational, or that the empirical logic of the sciences can provide such a foundation for fundamental questions of ontology. Instead, Heidegger reflects on how our sense of objectivity as truth comes to be constituted as a phenomenon that appears within and is inseparable from the subject's experience of the world. He examines the ways in which being a self in the world appears to the self in the world, and his works discuss everyday aspects of being in an attempt to uncover their necessary conditions, such as our experience of time, our sense of inhabiting or being in any given place, the dispositions we have toward our surroundings in terms of projects, moods, and inherited beliefs, the nature of language in its relation to thought and subjectivity, and the different ways in which earlier philosophical traditions have shaped our sense of self.

Heidegger's development of phenomenology is best approached as a project that seeks to return us to a coherent self-understanding, or authenticity, that will allow properly ethical relations. His thought can be understood as a lifelong response to the paradoxical foundations of our technological late modernity, and the several obstacles to an authentic life that it represents: the assumption that instrumental technological ends can reveal essential human truths; the fact that social worlds are structured by relationships of material inequality and administrative equivalence; and the nihilism that results from depending on technical truths established by those who precede us. These concerns are clearly part of ecocritical thought, and so the relevance of Heidegger's work becomes clear for such a project.

There are many ways into Heidegger's thinking about authenticity, about the truth of experience, and the obstacles to its realization. In what follows, I want to discuss just one thread, that is, the way that truth can be uncovered or revealed in aesthetic experience. I do so by considering Heidegger's well-known lecture "The Origin of the Work of Art," given in 1935 and published in 1950. At various points, I also refer to ideas and arguments found in the literary and critical works of the English writer D. H. Lawrence (1885–1930). Very often, Lawrence's work shows him struggling with a new conception of being that is strikingly comparable to Heidegger's.

Lawrence and Heidegger were contemporaries, and although their work is not explicitly related, there are many correspondences of thought that make a joint reading fruitful for anyone trying to understand the struggles of an earlier generation of writers, particularly where they hope to formulate an account of being that can counter the excesses of modernity. Both writers' concerns fall within the perspective of ecocriticism because they reflect explicitly on what it means to be the inheritor of industrial and scientific modernity, and think carefully and persistently about its environmental, aesthetic, and spiritual transformations.

D. H. Lawrence was profoundly concerned by what he saw as a crisis of civilization, most obviously represented by World War I. Like many people at the time, Lawrence understood the war as the uncontrolled effect of Western societies' industrialization, and he described it as an expression of "mechanical, obsolete, hideous stupidity."[2] As with Heidegger, the subjection of human life to uniformly technological ends without clear ground or direction is a major theme of his work. The characteristic anxiety of modernism, that civilized life has taken a wrong turn somewhere, informs both writers' work, and both are interested in the movement from pre-Socratic thought to Platonic Idealism, which they identify as a fundamental metaphysical error that skews our understanding of nature, and of our place in it.

Both find in the fragmentary writings of Heraclitus, the pre-Socratic

Greek philosopher who lived in Ephesus at the turn of the sixth and fifth
centuries BCE, the promise of a different relationship between self and
world. Heraclitus's thoughts on strife and opposition, enigma and uncertainty inform both Heidegger's and Lawrence's attempts to think the nature
of being differently, and through their reading of Heraclitus they develop a
conviction that the poetic artwork has a central relationship to truth. For
both writers, it is the enigmatic nature of poetry that reveals an essential
aspect of our being.

The final part of this discussion considers Heidegger's argument about
the pre-Socratic sense of the natural world, of being as *phusis*, from which
we derive our word physical. *Phusis*, or what Lawrence calls *the physic*, is a
dynamic conception of the natural world that stands in distinction to the
conventional attitude toward nature which imagines it as the material sub-
strate of being, as mere matter awaiting the purpose and utility of man. For
both writers, the essential function of poetic language is that it returns our
attention to nature as *phusis*, and counters a deadened approach to our
environment. Heidegger's and Lawrence's treatment of poetry and poetic
attention approaches the question of being as an ecocritical concern.

In his discussion of Heideggerian poetics in *The Song of the Earth*, Jonathan Bate suggests that "the poem is a clearing in that it is an opening to the
nature of being."[3] Bate uses Heidegger's own term, the clearing, for the
moment of revelation offered to us in the poem. We can understand this by
imagining ourselves on a forest walk. As we walk along a densely wooded
path, we pay attention to the unstable ground, to the mossy rocks on which
we might slip, to the branches that need to be held aside and the brambles
that might tear at us as we pass. The going is hard and demanding, and we
are preoccupied by the practical demands to which we need to attend in
order to guarantee our passage. Suddenly, we come across a clearing in the
forest, and it is in this moment that we might first become properly attuned
to the nature of the environment we have been passing through, to our sense
of ourselves, our sense of relatedness to an environment which a moment
before had seemed only partial, fragmented, and dominated by practical
urgencies.

For Heidegger, poetry is a kind of clearing that allows attention to
aspects of being normally covered over by everyday demands. Bate's argument is essential reading for anyone interested in an ecocritical project,
and importantly he argues against the usual presumption that literature
and poetry have less power than technical or political programs for change.
However, he is more concerned with Heidegger's later essays on technology
and poetry. By beginning with "The Origin of the Work of Art" and thinking
about how it corresponds to themes in D. H. Lawrence, we can move toward

an understanding of how poetry is related to Heidegger's sense of being as *phusis*.

Heidegger sets out to counter the assumption that the nature of truth in art is a basic question of representation. Judging a work of art according to how well it represents an object is a common attitude of mind. Heidegger's observation is that this attitude rests on an unexamined assumption about the nature of truth: that truth is a relationship of correspondence between statement and world. In this picture, working out whether something is true is a question of how well the statement (or painting, etc.) fits the world to which it refers, but for Heidegger truth as correspondence or representation is only possible because it depends on a more fundamental sense of truth: our pretheoretical sense of *Dasein*, of just being there in a given situation.

Heidegger argues that we are more attuned to truth as representation because we are surrounded by technical instruments and forms of life that result from those disciplines and practices that emerge from it. Take a moment to look around you, and it is likely that unless you are reading this in a secluded woodland glade, you are surrounded by mass-produced objects and mechanisms, enclosed in the hum of home, office, industrial or transport systems, and dependent on the reliability and constancy of that technical environment. The practical truth of this kind of environment is exactly that of representation and correspondence.

However, Heidegger's point is that, despite its dominance, this kind of truth is neither originary nor exclusive. More than this, our immersion in a world of technical objects and goals means that we are always involved in or set to a particular project, and moving in a world in which things have already been interpreted by others. We are therefore largely exempted from the need to rediscover correspondent truths over again for ourselves. This leads both to nihilism, since we become passive in the face of a world whose function has been largely decided by others, and to anxiety about how what we say is related to the world it purports to describe.

However, it is a mistake to cast this historical exemption from interpretation as an epistemological uncertainty about our relatedness to the world. Truth is not something that precedes us in the world as a kind of object whose adequacy we latecomers must determine. Heidegger suggests that our technological form of life hides a more basic kind of truth: the environmental dynamism, becoming, and relatedness that is the foundation of *all* claims to truth. Heidegger discusses this originary aspect of truth in many works, and his term for it in English translation is *unconcealment*, romanized from the Greek as *aletheia*. Here, the *a*- is privative, that is, it represents the absence of something, specifically the absence of *lethe*, or forgetfulness. In "The Origin of the Work of Art," the truth available to us in the artwork awakens us from our forgetfulness by uncovering, or unconcealing, a foundational aspect of our being.

In the essay, Heidegger asks us to imagine a Van Gogh painting of a pair of shoes. He attributes the shoes to a peasant woman and suggests that they allow the world of the peasant woman to "shine forth" from the painting. The artwork reveals the intentional, phenomenological world of the shoes in its earthy materiality. The mud, the sounds, sensations, and habits of rural life, the sensuous whole of the peasant woman's world, are evoked in a way of which perhaps a peasant woman is not aware, or more probably that our encounter with such a woman in ordinary life would not reveal, submitted as our everyday experience is to the usual means-end way of being. Through the discussion of the painting, Heidegger hopes that we will think of the artwork as something that shows the thing in place in its world.

The second work Heidegger discusses is a Greek temple standing in a valley. The point of this example is that unlike the painting, the temple is not a copy of an original elsewhere. It is not a representation of anything. The example of the temple reminds us that something happens in the artwork apart from the question of representation. As we contemplate the temple, we are aware that a worldview exists which brings forth temples out of stone. People made this, and we know that people must live within a perspective on their world. The stone, in its materiality, has meaning only by virtue of a particular worldview that, among other things, brings temples into being here and leaves stone unquarried there. Whatever the stone is, it is so only within a given worldview. Although the temple is made out of stone, nothing in the materiality of the unworked stone in the ground anticipates or justifies the temple-making worldview, and the stone used in the creation of the temple exists within a worldview in which stone also has many other uses, only one of them being the construction of temples. This complex relation between stone, temple, and worldview is an intrinsic part of our contemplation.

Heidegger calls the thingness of the stone *earth* and calls the worldview *world*. The temple, or the artwork, is the place where both meet, but importantly for Heidegger, the worldview can never reveal the stone in its absolute nature. We can never know in advance the world-interpreting perspectives that are to come, and we can never retrieve the world-interpreting perspectives that have passed from history. We can therefore never exhaust or master all possible interpretations of the earth. This means that while in one way the world brings forth the earth in its meaning, in another way the earth withdraws from the interpretation of the world. In other words, the earth is not intelligible without a world, but no world can reveal the earth in its absolute finality. Earth and world are in perpetual tension.

In his novel *The Rainbow,* D. H. Lawrence writes the following about Will Brangwen's experience of Lincoln Cathedral:

> In a little ecstasy he found himself in the porch, on the brink of the unrevealed. . . . Here the very first dawn was breaking, the very last sunset sinking. . . . Away from time, always outside of time! Between east and west, between dawn and sunset, the church lay like a seed in silence, dark before germination, silenced after death. Containing birth and death, potential with all the noise and transitation of life, the cathedral remained hushed, a great, involved seed, whereof the flower would be radiant life inconceivable, but whose beginning and end were the circle of silence. Spanned round with the rainbow, the jewelled gloom folded music upon silence, light upon darkness, fecundity upon death, as a seed folds leaf upon leaf and silence upon the root and the flower, hushing up the secret of all between its parts, the death out of which it fell, the life into which it has dropped, the immortality it involves, and the death it will embrace again. Here in the church, "before" and "after" were folded together, all was contained in oneness.[4]

This is a beautiful account of the field of being of the church, which Lawrence observes has as much to do with the unrevealed as with what is open to display. It is both what lies before and after life that the church gestures toward, but it can only do so from within the terms of its own materiality. The tension between what it offers and what it withholds is so productive that the church is "a great, involved seed" of the same order of being as the coming-to-presence of a flower.

The parallels here between Lawrence and Heidegger are insistent. In "The Question Concerning Technology," the "bursting of a blossom into bloom" and "artistic and poetical bringing into appearance" are both versions of truth as *aletheia,* as unconcealment.[5] The way in which being emerges into appearance, demanding and yet resisting interpretation, is the mystery to which both writers allude. For both, the materiality of the church or temple is a space experienced through the religious lifeworld whose field of being it enacts, but the passage from *The Rainbow* clearly shows us that a necessary part of the experience is the observation that the church is full of darkness, silence, and the involuted secrecy of its central mystery.

Importantly, the epistemological gap that interpretation of materiality seems to open up in the world is a gap *in appearance only.* In the technical attitude, we respond to this epistemological gap, to the indeterminacy or uncertainty of the material world, by imaginatively tunneling into or stripping away the surface appearance of the earth instead of dwelling in the poetic attitude, which recognizes that indeterminacy is the intrinsic feature of all appearances. There is a paradox in the urge to overcome uncertainty by stripping away surfaces in an attempt to reveal hidden depths: whatever is revealed to us is always revealed, necessarily, in the mode of appearances. No matter what the scale of encounter, there is nothing other than ambiguous appearance and interpretation, and it is this paradox that we contemplate when we consider the work of art.

We can misconceive the paradox as a problem of how appearance relates to a more fundamental reality, but this is to devalue the essential nature of appearance *as* reality. The indeterminate nature of appearance is central to the mystery of being. This observation in Lawrence is fruitful since it is a path toward the kind of holistic thinking that Heidegger wishes us to undertake. Heidegger calls this enigmatic gap in appearance *the rift between world and earth,* and importantly he identifies the artwork as a figure within this rift. In other words, it is the tension and play between appearance, concealment, and relatedness that is the mode of being of all works of art, and consideration of this leads us toward a more profound understanding of our being. We experience this tension by the way that the work reveals and yet conceals at the same time. The artwork reminds us that the stuff out of which we bring forth works has no meaning prior to a lifeworld of values, but it also reminds us that anything that we might like to call the world of values only properly appears in this kind of relation.

In his reading of Heidegger's essay, Julian Young observes that "in apprehending the artwork we become aware of the inadequacy of all our 'projections' fully to capture the nature of the material, aware that there is infinitely more to nature, to beings, than we can ever make intelligible to ourselves."[6] Heidegger's sense of truth as *aletheia* is bound up with this play of concealment and revelation. The example of the temple reminds us that the artwork is not primarily a representation but a field of experience in which crucial relations of being come to light.

D. H. Lawrence's novel *The Rainbow* was first published in 1915 and immediately banned. Its continuation, *Women in Love,* was published in 1920 in the United States and following the absence of legal action was published in England in 1921. Together the novels show the Brangwen family over three generations from rural to industrial England, between the 1840s and the new century. Like all of Lawrence's work, these novels are concerned with the nature of knowledge, truth, art, and human relations in a world transformed by technology. *Women in Love* takes the questioning impulse in *The Rainbow* and matches it to a prose style that enacts the earlier novel's questions in a very different way. The action of the novel is contemporary to the moment of its composition, which is the disaster of World War I.

Lawrence's disgust at the mechanization and intellectualization of life informs *Women in Love* and explains his search for a more holistic picture of human relations. In a well-known passage from the chapter "Excurse," we can see how his prose enacts the kind of strife between earth and world, reality and appearance, that Heidegger claims for the artwork.

> She had her desire of him, she touched, she received the maximum of un-speakable communication in touch, dark, subtle, positively silent, a magnificent gift and give again, a perfect acceptance and yielding, a mystery, the reality of that which can never be known, vital, sensual reality that can never be transmuted into mind content, but remains outside, living body of darkness and silence and subtlety, the mystic body of reality. She had her desire fulfilled. He had his desire fulfilled. For she was to him what he was to her, the immemorial magnificence of mystic, palpable, real otherness.[7]

This is just a fragment from a chapter full of oblique imagery and strangely modulated phrasing. Without clear indication of the referent or the explanatory commentary of the narrator, the text appears mysterious, enigmatic. We are thrown back on its poetic opacity and density, but this is the clue to its value and shows Lawrence's proximity to the thoughts about art and poetry that we find in Heidegger. It is the central intuition of modernism to reach toward something that is seemingly left out of representation in order to lead away from an insistence on representation as the ground of art. Lawrence was drawn toward intuitive aspects of experience that could not be shown but rather only felt, and in "Excurse" the prose enacts just such an ambiguous relationship between material and understanding.

The revelation requires this opacity and density of language, which is also its movement away from representation. The poetic density of the prose at first seems to hide but in fact reveals exactly the experience that Lawrence wishes us to contemplate. The prose offers us the same order of experience as that given to the protagonists, that is, the feeling of being immersed in a powerfully significant experience but one whose meaning is as yet undisclosed. In essence, this is poetic truth emerging in the play of concealment and revelation.

Lawrence recognized that the strangeness of his prose, and the revelation of aspects of being not normally considered, would have to be apprehended by an effort of feeling that some readers would most probably not want to discover in themselves. In a letter written to David Garnett on 5 June 1914, he suggested that reading the novel "necessitates a different attitude . . . which you are not as yet prepared to give."[8] Lawrence's ambition was to renew the language of prose in such a way that it communicates something that has been forgotten or covered over. He wants a new way of feeling about self, being, and world and knows that the density and opacity of poetic language is somehow involved.

Michael Bell points out the paradoxical inefficacy and success of *Women in Love* as communication. He suggests that the rhetorical strain of the text is the clue to its existential vision. The densely poetic prose points toward something that remains stubbornly ungraspable and so reminds us that language both is and is not communication, and that while every representation is a relation, not every relation is one of representation or correspondence.[9]

How can the density of poetic language lead us toward an observation about truth? In "The Origin of the Work of Art," Heidegger's thoughts about the truthfulness of the artwork ultimately derive from the status that he accords to poetic language. It is a dense, opaque, and enigmatic form of revelation. Rather than taking us away from the nature of being toward mere appearances, the field of the poetic returns us to the play of disclosure and concealment within appearances, which *is* the nature of being and the original possibility of art. For Heidegger, poetry reminds us of the essential tension that our language holds for us. On the one hand, it is thing-like, debated as faithless representation and serving as a locus of anxiety about truth and authenticity. Yet, on the other, it is also a profound index of embodiment, a sensuous experience and a form of revelation.

The value of Heidegger and Lawrence for ecocriticism is that both are concerned to make us pay careful attention to the limitations of our conceptual grasp of the world, and to weigh up the consequences of imagining we understand where clearly we do not. By bringing the dense materiality of language into relief, their work enacts a poetic attitude in which both the limits and instrumentality of conceptual thought and a contemplative attention to embodied language are held together.

In a 1928 review, Lawrence makes clear his sense of poetry as the play between appearance, concealment, and relatedness: "Poetry is a matter of words. Poetry is a stringing together of words into a ripple and jingle and run of colours. Poetry is an interplay of images. Poetry is the iridescent suggestion of an idea. Poetry is all these things, and it is still something else. . . . The essential quality of poetry is that it makes a new effort of attention, and "discovers" a new world within the known world."[10] In both writers' observations about poetic experience, various aspects of our being are brought to light, most notably dynamic relatedness, being as revelation, and the enigma of nature. Taken together, these three aspects offer an insight into the ancient Greek sense of being as *phusis*.

The conventional sense of nature entails the breaking apart of being into world and representation, matter and form, etc. This is a metaphysical problem to which Heidegger returns in many different works. He counsels us against the misinterpretation of nature as matter endowed with force, as underlying substratum of being, as something unformed or something opposed and contrasted to mind, culture, or history.

All of these dichotomies, however, reveal something important about being. Being as *phusis* is dual. It contains within itself two seemingly contradictory movements that in various interpretations become essentialized as the oppositions above. Being is appearance in the sense of presence. It is what is present to us, what is enduring and lasting. But being is also what becomes, what comes into presence, and what ceases to be. Beings remain the same. Beings change. Beings emerge into being. Beings cease to be. Plants, human beings, animals, and the processes of nature are of the order of being that Heidegger describes as *phusis*. In Heidegger's terms, being as *phusis* contains as its essential nature both *coming to presence* and *absencing*, or ceasing to be.

The wrong turn that Heidegger attributes to Platonism and to the subsequent history of Western metaphysics is the misconception of what appears, what comes into presence, as the expression of an *eidos*, an independent essence common to and present in all beings that have that appearance. It is therefore something that endures ideally once any given being has ceased to be. Through this misinterpretation, the singularity of beings is displaced into the mode of a derivative, secondary, and degraded appearance. By consistently closing down our responsiveness to the ways in which being comes to light in what appears and what is present in appearance, and by misconceiving appearance as the superficial expression of an underlying equivalence of matter, we implicitly devalue what is present to us. More significantly, we simplify the field of our being into something temporary and structured by equivalence, thereby giving its preservation an equally superficial character.

Heidegger observes that we only ever encounter being in the singularity of its appearance: "we find what is [*phusis*-like] only where we come upon a placing into the appearance; i.e., only where there is [*morphe*]."[11] In other words, being is inseparable from its appearance within a world. It is a metaphysical illusion to think that there exist several layers of being, trapped inside one another, each less superficial and more objective than the last, and that human intervention will eventually allow them to emerge, thereby dispensing finally with the need for interpretation. Whatever can be said to be can only appear to us in the interpretative play of presencing and absencing that is the dynamic condition of the natural world.

What is the relationship between this observation about nature and the function of poetry? In an essay on the concept of *phusis* in Aristotle, Heidegger translates the familiar Aristotelian maxim in a rather different way.

Rather than "Man is a rational animal," Heidegger suggests that ανθρωπος ζωον λογον εχον should be translated as "the human being is the living entity to whom *the word* belongs." He explains further that "the distinguishing characteristic of the essence of the human being consists in the fact that one has, and holds oneself in λογος."[12]

In a characteristic move, Heidegger depends for his argument on the etymology of *logos* and the verb *legein*. *Legein* means to collect, to gather, or "to bring together into a unity . . . it means the same as to reveal what was formerly hidden, to let it be manifest in its presencing."[13] Here Heidegger reminds us that language is a means of ordering and revealing but that it is not simply a means of revealing what is present. He insists on the authentic sense in which language is related to *phusis* and turns to two fragments of Heraclitus in which the cryptic quality of the *logos* is emphasized in its relation to *phusis*.[14]

In Heraclitus, and for both Heidegger and Lawrence, the *logos* is *that which reveals and conceals at the same time*. Language is a part of nature, and it is therefore in the nature of language to make manifest the nature of being as both concealment and revelation: "only because human beings *are* insofar as they relate to beings as beings, unconcealing and concealing them, can they and must they have the 'word,' i.e., speak of the being of beings."[15] Here, language is not to be understood in the degraded sense of representation, obscurely related to the world, but in the sense of a mode of being through which the essential nature of being is revealed.

Poetic language, in its attention to the singularity of beings in appearance, to the relatedness of the seemingly unrelated, and in its emphasis on the play of indeterminacy, uncertainty, enigma, and revelation, moves us closer to Heidegger's sense of authentic being. The act of poetic attention returns us to the dynamic presencing and absencing of *phusis*, to language as a locus of the truth that Heidegger calls *aletheia*, and to an originary sense of nature.

In her essay on ecopoeisis, Kate Rigby wonders whether this privileging of poetic language in Heidegger is a kind of anthropocentric hubris, but we remember that for Heidegger, the poetic reminds us of the *limits* of our interpretative mastery of the world and of the essential importance of dwelling in uncertainty. Rigby usefully calls this a "negative ecopoetics,"[16] and as we have seen in both Heidegger and D. H. Lawrence, the cryptic nature of being is not a problem to be overcome, but rather a path toward a greater holism.

Heidegger concludes his essay on the concept of *phusis* in Aristotle with an observation that "today we are all too inclined to reduce something like this presencing-by-absencing to a facile dialectical play of concepts rather than hold on to what is astonishing about it."[17] If poetry can return us to an awed appreciation of the mystery of *phusis*, then it has its place in a project whose task is the preservation of being.

NOTES

1. Heidegger, *Basic Writings*, 322.

2. Lawrence, *Selected Letters*, 79.

3. Bate, *Song of the Earth*, 280.

4. Lawrence, *Rainbow*, 168.

5. Heidegger, *Basic Writings*, 317.

6. Young, *Heidegger's Philosophy of Art*, 48.

7. Lawrence, *Women in Love*, 320.

8. Lawrence, *Selected Letters*, 77.

9. Bell, *D. H. Lawrence*, 226.

10. Lawrence, *Introductions and Reviews*, 109.

11. Heidegger, *Pathmarks*, 212.

12. Ibid.

13. Ibid., 213.

14. See fragments X & XI, Heraclitus, *Hippocrates*, 472.

15. Heidegger, *Pathmarks*, 213.

16. Rigby, "Earth, World, Text," 437.

17. Heidegger, *Pathmarks*, 227.

Merleau-Ponty's Ecophenomenology

Maurice Merleau-Ponty is the only major European philosopher who embraces the consequences of evolution and sees humans as interdependent members of the ecosystem. His thinking manifests a lifelong engagement with modern science, which he saw in a necessary complementarity with philosophy. Although his untimely death prevented the completion of his ambitious philosophy of nature, enough of the work in progress exists in manuscript to indicate its shape and importance as a radically ecological philosophy.

In contrast to the long tradition of Western philosophical dualism, phenomenology from Husserl to Heidegger and Merleau-Ponty restores attention to the human immersion in nature and the meaning immanent in ordinary experience. Both Heidegger and Merleau-Ponty saw literature as a central mode of biocentric dwelling. Heidegger argued that humans are the shepherds of Being who care for the earth by "letting things be." However, he was horrified by the bodily resemblance of humans to other animals and argued that an abyss yawns between us and them.[1] Merleau-Ponty, in contrast, came to embrace the kinship of living organisms through coevolution and described language as an embodied force emerging in many dimensions and beings in the natural world. He argued that that each human—like any other organism—exists in a chiasmic embrace with the surrounding world. Posthumanist theory and a new wave of theoretical attention to human/animal relations, such as Derrida's late writings, are congruent with much of Merleau-Ponty's thought and extend its concerns into interdisciplinary work in evolutionary biology and recent studies of animal sentience and culture.

Merleau-Ponty's thinking moved from early assumptions about human superiority to other beings, in *The Structure of Behavior*, to an exhaustive examination of embodiment in *Phenomenology of Perception*. His late work developed a chiasmic ontology of wild being in *The Visible and the Invisible* and a simultaneous exploration of the philosophical dimensions of modern science in lectures published recently in English as *Nature*. He saw human language as a late event in biological evolution, growing out of immanent structures of meaning throughout the natural world.[2]

Merleau-Ponty suggests that all organisms exist intertwined and in constant interaction with the flesh of the world around them. He explained, "This environment of brute existence and essence is not something mysterious: we never quit it, we have no other environment."[3] Such a philosophy is congruent with sciences such as quantum physics and molecular biology which revolutionized the understanding of the natural world in the twentieth century, and whose philosophical ramifications Merleau-Ponty was considering in the Nature lectures. Though he did not live long enough to know the genetic and molecular discoveries which would demonstrate a common heritage and sharing of genetic material for all organisms, his concept of the flesh of the world anticipated it. His understanding of its dynamic unfolding through geologic time accords with Lynn Margulis's recent assertion that "all beings alive today are equally evolved. All have survived over three thousand million years of evolution from common bacterial ancestors."[4] We share the same fate as equal participants in the biota with its dense ecological texture of interdependence.

Merleau-Ponty's lifelong relationship with science was appreciative yet critical. In the preface to *Phenomenology of Perception*, where he seeks to place his own enterprise in the context of Husserl's and Heidegger's work, he defines uncritical scientific thought as "both naïve and at the same time dishonest" because it fails to admit that its access to the world comes only indirectly, mediated by human consciousness. In contrast, phenomenology seeks to restore awareness of that world "which precedes knowledge, of which knowledge always *speaks*, and in relation to which every scientific schematization is an abstract and derivative sign-language, as is geography in relation to the countryside in which we have learnt beforehand what a forest, a prairie or a river is."[5] Nevertheless, Merleau-Ponty's work was consistently engaged with the science of his day, particularly with Gestalt psychology and the disciplines of neuroscience during the 1930s and 1940s, and with physics, animal studies, human physiology, and evolutionary biology in the 1950s. There is no contradiction between his insistence on recognizing the limitations of scientific knowledge and his lifelong interdisciplinary involvement with its major disciplines. He valued the careful attention to nature that science alone provides, while at the same time his critical distance enabled his style of phenomenology to complement scientific findings by identifying their limitations and placing them within a larger, more complex frame of interpretation.[6]

Near the end of his life, he commented on how many scientists were themselves thinking about these limitations. Because of the indeterminacy resulting from relativity theory and quantum mechanics, the thinking of many modern physicists became tentative in ways unthinkable for classical Newtonian mechanics, as Merleau-Ponty explained in his late lectures entitled "Classical and Modern Physics."[7] By the middle of the twentieth century, scientists in other fields as well were aware of the contingency of their work, and he believed that the point had been reached at which we could not think about nature without taking serious account of how our understanding is culturally conditioned and "impregnated with artifice."[8] Although for him science was a privileged site for the experience of nature in its most carefully regulated form, its description of that experience is radically limited by its reductionist methods and partial access to a reality which can never be fully captured by observers from within its very texture.

Conceptual/political struggles within biological sciences at present reveal how some researchers continue to assume a Cartesian mechanistic paradigm while others contest its reductionist premises along the lines that Merleau-Ponty suggested. Steven Rose, for example, explains that biology needs an epistemological pluralism to approach "the radical indeterminacy of living processes . . . inherent in the nature of life itself."[9] As Bruno Latour points out, the history of modern science begins with the development of the laboratory which can drastically reduce this indeterminacy.[10] Rose reminds us that such simplification comes at a price: "Effective experiments demand the artificial controls imposed by the reductive methodology of the experimenter, but we must never forget that as a consequence they provide only a very simplified model, perhaps even a false one, of what happens in the blooming, buzzing, interactive confusion of life at large, where things rather rarely happen one at a time and snakes intervene inconveniently."[11]

Biologists like E. O. Wilson and Richard Dawkins continue to rely on simplified mechanistic explanations for living processes that others such as Rose and Richard Lewontin describe as far more complex. "Ultra-Darwinism," as Rose terms the reductionist approach, is a sort of Hobbesian vision of ruthless struggle for reproductive success and adaptation at the level of what Dawkins calls "the selfish gene" that renders organisms mere robots or survival machines for our genes.[12] Rose exposes the dualism of such a model and explains that it leaves no room for the processes of development, for the internal physiological activities of the organism, or for the organism's agency in shaping its own destiny.[13] Richard Lewontin, like Rose, urges biologists to move beyond a mechanistic focus on genes and to acknowledge the dynamism and complexity of organisms in their interactions with their environments: "Everybody 'knows' at some level of consciousness that DNA is not self-reproducing, that the information in DNA sequences is insufficient to specify even a folded protein, not to speak of an entire organism, that the environment of an organism is constructed and constantly altered by the life activities of the organism. But this in-principle knowledge cannot become folded into the structure of biological explanation unless it can be incorporated into the actual work of biologists."[14]

Merleau-Ponty's late work sought to explain this situation on the basis of an ontology that complemented the work of scientists by defining a non-dualistic nature consisting of a flesh that is not only materiality but also "expression, and ideas 'encrusted in the joints' of things, and a Logos rooted in the world."[15]

In order to reach this position, Merleau-Ponty began by turning phenomenology to an examination of the body. Such an emphasis is radical in the dualistic tradition of Western philosophy, which has tended to ignore or denigrate body in favor of mind, just as the natural world has been denigrated in favor of a nonmaterial realm of spirit. For Plato, the body was a flawed part of a changeable material world that itself was only a flawed copy of an eternal realm of ideal forms. Descartes saw human essence as Mind, a substance distinct from the material substance of a world in which our physical body and all other living things are mere machines.[16] Essential human existence would therefore not really be part of material nature, although the body obviously is.

Merleau-Ponty's close examination of the body is designed to erase that dualism. In the preface to *Phenomenology of Perception,* he announces, "The world is not what I think, but what I live through," and meaning is bodily attunement to that world.[17] The body is "a nexus of living meanings" clinging to its particular experiences as it moves towards its equilibrium.[18] Things in the world around us withhold their full being from our perception: "From the point of view of my body I never see as equal the six sides of the cube, even if it is made of glass, and yet the word 'cube' has a meaning. . . . The thing, and the world, are given to me along with the parts of my body, not by any 'natural geometry,' but in a living connection comparable, or rather identical, with that existing between the parts of my body itself."[19]

The relations between ourselves as sensing bodies and the sensible things in the world are dynamic, continually unfolding in vital reciprocities. We have no choice to disengage, for our very life emerges within the intertwined and cooperating cells and organs of our bodies, just as those bodies have always moved in participation with the things and forces surrounding them.

In spite of this account of the subject's immersion in the world, Merleau-Ponty was criticized for retaining an emphasis on the unitary consciousness of the perceiver in *Phenomenology of Perception.* Indeed, the Cartesian *cogito,* or separate Mind, remains. He himself recognized this problem, noting in July 1959 that "the problems posed in *Ph.P.* are insoluble because I start there from the 'consciousness'-'object' distinction."[20]

In *The Visible and the Invisible*, he worked to solve this problem by developing an ontology in which individual beings are intertwined with the basic stuff, or flesh, of the universe, existing in a kind of *reversibility* with other beings and things. Unlike what he calls the *kosmotheoros* of traditional philosophy—"a pure look which fixes the things in their temporal and local place and the essences in an invisible heaven . . . a ray of knowing that would have to arise from nowhere"[21]—each of us is enmeshed within the visible present and is both seeing and seen, touching and touched by the things around us.

Merleau-Ponty used the term *chiasm* for the reversibility within the tissue or flesh that sustains and nourishes all things, and he illustrated it with the metaphor of a person's two hands both touching and touched by each other. There is a similar kinship between the body's movements and what it touches:

> This can happen only if my hand, while it is felt from within, is also accessible from without, itself tangible, for my other hand, for example, if it takes its place among the things it touches, is in a sense one of them, opens finally upon a tangible being of which it is also a part. Through this crisscrossing within it of the touching and the tangible, its own movements incorporate themselves into the universe they interrogate.[22]

And yet, this reversibility is "always imminent and never realized in fact,"[23] so that there is no coincidence or merging but instead a divergence or "incessant escaping" (*écart*).[24] Similarly the relation of any creature to others within the flesh of the world is never fully realized or identical; this dehiscence, or *écart*, generates differentiation even as the intertwining of things and creatures ensures their kinship: "Why would not the synergy exist among different organisms, if it is possible within each? Their landscapes interweave, their actions and their passions fit together exactly."[25] The emphasis is no longer on the *cogito*, the thinking consciousness of the perceiver, as it was in *Phenomenology of Perception*, but rather upon the ecological interrelationships of beings that temporarily emerge in particular forms within the flesh of the world and then merge back into its body again.

These relationships carry with them the weight of time and entanglements with space, woven into an Einsteinian fabric of space-time: "In short, there is no essence, no idea, that does not adhere to a domain of history and of geography. Not that it is *confined* there and inaccessible to the others, but because, like that of nature, the space or time of culture is not surveyable from above, and because the communication from one constituted culture to another occurs through the wild region wherein they all have originated."[26] Within this primordial nature or brute being, each developing life is an upsurge of the flesh of the world, coiling over upon itself, which will eventually return to the whole.

Such an account of the natural world is congruent with evolutionary biology's picture of the coevolution, symbiosis, and genetic sharing of plants and animals with the stuff of the biotic microcosmos from which the millions of particular species developed. As Lynn Margulis has explained, symbiosis among bacteria was one of the drivers of evolutionary novelty and the development of complex organisms. Such literal, physical intertwining was not necessarily peaceful or beautiful; indeed, it may well have begun as predation.[27] But Merleau-Ponty's description of the promiscuity and enormous, messy vitality of the natural world with its ontological vibrations and generativity of brute essences matches evolutionary history that continues to unfold in the biotic soup of our present world. Alphonso Lingis, translator of The Visible and the Invisible, points out that we humans live in symbiosis with thousands of species of anaerobic bacteria that colonize our bodies and perform necessary functions such as neutralizing plant toxins, digesting our food, and cleansing our blood. The number of these microbes vastly exceeds the number of our own "human" cells. We live in external symbiosis with all the other mammals, the birds, the insects, and with "rice, wheat, and corn fields, with berry thickets and vegetable patches."[28] This chiasmic understanding of the human place in the biota for Merleau-Ponty includes thought and language.

As early as the preface to Phenomenology of Perception, Merleau-Ponty suggested the immanence of language and thought in the natural world by insisting that "the only pre-existent Logos is the world itself."[29] Human language is described, in a chapter entitled "The Body as Expression, and Speech," as essentially gestural, and "the words, vowels and phonemes are so many ways of 'singing' the world."[30] As part of that world, our bodies from infancy are oriented meaningfully toward things, and we learn to speak by being surrounded by the gestures of adults, enticed by the style of their language until "a single meaning emerges from the whole."[31] This is only the human translation or expression of the world's meanings, a second-order reference that makes sense of things from within our limited perceptions. The universe will always elude efforts to capture its full meaning, but from within its depths, language witnesses its revelations and questions its mysteries.

In The Visible and the Invisible, Merleau-Ponty speaks of the proper exercise of language as an openness to Being rather than an attempt to fix meaning precisely.[32] For both Heidegger and Merleau-Ponty, this is the work of the philosopher as it is also that of the poet. But Merleau-Ponty goes on to develop his own explanation of language as articulating "the bond between the flesh and the idea, between the visible and the interior armature which it manifests and which it conceals."[33] He claims that "no one has gone further than Proust in fixing the relations between the visible and the invisible, in describing an idea that is not the contrary of the sensible, that is its lining and its depth. . . . Literature, music, the passions, but also the experience of the visible world are—no less than is the science of Lavoisier and Ampère— the exploration of an invisible and the disclosure of a universe of ideas."[34] Garth Gillan says that for Merleau-Ponty the experience of language is that of "a truth lived in the thick and embroiling relations we have with others and is thus groping, emotionally turbulent, giving our contact with ideas a savage quality."[35] Chapter 4 of The Visible and the Invisible, "The Intertwining —The Chiasm," ends with a definition of philosophy that sounds like a literature of wildness:

> The meaning is not on the phrase like the butter on the bread, like a second layer of "psychic reality" spread over the sound: it is the totality of what is said, the integral of all the differentiations of the verbal chain; it is given with the words for those who have ears to hear. And conversely the whole landscape is overrun with words as with an invasion, it is henceforth but a variant of speech before our eyes, and to speak of its "style" is in our view to form a metaphor. In a sense the whole of philosophy, as Husserl says, con- sists in restoring a power to signify, a birth of meaning, or a wild meaning, an expression of experience by experience, which in particular clarifies the special domain of language. And in a sense, as Valéry said, language is every- thing, since it is the voice of no one, since it is the very voice of the things, the waves, and the forests.[36]

Granted that this vatic passage is part of an unfinished and often cryptic manuscript, it nevertheless demonstrates how Merleau-Ponty's theory of language makes it far broader than a simply human creation; it is deeply integrated into the dynamism of nature as a dimension of the flesh of the world.

At the same time that he was developing the more general ontology of The Visible and the Invisible, Merleau-Ponty was exploring in his courses at the Collège de France the philosophical dimensions of the twentieth-century knowledge of the natural world provided by the main branches of science. These courses were one facet of a three-part enterprise described in some of his "Working Notes." Two months before he died, he had outlined the plan of his work in progress:

I. The Visible
II. Nature
III. Logos

He wrote that the project "must be presented without any compromise with *humanism*, nor moreover with *naturalism*, nor finally with *theology*—Precisely what has to be done is to show that philosophy can no longer think according to this cleavage: God, man, creatures."[37] Instead he proposed to describe "the man-animality *intertwining*," and it was in his lecture courses from 1956 to 1960 that he developed part 2 of his project, as the book manuscript was shaping parts 1 and 3. Notes from the courses, primarily taken by students but including some of his own lecture notes, were published as *La nature* in 1995 and in English as *Nature* in 2003. Though sketchy, they offer a crucial glimpse of how he was exploring the philosophical implications of classical and modern physics, animality and the study of animal behavior, the animality of the human body, cybernetics, contemporary developments in Darwinism, and such aspects of evolutionary biology as ontogenesis and phylogenesis.

Nature shows how deeply Merleau-Ponty engaged with the advanced sciences of his day in an effort to redefine the situation of humans within the natural world. Because this work has only become available recently, its significance and articulation with *The Visible and the Invisible* will take some time to evaluate. But already it is clear that the 1956–57 course entitled "The Concept of Nature" offered a radical philosophical critique of Aristotelian and Cartesian descriptions of the natural world and explored the philosophical consequences of relativity theory and quantum mechanics. Physicists' difficulty in reconciling particle theory with wave theory created an internal critique within their discipline that led Merleau-Ponty to conclude: "The perceived world is no longer an immediate given. The mediation of knowing allows us to retrieve indirectly and in a negative way the perceived world that anterior idealizations had made us forget."[38]

The 1957–58 course entitled "Animality, the Human Body, and the Passage to Culture" assumes the evolutionary relationship of *homo sapiens* to other creatures and considers the work of ethnologists such as Jakob von Uexküll and Konrad Lorenz. In particular, Merleau-Ponty examines the implications of von Uexküll's notion of the subjective environment, or *Umwelt*, that each species and individual creates in its reciprocal interaction with the world around it, as determined by its perceptual and motor abilities.[39] Operating within its own *Umwelt*, Merleau-Ponty explains, each animal "defines its territory as a privileged emplacement" and functions in a symbolic realm.

A crab, for example, can use a sea anemone to camouflage its shell and protect it from predators, or indeed to replace a lost shell, or it can use the sea anemone as food: "The architecture of symbols that the animal brings from its side thus defines within Nature a species of preculture. The *Umwelt* is less and less oriented toward a goal and more and more toward the interpretation of symbols."[40] Lorenz's work on animal instinct and imprinting offers another approach to the question of animal consciousness. Together with von Uexküll's work, and E. S. Russell's study of relations among cells, Lorenz's affirmation that "none of those who have a familiarity with animals would deny them consciousness" sets up for Merleau-Ponty the project of investigating the sentience in other animals: "Is there animal consciousness, and if so, to what extent?"[41]

"Nature and Logos: The Human Body," the 1959–60 course, moves on to explore the human place in evolution, defining species uniqueness and yet essential kinship with other animals. Teilhard de Chardin figures prominently in this course for his philosophical consideration of human evolution, though Merleau-Ponty criticized his idealism in seeing evolution progressing toward a divine goal.[42] Teilhard leads Merleau-Ponty to suggest a definition of the "man-animality intertwining" he had been considering in his own "Working Notes." From Teilhard's description of the silent, almost imperceptible appearance of humans in evolution, it follows that "the relationship of man to animality is not a hierarchical relation, but lateral, a moving beyond that does not abolish kinship."[43]

Clearly for Merleau-Ponty the description of nature in these courses was tentative and preliminary. Nevertheless, the lectures initiate a radical departure from traditional philosophy. Writing before the *Nature* lectures were published, David Abram could already predict, in "Merleau-Ponty and the Voice of the Earth," that Merleau-Ponty was moving toward a recognition of animal consciousness and the continuity among species while still acknowledging a distinctive way of being for *homo sapiens*.

For ecocritics it is especially important to notice how carefully Merleau-Ponty engaged the life sciences and the questions that increasingly concern the various branches of environmental studies, animal studies, and cultural theory. But Merleau-Ponty's ontological perspective can also illuminate literary works from any period or culture and offer insights of startling environmental relevance. Particular applications include examination of ecophenomenological descriptions of the world in poetry and fiction; treatments of embodiment and human-animality intertwining; and attention to science fiction that interrogates interrelations between science and the shapes of nature in possible future worlds. As I have explained elsewhere, Merleau-Ponty's contemporary Virginia Woolf explored many of the same questions of embodiment and human perception of the phenomenal world in her fiction; I have also examined the profound anxiety about human/animality intertwining in ancient literary works such as *The Epic of Gilgamesh* and Euripides' *Bakkhai*.[44]

For present purposes, however, I offer ecophenomenological readings of two brief examples: a description of a meditative baptismal swim from Eudora Welty's "The Wanderers" and W. H. Auden's poem "A New Year Greeting." In Welty's story, on the evening of her mother's sudden death, Virgie Rainey walks down from her farm to the Big Black River for solace. Like Woolf, whose fiction she admired, Welty uses her prose to explore consciousness as embodied participation within a dynamic, intertwining community of plants, animals, and nonliving things. Virgie's swim is an epistemological journey into the texture of spacetime that Merleau-Ponty defines as "the wild region" wherein all things have originated. Virgie comes to know with her whole body the enormous scope of history lying within primordial nature and dwarfing the temporary coiling up of individual be-ings and objects. Her mother's death is only a tiny episode amidst continual metamorphoses such as the vast geological changes crushing shells and stones as the earth's skin flexes with the movements of earthquake and glacier:

> She stood on the willow bank. It was bright as mid-afternoon in the open-ness of the water, quiet and peaceful. She took off her clothes and let herself into the river. She saw her waist disappear into reflectionless water; it was like walking into sky, some impurity of skies. All was one warmth, air, water, her own body. All seemed one weight, one matter—until as she put down her head and closed her eyes and the light slipped under her lids, she felt this matter a translucent one, the river, herself, the sky all vessels which the sun filled. She began to swim in the river, forcing it gently, as she would wish for gentleness to her body. Her breasts around which she felt the water curving were as sensitive at that moment as the tips of wings must feel to birds, or antennae to insects. She felt the sand, grains intricate as little cogged wheels, minute shells of old seas, and the many dark ribbons of grass and mud touch her and leave her, like suggestions and withdrawals of some bondage that might have been dear now dismembering and losing itself. She moved but like a cloud in skies, aware but only of the nebulous edges of her feeling and the vanishing opacity of her will, the carelessness for the water of the river through which her body had already passed as well as for what was ahead.[45]

This passage captures the erotic *chiasm* Merleau-Ponty defines for the hu-man body with the world, in which surfaces or boundaries are not frontiers but rather contact surfaces.[46] Virgie's skin becomes the organ of her perception of both visible things and invisible rhythms of time, emotion, and memory. Welty intensifies what Merleau-Ponty sees as the natural magic of language "that attracts the other significations into its web, as the body feels the world in feeling itself."[47] In spite of Virgie's sense of merging with the world around her, she remains a separate being, aware of the otherness of insects, snakes, ribbons of grass, and fragments of ancient shells. Merleau-Ponty's concept of *écart* accounts for the simultaneous human kinship with and separateness from other creatures and things in this moment of Virgie's release from grief. His philosophy illuminates the significance of the epiphany Welty has given to Virgie and, through her, to her readers.

Auden's "A New Year Greeting" is far different in tone from Welty's lyrical celebration of the body's chiasmic relation to its *Umwelt*. He comically salutes all the tiny creatures for whom his "ectoderm / is as Middle-Earth to me,"[48] but the poem darkens and sharpens as it moves toward a bleak acknowledgment of destructive forces intertwined with creation and flourishing. In greeting the yeasts, bacteria, and viruses who live on his body, he explains:

> For creatures your size I offer
> a free choice of habitat,
> so settle yourselves in the zone
> that suits you best, in the pools
> of my pores or the tropical
> forests of arm-pit and crotch,
> in the deserts of my fore-arms,
> or the cool woods of my scalp.

After an invitation to build colonies and enjoy the warmth and nourishment his body supplies, however, he cautions his tiny symbiotic intimates against creating annoyances like acne or boils. This negative turn intensifies as the poem considers disasters caused by ordinary human movement. Taking a shower broils and drowns millions; changes of clothing bring hurricanes:

> Then, sooner or later, will dawn
> a day of Apocalypse,
> when my mantle suddenly turns
> too cold, too rancid, for you,
> appetising to predators
> of a fiercer sort, and I
> am stripped of excuse and nimbus,
> a Past, subject to Judgement.[49]

Here is a teasing, intimate meditation on human/animality intertwining, that cheerily and sardonically undercuts the godlike anthropocentric illusions of its opening largess. Human exceptionalism is nibbled away as the conscious individual disappears back into the mass of pullulating life forms that Merleau-Ponty describes as the "perpetual pregnancy, perpetual parturition, generativity and generality, brute essence and brute existence, which are the nodes and antinodes of the same ontological vibration."[50]

Like Merleau-Ponty, Auden read science all his life and incorporated it into his writing. This poem was inspired by a 1969 *Scientific American* article about the myriads of tiny symbiots living on and in our bodies, and he turned it into a whimsical musing about the simultaneously sustaining and destructive interrelationships of living creatures within the scope of their limited existences.

Merleau-Ponty's ecophenomenology offers a deeply nuanced theoretical description of reality that corresponds to the implications of modern life sciences and one that values the kinds of literary openness to the mysteries of experience in the physical world that Welty and Auden provide. His account of the human place in nature accords with deep ecology's insistence on the common fate we share with other forms of life, yet avoids the erasure of distinctions which Val Plumwood decries in deep ecology.[51] Merleau-Ponty's thought seeks to avoid anthropocentrism, acknowledging the immanence of meaning in the world itself and therefore communicative modes outside human language, while at the same time describing the particular ways human art and literary forms allow the exploration of the invisible armature of the world we can see. Human language, literature, and the other arts are for him the continuing efforts of our species to sing the world in call-and-response, carrying with them the past and anticipating the future.

NOTES

1. Heidegger, "Letter on Humanism" in *Basic Writings*, 227–30; Heidegger, *What Is Called Thinking?* 16.

2. Merleau-Ponty, *Phenomenology of Perception*, 187.

3. Merleau-Ponty, *The Visible and the Invisible*, 116–17.

4. Margulis, *Symbiotic Planet*, 3.

5. Merleau-Ponty, *Phenomenology of Perception*, ix.

6. See Joseph Rouse's philosophical analysis of Merleau-Ponty's position in "Merleau-Ponty's Existential Conception of Science." I am also indebted to Ted Toadvine for suggestions about how to characterize Merleau-Ponty's attitudes toward science.

7. Merleau-Ponty, *Nature*, 88–100.

8. Ibid., 86.

9. Rose, *Lifelines*, 14–15.

10. Latour, *We Have Never Been Modern*, 16–27.

11. Rose, *Lifelines*, 28.

12. Ibid., 21; Dawkins, *The Selfish Gene*, 215.

13. Rose, *Lifelines*, 214–15.

14. Lewontin, *The Triple Helix*, 129.

15. Toadvine, personal communication, 27 August 2007.

16. Descartes, *Philosophical Works*, 1:116, 150–51, 190–91.

17. Merleau-Ponty, *Phenomenology of Perception*, xvi–xvii.

18. Ibid., 147, 151, 153.

19. Toadvine, "Primacy of Desire," 203–5.

20. Merleau-Ponty, *The Visible and the Invisible*, 200.

21. Ibid., 113.

22. Ibid., 133.

23. Ibid., 147.

24. Ibid., 148.

25. Ibid., 142.

26. Ibid., 114–15.

27. Margulis, *Symbiotic Planet*, 38–49, 89, 99–103.

28. Lingis, "Animal Body, Inhuman Face," 166.

29. Merleau-Ponty, *Phenomenology of Perception*, xx.

30. Ibid., 187. George Lakoff and Mark Johnson, in *Philosophy in the Flesh*, have developed an extensive description of how this might work, using both cognitive neuroscience and linguistic theories of the embodied, metaphoric grounding of abstract thought.

31. Merleau-Ponty, *Consciousness and the Acquisition of Language*, 35, 51.

32. Merleau-Ponty, *The Visible and the Invisible*, 101–2.

33. Ibid., 149.

34. Ibid.

35. Gillan, "In the Folds of the Flesh," 56–57.

36. Merleau-Ponty, *The Visible and the Invisible*, 155.

37. Ibid., 274.

38. Ibid., 100.

39. Merleau-Ponty, *Nature*, 167–78.

40. Ibid., 176.

41. Ibid., 199.

42. Ibid., 269.

43. My translation from Merleau-Ponty, *La nature*, 335; in Merleau-Ponty, *Nature*, 268.

44. Westling, "Virginia Woolf and the Flesh of the World" and "Darwin in Arcadia."

45. Eudora Welty, "The Wanderers," in *The Collected Stories*, 439–40.

46. Merleau-Ponty, *The Visible and the Invisible*, 271.

47. Ibid., 118.

48. Auden, *Selected Poems*, 292.

49. Ibid., 292–93.

50. Merleau-Ponty, *The Visible and the Invisible*, 114–15.

51. Plumwood, "Nature, Self, and Gender," 166–67.

Gernot Böhme's Ecological Aesthetics of Atmosphere

In *The Ideology of the Aesthetic,* Terry Eagleton acclaims A. G. Baumgarten's "discourse of the body" as "the first stirrings of a primitive materialism—of the body's long inarticulate rebellion against the tyranny of the theoretical."[1] While Baumgarten is widely acknowledged as a founding figure in modern philosophical aesthetics, the counterideological potential that Eagleton locates in his valorization of corporeality failed to be realized, as the emergent discipline of aesthetics fled the flesh, restricting itself instead to a consideration of the formal properties and moral-intellectual significance of the work of art. Gernot Böhme, a leading figure in contemporary German ecological thought,[2] has set about reversing this historical trajectory by returning to Baumgarten's theory of sensuous cognition as a point of departure for a new "ecological aesthetics of nature."[3] Here, nature no longer figures primarily, as it does in Adorno's aesthetics of natural beauty (another important precursor for Böhme), as the locus of a *promesse de bonheur* situated beyond the realm of social oppression, but rather as itself a site of suffering: one that we can more readily recognize as such as we begin to experience in our own bodies what our society has done to the earth.[4] While Böhme's ecological aesthetics promises to take us "beyond the frame" of the work of art, it also offers an ecocritically valuable perspective on the arts, including literature.

Böhme's work on aesthetics is part of a wider project entailing the rehabilitation of the German tradition of *Naturphilosophie* (natural philosophy) in the guise of a critical theory of social-natural relations, interweaving (post)Marxist social critique and the "new phenomenology" of Hermann Schmitz. This project is underwritten by a sober recognition that "we no longer stand on the brink of environmental catastrophe: we are in the midst of it."[5] Under these circumstances, Böhme calls for a pragmatically oriented *Naturphilosophie,* which, like the older Critical Theory as defined by Max Horkheimer, would be "driven by the interest in reasonable conditions,"[6] while nonetheless recognizing that what constitutes "reasonableness" with regard to social-natural relations cannot be presupposed, but must be communicatively elucidated over time, and oriented toward safeguarding the reproduction of natural systems as the necessary foundation for human society. The urgent need for such a critical theory of social-natural relations arises from the increasingly anthropogenic character of our earthly environs, or "the nature that we are not," coupled with the growing technologization of the human body, or "the nature that we ourselves are." This implies that at least on the scale that is most relevant for human life, the nature/culture binary that has for so long structured Western understanding, while perhaps always partially illusory and certainly culturally contingent, has now become highly problematic, and with it, the modern division of the natural and human sciences must also be challenged. What is required is a new "social-natural science" which acknowledges both the social production of other-than-human nature and the bodily dimension of human subjectivity.[7]

With the disappearance of "nature" as pre-given, it makes little sense to talk of "conservation" or even of "sustainability." This is not necessarily a cause for despondency, however. Perilous though our current situation might be, Böhme has so far remained remarkably upbeat. If the impact of industrial societies on other-than-human nature is rendering our planetary home increasingly uncongenial to human life, while the encroachment of technology on our own nature as bodily beings challenges our very sense of what it is to be human, then the onus is on us to figure out what kind of a "nature" we actually want to inhabit collectively and to embody individually. Picking up a resonant expression from Ernst Bloch, Böhme insists that although the global environment might everywhere bear traces of human impact, that does not mean that we should simply consign "nature" to the past, as promodernists (and "postmodernists") would have us do: on the contrary, "nature" represents a possibility that as yet lies "before us."[8] This Böhme identifies as the transformation of our industrially degraded earthly environment into a humane living space, in which a decent life might be enjoyed by all, together with the limitation of the technologization of the body to levels that we, individually, deem compatible with human dignity: a dignity, that is to say, which is proper to humans, not as in the past, in contradistinction from animals, on the one side, and God, on the other, but rather from machines.

To construe "nature" as a cultural project might well seem overweeningly anthropocentric. Böhme's philosophy is nonetheless far from endorsing human supremacy. To begin with, he assumes an understanding of natural phenomena as autopoietic, interdependent, and communicative, and he follows Bloch in advocating a technology of "alliance" rather than domination. Moreover, in his work on ethics, Böhme argues that the imperilment of the natural foundations of human life obliges us to consider anew the moral dimension of our relations with nonhuman others. In becoming more respectful of our earth others and of the network of interrelationships that facilitate our collective flourishing, we also secure a practical advantage: rather than burdening ourselves with the impossible task of global environmental management, the ethos of alliance could enable us to create largely self-regulating ecological (i.e., social-natural) complexes (*ökologische Gefügen*), which would be conducive to human well-being while simultaneously respecting the interactive autopoiesis of other-than-human nature.

In order to create humane living spaces within which other-than-human entities might also thrive, we certainly need the guidance of the natural and technical sciences. Scientific and technical knowledge is nonetheless insufficient to the task of grounding an ethical relationship with other-than-human nature, let alone an ecological aesthetics: science might be able to define limit conditions for healthy environments, but it cannot tell us why we might desire to share our living space with a diversity of plants and animals, or why we should treat them with respect. If we are to reposition ourselves as allies rather than conquerors of nature in the production of a newly "habitable earth,"[9] we need to supplement the sciences with a different type of knowledge, premised not on objectification, but on recognition: a carnal kind of knowing, whereby we come to understand the other, if never fully, on the basis of a relationality that is given in and through our shared physical existence. In this way, the discovery of other-than-human nature is necessarily conjoined with the recovery of our own naturality. And that is where aesthetics comes in.

In order to answer the question as to what kind of nature we wish to inhabit and embody, we need to begin by ascertaining what "nature" means to us from a noninstrumental perspective. On one level, as Simon Schama has demonstrated in *Landscape and Memory*, this is a question for the cultural historian who traces the ways in which such things as oral narratives, books, and paintings invest certain entities and places, whether near or far, with meaning, and inscribe them in our affections. What is it, though, about, say, roses, that have invited the symbolic significance that European culture has ascribed to them? For Böhme, this is a question for the phenomenologist, for it concerns the way in which things manifest themselves to human perception in potentially mood-altering ways. Somatics, in other words, precedes semantics.

With regard to talk about "the body," though, a bit more semantic precision is called for. German makes this easier than English, since in Böhme's mother-tongue the body is doubled, appearing as *Leib* in one aspect and *Körper* in another. The latter refers to the body as physical object: this is the body you "have"; the body you "use" to type with, for instance; the body that contains the kind of heart that you "take" to the cardiologist when it is ailing. The former is something altogether different: it is the body that, ineluctably, you "are"; the body that aches when you have typed too long; the body that incorporates the kind of heart that "skips a beat" when you catch sight of your lover. Unlike your *Körper*, your *Leib* lacks clear physical boundaries, expanding and contracting by turns, flowing out into the circumambient space, mingling with other entities, or recoiling in the face of something frightening or repugnant. In the body qua *Leib*, as the Australian poet and ecocritic Mark Tredinnick puts it, "we are not finished at the skin."[10]

It is this radically porous body with its shifting contours that figures in the phenomenology of Maurice Merleau-Ponty and Hermann Schmitz. The trouble with purely phenomenological accounts of corporeality qua *Leiblichkeit*, though, is that they pay insufficient heed to the historicity of the body. The phenomenality of bodily existence, the particular ways in which people in different times, places, and social situations experience their own corporeality, is informed by the kinds of bodily praxis, incorporating modes of thinking as well as acting, into which they have been socialized. For instance, within that way of thinking and being commonly referred to as Cartesian, which infamously sunders mind from body while privileging the former, the body in question is the *Körper*. Such mind-body dualism is no mere illusion that can be dispelled by means of a more "holistic" account of human subjectivity, however. For the experience of the body as something external to the self, and the objectification and instrumentalization that this facilitates, has become a more-or-less habitual state of being for most moderns.[11]

In the context of our technological civilization, the reconstruction of a more corporeal sense of self assumes the status of an ethical imperative. Recognizing that ethical questions, and the answers we give them, are also historically contingent, Böhme argues that while it was formerly considered virtuous to exercise control over the wayward flesh, today we need to make a virtue out of heeding our bodily impulses and sensations (*leibliches Spüren*).[12] This is no easy matter, not only in view of our socialization into having a *Körper* rather than existing as *Leib*, but also because bodily being is intrinsically trying. Let's face it, our bodies are forever slowing us down and tripping us up, limiting what we can do and where we can be; in the body, we are vulnerable to illness and injury, along with sundry troublesome appetites; in the body, we grow old, if we are lucky, and sooner or later we die. In fact, in Schmitz's analysis it is precisely from negative experiences of fear and pain that the realization that we exist as a bodily being, bound ineluctably to a particular here and now, is borne:[13] small wonder that so many cultures have come up with strategies for variously denying, dominating, or transcending this pesky mortal frame of ours. Consciously incorporating the body qua *Leib* with its attendant messiness, discomfort, limitations, and peculiarities into our sense of self, far from promising the alleged pleasures of "letting it all hang out," entails conscious commitment and daily discipline: it is, in other words, a cultural practice informed by ethical choice, not simply a matter of doing "what comes naturally."

Corresponding to the project of transforming the "nature that we ourselves are not" into a humane living space, Böhme identifies the cultivation of the "nature that we ourselves are" as an ethical "task." Among other things, this might entail learning how to live graciously with incurable illness or unquenchable pain. It could motivate the decision to resist certain forms or degrees of technologization of the body. More pleasurably, it might mean cultivating a heightened sense of corporeal being-with-another in the medium of bodily love. For all of us, it implies enduring the tension between the limitations of our own bodily being, bound to a particular here and now, and the preconceived projects that we aspire to realize. Rather than assuming that this tension implies an irreconcilable opposition, however, Böhme recommends that we seek to mediate it through a practice of care for the self, incorporating a new dietetics oriented toward the acceptance, rather than the domination, of our own naturality.[14] This conscious cultivation of bodily existence begins with attending to how you feel in the flesh, from moment to moment, here and now. The articulation and theorization of this attentive sensing of one's own bodily existence in the presence of other people, things, and places constitutes the core concern of Böhme's ecological aesthetics.

The key concept of his new aesthetics comes from Schmitz: namely, "atmosphere." Schmitz's project is to overturn the baleful banishment of the body qua *Leib* from European philosophies of the subject since Plato. In particular, he seeks to undo what he terms the "introjection of feeling" associated with modern psychologism. In Schmitz's analysis, feelings do not originate "inside" the self; rather, they are given to experience as "unlocalized, poured forth atmospheres . . . which visit (haunt) the body which receives them . . . affectively, which takes the form of . . . emotion."[15] For Schmitz, atmospheres are "affective powers of feeling, spatial bearers of moods."[16] Such atmospheres constitute the "space of feeling" or "mood" (*Gefühlsraum*). As Böhme explains in "The Space of Bodily Presence," the "space of moods is the space which, in a sense, attunes my mood, but at the same time it is the extendedness of my mood itself."[17]

While Schmitz does discuss aesthetics, he does not relate it to atmosphere. In order to do so, Böhme corrects Schmitz's view of atmosphere as uncoupled from things and unlocalizable in space by drawing on Aristotle's notion of *ekstasis:* how things go forth from themselves, giving themselves to perception through particular qualities, for instance, of size, shape, color, or smell. Such self-disclosure always involves an element of self-concealment: no other is ever fully present to us, and we wrong the other that we take to be so. Being, according to Böhme's neo-Aristotelian ontology, is nonetheless always being-for-another, which is to say, as biosemiotics also teaches, being-in-communication.[18] In their "ecstasies," people, things, and places "tincture" the environment in which they are perceived, and in so doing, generate "atmospheres":

> Conceived in this fashion, atmospheres are neither something objective, that is, qualities possessed by things, and yet they are something thinglike, belonging to the thing in that things articulate their presence through qualities —conceived as ecstasies. Nor are atmospheres something subjective, for example, determinations of a psychic state. And yet they are subjectlike, belonging to subjects in that they are sensed in bodily presence by human beings and this sensing is at the same time a bodily state of being of subjects in space.[19]

We are most likely to become aware of the spatial dimension of feeling on first entering a place with an atmosphere markedly different from the one that we have left ("ingression"), or at those times when a prevailing atmosphere contrasts strongly with our own preexisting mood ("discrepancy").[20] The atmospheres that we encounter in such instances are initially experienced "synaesthetically" as "poured-forth indeterminately into the distance."[21]

Atmospheres are perceived in the form of an "appeal" or "impression" (*Anmutung*):[22] this is how things "strike us," altering our current mood or disposition (*Befindlichkeit*), filling us, for example, with desire or distaste, joy or sadness, cheerfulness or melancholy.[23] Recognizing our somatic susceptibility to the impressions that something, someone, or someplace make on us, our own emotional affectedness by the atmospheres they generate, we recognize ourselves as sharing with them a physical existence as a bodily being. Recovering a sense of our own corporeality, we discover that we are ecological selves, existing in environments and with others by whom or which our psycho-somatic disposition is inevitably inflected.

Sometimes the appeal of another in whose atmosphere we have been caught up acquires a moral force. Beholding the other in their *ekstasis,* we might find ourselves looked upon in turn, as occurs, for example, to the speaker of Rainer Maria Rilke's "Archaic Torso of Apollo" in the face of this sculpture: "there is no spot, / that does not see you. You must change your life."[24] "An aesthetic relation to nature," Böhme argues, "consists in allowing oneself to be spoken to by it. Sensual perception means participating in the articulate presence of things."[25]

Turning to Schmitz's New Phenomenology in connection with the social critique of the earlier Frankfurt school, Böhme returns aesthetics to its eighteenth-century origins as a general theory of sensual cognition, overturning its post-Hegelian restriction to the specialized task of making judgments regarding those privileged human artifacts defined within bourgeois culture as works of art. Böhme delineates three domains in which this expanded aesthetics might be deployed. First, an enhanced understanding of the connection between the physical properties of things, people, and places, and the atmospheres they generate is pertinent to many activities where a tacit knowledge regarding the production of atmospheres has long been practiced by a diversity of "aesthetic workers": for example, in cosmetics and fashion; costume and set design; architecture and interior decorating; "acoustic" and other kinds of furnishing; town planning and landscape architecture. Second, ecological aesthetics provides a vantage point from which to critique the ever-increasing "aestheticization of reality" within the "aesthetic economy" of capitalist consumerism, where particular atmospheric effects are strategically deployed in advertising, supermarkets, shopping malls, and product design and packaging in order to engender desires that are guaranteed never to be sated with their fulfilment.[26] Third, the arts have a crucial role to play in disclosing the negative consequences of the attempted domination of nature; helping to regenerate those places that have borne the brunt of this failed project; and overcoming our amnesia regarding the nature that we ourselves are by providing training in the experience, articulation, and production of atmospheres.

To a greater or lesser extent, art has always had an "atmospheric" dimension, but this only acquired programmatic status in response to the perceived deficits of rationalist reductionism: namely, within that strand of Romantic ecopoetics which seeks to foster an attunement to "the moods / Of time and season, to the moral power, / The affections and the spirit of the place," as Wordsworth puts it.[27] Romantic painting, music, and literature frequently foreground the phenomenon of atmosphere, which also found an early theoretical articulation in Goethe's research into the "sensual-ethical" effects of color, and in Alexander von Humboldt's concept of the "physiognomy" of landscape.

Unlike earlier conceptualizations of physiognomy as the art of deducing human character traits from facial features, Humboldtian physiognomics is concerned not with what might be revealed about a human other in their appearance, but rather with the impressions made by other things, especially

plants and landscapes, on a human observer. When Humboldt refers to the
"character" of a landscape, he is alluding not to an inner essence but to an
external "atmosphere" as measured by the mood it engenders in a perceiving
subject. It is this unconventional usage of physiognomy to refer to the
impressions formed by the "speaking face" of the land and sky that Böhme
adopts and adapts as one of the key terms of his aesthetic theory.[28]

In the wider context of Böhme's project of the recovery of the "nature
that we ourselves are" in conjunction with the regeneration of the "nature
that we are not," the translation of inchoate impressions into articulate
speech is the necessary precondition for raising the personal experience of
atmosphere to the level of a transformative social praxis: it is only by conversing about atmospheres, and the physical qualities of the things and
places that produce them, that we might reach agreement on how to reshape
our environment with a view to enhancing our collective well-being as
bodily beings among others, human and otherwise. From this perspective,
literature, in verbalizing the "space of feeling," has a key role to play within
the wider field of ecological aesthetics.

Literary invocations of atmosphere come in all genres. In fiction and
drama, for instance, spatial atmospheres feature whenever the moods or
motivations of characters are shown to be inflected by their surroundings.
Within nonfiction "nature writing," the affective force of place is often
explicitly thematized. Yet Böhme's own literary examples are most commonly taken from lyrical verse. This is no mere personal preference. Poetic
writing, in its use of metaphor, metonymy, rhythm and rhyme, alliteration,
and assonance, is a particularly effective medium not only for the depiction
of atmosphere, but also for its production: namely, in the bodily and affective responses of readers. In this way, the "space of poetry" itself constitutes
a *Gefühlsraum,* not so much through the detailed description of any puta-
tive "real" place, but through the use of figurative language and phonetic
effects to inflect the reader's state-of-feeling.[29] This reminds us that the
ideas elicited by words can just as readily affect our bodily disposition as can
the atmosphere generated by the physical environment affect our frame of
mind. This is the principle on which literary eroticism, no less than auto-
genetic training, operates. Similarly, we might recall how in everyday life the
atmosphere of a meeting, for example, can be "poisoned" by a wounding
word, and "brightened up" again by a verbal reassurance.[30]

In the remainder of this essay, I exemplify, but also to some degree
complicate, Böhme's approach to the analysis of atmosphere in the medium
of literary communication, with reference to a poem by the Australian
author Charles Harpur (1813–1868). "A Midsummer Noon in the Australian
Forest" belongs to the popular subcategory of nature poetry that turns on the

seasons, weather, or time of day.[31] "Daybreak," "Autumn," "the wind," "the heat": nouns such as these refer to atmospheres that have acquired a thing-like character, exemplifying what Böhme terms "the atmospheric."[32] The ecstasies of things, people, and places can also be experienced as quasi-things, as when we speak of the ominous buzzing of a mosquito; the coldness in someone's tone of voice; or the coziness of a pub. In the era of "Global Warming Criticism,"[33] however, when the weather itself bears witness to the industrial disruption of natural systems, the literature of weather-borne atmospheres acquires a special interest. In the phenomenon of the weather, the aesthetic and meteorological meanings of atmosphere are bridged.[34]

Harpur's "Midsummer Noon" begins by staging an ingression experi-ence, leading the reader into an imagined space giving the impression of profound quietude:

> Not a sound disturbs the air,
> There is quiet everywhere;
> Over plains and over woods
> What a mighty stillness broods!

The atmospheric quality of this virtual locale is imaged initially as "poured-forth indeterminately into the distance." Only in the second stanza are some of the things that contribute to generating this mood of quietude particu-larized: the grasshoppers, keeping to "Where the coolest shadows sleep"; the ants, "Resting in their pebbled mound"; and the locust, which has fallen silent on the "barky bough." This insistence on the all-pervasive silence of this place at this time, where "Quiet, vast and slumberous, reigns," is seem-ingly contradicted in the third stanza when the speaker proceeds to register "a drowsy humming / From yon warm lagoon slow coming." Far from break-ing the prevailing mood of quietude, though, the sound of the "dragon-hornet" (cicada), ringing out all the more strikingly in the absence of other noises, only adds to it. Qualifying its humming as "drowsy" and later "dron-ing," the poet foregrounds its soporific effect, heightening the prevailing stillness, which is now disclosed as connoting not the literal absence of sound or movement, but a general feeling of restfulness. Catching sight of its source ("Tis the dragon-hornet—see!"), the speaker is dazzled by the radiant *ekstasis* of this "bright beetle," "all bedaubed resplendently / With yellow on a tawny ground," as it "gleams the air . . . in its droning flight, / With a slanting track of light, / Till rising in the sunshine higher, / Its shards flame out like gems on fire."

Contrasting with the fiery radiance of the cicada and the bright sunlight in which it has been revealed, the "cool murmur" of "the ever wakeful rill" and the breeze that periodically ripples the "sea / Of leafy boughs" in the following stanza convey the sense of refreshment that, as we discover in the final lines of the poem, the speaker has found in the relative coolness and shade of his forested "recess":

> O 'tis easeful here to lie
> Hidden from Noon's scorching eye,
> In this grassy cool recess
> Musing thus of Quietness.

In keeping with the tradition of European pastoral poetry, the atmosphere attributed to this midsummer noon induces a pleasantly drowsy disposition, in which the self seems on the verge of melting into its surroundings. This mood was traditionally personified in the mythic figure of Pan, whose mesmerizing music is naturalized here in the dragon-hornet's humming, in keeping with the allegory of languorous Summer explicitly invoked by Harpur:

> Tired Summer, in her forest bower
> Turning with the noontide hour,
> Heaves a slumberous breath, ere she
> Once more slumbers peacefully.

Sinking into the "slumberous" state engendered by the peaceful atmosphere of the bush this midsummer noon, in company with grasshoppers, ants, and locusts, the speaker reaffirms the creaturely dimension of human subjectivity. Verbalizing this atmospheric experience of place and season, the poet reminds the readers of their own bodily affectivity by inviting them to share in the feeling of quietude invoked by his words.

In literary communication, seasonal atmospheres are commonly summoned by means of what Böhme terms verbal "insignia," such as the "bright paths," "late roses," and "last asters" that create the autumnal mood of a well-known Stefan George poem, "Komm in den totgesagten Park und schau."[35] Functioning metonymically, such culturally familiar insignia frequently convey a comforting sense of the continuity of natural cycles. While seasonal weather patterns clearly hold practical importance in agrarian societies, they become salient in a new way when the terrestrial environment is altered by industrialization: within modernist poetry such as George's, the weather is invoked as a primary medium through which city dwellers continue to experience their corporeal connection with the nature that they are not.

But what if the conventional insignia of seasonal atmospheres no longer correspond to the lived experience of weather? For settler Australians in the nineteenth century (as for ever-more people around our warming world today), the weather, far from offering reassurance, was itself a locus of intense anxiety. Together with its weird biota, fickle waterways, and odd topography, Australia's erratic climate, which even in the temperate regions fails to conform to the regular four seasons that we nonetheless project onto it, contributed to the environmental alienation that assailed many European settlers (as well as hampering their endeavors to induce the land to grow European crops). Harpur's poetry is significant historically not least for its attempt to overcome this sense of alienation by affirming the beauty of the bush, which is reconstituted in "Midsummer Noon" as a pastoral *locus amoenus*—albeit at the price of banishing all traces of the colonial battle with, and for, the land, of which he gives glimpses elsewhere. Even so, it is evident that the European insignia of summer cannot be translated seamlessly to the Australian environment. Among these, traditionally, are ripening grain and swelling fruits, harbingers of the harvest to come. Harpur, however, has fled the troubled agricultural landscape in order to find refuge in the forest. Moreover, the tenuous quality of this refuge is hinted at in the reference to "Noon's scorching eye." Here, Harpur lets slip that Australian summers are not as benign as might be suggested by the mood of easefulness that he invokes in his somewhat strained effort to adapt the insignia of European seasonal poetry to the antipodean environment:[36] Harpur was well aware that there would be many years when that "rill" would fall silent, while the oil-laden "leafy boughs" above it were bound, sooner or later, to burst into flame.

There is also a more fundamental problem of translation here, though, namely from bodily experience to verbal expression. While the corporeally affective force of language is indisputable, Böhme's confident assertion that "the same atmospheres . . . can be produced through words" elides the shifts and slippages that inevitably occur both in the process of translating feelings into words and that of responding to words with feelings.[37] If it were true that words could mediate atmospheres without loss or alteration, then it would appear that bodily presence is not really necessary to ecological aesthetics after all. In that case, should I seek to enjoy, say, the *Anmutung* of a rose, I could happily make do with a poetic depiction (which would have the added advantage of protecting me from the risk of bloodshed, since its thorns, like its luscious folds and heady scent, would be merely virtual). Gloriously, though, reading a poem about a rose is not at all the same thing as having a risky encounter with a real one in the flesh. Indeed, it is only to the extent that the literary text falls short of replicating the bodily experience to which it alludes that it might have the effect of calling us to lay aside our books and venture "forth into the light of things," to cite Wordsworth once again.[38] Böhme admits as much himself in conceding that his own book, *Leibsein als Aufgabe*, "can only point beyond itself and thereby motivate the reader to seek out modes of bodily existence in their own practice."[39] While providing training in those extratextual experiences of atmosphere that it cannot fully mediate, literature serves also to remind us of the role of words, and the complex and mobile networks of intertextual connotation they activate, in inflecting those states of feeling engendered by our physical encounters with other people, things, and places. Creatures of flesh and blood though we most certainly are, as Judith Wright reminds us in "Summer," we "live though a web of language."[40]

The atmosphere engendered by Wright's "burned-out summer" contrasts sharply with earlier Australian poetry that sought to accommodate "antipodean" environments to European seasonal memories in a manner analogous to the physical reshaping of the land in accordance with colonial notions of "humanization." It is the devastation that this has wrought both for Indigenous people and their land that Wright stresses in speaking of the "quality" of the place invoked in this emphatically post-pastoral poem as "not its former nature / but a struggle to heal itself after many wounds."[41] Linking a seasonal mood marked by the aftermath of fire with the historical memories of massacre and mining that can also be traced in this place, Wright recalls that bodily presence is never pure: living in the web of language, our corporeal affectivity, insofar as we can verbalize it, is always tinctured by sociality. Moreover, admitting her inability to ever "see without words" as do the jenny lizard and wolf-spiders, whose strange physiognomies are revealed in the speaker's torch-light, Wright points beyond the aesthetics of atmosphere toward an ethics of alterity. But that is another story.[42]

In the wake of Marcel Duchamp's modernist *pissoir* and in the midst of a warming world, any artist who depicts that atmosphere of, say, rural Suffolk on a warm summer's day in the manner of Constable is bound to have their work consigned to the category of nostalgic kitsch. If it is to be more than mere botanizing, angry protest, or conciliatory mysticism, Böhme insists, contemporary ecological art should challenge our assumptions about the nature and status of both nature and art, and, in so doing, demonstrate how aesthetics qua sensual cognition can contribute to articulating and redressing the ecosocial ills of the present.[43]

NOTES

1. Eagleton, *Ideology of the Aesthetic*, 13.

2. Currently an Emeritus Professor of Philosophy at the Darmstadt University of Technology, Böhme has expertise in the history and philosophy of science, as well as ethics, aesthetics, and the philosophy of nature, and he has held guest professorships at many foreign universities, including Cambridge and Harvard. He frequently collaborates

with his brother, Hartmut Böhme, a Professor of Cultural Theory at Humboldt University and a leading figure in German ecological literary and cultural studies.

3. Böhme, *Für eine ökologische Naturästhetik*. Böhme has published four other monographs on aesthetics and numerous articles, some of which have appeared in English translation. Art and aesthetics are also discussed in *Die Natur vor uns* (Nature Before Us); *Leibsein als Aufgabe* (The Task of Bodily Existence); and *Ethics in Context*. On the ecocritical significance of Böhme's work, see also Gersdorf and Mayer, *Nature in Literary and Cultural Studies*, 17–19; Goodbody, *Nature, Technology and Cultural Change*, 30–38; and Rigby, "Beyond the Frame" and "Tuning in to Spirit of Place."

4. Böhme, *Für eine ökologische Naturästhetik*, 6.

5. Böhme, *Die Natur vor uns*, 261.

6. Böhme, "Driven by the Interest in Reasonable Conditions."

7. See Böhme, *Natürlich Natur*; and Böhme and Schramm, eds., *Soziale Naturwissenschaft*.

8. Bloch, *The Principle of Hope*, 3:1353.

9. Shelley, *Queen Mab*, in *The Complete Works*, 1:122.

10. Mark Tredinnick, "We Are Not Finished at the Skin," *Philosophy Activism Nature*, no. 5 (2008), http://search.informit.com.au/documentSummary;dn=814875138782364 ;res=E-LIBRARY.

11. Böhme, *Leibsein als Aufgabe*, 48–52.

12. Böhme, *Ethics in Context*, 91–94.

13. Böhme, *Leibsein als Aufgabe* 24.

14. Ibid., 368–70.

15. Schmitz, qtd. in Böhme, *Atmosphäre*, 119.

16. Böhme, *Atmosphäre*, 119.

17. Böhme, "The Space of Bodily Presence," 5.

18. Böhme, *Atmosphäre*, 183–86.

19. Böhme, "Atmosphere as the Fundamental Concept," 122.

20. Böhme, *Aisthetik*, 46–48.

21. Böhme, *Atmosphäre*; Böhme, *Aisthetik*, 87–100.

22. Böhme, *Anmutungen*. According to the online Grimms Wörterbuch (Grimms' Dictionary), *Anmutung* can mean the incitement, demand, or appeal of another upon the self or one's own sense of attraction, inclination, or affect with regard to another (Grimms Wörterbuch, http://germazope.uni-trier.de/Projects/DWB). Many thanks to Michael Gratzke for this reference.

23. Böhme, *Aisthetik*, 73–86.

24. Ibid., 116.

25. Böhme, *Atmosphäre*, 187.

26. Böhme, "Contribution to the Critique of the Aesthetic Economy."

27. Wordsworth, *The Fourteen-Book Prelude*, 235–36.

28. On the history of physiognomy in *Atmosphäre*, 101–52. See also *Aisthetik*, 104–10.

29. Böhme, "Der Raum des Gedichts."

30. Böhme, *Atmosphäre*, 75.

31. The poem appears in Barnes and McFarlane, *Cross-Country*, 8–9. In *Aisthetik* (65), Böhme observes that nearly a third of the poems anthologized by Alexander von Bormann in *Die Erde will ein freies Geleit* fall into this category.

32. Böhme, *Atmosphäre*, 66–84; Böhme, *Aisthetik*, 59–72.

33. Jonathan Bate, "Living with the Weather."

34. Böhme, *Aisthetik*, 64. The association of meteorological and affective atmospheres is suggested also by the metaphoric use of terms derived from the semantic field of the weather to refer to states of feeling, for example, to "storm" into a room; "sunny disposition"; "icy" stare (Böhme, "Mir läuft ein Schauer übern ganzen Leib").

35. Böhme, *Atmosphäre*, 77–78.

36. On the challenges of writing pastoral in an Australian context, see Kane, "Woful Shepherds."

37. Böhme, "Atmosphere as the Fundamental Concept," 124.

38. William Wordsworth, "The Tables Turned," in *Lyrical Ballads, and Other Poems, 1797–1800*, ed. J. Butler and K. Green, 108 (Ithaca: Cornell University Press, 1992). For an elaboration of this point, see Rigby, "Earth, World, Text."

39. Böhme, *Leibsein als Aufgabe*, 10.

40. Wright, *Collected Poems*, 421.

41. Gifford, *Pastoral*.

42. See, for example, Timothy Morton's contribution to this volume.

43. Böhme, *Die Natur vor uns*, 255–58.

4

ETHICS & OTHERNESS

Dialoguing with Bakhtin
over Our Ethical Responsibility
to Anothers

The Russian theorist Mikhail Bakhtin (1895–1975) provides a valuable set of tools for ecocritical analysis and a method of approaching literary works and their interrelationship with the material world. Bakhtin's attitude toward language positions him in opposition to Ferdinand de Saussure and Saussurean linguistics. Instead, he can be aligned with his contemporary, Émile Benveniste, as well as current linguists such as George Lakoff and Mark Johnson, who have emphasized discourse over language. This emphasis leads to seeing speaking and writing as individual acts undertaken at particular moments in specific configurations of the world. That recognition of immersion leads to emphasizing the speaker/writer as a social individual on the one hand, and as a physical being on the other hand.

As Michael Holquist notes, in his introduction to *Art and Answerability*, the ideas of Henri Bergson significantly influenced Bakhtin, in particular the recognition that "the sheer physicality of my body cannot be understood as the locus of my existence without *also* taking into account the fact that as a living organism I must, whether I will it or not, pay *attention to life*. . . . A total description of an act would have to include a body, objects (or images of objects) external to it, and a *change in the relations* between the body and the other images."[1] This influence causes Bakhtin to recognize discourse as an embodied and material activity.

Bakhtin's *Art and Answerability* opens with a brief note that provides the title for this collection. There he stakes out the ethical orientation of his lifelong philosophical project, which can provide a starting point for an ethical literary ecocriticism: "But what guarantees the inner connection of the constituent elements of a person? Only the unity of answerability. I have to answer with my own life for what I have experienced and understood in art. . . . It is not only mutual answerability that art and life must assume, but also mutual liability to blame."[2] What a clear and profound statement, which moves beyond a vague sense of "responsibility" and clarifies that concept as an act of "answerability."

Critics exist as such because we reply to phenomena that we observe and in which we participate through answering. But answerability represents more than the description of that speaking back; it also represents the necessity of our responsiveness to be ethically grounded and morally justifiable. Hence, Bakhtin emphasizes the "liability to blame" for the shortcomings of our critical responses. Answerability imposes obligations on the ecocritic in relation to environmental issues, representations of ecology, and the quality and functionality of artistic images of nature, environments, ecologies, and human practices.

In the second essay in *Art and Answerability*, Bakhtin adds another crucial concept: transgredience. For the author to represent life, and for the critic to evaluate those representations, Bakhtin argues that he "must take up a position outside himself, must experience himself on a plane that is different from the one on which we actually experience our own life. . . . He must become another in relation to himself."[3] The concept of "transgredience," then, connects with the issue of anthropocentrism versus ecocentrism. It addresses the problem of trying to "speak for nature" or to let nature speak through oneself as an author. It also pertains to the task of evaluating artistic representations from a perspective that includes but transcends one's own tastes and uses for a particular work in order to consider the impact of art on perceptions of human and rest-of-nature relationships. It encourages authors and critics to see themselves through another's perspective: those of the rest of the natural world at the general level, and of specific ecosystems, plants, or animals at the particular level.

The practice of transgredience can lead to a critical autobiographical stance that requires a persistent ethical evaluation of one's moral behavior: "After looking at ourselves through the eyes of another, we always return—in life—into ourselves again, and the final, or, as it were, recapitulative event takes place within ourselves in the categories of our own life."[4] The experience of adopting the perspective of another must be consolidated as an act of consciousness. The practice of ecocriticism and the promotion of reading environmental literature, then, would always include the potential for, whatever else the reader or critic might want to think about, the evolution of a more ethical interaction with the rest of the world. This interaction requires that we make the same kind of distinction in English that is possible in Russian: that between alien other—*chuzhoi*—and familiar other—*druzoi*. Caryl Emerson notes that "the *another* Bakhtin has in mind is not hostile to the *I* but a necessary component of it, a friendly other, a living factor in the attempts of the *I* toward self-definition."[5]

As a result of his emphasis on answerability, Bakhtin bases all of his work on an ethical orientation that emphasizes the responsibility of speakers/writers for the potential impact of their utterances on others. He also anticipates the feminist concept of "situated knowledges" discussed by Donna Haraway and others when he brings the limits of human sensual perception into the consideration of aesthetic activity. He rightly notes, "While my thought can place my body wholly in the outside world as an object among other objects, my actual seeing cannot do the same thing."[6] This point becomes particularly acute in regard to autobiographical and semi-autobiographical nature writing and the degree to which the author identifies his observational point of view as one perspective among many and represents the perceptions of "anothers," including nonhuman ones.

This kind of different authorial point of view is invariably remarked upon by my students when we read John Burroughs, John Muir, and Mary Austin back to back to back. Students comment on how Muir makes himself the hero of many of his stories and a unique observer who cannot be imitated by his readers. Burroughs, in contrast, frequently makes himself unheroic and includes representations of how he thinks he is being viewed by other animals. Austin, in turn, often makes others the heroes of her stories and frequently internal narrators, so that she presents her own perspective as a relative one, commenting on its limitations and bringing herself onto an equal plane with her readers.

All of these writers' works have their place, but they perform the representation of being-in-the-world and the limitations of human perception quite differently. The importance of adopting, even though temporarily, ecocentrism as a subjective orientation, provides a means by which to utilize transgredience in the service of ecocritical comprehension. It enables self-objectification as part of another-subjectification. Bakhtin believes that "one can speak of a human being's absolute need for the other, for the other's seeing, remembering, gathering, and unifying self-activity. . . . This outward personality could not exist, if the other did not create it."[7]

Part of the crisis of humanity is precisely the degree to which human societies and individuals do not allow nonhuman others to participate in aesthetic memory and in the generation and self-understanding of our outward personalities and perceptions of ourselves as characters within our own stories. Nor does humanism enable the aesthetic rendering of nonhuman others as formative influences, as subjects—rather than setting or objects of attention—that facilitate the author and his or her human characters as "perceiving myself as another."[8] This point holds true whether one argues that a core personality exists that shapes all variations of its manifestation in society or that personality is a performance affected by a sense of audience.

As Bakhtin asserts: "I myself cannot be the author of my own value. . . . The biological life of an organism becomes a value only in *another's* sympathy and compassion with that life."[9] Repeatedly we see in environmental writing the effort to include the voices of nonhumans as others and anothers, literally and figuratively, as in Starhawk's political council in *The Fifth Sacred Thing* and Ursula K. Le Guin's short stories in such collections as *Buffalo Gals and Other Animal Presences*, or in Bernard Werber's *Empire of the Ants*.

This focus on representing anothers and the ethical obligations it imposes become the starting point of Bakhtin's unfinished essay *Toward a Philosophy of the Act*, written around the same time (1919–21) as the texts included in *Art and Answerability*. Bakhtin opens it with the declaration that each thought "is an act or deed that I perform," thereby interdicting the effort to separate thought and action, mind and body, and other dualisms of the Enlightenment tradition. He further recognizes that the thought needs to be understood as a whole in terms of "its content/sense" and in terms of "its presence in my actual consciousness."[10] The generation of a thought is an act for which a person is answerable because that thought forms part of consciousness and, by extension, part of behavior.

Thought becomes an environmental act because its presence in consciousness cannot be separated from the human being holding that consciousness. Further, my thoughts become part of the habitual, unconscious ethics of another individual, just as the thoughts of others have habituated my ethics.[11] The act of our thoughts taking up residence in another, influencing and forming their thinking, results in behaviors and practices—what V. N. Vološinov calls "behavioral ideology"—that affect human interrelationship with the rest of nature.[12] Therefore, each of us is answerable for the way we think in relation to the way that human beings affect local and global environments.

Supportive of this position, Bakhtin emphasizes that thought remains always embodied, both to occur and to be implemented.[13] It never gains the status of pure objectivity, although particular thoughts can gain the status of a perspective situated outside one's self-centeredness. In what today sounds amazingly prescient in light of nuclear weaponry, carbon emissions, species extinction, and the energy consumption crisis, Bakhtin remarks: "All that which is technological, when divorced from the once-occurrent unity of life and surrendered to the will of the law immanent to its development, is frightening; it may from time to time irrupt into this once-occurrent unity as an irresponsibly destructive and terrifying force."[14]

Each person's life is a "once-occurrent" event, and each action as thought and practice is also once-occurrent, and for them we remain responsible.

Thus Bakhtin emphasizes the need to link theory and practice in individual "moral being" as a result of each moment of time, each individual, and each event being specifically unique.[15] We are not then looking for formulas to guide ecological practice, but for methods, guidelines, and ethics that allow for an ongoing cascade of unique moral decisions.

The effort to get students and readers to appreciate the distinction between ethics and morals, guidelines and practices, pertains continuously to reading environmental literature and discussing specific environmentalist strategies. *Critical Political Ecology* by Tim Forsyth makes this case in regard to specific issues pitting first-world environmentalists against third-world inhabitants, such as desertification, deforestation, and population control. More recently we can see the complexity of first-world versus third-world dynamics in food crops being replaced with biofuel crop cultivation.

This caveat paragraph leads me to Bakhtin's argument about "aesthetic empathizing."[16] Bakhtin warns that in observational writing, no matter how empathetic the writer, he or she must recognize the interrelationship of the observer and observed and the moment in which the interrelationship is being understood. In so doing, the writer necessarily steps outside the relationship in order to write about it. This necessity is both an aesthetic and a moral action because the writing down acts as a testament to what has occurred and can also act as a warning or a recommendation of what could or should occur. This understanding of the necessity of subjectivity, of interacting from within oneself—although not necessarily for oneself—addresses the complaints that students often make that an environmental author ought to be a full-time activist and not a writer. Or it helps students come to an understanding of how Gary Snyder could have ended up working in logging as a youth, which he records in *The Practice of the Wild*, and could continue to chop firewood for heat, which seem to them imperfect or hypocritical behaviors from an all-or-nothing perspective.

People who don't want to come to terms with their own environmental responsibility frequently raise these kinds of overgeneralized objections so they can avoid thinking through their own responsibilities. Bakhtin speaks precisely to this tendency when he emphasizes *participative* consciousness and *answerability*. As he notes: "Contemporary man feels sure of himself, feels well-off and clear-headed, where he is himself essentially and fundamentally not present in the autonomous world of a domain of culture and its immanent law of creation. But he feels unsure of himself, feels destitute and deficient in understanding, where he has to do with himself, where he is the center from which his answerable acts or deeds issue."[17]

This reliance on "some domain of culture" appears frequently through appeals to a notion of stasis, whether in some image of unchanging human

nature or some form of cultural fundamentals, such as American exceptionalism or God's blessings. Because of such anti-environmental inertia, it
becomes ever more pressing to promote within ecocritical theory Bakhtin's
emphasis on answerability for everyday behavior. One is always moving
from possibility to performance to effect within the context of *"what is once-
occurrent."*[18]

As a result, Bakhtin moves toward "This fact of *my non-alibi in Being.*"[19]
Because each entity is unique, not just us but also all other organisms and all
other material formations, every entity plays an irreplaceable and nonsubsti-
tutable role in events at the level of maximum particularity. That is not to
exclude significant similarities or to deny that nearly identical entities exist
synchronically and diachronically together, but rather to emphasize that no
one totally substitutes for another one.

As with *Art and Answerability,* in *Toward a Philosophy of the Act,* Bakhtin
emphasizes that our starting point from within our own existence need not
be our ending point in ethical decision making. We need not be anthropocentric: "to live from within oneself does not mean to live for oneself, but
means to be an answerable participant from within oneself, to affirm one's
compellent, actual non-alibi in Being."[20] Understanding generates obligation and also enables a person to practice an orientation not always of I-for-
myself, or even I-for-humanity, but an "I-for-the-other,"[21] with that other
encompassing entire ecologies from one's locale to the entire biosphere.

In addition, in the same section of *Toward a Philosophy of the Act,* Bakhtin writes about the idea of "compellentness," an inner conviction guiding
and requiring one's own living as deed. Hence, ecocritics can argue for the
value and significance of nature-oriented literature in general, in contrast
with other forms of literary production, and argue for the value of generic
stylistic diversity among such literature. We can do so precisely because we
understand that the affectivity of literature varies widely from one audience
to another. Nonfiction is not the *best* or preferred form of nature-oriented
writing on the basis of its apparent facticity or its outer mimesis. Nor is
environmental poetry more likely to move readers because it is an affective-
expressive genre rather than a narrative one.

Rather, promoting the widest diversity of nature-oriented literature,
from traditional nature essays to postmodern performance pieces, has
the greatest potential to move audiences precisely because that diversity
matches the diversity of audiences who need to be moved. For example, my
graduate students have been amazed at how the scientific writing of Rachel
Carson in *Silent Spring* and the rhetorical harangues of Wendell Berry in
The Unsettling of America have moved them emotionally. Some were moved

more by these works than by the poetry of Robinson Jeffers or the narratives of John Burroughs and Mary Austin, which they had read earlier in the same course.

These students' affective responses to the texts assigned for the course, "Literature of the Environmental Movement," help us understand Bakhtin's concept of "aesthetic empathizing."[22] Readers can through literature vicariously experience and engage with the perspectives of others and anothers through entertaining within themselves differing perceptions of reality and right behavior without immediately threatening their own positions and behaviors in the world. The distantiation that aesthetic works provide enables readers to explore empathetically, and not just intellectually, behaviors, practices, and beliefs that directly contradict their own or open up previously unexplored worlds, such as animal intelligence, without imposing upon them a loss of identity.

Aesthetic empathizing is precisely most successful when readers can retain their own sense of uniqueness while vicariously embodying the uniqueness of other entities. It constitutes an immersion without risk of drowning, yet at the same time to the degree to which readers become conscious of the others that interpellate them in the course of aesthetic empathizing, it imposes on them an obligation to think and act differently.[23]

It is important to consider the ways in which different literary genres and styles set up varying degrees of distantiation that increase or decrease a reader's comfort zone, that focus on small differences close to home or differences realized on other planets, or that pose differential human perspectives across times and cultures or eukaryotic distinctions across species and ecologies. Realist fiction and literary nonfiction tend to construct a zone very close to home and very close to known human experience and individual perceptions.

Science fiction, in contrast, often focuses on the largest possible distantiations in terms of locations, temporality, and species. Magic realism and postmodernist fiction often generate a distantiation based on tweaking contemporaneous reality or introducing irruptive and disruptive nonrealist phenomena to change the gestalt framework of character or reader orientation. Poetry manifests distantiations in its own stylistic ways, such as through nonhuman points of view or descriptive defamiliarization.[24]

Such an attention to distantiation is just one element of thinking through writing styles, genre choices, and strategies in terms of Bakhtinian dialogics. Two other elements are Bakhtin's differentiation of monological and dialogical discourses and authoritative and internally persuasive discourses. While those two binaries often overlap, they are not identical. The most developed remarks on both of these binaries are to be found in *The Dialogic Imagination* and elaborated in *Problems of Dostoevsky's Poetics*.

In the first instance, Bakhtin focuses on literary and rhetorical texts that are written as if the author of the text is addressing no one who might have a response to the claims being made or the stories being told. He contrasts these to dialogical discourses that tend to contain within themselves recognition of other voices that have addressed the subject and possible responses to claims and stories. Bakhtin sets up a dichotomy, but we might more profitably consider the concepts as two poles of a continuum, on which can be plotted the location of various environmental novels, ecological poems, and nature essays. And we might evaluate this plotting in terms of the relationship among author, reader, and text, on the one hand, and content, theme, and ethical response, on the other hand.

In the second instance, Bakhtin focuses on the degree to which a text relies on narrative voicing or rhetorical structure to represent the writer's words as the authoritative word on a subject, as in the case of sacred texts or political dogma, which brook no resistance of rejoinders from the readers. He contrasts that with internally persuasive discourse, which relies not on the authority of the narrator or the rhetorical category of the text for its claim to truthfulness or accuracy, but rather on the degree to which the reader is encouraged to interrogate and evaluate the voice or voices heard in the text, in terms of the reader's decision to deem the text accurate or truthful.

Certainly, a monological text can more easily pass itself off as authoritative, but it need not do so. Many first-person nature narratives present only a single speaking voice, yet the often self-questioning style and learning-curve plot enable these works to develop in an internally persuasive manner, in which the author claims for himself or his narrator no particular official authority, but only the sincerity of experiential learning. In like manner, a dialogical text will initially appear more internally persuasive, but the degree to which it actually encourages active critical interrogation by a reader depends more on the degree to which the differing voices within the text genuinely contend with one another.

Bakhtin would argue that we find the potential for dialogical and internally persuasive discourses in the modern period across all genres because modern fiction produced a novelization of other genres, altering the ways in which they are written and received.[25] Even if we do not concur that the rise of the novel in Western societies caused other genres to become novelized, we still must recognize that the voice of authority as an absolute, god-given or politically endowed, truth stater has declined in both intellectual public acceptance and rhetorical and literary preference.

Even the memoir takes on more of an internally persuasive character in the contemporary world because it focuses on contemporaneity and identity; the memoir's obvious subjectivity reduces its authoritativeness. Sincerity begins to become a more significant factor in first-personal narratives than facticity. As a result, novelization and the movement toward the internally persuasive in first-person accounts tend to place greater weight on the affective-expressive qualities of the text than on authority.

In like manner, in treating the literary nonfiction category of nature writing as arising from the amateur natural history essay, I would consider the term "amateur" most important here. The author's believability is not conferred on the basis of certification or institutional affiliation but rather on the basis of personal experience and effort. The text that results may retain the qualities of a monological voice, but its persuasiveness is internally derived, based primarily on a perception of the authenticity of direct and immediate experience.

As a result, the success of nature writing in moving readers comes from a comic structure, where readers can view themselves as on the same plane as the author, with the ability, if not always the opportunity, to undergo similar experiences and reach similar conclusions.[26] In discussing parody, Bakhtin claims that "language is transformed from the absolute dogma it had been within the narrow framework of a sealed-off and impermeable monoglossia into a working hypothesis for comprehending and expressing reality."[27] This observation can be applied as well to the self-consciously amateur style of the nature writer, who is often aware of his own limitations and ignorance, and, especially, to the nature writer willing to laugh at his own failings and foibles.

The novel, of course, has a far greater ability to become internally persuasive by the freedom of representation of ideas through a variety of characters, with none of them obviously the voice of the author. This internally persuasive character is not limited by whether the novel is written in a first-person or third-person narrative style. For example, Neal Stephenson's *Zodiac* is written as a first-person memoir of his exploits in unraveling a toxic-dumping mystery in Boston harbor. Yet, the self-parodying style of his narration and the author's careful efforts to maintain a certain degree of reader dislike for the hero's obnoxiousness and arrogance work to ensure that the reader will not accept his statements as authoritative, but will resist accepting them because of the speaker's personality. As a result, readers find themselves agreeing with his conclusions by the force of experience and evidence, rather than by the force of personality or scientific authority.

Given that a novel can easily accommodate as much factual information as a book-length work of literary nonfiction, neither can claim generic superiority in terms of reader education. Rather, the difference in genres has more to do with differences in the writing styles and strategies of individual writers and in the receptiveness of different groups of readers to those styles. Bakhtinian dialogics can help us understand the differences and strategies for writing as well as their varied reception without having to build a genre hierarchy or exclude works from consideration because they are fictional.[28]

Indeed, cautionary tales have played a significant role in various ethical campaigns, such as the antinuclear movement, and these necessarily are not based on what has happened but on what can happen. They depend for their effectiveness on choosing the right construction of the moment of crisis. Understanding the function of this focal moment as either the setting for the novel or as the crux of the plot can benefit from a reading of Bakhtin's concept of the *chronotope*. This is worked up in his essay "Forms of Time and Chronotope in the Novel" in *The Dialogic Imagination*.[29] The chronotope defines the "intrinsic connectedness of temporal and spatial relationships that are artistically expressed in literature."[30] As such, these nodes are crucial for shaping reader response to the theme, plot, or argument of the literary or rhetorical text.

To the degree to which nature writing and nature poems, for instance, appeal to or invoke reader associations with the pastoral and the idyll, they take the reader out of time, either nostalgically or mythically. By focusing, in contrast, on specific crises, such as the hole in the ozone layer or the sudden release of methane from under the Arctic Ocean or out of tundra peat bogs, authors generate a chronotope that encourages the reader to interpret plots and themes not only intratextually but also extratextually.

The appeal to the idyll is highly contradictory and needs to be understood as such. On the one hand, it fruitfully reasserts an organic and holistic relationship of humanity and the more-than-human that needs to be revitalized in the increasingly de-natured life of urban consumerism.[31] On the other hand, the carrying away of the reader from the present may lessen the sense of crisis and decrease feelings of need for engagement with the environmental issues of the day. This decrease of intensity cannot be considered always a bad thing, but it becomes problematic from an ethical perspective when it becomes a form of escapism. Bakhtin, for instance, tends to view the idylls of contemporary life in the former way. Their "organic fastening-down, a grafting of life and its events to a place, to a familiar territory" provides a sense of refuge and respite.[32] If, however, they generate the illusion that multitudes can opt out, then they may very well hinder the preservation of those places of refuge that the authors so lovingly render. Charles Siebert in *Wickerby: An Urban Pastoral* does an excellent job of threading the needle between these tendencies, seeing the rural retreat as just that, a temporary period of reprieve and reflection that enables the narrator to reintegrate himself into the city with a renewed awareness of human and more-than-human interdependence.

Those writers setting up chronotopes focused on immediate moments of crisis, however, have to risk the limitations of timeliness. Their works may lose reader interest if they have chosen a crisis that does not materialize or is quickly ameliorated. Some works, though, even when their chronotope moves from the near future to the near past, may very well retain their thematic power as well as their aesthetic merits. John Brunner's *The Sheep Look Up* serves as a noteworthy example. Its future at the time of its writing has now become our immediate past, yet readers find it engaging as they realize how many of the environmental dangers about which we are warned have had to be addressed or remain unaddressed.

Resisting readers, to borrow a term from Judith Fetterley, may very well shy away from literary styles that smack of authority. For them, the internally persuasive may be more acceptable and interesting. As a result, the econovel, particularly cautionary tales set in the present day or the near future, may hold the most promise for eliciting their ethical engagement with environmental issues. And, in particular, they might find travesties, parodies, and other forms of carnival particularly appealing. As a result, it is also important for ecocritics to bring Bakhtin's theory of carnival into their theoretical repertoire. Space does not permit a full development of this aspect of Bakhtin's theory, but it holds great promise, as suggested by a recently completed Australian dissertation.

In that study, "Carnival in Space and Time: Shared Metaphors of Change in 'Post Neo-Darwinian' Evolutionary Theory and Feminist Science Fiction," Tess Williams brilliantly expounds on the key features of Bakhtin's concept of carnival as developed in *Rabelais and His World* (written in the late 1930s but not published until 1965). She links his theory of carnivalization as a process consisting of subversion through laughter, ambivalence, and hierarchical reversals with the feminist performance theory of Karen Barad. Williams makes a compelling case for the way that carnivalization works in scientific debates over paradigm shifts. Her study demonstrates the need to become more attentive to the ways in which carnivalization can work ethically to promote internally persuasive narrative and rhetorical strategies for representations of environmental philosophies, ecological ontologies, and activist issues.

To date, probably the most attention in ecocriticism given over to carnivalization has occurred in relation to Native American literature, particularly the trickster figures in both oral and written stories. Those working with fiction have had to address carnivalization in such works as Edward

Abbey's *The Monkey Wrench Gang,* Karen Tei Yamashita's *Through the Arc of the Rain Forest* and *Tropic of Orange,* Julian Barnes's *England, England,* and Günter Grass's *The Rat.*

At the same time that Bakhtin's theory of carnival facilitates analysis of trickster figures across literary genres, it also enables the formation of a different perspective in the analysis of scientific discourse. But Bakhtin's theories work for more than just the carnivalization that Williams identifies in such debates as those over genetic determinism, aquatic ape theory, and sociobiology. The dialogic method itself and the distinctions between monological and dialogical and authoritative and internally persuasive discourses help to clarify an increasingly sharp division in genetics. In opposition to the unidirectional authoritative command model of single genes determining epigenesis and identifiable inherited traits, a variety of countertheories have been broached, such as development systems theory, ecosemiotics, and semantic biology. All of these rely on a dialogical model of interdependent activity and communication. In "Where Do Your Borders Lie?" for instance, Timo Maran cites Bakhtin's dialogics as one of the possibly productive humanist theories for elaborating ecosemiotics.[33]

I began by focusing on ethics and end by focusing on responsiveness. Bakhtin wants to promote the foregrounding of the multifacetedness of the "living word." This living word, "having taken meaning and shape at a particular historical moment in a socially specific environment . . . cannot fail to become an active participant in social dialogue."[34] The recognition of this dialogical contingency for meaning and its ongoing interpretation under changing circumstances hails listeners and readers. It calls on them to engage in "responsive understanding."[35] As such, it makes readers as responsible as speakers and writers in their nonalibi of being.

While the specific tactical or strategic practices that may result from the writing and reading of nature-oriented literature and environmental writing remain in dispute, under negotiation, and subject to critique as they are implemented, they nevertheless witness an ethical responsibility. Bakhtinian dialogics helps us to understand that ongoing dialogue and its underpinnings, as well as providing specific concepts and categories of analysis for studying such writing.

NOTES

    1. Holquist, introduction to Bakhtin, *Art and Answerability,* xxxiv, original emphasis.

    2. Bakhtin, *Art and Answerability,* 1.

    3. Ibid., 15.

    4. Ibid., 17.

    5. Bakhtin, *Problems,* 302 n. 15; see also Murphy, *Literature, Nature, and Other,* 35:114–15.

6. Bakhtin, *Art and Answerability*, 28.

7. Ibid., 36.

8. Ibid., 59.

9. Ibid., 55, original emphasis; see also 105.

10. Bakhtin, *Toward*, 3.

11. See Murphy, *Literature, Nature, and Other*, 9–10; and Vološinov, *Freudianism*, 14–15, 23–24.

12. Vološinov, *Freudianism*, 88. Some biographers contend that Bakhtin either wrote the books published in V. N. Vološinov's name or was significantly responsible for their content. While others dismiss this claim, most critics consider *Marxism and the Philosophy of Language* and *Freudianism* to qualify for inclusion in a loose unity of works by a group known as the Bakhtin Circle: Bakhtin, Vološinov, and P. N. Medvedev.

13. Bakhtin, *Toward*, 6–7.

14. Ibid., 7.

15. Ibid., 12.

16. Ibid., 17.

17. Ibid., 20–21.

18. Ibid., 29, original emphasis.

19. Ibid., 40, original emphasis.

20. Ibid., 49.

21. Ibid., 54.

22. Ibid., 72–75.

23. On interpellation, see Louis Althusser, *Lenin and Philosophy and Other Essays* and *On Ideology*.

24. *Defamiliarization* is developed as the term for a particular type of literary technique by Victor Shklovsky, in "Art as Technique," originally published in 1917.

25. Bakhtin, *Dialogic Imagination*, 7–14.

26. See Meeker, *Comedy of Survival*.

27. Bakhtin, *Dialogic Imagination*, 61.

28. See Murphy, *Farther Afield*.

29. Bakhtin, *Dialogic Imagination*, 84–258.

30. Ibid., 84.

31. Ibid., 225–26.

32. Ibid., 225, see also 233.

33. Maran, "Where Do Your Borders Lie?" 469.

34. Bakhtin, *Dialogic Imagination*, 276.

35. Ibid., 280–81.

Coexistence and Coexistents:
Ecology without a World

What we need is an ecology without nature: the ultimate obstacle to protecting nature is the very notion of nature we rely on.—Žižek, *In Defense of Lost Causes*

Environmental ethics sometimes depends upon ideas of life forms immersed in a surrounding "world."[1] For Trevor Norris, "world" is the "dynamic relatedness that grounds our identity" (see his essay in this volume). The philosopher Martin Heidegger derives the notion of "world" from his study of Jakob von Uexküll's biological research, which suggested that different sentient life forms have different experiences of their surroundings, and hence phenomenologically (that is, experientially) different worlds. A "world" in this sense is a zone of things that surround the sentient being, which have various kinds of significance for that being.

On this view, life forms have worlds, and worlds have life forms: to destroy a life form, therefore, is to end ways of seeing and being in the world. There are, however, serious questions about whether there is such a thing as "world," and whether world-making ("worlding") provides a sufficient reason for respecting life forms. Is it ethically powerful and politically efficient to say that ideas about nature are instances of "worlding"—they construct worlds for living in, and so we should not tamper with them? There was a "world" of witch-ducking stools. Nazi ideas constituted a "world." If the "worlding" argument is valid, we should perhaps have allowed the Nazis to have their world and not intervened in the Holocaust.

A further problem arises concerning the number of worlds: Are there as many worlds as there are individual life forms? Or species of life forms? And do these worlds overlap, in which case, does the overlapping itself constitute a larger world, in which all the worlds coexist? Sensing the danger, some philosophers try a different word, such as "surround," that does not perhaps convey the same depth and significance as "world."[2] In doing so, they tacitly acknowledge that "world" is an aesthetic construct—it's more compelling than it is real. For there is a more fundamental problem with worlds: they do not exist. It is ecological thinking itself that implies that there is no world. The system of life forms is open-ended and infinite. Since there is no such thing as "species" (just read Darwin), the life/nonlife distinction is untenable; thus there had to be a pre-living "life," as the biologist Sol Spiegelman showed.[3] Since all life forms coexist (symbiosis, explored by Lynn Margulis), we cannot draw a line around them, a horizon, and construct a "within" (where life lives) and a "without" (where it doesn't).[4] Where do you stop? The biosphere? The earth's gravitational field? The sun? The solar system? Life forms are connected in a mesh without a center or an edge. There is no way to achieve the appropriate distance from which to observe anything like a world. The ecological mesh makes Heidegger's proclamation that "the human being is a creature of distance!" problematic at best.[5]

What happens when you think ecology without a "world"? It seems paradoxical that the infinite mesh of life forms is both real and not solid. But the paradox is only the result of thinking nature as a "thing" that is "over there"—even when we upgrade that "thing" to be a squishy "surround" that immerses us. (There's something of the language of the virtual-reality couch potato in this talk of surrounds, invoking the distance from which ecological thinking struggles to escape.) Since thinking ecologically abolishes distance, what remains is intimacy with all life forms. This is the (not so bad) alternative to the language of worlds. Thinking ecology without worlds (singular and plural) means thinking coexistence and intimacy in constant flux.

It gets worse (or better). If there is no world, there can be no ontology as such. Ecology confronts us with a pre-ontological level of "existence" (I use this word knowing that we are dealing with an attenuated version), which is coexistence. Some of the implications disturb "environmentalist" ideology: we are not living in a "world"; there is no nature; holism is untenable; personhood is a form of artificial intelligence; life forms are queer down to the genomic level; and so on.[6] Thinking coexistence, coexistence as thinking, force these counterintuitive conclusions on us.

In this essay, the anti-ontological philosopher Emmanuel Levinas shall help steer us through these paradoxical ideas. Heidegger is the principal philosopher of world and "worlding." Levinas's project was not to ignore Heidegger, but to try to go underneath him, "below" ontology and "worlding"— in particular because he sensed strongly the political threat that lurks there. It's Levinas who allows us to think our coexistence not as a world, but as a disturbing proximity between strangers, for whom I, in the core of my existence, am formally responsible, even when they cause me harm. This opens a way of thinking ecological ethics without a world. Wouldn't this be helpful in an era of climate catastrophe, in which our "normal" world is melting, and furthermore, our ideas of what a world is are also melting?

What can art do to help us achieve this opening? Does reading a poem have anything to do with ecology? Think of a Rorschach blot: as well as looking like a cloud or a person, it is just a meaningless stain. Aside from content and form, texts are blobs of others' enjoyment, literally—they are made of ink—and less literally, but fantasy is part of reality. Reading is co-existence. To read a poem is a nonviolent political act of appreciation, with no particular reason, of another's enjoyment, which, transcending mere toleration, may involve disturbing encounters with enjoyment. Samuel Taylor Coleridge's "The Rime of the Ancient Mariner" (1798, 1817) is about reading as coexistence beyond toleration. This poem, about a story that someone "cannot choose but hear," forces us to coexist with coexistence itself.[7]

Coleridge's poem and Levinas's philosophy face up to horror—a visceral reaction to the proximity of "inhuman" matter. This "facing" has an aspect that some would call spiritual: it goes beyond what we often imagine to be aesthetic and ethical ways of responding to things, because it isn't pretty or sublime, and because it isn't an action in a narrow sense. Levinas, a profoundly Jewish writer, mirrors Coleridge's profound theism—Coleridge could have become a Unitarian minister. The encounter with the "other" which ecology forces us to acknowledge does have a dimension that some have called spiritual or religious. Even if you are a materialist, you should not be afraid to explore this dimension: it contains reserves of materiality and sensuality not yet embodied in social forms. Marxism's big complaint is not that modern life is too materialistic, but that it is not nearly pleasurable enough. Could religious language, which as Georges Bataille says, often substitutes for kinds of intimacy that we don't fully acknowledge, help us to think materialism in a more profound way?[8]

Now the problem is that Levinas, like many Continental philosophers, proudly cleaved to differences between humans and animals. Much Continental thinking assumes no continuity between humans and animals, adopting a haughty "everyone knows that" tone, and saying that thinking otherwise is "asinane" (worse than asinine—and worse because we're behaving like donkeys).[9] This is the language of condescending exclusivity. Some are proud to "refuse to accept the theory of evolution," which to a biologist sounds like someone refusing to accept that the earth is round.[10] Even creationists take evolution more seriously than that.

It seems counterintuitive to ask Levinas to help us steer toward new directions in ecological criticism. But is this really the case? Levinas grounded his ethics in a nonontological, literal proximity of the other, which he calls "the face." Now this face isn't a literal face, but it often seems as if Levinas is thinking of coexistence and proximity as a (human) face; metaphors are not just decoration, particularly for a writer who argues in an intuitive, experiential manner. In places, Levinas concedes that nonhumans such as snakes may also have a "face"—doesn't this concession cut two ways?[11] It allows other beings to have faces. Yet doesn't it also say, in effect, "Yes, there is a face, a human face with nose, eyes, mouth, and so on."

Would Levinas allow coral to have a face? How about bacteria? How about viruses? If we are going to use Levinas, we must address these questions. Coleridge's poem explores these very issues, which boil down to the fact that we coexist, symbiotically, with life forms inside and outside our bodies (if "our" and even "body" mean anything in this context). So this essay will be difficult, because it demonstrates not only the value of reading Coleridge via Levinas, but also the value of reading Levinas via Coleridge.

Our poem is about the face, the nonhuman face, and also the inhuman face. The ancient Mariner encounters a nonhuman other in the face of the albatross. And he encounters an inhuman face in the leprosy-like whiteness of Life-in-Death. Debbie Lee has convincingly shown that while writing "The Rime of the Ancient Mariner," Coleridge was thinking about the yellow fever virus, which turns the flesh to brown ("I fear thee ancient Mariner! . . . And thy skinny hand, so brown," 4.224–29).[12] Significantly, leprosy is indeed a virus that eats the literal face away. Coleridge works with a notion of "face" that goes beyond eyes, nose, and bilateral symmetry.

Don't shoot albatrosses! Is this really Coleridge's moral? Senseless violence against animals is wrong—so sensible violence against them is justifiable? After editorializing about "All things both great and small" (7.615), the Mariner leaves the Wedding Guest "as if he had been stunned, / And is of sense forlorn" (7.622–23). Is that the reaction we expect from so trite a sentiment? Even by the late eighteenth century it was trite. Traditional readings of the shooting of the albatross are about disrupting a natural continuum. Why is this any worse than, say, shooting a turkey for Thanksgiving?[13] Coleridge sketches out a radical democracy beyond the politics of pity, whose pith is the necessarily traumatic encounter between strangers, or as I call them, *strange strangers*—the ultimate strangers, whose strangeness is irreducible, translating Derrida's *arrivant*.[14] The *arrivant* is a hypothetical visitor whose arrival cannot be predicted or accounted for. One of these is the albatross itself; another is the Mariner; another the Wedding Guest; Life-in-Death; and several million water snakes. Coleridge stages the traumatic encounter with the strange stranger, who emerges from, and constitutes, the environment.

Consider the existential "thereness," the Levinasian *il y a* of the Mariner himself, Life-in-Death, and the snakes surrounding the dead ship at the dead center of the poem. For Levinas, intransitive language about environmental processes reveals something about existence. When we say, "It is raining," what is the "it" that is raining? Levinas concludes that the "it" is existence as such, which we experience as a disturbing environmental presence.[15] Coleridge moves this presence from the background to frontal foreground. It is the inert density of the albatross, not the fact that it is a cute creature, great or small, which disturbs. We cannot establish who or what the strange stranger is, or even whether they are a "who" or a "what." Isn't this presence of the stranger the dark gift of global warming? The environment as such has vanished; in its place is a disturbing presence manifesting as distinct, unique, suffering beings.

What Levinas says about the stranger—that we are "passive with regard to it"[16]—was what Coleridge's friend Wordsworth disliked about the Mariner. But it's what makes the Mariner the hero of a Levinasian tale. This essay's title comes from Levinas's *Existence and Existents*, which showed how existence is ambient—it enmeshes our being prior to any ontological notion such as "world" or "system." Levinas consistently uses striking environmental images for existence such as rustling, splashing, rumbling, buzzing, murmuring, or the enveloping darkness of night.[17]

Without a world, we have no concern with inclusion and exclusion, because there's no inside or outside. Thinking can thus take responsibility for all life forms. Heidegger excludes animals from the "worlding" club.[18] Only humans can have a world, while animals are "poor in world." Like many Continental philosophers, Heidegger asserts that there is a radical discontinuity between humans and animals. "Below" Heidegger, animals reappear in the more intimate form of the strange stranger, and it is at this level that Levinas meets Darwin.

Coexistence as Infinity

Let's begin exploring the twenty-four lines in which the Mariner discovers and shoots the albatross:

> The ice was here, the ice was there,
> The ice was all around:
> It cracked and growled, and roared and howled,
> Like noises in a swound!

> At length did cross an Albatross,
> Thorough the fog it came;
> As if it had been a Christian soul,
> We hailed it in God's name.

It ate the food it ne'er had eat,
And round and round it flew.
The ice did split with a thunder-fit;
The helmsman steered us through!

And a good south wind sprung up behind;
The Albatross did follow,
And every day, for food or play,
Came to the mariner's hollo!

In mist or cloud, on mast or shroud,
It perched for vespers nine;
Whiles all the night, through fog-smoke bright,
Glimmered the white moon-shine.

"God save thee, ancient Mariner!
From the fiends, that plague thee thus!—
Why look'st thou so?"—With my cross-bow
I shot the Albatross. (1.59–82)

The "here . . . there . . . all around" trope evokes the atmosphere, a zone of existence as such, Levinas's "splashing of the there is."[19] Global warming is like this. You can't have that neutral, easy conversation about the weather any more. Either it trails into silence, or slides toward the phrase "global warming"; then the conversation is practically over. There is no longer *weather*. There is *climate*—something we cannot see directly without tremendous computing power (terabytes of RAM). Coleridge puts his Mariner in the extreme, threatening ambience of ice: the "world" loses its bearings and looms forward. Then the fateful bird emerges "Thorough the fog" (1.64), the intense, oppressive atmosphere of sheer existence. The ice and fog imply coexistence, beyond the "world": something not "handy," not pertaining to a horizon of meaning (you can't see through the fog).

"Thorough" the fog (1.64) means right the way through it, to "this" side: not from some beyond "outside" the fog, but from within it, within existence itself. The fog stands for "very large finitude"—things that are profoundly hard to grasp on "this" side of reality. Abstract infinity is easier than, say, 4.5 billion years (earth's age), or global warming. Ecology presents us with this "very large finitude." Like Copernicus and Darwin, ecology humiliates us (brings us closer to earth). Now put a face on life forms. Assume they are people: this is infinity on this side of reality. Abstract void is easier than the void of another person. This personal void is the albatross, the face of the fog below "personification."

Now we are thinking like Levinas. "Thorough the fog it came"—re-

sembles "Out of the sea came he" (the sun [1.26]). The albatross is not far
away, then closer, then. . . . There is no smooth transition between the "very
large finitude" of the freezing fog, and the sudden presence of a sentient
being. While the sun is personified as "he" (1.64), the albatross is reified as
an "it," emphasizing the inertia of life forms. This gives "As if it had been a
Christian soul" a sense of fetishistic disavowal: "We knew very well that the
albatross wasn't a human soul; nevertheless, we acted as if it did have one."
Isn't this the beginning of the end for the punch line—that you should love
"All things both great and small" (7.615) because God made and loves them?
The sailors suspend their belief, their "lifeworld" (a good God made and
loves all creatures, in a paternalistic, safe fashion), and treat an "it" as
a "soul."

The sailors voice a radical form of nontheistic Christianity, taking seriously the idea that God died on the cross. The death of God and the death of
the theistic cultural lifeworld ("To walk together to the kirk, / And all
together pray" [7.605–6]—Coleridge's use of Scots dialect localizes the sentiment within a certain cultural horizon), with its comforting concentric
hierarchies (the "goodly company" of "Old men, and babes, and loving
friends" [7.604, 7.608]), explain why the Wedding Guest leaves the "bride-
groom's door" "like one that hath been stunned, / And is of sense forlorn"
(7.621–23), better than the editorializing injunction to love "all things"
(7.615).

The ancient Mariner causes the bottom to fall out of the Wedding
Guest's world. What makes the poem "ecological" is what makes it least
pantheist: its disturbing, relentless intimacy with the "it": Death and Life-in-
Death, with "slimy things" (4.238). This intimacy is on the way to love at its
extreme: out of "all things" in the Universe (7.615), I pick you. It already has
something "evil" about it, disrupting cozy lifeworlds. Far from pantheist
inclusiveness and holism, the welcome radically disturbs the "balance of
nature." To love another creature is a perverse choice, not "letting be" or
snuggling in a predetermined surrounding. Coleridge's albatross is the messianic, absolutely unexpected arrival, whose shadow falls into our world in
the disturbing proximity of strangers.

The albatross is the second disturbing "face" in the poem. The ancient
Mariner himself already ruptured the lifeworld. To the Wedding Guest, he
appears as an "it": "It is an ancient Mariner" (1.1). This phrase makes us
imagine that he is already there, as if some lines were missing: "Who on
earth is that? It is an ancient Mariner." This stranger has the disturbing
inertia of the Levinasian "there is," evoked by the night: "I pass, like night,
from land to land" says the Mariner, a walking poem (7.586). This walking
poem outlives and dominates the Mariner as flesh and blood, "wrenching"

him with "agony" (7.577–78), compelling him to speak. While the Mariner tacks on the sentiment that we live in a lifeworld that should not be disrupted, the "Mariner-poem" speaks a more disturbing truth. "Before" lifeworlds, "before" Being, there is intimacy with the strange stranger. The Judeo-Christian reading of this poem is by no means at odds with the most profoundly ecological one.

The infinity to which Levinas refers when he writes of the other (*autrui*) is not "beyond" reality, if by "beyond" we mean "outside." Levinas's view implies an ontologically incomplete universe where there is no neat nesting of parts in wholes. Rigorous materialism must take seriously the seemingly theological idea that infinity is "here." Burying our heads in the vulgar materialist sand, or the utilitarian environmentalist sand, won't work.

Hailing Frequencies

The sailors encounter the albatross: "We hailed it in God's name" (1.66), then the albatross "Came to the Mariners' hollo" (1.74). The sense of "hello" as a greeting was emerging while Coleridge was revising the poem.[20] The second edition of the *Oxford English Dictionary* puts it eloquently: "An exclamation to call attention; also expressing some degree of surprise, as on meeting any one unexpectedly." Levinasian ecology restores to this part of Coleridge's masterpiece the profoundly ambivalent gravity that marks the seemingly casual appearance of the albatross. It would be too easy to claim the bird stands for nature, or for supernature—unless by supernature we mean something like the toothpaste ads when they claim that there is "30 percent extra" in the tube: more existence than we bargained for.

Hello is bound up with the history of telephones. If you express surprise "on meeting any one unexpectedly," it's as if you are not yet conversing, but signaling that talking may or may not happen. *Hello* brings into language the proximity of an other, drawing attention to the medium in which the message is transmitted.[21] When you use it sarcastically, it's as if you are pointing out an imaginary communications breakdown, like knocking on a glass helmet.

"Hello" is a variant of "hallo," which derives from "hollo" (Coleridge's word), "hullo," "hillo," and "holla." "Hollo" dates back to the sixteenth century and is used either as "a call to excite attention, also a shout of encouragement or exultation" (*OED*, "hollo," A.int.), or as "a loud shout; esp. a cry in hunting" (B. n.). "Hey" and "hi" coincide with "hollo" to this extent.[22] The conventional way to read the albatross passage would be as a progressive degradation in communication. The bird is "hailed . . . in God's name"; then it "came to the Mariners' hollo" like a hunting dog; then, like a hunted bird, it's shot. The albatross descends from lofty, almost angelic being to hunted animal in a few verses: from "hail," to "hello," to "hi!" or even "oi!" (the 1936 variant). Heidegger would readily conclude that the telephonic *hello* had turned us away from Being, had turned us all into hunting dogs.

Even the "hunting dog" sense of "hollo" slides between a call to play, and a call to return to the master, unless play were always a simulation of hunting. Surely the bird comes "for food or play," not to retrieve other dead birds! It is no hawk. The sailors themselves are playing, pretending that the bird is a pet, like pretending that an ungainly golden retriever were a wolf. The albatross is not "domestic." But it's not hawk-wild, not majestic-wild: it's ungainly, disturbing, "abject-wild." This reflects a hesitation within the word "hello" itself, a hesitation that addresses the matter of strangeness. You can say "hello" in speaking to yourself—"hello, how curious"—as if wonder at an unexpected encounter (with an other) provoked a self-reflexive version of the sarcastic "hel-lo"—a gentler version. Or perhaps self-reflection noticed that an opening was already there, as if one had cut oneself. "Hello" is the sound of someone noticing a wound: a gentle wound, a "delightful 'lapse' of the ontological order" (Levinas).[23]

Then there is the tentative "hello?" that someone utters in a dark room, unsure whether anyone is there. It's like the echolocation of a bat or the sonar of a dolphin. This *hello* tests the medium of transmission itself, like a "ping" command to a URL when you're not sure the Internet is working. This *hello* says, "I am here" and, "This is here." Some bird cries are phatic in this sense. This hello is highly ambivalent, as if it meant, "Is this a medium?" or, "Is this thing on?" The ambivalence magically activates the realm of meaning. This illocutionary *hello* conjures something: "Is this on?" becomes "This is on!"

Hello is a minimal mark, an on switch. But doesn't the on switch imply the existence of an electrical circuit, a house, a shared existence? As if the darkness itself of the dark room, the Levinasian "night" of sheer existence, were already populated, already a communicative field, an electrical circuit. Space is already warped by language. As Levinas argues, the "third" is already in the other, waiting in the darkness, even when there's no one.[24] Coexistence subtends and subverts models of perfect communication. "Hello" implies a preexisting boundary between information and noise: an unspeakable coexistence.

Does this coexistence constitute a world? When you "hail" something "in God's name," are you welcoming a predictable being into an established domain? Is the bird an ambassador from God's realm, or are the sailors ambassadors for God, welcoming a foreigner to their "far countree" (7.518)? The ecological irony is that the sailors are in the albatross's hostile ecosystem. This welcome "in God's name" would thus be a colonial greeting to an indigenous person. The bird should beware, in that case. It is already as good as dead. Is the hailing already a hunting cry, summoning a predictable tool (living or inanimate) to a predictable place? As when a car mechanic you called arrives on the deserted highway? "Hello! Thank God you're here!"

For Heidegger, poetry is hailing (*Heil*—hel-lo!).[25] The curtain swishes back to reveal a world. There is a sheen of otherness, a shimmering of the veil as he puts it, in the theater of the Same. Hailing implies a lifeworld, a Norse one to boot. Like "life" and "world," "hail" has an Old English root. The verb "to hail" is a metonymy of the noun "hail," which means a mixture of "Health, safety, welfare. In northern ME. taking the place of the native Eng. hele, HEAL." The origin of the word is Old Norse, "heill health, prosperity, good luck."[26] "Heal" or "hele" is an amalgam of health, good fortune, spiritual well-being—there's an integrated world, a horizon of meaning, a mind-body manifold.

Perhaps the lifeworld already had some tatters in it by the time *hail* acquired its nautical sense (1546), the sense we use when we hail a taxi.[27] We are detecting a proto-telephonic register—a calling or summoning from afar. Ironically, when Heidegger says that poetry makes the absence of things present, brings the farness of things near, is he not nudging *hele* and hail and health toward their modern, telephonic senses?[28] However much the ambassadors have prepared to receive their guest, there is always a trace of radical uncertainty, effaced in the pomp and circumstance of welcome, yet all the more visible in its effacement. Thus "in God's name" strives to efface this uncertainty, to underwrite the encounter with God's name. It enfolds the albatross within a theistic symbolic order, functioning like the police officer's "Allo, allo, allo!"—an expression of feigned surprise. Something fishy is going on in the ice.

This deep ambivalence affects "As if it had been a Christian soul." It is as if the sailors can't tell, or don't want to tell, whether the bird is an emissary from God, or actually is God. For there is yet another *hello*—the abject *hello*, said when we see someone who's already there, whom we do not like, or who does not like us: "Oh, it's you." Isn't there something like this in "It is an ancient Mariner" (1.1)? Even though we don't technically like or dislike him yet, his presence disgusts and disturbs us. Surely this is not the hello the sailors want to say. But it haunts their greeting all the same. The abject hello is the underside of reverence, the dark side of hailing.

We are embarrassed by the fact that the strange stranger is already there, in the most intimate possible sense, for existence is coexistence. The strange stranger is not an integrated being greeting another integrated being in a more or less well-established medium. *Hello* contains a trace of an awkwardness, even hostility, which it struggles to edit out.[29] The *hello* of automated customer service contains this trace in its very smoothness. The sailors' joy and relief has an exorbitant element. The albatross eats their biscuit worms, shares their ship, seems to guide them through the ice. As Kate Rigby argues, their unbearable dependency on it is precisely what provokes the shooting.[30] Aware of their humiliation (the bird sees it, even plays along with it), they kill what they welcomed with relief.

What Western cultures reify as nature, Indigenous cultures view as a shifting, shifty being who cannot be pinned down. The trickster flies, on ponderous wings, into Coleridge's poem. The albatross appears to come from a beyond, but who knows? Do the sailors know? Is there not some recognition that the appearance of the bird and the sailors' joy close off the beyond forever? The albatross does not hail from a beyond that bestows meaning on a world bounded by a horizon. It appears abruptly on this side of a radically incomplete universe, too close for comfort. At the end of part 2, when the "death-fires danced at night" in a sickening reel ("About, about, in reel and rout" [2.127]), the bird is hung from the ancient Mariner's neck. There is a phantasmagorical increase of the play and fantasy that seemed innocent in the sailors' play with the albatross. It worsens in part 3, when Death and Life-in-Death are playing for possession of the crew ("casting dice" [3.196]). The face of Life-in-Death is defaced, a zero-level face that is horrifying and dissimulating at once ("as white as leprosy" [3.192]). Life-in-Death is an apt way of describing life without concepts of nature and world. Is a virus like leprosy alive or not? Is life as such in fact a form of undeath—a zombie-like persistence? This undeath is imagined as the water snakes of part 4—squirming, horrifyingly "there," and the zombified sailors of part 5.

The trite connotation of the albatross is of a karmic weight around your neck. This weight is detachable from the poem, as if this part of the poem were itself the albatross of the poem. Doesn't the trite meaning capture something profoundly true? We are witnessing gravity—matter pinning us to this side of reality. Fog and mist horrifically abolish the background. Suddenly everything is foreground. The lifeworld goes up in smoke. The apocalyptic curtain is drawn around the beyond. The albatross comes out from behind the curtain of mist, from out of its endless folds—we have no idea from how far (or near). In this anti-Wagnerian art, you see the curtain wafting around, you see that it enfolds not a world, not a horizon or a beyond, but a creepy nothingness. This is the meaningless contingency in the face of which the sailors desperately try to rig up superstitious meanings.

Mystery dissolves, yet infinity appears on this side of things. What if environmental ideologies were not part of the solution but part of the problem—what if they were cunning obstacles to coexistence? A Levinasian reading of Coleridge suggests that there is more on earth than has been dreamt in the environmental philosophy of world and "worlding." At this moment of peril, as we lose our grounding and the actual ground beneath our feet, it might be salutary to reflect on why we keep wanting to be somewhere or sometime else: wishes that some environmental writing strives to fulfill.

All destructive projects might be summed up in Heidegger's axiom, "The human being is a creature of distance!" What happens when distance collapses, when we know that what happens anywhere on earth affects what happens everywhere else? Should we replace the dream of distance with another dream, say of embeddedness or world? Knowing what we know, we would only dream in bad faith, a little island in the nightmare of our ecological history from which we're struggling to awaken. How do we live awake on this side of reality, so easy to negate with apocalypticisms that assume environmental forms such as the revenge of Gaia?[31] Green Schadenfreude finds it too easy to imagine human extinction—that'll teach those Cartesians! They'll be laughing on the other side of their face when they're dead! Is this why we write ecological criticism? Aren't we just like the sailors, humiliated when our dreams (of nature) are disturbed, wishing not for a genuine coexistence with other beings, but for a return to sleep, to green dreams?

NOTES

1. See for example Mazis, *Humans, Animals, Machines*, 24–32, 44–48.

2. Ibid., 186–91 and passim.

3. Dawkins, *The Ancestor's Tale*, 582–94.

4. Margulis, *Symbiosis*; Margulis and Sagan, *Microcosmos*.

5. Heidegger, "Supplement," 221.

6. See Morton, *The Ecological Thought*, chap. 2.

7. Coleridge, "The Rime of the Ancient Mariner," in *Coleridge's Poetry and Prose*, hereafter cited parenthetically.

8. Bataille, *Religion*, 52.

9. Derrida uses the term "continuism" in *The Animal That Therefore I Am*, 30. The assumption that Derrida always knows what he is talking about is not Derridean. Derrida is also responsible for "asinane" (18, 31). He finds himself in company with Ferry, "Neither Man nor Stone," in Atterton and Calarco, *Animal Philosophy*, 155. For a different view, see Fernández-Armesto, *So You Think You're Human?* 37.

10. Atterton, "Ethical Cynicism," in Atterton and Calarco, *Animal Philosophy*, 61. Incredibly, Gilles Deleuze and Félix Guattari assert that they are beyond evolution, proposing the codevelopment of all beings in "alliance." Contrary to what they claim, symbiosis, far from being the opposite of evolution, is deeply entrenched in it ("Becoming-Animal," in Atterton and Calarco, *Animal Philosophy*, 88).

11. Quoted in Atterton, "Ethical Cynicism," in Atterton and Calarco, *Animal Philosophy*, 58.

12. Debbie Lee, "Yellow Fever and the Slave Trade."

13. Thanks to Ashton Nichols for suggesting this to me.

14. Derrida, "Hostipitality," 356–420.

15. For further discussion, see Levinas, *Existence and Existents*, 45–60.

16. Levinas, *Otherwise Than Being*, xxiii.

17. Levinas, *Existence and Existents*, 45–60.

18. Heidegger, "The Origin of the Work of Art," 45.

19. Levinas, *Otherwise Than Being*, 140.

20. *OED*, "hello," A.int.1.

21. See Morton, *Ecology without Nature*, 36–39.

22. Compare "hey," as in *The Tempest*, when Prospero and Ariel pretend to be commanding hunting dogs—"Hey, Mountain, hey!" (4.1.255).

23. Levinas, *Totality and Infinity*, 150.

24. Levinas, *Otherwise Than Being*, 99–129.

25. Heidegger, "Language," 198–99.

26. *OED*, "hail," n.2.1.

27. Ibid., "hail," v.2.3, 4, and 4b—c.f. "where do you hail from?"

28. See Ronell, *The Telephone Book*.

29. Derrida, "Hostipitality."

30. Rigby, *Topographies of the Sacred*, 205.

31. I am thinking of Lovelock, *The Revenge of Gaia*.

The Matter of Texts: A Material Intertextuality and Ecocritical Engagements with the Bible

Preserved in the British Library, the fourth-century CE *Codex Sinaiticus* and the fifth-century CE *Codex Alexandrinus* recall both a colonial history of appropriation and custodianship of ancient artifacts, and a long tradition of production and reproduction of Bibles. Along with *Codex Vaticanus* and major papyri, these codices provide key witnesses for the authenticity and authority of particular textual variants in the Greek New Testament. By their material difference from contemporary mass-produced Bibles, they also remind me of the materiality of the text.

Very early, Christian usage moved from papyrus scrolls, to papyrus codices, to the codex manufactured from parchment. Thomas Pattie writes:

> The production of a large fine book on parchment required several hundred animal skins. A gathering of eight folios became the norm as one animal skin produced one gathering of eight folios of an average sized book. . . . There would be 32 gatherings of eight in a book of 256 average-sized folios, that is, 32 sheep. An average book has many flaws in the parchment when wounds in the skin have expanded when the skin was stretched. Even a fine manuscript like Vaticanus has many flaws of this nature, including a significant number in the text area, that force the scribe to write around the holes. Sinaiticus has many fewer flaws and most were repaired before the text was inscribed. Its pages are very large: even after trimming they measure 380 × 340mm, and before trimming perhaps 400 × 360mm. A sheet of two folios would then have measured 400 × 720mm, and one sheep, smaller than modern domestic sheep, might have produced enough parchment for only one sheet, taking into account the need to trim off the imperfections at the edges. In that case Sinaiticus, which seems originally to have had 730 folios, would require the perfect skins of 365 sheep or goats. The labour involved in the scraping, washing, stretching, and polishing would have been substantial.[1]

Pattie notes, moreover, that in 331 CE, in the wake of the Bible burnings of previous persecutions, "the Emperor Constantine wrote to Eusebius, Bishop of
Caesarea, ordering fifty parchment Bibles written by skilled calligraphers for
his new foundations in Constantinople."[2] Three important points emerge.
First, the more-than-human others who give themselves, through plant, skin,
or labor, to the production and reproduction of the text influence the way in
which the text presents itself to be read (for example, through an interruption
of script by holes in the skin). Second, the lives and deaths of more-than-
human others are given *to* or *at the command of* members of the ruling elite.
Third, these same lives and deaths are given *for* a sacred purpose. Human
social relations and their more-than-human contexts form a complex understory for the production, transmission, and preservation of Bibles. If we were
to read the written text of a Bible (either in the mode of scholarly criticism or
prayer), how would our reading account for, or open itself to, the myriad
more-than-human others whose lives, labors, and deaths form an understory
for the text? I draw on Julia Kristeva's *Revolution in Poetic Language* to suggest a
framework for engaging ecocritically with the materiality of biblical texts.

The Material Given

Papyrus grows in the swamps of Egypt and in the sluggish waters of the Nile
where they have overflowed and form stagnant pools. . . . Paper is manufactured
from papyrus by splitting it with a needle into strips that are very thin but as long
as possible. The quality of the papyrus is best at the centre of the plant and
decreases progressively towards the outsides. The first quality used to be called
"hieratic" paper and in early times was devoted solely to books connected with
religion, but to flatter the emperor, was given the name "Augustus"; the second
quality was called "Livia" after his wife, and so the term hieratic was relegated to
the third category.—Pliny the Elder, *Natural History*

Underlying my concern with the Bible as material artifact is the notion of
the "material given," a term referring to the givenness of material phenomena.[3] Earth, bodies, and pregnant bodies are paradigms of a material
givenness that is necessary to produce and sustain human species-life. This
necessity has the character of (1) a gift that cannot be defined wholly in
terms of exchange, property, or what is proper; and (2) a space, like the body
in pregnancy, in which self and other are interconnected. Both human sociality (hereafter, the social) and a wider more-than-human sociality (hereafter, sociality) are aspects of the material given.

The Bible has a relation of dependence on, and indebtedness to, the
material given. Because Bibles are material artifacts of certain human cultures, the Bible is plural. Not only is there a variety of canonical collections

which are called Bibles (e.g., the Hebrew Bible, the Roman Catholic Bible), but any one of these collections is a site of interconnectedness between plants, minerals, fossils; habitats and climates; bodies, breath, languages; oral and written traditions; societies and their stories; and the convergences and dissonances among these. Moreover, since the production, reproduction, and transmission of Bibles require plants, animals and human labor, and since biblical texts have been interpreted to support both destruction of, and care for, earth, the Bible affects the unfolding of the material given over time.

Only partially at best, and somewhat impossibly, do notions of matter and materiality relate to the underlying "stuff" to which the concept of the material given points, but which language cannot contain. Recalling metaphysical concepts of substance and Marxist concepts of commodity, the terms "matter" and "materiality" are unstable.[4] The relation between language and the material given is uncertain. Since the pregnant body offers one paradigm for the material given, this uncertainty resonates with Kristeva's consideration of the unsettling relationship between the maternal body, language, and texts. To explore this relation, two further concepts—embeddedness and embodiment—require comment.

Embeddedness refers to human interdependence with, and rootedness in, the sociality of earth. An underlying interrelatedness of self and other unsettles the notion of individual separate selves. Embodiment is the mode of human embeddedness in this sociality. Initially for the child, the pregnant body mediates sociality, so that the sociality of the pregnant body is already more-than-human. From the interconnectedness of self and other in the pregnant body, child and mother are born separate from one another. The child enters a more-than-human world which for a time remains largely the world of the maternal body (and this term needs to be understood more broadly than the body of the birth mother, as that which stands in relation to the infant as maternal).

Language and the Maternal Body

Bible paper, as the name implies, was developed for lightweight, thin, strong, opaque sheets for such books as bibles, dictionaries, and encyclopaedias. Bible papers are pigmented (loaded) with such pigments as titanium dioxide and barium sulfate and contain long fibres and artificial bonding agents to maintain strength.—"Bible paper," *Encyclopaedia Britannica*

Kristeva's consideration of the relationship between the semiotic and the symbolic is useful for my exploration of the relation between the maternal, language, texts, and the material given. Several key terms appear as central to this consideration: the speaking subject, the semiotic and the symbolic, the thetic phase, and mimesis. For Kristeva, the emergence of the speaking subject occurs as a separation from the maternal body. First, through language the child separates from the mother, so that even pregrammatical language parts "an object from the subject," self from other, where the mother is the paradigmatic other. Second, the connection with the maternal body (and hence also the other more generally) remains a trace in, and space for, language.[5]

The semiotic and the symbolic describe "two modalities" of the signifying process. Language does not exist as an abstraction separate from its human users; rather the semiotic and symbolic functions of the signifying process represent two aspects of the subject her- or himself. The subject is constituted through language, initially through the dynamic of connection with, and separation from, the maternal body. Within this broad framework, the semiotic describes the language of desire, eros, the body, and drives, associated in psychoanalytic terms with the prelinguistic, infant stage. The symbolic describes socially significant language that presupposes reason, logic, and the possibility of unified, singular communication.[6]

Kristeva uses the term *chora* to describe the semiotic modality. The semiotic *chora* is presymbolic. Here signification does not rely on the absence of an object. The maternal body orders the *chora*, which is analogous to the rhythms of movement and voice. Through the mother's management of her response to the child, the maternal body represents the regulation of social relations for the child. Maternal regulation precedes and informs "the law of the father," and, for this reason, the semiotic both supports the symbolic order and is an essential element in it.[7]

At the threshold of the realms of the semiotic and the symbolic is the thetic phase, which entails a break that enables the process of signification. This break (between subject and object; signifier and signified) occurs through two transitional moments in the relation between child and mother: (1) a moment of identification and difference, denoted as the "imaginary mirror stage"; and (2) a moment of desire and its (non)fulfilment, denoted as the "symbolic castration complex."[8] In the thetic phase, the child recognizes both that the other is other and that the child's interactions with others are socially regulated. Through this recognition, the child experiences a lack that returns as "the space of language, sociality and identity."[9] Moreover, the lack "implies that the child is fundamentally social: it needs the other for its survival."[10]

As paradigm of that necessary to the child's survival, the maternal body can stand for the material givenness of (more-than-human) sociality. This appeal to the maternal is not an essentialist overvaluation of the mother.

Rather, always in a relation of tension with the symbolic order, the maternal body is an instance of the *subject in process* (or *on trial*), where the other is interimplicated with the self.[11] Any ethics, ecological or otherwise—and I take ecocriticism to be an expression of an ecological ethics—needs to be articulated based on an interrelationship of self and other, which unsettles the self and the social even as it constitutes them.

Kristeva's work is pertinent, therefore, for a critical affirmation of human interrelationship in this sociality, precisely where her work announces as central to the processes of signification: (1) the continuity and difference between self and other; and (2) the gap between desire and gratification (and an attendant unsettling of an imaginary of human agency as control of the other, particularly the other-than-human). While the focus on castration suggests a founding violence in signification, problematic from both feminist and ecological perspectives, Kristeva's analysis of signification describes a patriarchal social economy and its accompanying imaginary (or worldview).[12] She offers one understanding of this imaginary's simultaneous resilience and instability.

This interplay of resilience and instability echoes across the boundary between the symbolic and the semiotic. By an invocation of language open to the semiotic and tending toward an imitation of its object, *mimesis* can transgress the thetic break from the *chora*. Mimesis is less a construction of, than a verisimilar approach to, the other. While affirming that the unifying and structuring character of the symbolic is necessary for a text to be a signifying practice, Kristeva signals the transgression of the thetic through poetic language, especially when it departs from grammatical construction. The language of biblical narration also has this transgressive capacity.[13]

Intertextuality

When a great crowd gathered and people from town after town came to him, he said in a parable: "A sower went out to sow his seed; and as he sowed, some fell on the path and was trampled on, and the birds of the air ate it up. Some fell on the rock; and as it grew up, it withered for lack of moisture. Some fell among thorns, and the thorns grew with it and choked it. Some fell into good soil, and when it grew, it produced a hundredfold." As he said this, he called out, "Let anyone with ears to hear listen!" . . . "Now the parable is this: The seed is the word of God."—Luke 8:4–8, 11 (NSRV)

The Bible is the best-selling and the most widely distributed book with 50 million copies sold annually and translations in over 2,200 languages and dialects.—*Faiths and Environment: World Bank Support 2000–05*

The thetic break from the *chora* necessary for signification is dynamic. A position occurs when previous positions are unsettled by a semiotic trace in the articulation of those positions. For example, a new signifying system, such as a novel, appears as a passage from one or more signifying systems. "The term inter-textuality," writes Kristeva, "denotes this transposition of one (or several) sign systems into another."[14] Transposition (hence, inter-textuality) characterizes any signifying practice.

Working with the textual multiplicity evoked in the concept of inter-textuality, four typical usages emerge in biblical interpretation:

1. The least subtle usage, which Kristeva describes as "banal," understands intertextuality as the "study of sources," identifying explicit and implicit traces of other texts within a particular text.[15]

2. A far more subtle usage focuses on the multivocality of the text, in particular tracing underlying sociocultural and communal voices that inform the text.[16]

3. A further usage notices the function of the repressed in the text, and the way in which the forgotten returns as an otherness not wholly suppressed in the text or later interpretations.[17]

4. Sometimes, intertextuality represents a mode of reading performance between later texts—such as literary works, visual arts, film, and multimedia—and biblical ones. The focus is less on the influence of the Bible on these works than on a mode of reading that intervenes deconstructively (and perhaps reconstructively) in the inter-influence between texts.[18]

While useful, the first mode remains largely in the frame of the symbolic. Reading Luke's parable of the sower, for example, I note several genres: a parable, a dialogue within the narrative, a saying, a quotation from Isaiah, and an allegorical interpretation.[19] These shifts of genre suggest a variety of oral and written sources behind Luke 8:4–15, including, as most biblical scholars maintain, the version found in the Gospel of Mark (4:1–20). A problem arises when one describes this mode of interpretation as intertextual, because it misses, and may be counter to, the focus of intertextuality on "the anonymous codes, the ruptures and registers of language itself, as it speaks through the text."[20]

The second mode indicates a wider view of the textual encoding of the sociality of self and other for which the maternal stands. One aspect of this encoding is the relationship between oral and written traditions. Where memory and forms of expression conducive to remembrance (for example, repetition) mark orality, literacy gives rise to greater possibilities of abstract thought.[21] In a literate culture, the development of speech in the child occurs within a subculture of orality shaped by writing. Within those same cultures, preceding oral cultures inform written texts. For an ancient text, such as the Bible, traces of orality cannot be discounted; they represent points of connection with the myriad layers of the social underlying the text.

For example, at least four ancient versions of the parable of the sower appear, one in each of the three canonical synoptic gospels (Matt. 13:1–23; Mark 4:1–20; Luke 8:4–15), another in the apocryphal Gospel of Thomas. The last has a version of the parable only, without the accompanying interpretation. Although form criticism might suggest a single oral tradition behind the parable, as Werner Kelber notes: "oral performance enacts multiple original speech acts, a situation that suggests a culture of speech quite different from that represented by the one, original form."[22] The emphasis on hearing—in the soundscape of the parable, where rhythm and repetition work on the ear (esp. 8:4); the appeal to hearing at its close (8:8); and the allegory (8:12–15)—resonates with a culture of oral performance, where even reading to oneself entailed reading aloud.[23] Such attention becomes particularly pertinent when biblical texts, as written documents, are introduced in primarily oral cultures, such as Australian Aboriginal and Torres Strait Islander ones. As Anne Pattel-Gray explains, Aboriginal exegesis, focused on interpreting the land, encounters in biblical exegesis practices often problematic for both people and land.[24]

In different ways, the first and second approaches suggest an intertextual multiplicity—by way of sources, voices, genres, and reading contexts—to some extent recoverable in reading. The third approach takes a different turn. While the first and second do not rule out the uncanny, the third orients itself toward it. Just as Kristeva suggests that certain forms of writing, for example, the poetry of Mallarmé and the novels of Joyce, are particularly expressive of the semiotic, biblical scholars allude to a quality of strangeness in the genre of parable.[25] C. H. Dodd, for example, defines the parable as "a metaphor or simile drawn from nature or common life arresting the hearer by its vividness or strangeness, leaving the mind in sufficient doubt about its precise application to tease it into active thought."[26] For Stephen Curkpatrick, a parable's strangeness becomes apparent in its kerygmatic framing, that is, its framing within the theology of the narrative as a proclamation (kerygma) of good news (gospel). The otherness of the parable appears in its very familiar details, suggesting the ambiguity of lived experience. But since this parabolic ambivalence resists theological interpretation, a "dissonance" may occur "between any particular parable and its frame."[27]

While the gospel frame for a parable may serve to fix meaning, framing can also open the parabolic world to the ingress of the other. For example, although an allegorical interpretation (8:11–15) focusing meaning in obedience to the word accompanies the parable of the sower (8:4–8), the same allegory stands in, and shapes, the theological imaginary of the Lukan gospel. Here, the metonymy ear/heart/earth crosses with the maternal body to open a wider field of meaning. Especially in the figure of Mary of Nazareth, the Lukan maternal is both paradigm for and in tension with an imaginary of obedience to the word, employing a metonymy—ear/heart/earth/womb—that is also metaphor (2:19, 51; 8:21; 11:27–28).

The agricultural imagery of seeding and the governing metaphor for the interpretation of the parable—"the seed is the word of God" (8:11)—are part of a dense patriarchal imaginary that in an ancient Mediterranean context links plant seed with human seed; field with womb; earth with woman. While alliteration may be neither common nor particularly significant in Greek poetry, the alliterative rhythm Luke brings to the opening of the parable unites sower (*speiron*), sowing (*speirai*), and seed (*sporon*) (8:5; cf. Mark 4:4; Matt. 13:3). Where both Mark and Matthew begin explicitly with a command, "Listen," the opening repetition and rhythm of Luke's version engages its hearer. Rhythm interweaves with imagery to suggest the more-than-human labor expressed in seeder/seeding/seed. The tension between the contingencies incumbent on and, the purpose of, an agricultural practice of broadcast seeding resonates in the repetition of *kata* in verses 5 and 6, a further divergence from Mark and Matthew, each of whom uses the prefix only once in the parallel verses.[28] The prefix *kata* refers to downward motion and destruction: *katepatethe* comes from *katapateo*, to "tread upon" or "trample"; *katephagen* from *katesthio*, to "consume, devour, swallow"; *katepesen* from *katapipto*, to "fall (down)."[29] The destructive resonances in the seed's downward motion reinforce the failure of full fruition. The prefix returns in 8:15, with *katechousin*, from *katecho* to "hold back" or "down," "hinder" or "suppress," but also "hold fast," "keep in . . . memory," "retain," signifying descent toward a holding that is fruitful.[30]

The allegory moves from a focus on the word (8:11) to those who hear it (8:12–15). The word (*logos*) appears in nominative (8:11) then accusative (8:12, 13, 15) forms. A survey of Luke's Gospel suggests that in the nominative the "word" has authority and power (4:32, 36), going about much (*dierchomai* [5:15]) and going out (*exerchomai* [7:17]) in the *whole* of Judaea and *all* the surrounding area. In the accusative, the "word" is the object of hearing (5:1; 8:12, 13, 15, 21; 10:39; 11:28), associated with keeping and doing (8:21, 11:28). The ear/heart/earth is locus of receptivity to the word/seed, whose seeder may be God or Jesus. By the time we get to John's Gospel, the word/seed is the word become flesh in Jesus (John 1:1–18). An interrelatedness between seed, word, earth, and embodiment suggests the interimplication of *an androcentric worldview*, in which the seed is *his* (8:5), and *a semiotics of receptivity*, that is not simply a passive reinscription of a woman/

nature subordination to the agency of the male seed/word. Through its rhythms, alliteration, and repetition, especially around *acouo* (to hear), Luke 8:4–15 invites the reader to hear differently, as if the body is a "sonorous cavity" for a scripture that arrives as parable. How might we hear differently?[31]

The fourth mode appears in this essay in the interrupting descriptions of ancient papyrus manufacture and contemporary issues around the making of Bible paper. One way of reading these interruptions may be to understand the prevalence of Bibles over two millennia (and their seeming increase in this era of celebrated post-Christendom) as an exemplar of, or evidence for, the wide and imprecise dissemination of the seed/word, to whose ecological effects we need turn. In what ways can we understand the matter of the text to be at play in ecocritical biblical studies accountable for these effects?

The Matter of the Text and a Material Intertextuality

The complexity of the paper issue means that firm conclusions are hard to draw. All paper manufacture causes harm to the environment and more often than not the determining factors in a paper mill's environmental performance are not the process, paper type or fibre source but the location, mill practice and mill operator.
—Friends of the Earth briefing sheet

When considering biblical texts, scholars usually refer to the interplay of author, text, and reader, aware of the different social and cultural contexts of all three. Taking shape in relation to specific readers/hearers, the text relies on, but is other than, the material artifact in which particular words, spaces, punctuation, and structure present themselves to reading. For a biblical passage, myriad such material artifacts, versions, translations, and readings exist. The transferability of a passage to a variety of material media and reading contexts over many centuries gives priority to its words rather than the matter supporting them. Indeed, the priority of the word all but effaces the material medium that supports it.

Although effectively invisible in most contemporary biblical studies, the material medium of a passage is not without effect. While a survey of ways different media affect readings is beyond the scope of this essay, one may wonder what styles of interpretation seem most compatible, for example, with a parchment codex such as those produced at the order of Constantine as Christianity became the religion of empire. In what ways were the lives and labors of animals and humans reflected in interpreters' effacement, or otherwise, of the agency of animal and slave characters in biblical narratives? How different were the readings of these characters when Bibles were produced with illuminations of plants and animals and human scribes twining through and around the pages? With the advent of printing and then after the Industrial Revolution the mass production of standardized Bibles in Hebrew, Greek, and in translation, to what extent did the thin pages of modern Bibles influence interpretation of a scriptural world thinned of its material context?

In the second and third century CE, the codex form of the book came to prominence in Christianity before it was popular in the ancient Mediterranean. A Christian preference for the codex suggests a theological purpose and the early linking of texts in codices moves in the direction of canon. Moreover, both this early preference and the adoption of Christianity by Constantine in the fourth century SC are key moments in Western book production, leading to contemporary industrialized manufacture of Bibles and all that entails in terms of ecological cost.[32]

In the context of the history of Bible production, it is insufficient to describe the text as completely separate from the material artifact by which it presents itself to be read, because this then separates the text from its underlying material givenness. Instead, a *text* can be defined as an interrelationship between the written, proclaimed, or remembered text, its readers/ hearers/interpreters, and the medium/media in which the text presents itself. This text holds a complex relationship of dependence on, and embeddedness in, a more-than-human earth community. Can we extend intertextuality to *a material intertextuality* in which the material givenness of the text irrupts in our reading?

For Kristeva, because the *chora* is ordered by the maternal body, the intertextual interruption of the semiotic returns us to our embodiment as living organisms, marked by biochemical processes of separation and connection and biological limits and controls as well as social ones.[33] To describe the intertextual operation of the semiotic, Kristeva introduces two further terms: (1) the *genotext* is a process foundational to language, in broad terms the underlying and dynamic social, familial, biological, ecological environment of language, through which the semiotic functions; and (2) the *phenotext* is a structure of language, serving to communicate.[34] Because humans are embodied and embedded in a (more-than-human) sociality, the material given, through the genotext, is already intertextual with texts.

Nevertheless, no simple parallel exists between the relationship between child and mother that erupts in language and the relationship between texts and their more-than-human contexts. The intensity of the child/ mother relation, and the forgotten dramas of speculation and castration that produce the thetic phase, are not replayed in the relationship between texts and the material given. However, that pregnant bodies, bodies, and the social are each paradigmatic of the material given, that the maternal *via* the semiotic and the social *via* orality remain as traces in sign systems, suggests that the rhythms of the semiotic *chora* may be evoked in modes of reading texts intertextually with their more-than-human contexts.[35]

Reading the Gospel of Mark, Stephen Moore offers an example:

> Writ(h)ing in pain on his cross, Jesus can at last be read: "Truly this man was a son of God" (15:39). He is in the process of becoming book. Nailed, grafted onto the tree, Jesus' body is becoming one with the flesh of the wood. His flesh, torn and beaten to a pulp, joined by violence to the wood, is being transformed into processed wood-pulp, into paper, as the centurion looks on. As tree and budding book, Jesus is putting forth leaves, the leaves of a gospel book, whose opening sentence the centurion has just read: "The beginning of the good news of Jesus Christ, son of God" (1:1).[36]

In Moore's reading, the Bible as thing—both earth product and object of consumption within global markets—speaks back to the text through the imaginative mode of his reading.

Nevertheless, the physical medium of the text continues to occupy a relation of otherness to the meaning of the text, and the agency of the material givenness of a particular text cannot be articulated in a reading. Yet reading remains an embodied process, and bodies, embedded in a more-than-human sociality, are affected by reading.[37] Ecocriticism wagers that reading practices can shape relationships between readers and their environments, so that reading both emerges from and prompts embodied practices of ethical engagement in a more-than-human earth community critically at risk.

Ecomimesis is one form of reading and writing practice that seems to parallel the mimesis Kristeva celebrates. Timothy Morton understands the genotext to be the "environment" to the phenotext of ecomimesis. This environment, or ambience, both separates and connects the material subject and its representation in writing. While celebrating what cannot be said of the other, the ecomimetic performance of the uncertain relation "between" the word and the thing can also serve to reinforce the distance it was meant to negotiate. Morton suggests that, recognizing the extent of our responsibility for ecological destruction, ecocritics acknowledge and live with this distance and engage with a "dark ecology" of ecological lamentation.[38]

Accepting that the material givenness of a text is withdrawn from us as we read, we confront a loss that we can allow to resonate with the losses the text's production brings about. If the Bible is "a text that thrusts its words into [our] losses," biblical readers attentive to the matter of the text can allow these losses to resonate in modes of "reading Earth" intertextually with the text.[39] As we move from seed to word to book (and screen), we engage with reading practices both colonizing of, and attentive to, an Earth community where parable becomes lament: *A seeder went out to seed the seed and as he seeded some fell into papyrus swamp, some into sheep fold, some into old growth forest and some into recycling bin. . . . And the parable is this: the seed is the book, produced a billionfold . . .*

NOTES

1. Pattie, "Creation," 62, 64–65.
2. Ibid., 63.
3. I develop the notion of the material given in Elvey, *Ecological Feminist Reading.*
4. Ayers, "Materialism and the Book."
5. Kristeva, *Revolution,* esp. 43–51, 57–71.
6. Ibid., 24, 27, 29; Grosz, *Sexual Subversions,* 42–44; Moi, *Sexual/Textual Politics,* 161. It is beyond the scope of this essay, but not irrelevant to an ecocriticism informed by feminist ethics, that Kristeva's subject is cast as masculine. Grosz, *Jacques Lacan,* esp. 167.
7. Kristeva, *Revolution,* 26–27; Oliver, *Reading Kristeva,* 22–23, 46–47; Payne, *Reading Theory,* 169.
8. Kristeva, *Revolution,* 43, 46–51; Grosz, *Sexual Subversions,* 45–47.
9. Grosz, *Sexual Subversions,* 47.
10. Ibid.
11. Oliver, *Reading Kristeva,* 48–50; McCance, *"L'écriture limite";* cf. Grosz, *Jacques Lacan,* 160–67.
12. Grosz, *Volatile Bodies,* 57–61.
13. Kristeva, *Revolution,* 57; "From One Identity," esp. 101–4; Kristeva, "Reading the Bible."
14. Kristeva, *Revolution,* 59–60.
15. Ibid., 60; Robbins, "Historical, Rhetorical." See, for example, Brawley, *Text to Text.*
16. See, for example, Wainwright, *Shall We Look?* esp. 35–49. Cf. Kristeva, *Revolution,* 60.
17. See, for example, Keller, *Face of the Deep,* esp. 30.
18. See, for example, Nutu, *Incarnate Word.*
19. See Luke 8:4–8, 8:9, 8:10a, 8:10b (cf. Isa. 6:9), and 8:11–15, respectively. Scripture quotations are from the New Revised Standard Version Bible, hereafter cited parenthetically.
20. Boyarin, "Question of Theory," 225.
21. Ong, *Orality and Literacy.*
22. Kelber, "Oral Tradition," 41.
23. Graham, *Beyond the Written Word,* 6, 32.
24. Pattel-Gray, "Dreaming."
25. Kristeva, *Revolution,* 82.
26. Dodd, *Parables,* 4.
27. Curkpatrick, "Parable Metonymy," 291.
28. I. H. Marshall, *The Gospel of Luke,* 320.

29. Bauer et al., *Greek-English Lexicon*, 415–16, 422.

30. Ibid., 422–23.

31. Nancy, *Listening*, 43.

32. Hurtado, *Earliest Christian Artifacts*, 43–93; Gamble, "Bible and Book," 16.

32. Kristeva, "System," 29.

34. Kristeva, *Revolution*, 87–88.

35. I am grateful to Julie Kelso for her emphasis on the mode of reading.

36. Moore, "Illuminating the Gospels," 262–63. See also Aichele, *Sign, Text, Scripture*, 19.

37. Bleich, "Materiality of Reading."

38. Morton, *Ecology without Nature*, 29–78, 181–201; cf. Rigby, "Earth, World, Text" and "Writing after Nature," where the focus is on response rather than mimesis.

39. Kristeva, "Reading the Bible," 119; see also Kort, "*Take Read*," esp. 117; and Habel, review of *An Ecological Feminist Reading of the Gospel of Luke*, by Elvey, 116.

There Can Be No Democracy
without a Culture of Difference

Ours is an age of sociology, of statistics, of mass media, and of politics. To be sure, other components can be included, such as technique, which is perhaps the one that underlies and unites the others. And also the one that today imperils the democratic model, at least as far as citizens, both men and women, are concerned. But is it not up to these citizens to judge whether a democratic system is well founded and well functioning?

Democracy at the Origin of Our History

What we call democracy, in fact, was born in ancient Greece and had as its more or less explicit stakes the differentiation of the masculine body from nature and the mother, who was assimilated to the natural world. It was a matter of favoring the emergence of man as such, especially of his sexuate body, thanks notably to the constitution of a language, of a logic, and of a society formed only by men and between men. In such a cultural context, democracy served human individualization, at least up to a certain point. Man asserted his own forms—including in art—but the difference between one man and another man was not really taken into account. What was important was to emerge from a lack of differentiation with respect to nature, to the mother, and to any wholeness that could, in one way or another, substitute itself for her and cause the masculine individualization that had begun to assert itself to once again be lost.

This masculine individualization was not carried out through a relation with the other. Man did not acquire an identity of his own by differing from a human individual other than himself—woman, beginning with woman in the mother—but by separating from her without any possible return thanks

TRANSLATED BY HEIDI BOSTIC, LUCE IRIGARAY, AND STEPHEN PLUHÁČEK to a relation between those who were the same, whose difference was only quantitative, or, one could also say, competitive.

We know the importance of physical, even warlike, strength in this competition between men. And the importance of intellectual competence is not really all that different from it, at least in its intention and its stakes. It is, however, at the level of the body that man remains closest to himself. This body will not receive an education that is truly appropriate to it. The culture that is put in place is a culture of the domination of matter, of the sensible, through a construction and a logic that are above all mental. One could say that the *logos* is the technique that Greek man defined and utilized in order to appropriate the world without wondering about the fundamental human alienation and exploitation that were thus put in place. Without the *logos*, the technological universe that is ours would not have become possible, nor its power of domination over humanity.

In order to begin to individualize himself, man thus did not make use of the way of a relation to the other, in particular to the mother, but of a competitive conquest of the universe by and between those who are the same: men. In addition to sporting or even warlike competition, competition takes place through the appropriation of material or mental things. Man gains his individualization through appropriating a pregiven universe that becomes thing, object, body, and world that separate him from an original lack of differentiation from the living natural world.

At first, this appropriation served a process of individualization in the masculine. But a concern for objectivity and universality gradually rendered neuter this construction of a world by the Greeks. The neuter has in a way occupied the place of relation in difference, an unrecognized qualitative difference this time. The neuter has become the arbiter of quantitative competitions between men, notably and exemplarily in the praetorium, but also in civil and political discourses and debates. A democracy established by and for men alone must be governed in the neuter, it alone being able to mask and regulate the competitive passions between those who are the same. The neuter has assumed a double function: to arbitrate the competition between quantitative differences, and to occupy or to cover up the place of a qualitative difference not taken into account and even repressed in this culture between men. The individualization considered to be human has thus been carried out only in the masculine with an individuation between men that is solely quantitative.

What had been excluded of qualitative difference was transferred into a religious or philosophical Absolute that always obeys quantitative norms but with an extrapolation that rules out any possible comparison or competition.

This constitution of a cultural universe and of its democracy still remains structurally our own. But the neuter has progressively ruined the process of individualization that the Greeks tried to promote, notably through a democratic system. The most destructive stage in this evolution is the progressive substitution of the neuter—exemplarily in the guise of money—for any emergence of the masculine thanks to man being confronted with the task of building himself a world. Where man attempted to define himself by appropriating a pregiven natural world, he henceforth disappeared into a universe lacking in differentiation that, despite himself, he has again created, that of money. The degree of humanity is assessed according to the amount of capital one possesses, or at the very least by one's buying power. The relation between humans becomes more and more quantitative and competitive, but measured by a standard that does not allow a real human individualization. Democracy, in particular, has lost this concern, and it risks, such as it appears today, serving a loss rather than a conquest of individualization. Moreover, the more the evaluation of human identity becomes abstract, quantitative, and measured between those who are supposedly the same, the more violence grows, a pure and partially arbitrary violence. It is a means of asserting oneself without referring to a human identity properly speaking: a sort of uncultivated energy that society is no longer able to channel or control, except occasionally, and less and less, in sport itself.

But the body in sports is henceforth a place of quantitative evaluation for which the fundamental standard of reference is money. The athlete's muscles correspond to a market value, artificially sustained by biological or medical science; they are no longer the expression of the affirmation of man as man in relation to what he experiences as a lack of differentiation with respect to the world in which he is. The athlete's body is at the service of the deluge that submerges us in the power of money and other values based solely on calculation. The global violence that goes hand in hand with this submersion bears witness to an ultimate will of masculine self-assertion. But it ends up yielding death more than cultivating life. In his impotent rage, man destroys himself and his fellow humans as well as the natural surroundings that have allowed him to survive up until today: not only humanity is thus in danger, but the earth itself.

A Necessary Return to the Process of Individualization

To continue wanting to govern humanity without asking oneself some radical questions about the means and the reasons for this government appears as complete madness to anyone who takes the time to think about it. The fact that the democratic ideal has become alienated from itself in a quantitative evaluation arbitrated by money is particularly problematic, notably because this process leads entire populations to demand their own loss of individuality. Power, from then on, is available for all the more or less latent or patent forms of totalitarianism. That goes from "political correctness" to the designer clothing that young people, and in particular young women, are expected to wear in order to not feel excluded, and includes the "trendy" discourses that publishers and mass media adopt as the only ones of value, all the while complaining about the lack of intellectuals capable of thinking.

All these forms of authoritarianism, harmful in various ways, are often supported by democratic arguments, which, more and more, contribute to the alienation instead of the affirmation of the individual. It is urgent that we return to the affirmation of the individual, and not by way of a mere appeal to vote for elected representatives, be they men or women. We know henceforth to what point a vote can be induced from the outside more than resulting from reflection or will by the individual himself. We also know that we cannot agree with the electoral decisions of certain populations of voters. In what terms is it thus still possible to speak and work toward a government truly shared by individuals?

Some decisions remain possible for promoting the participation of individuals in the government of the city with a view toward a positive becoming of humanity.

First, changing the very stakes of the legislation that supposedly supports a democratic politics. The law that rules our societies is concerned, above all, with property, possessions, goods. The body itself is assimilated to a good of which the owner is not always the man or the woman to whom the body really belongs. The fact that civil law is defined in terms of goods leads to subtle forms of enslavement, from citizens but also from states, notably with regard to women and children; something of which our supposedly democratic societies are not sufficiently aware. It is imperative that we shift the emphasis of the law from having to being, that is to say from the right to possess goods to the right to be a person. In order to return to a necessary process of individualization and pursue it, legislation today must start again from the person's right to exist in his or her singularity, and from the duties toward himself or herself as a person and toward other persons respected in their differences, that is to say from duties regarding coexistence.

To change the stakes of the law means modifying the relation of the citizens to themselves and to other citizens, but also the relation of elected representatives to citizens. Citizens will be recognized as full individuals and not as possessors of a more or less alienable part of the goods of the state, of the nation, or of a more global community. Modifying the emphasis of the law is essential if we are to preserve a democratic ideal inasmuch as the law is supposed to protect citizens individually, between one another, and from the state—and not to serve, as many understand it, as a means of subjecting citizens to the state. Modifying legislation is also imperative, which in a certain way amounts to the same thing, in order to change the connection between civil law and penal law, the latter often being exercised without the citizens being informed of the juridical fault that was committed.

To put the accent back on the right of persons to exist is also to put the accent back on the respect for life rather than on the ownership of goods. The most precious good—if I continue to use this word in order to speak according to the terms of existing legislation—which the individual enjoys is life. Now this is threatened by multiple dangers: our irreducible place of life, our planet, is itself in peril; our daily atmosphere is polluted in various ways; our food is often toxic; our place of habitation, when it exists, is in various ways subjected to the law of profit rather than that of respect for life; murderous wars are carried out by supposedly democratic regimes with arguments and economic means and technologies beyond the reach of their adversaries; the death penalty exists in countries that present themselves as models of democracy, etc. To put the accent back on life is simultaneously to begin with the individual citizen and to provide him or her with a chance equivalent to that of every other citizen of resuming a process of human individualization. If one wishes to speak of an equality of opportunities, it is from this reality and elementary and universal value that it is necessary to begin again.

Any democratic model that does not consider life as the first and irreducible value to be protected is already unfaithful to the ideal that it is intended to respect and command respect for. Life must be respected at the level of the natural world where it is a matter of cultivating it without appropriating or destroying it. It must be safeguarded as the place of existence for living beings. It must be preserved in its present and future possibilities.

The Individual Is Two

Taking gender into account is a democratic concern tied to the respect for life. The conservation and cultivation of life require respect for gender and its properties. This is true at the level of the living in general. And it is particularly true at the human level inasmuch as life cannot be reduced there to an exclusively natural process. Human life is always woven with culture. In order to be democratic, culture must take into consideration the duality of genders and the quality of their relation. Our supposedly democratic culture has been elaborated starting from the necessities of only one gender and in opposition to the other gender, considered as a natural pole to be overcome in order to differentiate oneself from it. One of the most fundamental issues for current democratic politics is recognizing that it cannot confine itself to the needs, in particular with regard to individualization, of only one gender; which, moreover, endangers it, as has been mentioned. It cannot be a matter of granting to the gender that for centuries has been kept in a status of naturalness a simple right to vote nor even a right to represent other citizens within the existing type of democracy. It is rethinking and refounding democracy that is in question. And doing so, most radically, starting from the existence of two different human beings, man and woman, whose necessities, notably with regard to individualization, are not the same. A political thought that claims to represent citizens must begin again with what they really are. This is not the case, and it cannot be the case, without resuming again a process of individualization adapted to each citizen. This task should be the most fundamental task of a democratic mode of government that, in this day and age, is satisfied with a loss of identity of individuals in order to assure a power founded, most often, on economic and competitive considerations that are difficult to distinguish from the most liberal theories and practices. And the egalitarian slogans, which nourish many so-called democratic discourses, then end up drowning individuals in anonymous and undifferentiated masses. This gesture is particularly dangerous as regards all sorts of the more or less latent totalitarianisms that are now attaining a planetary magnitude.

The opportunity that women's liberation offers to democracy is to allow it to take up again a process of individualization for the species and of individuation for each one, man and woman, starting from the qualitative difference of gender. Consequently, it is no longer starting from and against a mother-nature that neuter individuals—in fact, originally, men—differentiate themselves as human beings, but as humanity itself is composed of two different subjects who are entitled to recognition and rights that are equivalent but, in part, specific, and thus different. And the first right to which they can lay claim as humans is that of being respected for what they are: men or women and not neuter and undifferentiated individuals.

To take up again the task of individualization at work in Greek democracy seems at once a work of justice in accordance with the democratic ideal and a means of saving democracy itself, in particular from all the forms of totalitarianism that threaten it. To be sure, this cannot take place while remaining within a politics conceived of as the more or less legitimate and honest simple technique of governing: a conception of politics that is a priori not democratic. This requires rethinking politics itself without allowing politics to subjugate thinking, as is too often the case today. Rethinking politics is necessary if we are to put it once more at the service of citizens by proposing to them a happy medium to respect in order to live and to live together without anarchy or authoritarianism.

Thus, to turn again toward the task that is essential for women, it is important that their access to public life correspond to a means of winning an individuality of their own, beyond, which does not mean against, the natural belonging to which our tradition has confined them. To enter into public life must represent, for them, a task of individualization and not a competitive claim in relation to men. This task of individualization is specific to feminine identity. It is a matter, for women, not so much of opposing a simple indifferentiation with the mother than of opposing a reduction of themselves to an undifferentiated nature. Certainly a link exists between these two issues, but it is not simple. Women must go beyond a patriarchal world by drawing nearer to their feminine genealogy and, at the same time, they must develop a natural belonging, which they share with their mother, into a civil and cultural identity of their own. And this cannot amount to entering as a full subject into a culture constructed to respond to the requirements of an individualization in the masculine.

If man has to separate himself from his maternal origin, it is instead from her own maternal-natural power, embodied above all in the son, that woman must differ in order to be a woman. Caricaturing things somewhat, it would be possible to say that man's individualization has more to do with an ascendant genealogy and woman's individualization with a descendent genealogy. At least if one starts off again, as seems necessary, from the natural belonging of each one, a belonging that must be both safeguarded and cultivated in order to carry out a differentiation, not only in relation to other species or kingdoms but also within the human species itself, the place where humanity as such is realized.

In order to differentiate herself as woman, a woman thus has to go beyond a purely natural status which our tradition has assigned to her, a natural status not managed by her and confined to certain spaces where the head of the family, assisted in this by the state and religious ideologies or communities, had the responsibility of managing this simultaneously productive and reproductive capital. The first gesture to be accomplished, on the part of a democratic society, would be to entrust to women the management of what or who they are by defining rights appropriate to their identity. Before being recognized as adults capable of voting, and even of being elected, women must first be recognized as capable of responsibility toward themselves. If they are not acknowledged as having this right, to what do the other rights that they enjoy today correspond? Without first being responsible for oneself, what can be the value of the responsibility expressed in a vote, moreover the responsibility at play in the government of others?

It is thanks to the existence of positive civil rights that a woman can pass from a merely natural identity to an appropriate civil identity. These rights also represent duties. If, for example, it is in accordance with democracy that women can legally own and control their bodies—in love and motherhood, and more generally in civil and cultural life—this does not imply that they can do so without respect or responsibility for themselves and the community in which they live. To this community belong the sexual partner and the father of a child. The rights that a woman must enjoy in the domains of love and motherhood are especially indissociable from duties concerning the respect for the natural and psychic life of those who are involved in these relations. Such duties, moreover, are also incumbent on the man. In fact, to define the rights that women need in order to pass from a natural identity to a civil identity contributes to imperceptibly displacing the emphasis of positive civil law from the possession of goods to the respect for persons. And that can represent a pedagogy of respect for a difference between individuals that is not only quantitative and founded upon having, but qualitative and founded upon being.

To obtain the rights appropriate for passing from paternal or marital tutelage, or state supervision, to the liberty and responsibility concerning civil and cultural life should be the first education to be given to girls in order to help them to acquire a cultural identity. Without this preliminary formation, the education within schools, under cover of the democratic right to equality with men, risks representing a double alienation for women: the obligation to submit to a culture in the masculine that is foreign to their original identity, the demand of a purely affective subjectivity that does not exceed natural belonging. Neither of these two solutions allows women to acquire a human individuality that renders them capable of affirming themselves for what or who they are and of coexisting with men in a society.

A Culture in the Feminine

The individualization in the feminine must start again from a natural given and cultivate it. In particular, it must consider all the aspects of feminine identity in its complexity and discover a way to cultivate them. Some traditions have celebrated, in a more or less worthwhile manner, the diverse stages in the life of a woman: puberty and the first menstruation, deflowering and life as a lover, pregnancy and childbirth, motherhood, menopause, the status of being single, of being married, and of being widowed, etc. Our Western tradition has believed it good to erase what relates to sexuate belonging for the benefit of a supposedly neutral and universal culture. This only apparent erasure of gender no doubt endangers humanity today. It gives rise to all kinds of substitutions of abstract and totalitarian powers, among them those of money and technique, for human being. The erasure of gender is certainly not without relation to the ideology of the superfluous or surplus human, made possible by the pretension of a civilization to want to overcome our bodily, and in particular sexuate, belonging, and to consider that the abstract universal and the neutral or neuter are superior to the living being itself. The neuter universal corresponds to the fiction of a reality foreign to our human nature, a reality to which our tradition has submitted since its constitution and which, periodically, turns against humanity in the form of genocidal totalitarianisms. The most originary of these, and the one that makes them possible, relates to the abolition of the human through the abolition of gender.

It is distressing, but in complete coherence with Western culture, to see women claim their full admission into a tradition founded upon their exclusion, and more generally upon the exclusion of human being itself. The superfluous human being in cultural and political circles is first of all, and is always, the feminine sexuate being, unless she can act as a foil to man or his values. The opportunity for humanity would rest in this exclusion being recognized as such and its reasons being interpreted.

For women, to set as their ideal simply entering into a society of between-men is to renounce the differentiation of an identity of their own. That constitutes a mistake and, in a way, a fault toward not only themselves but toward the whole of humanity. Humanity can take up again the work of its individualization only by substituting for the traditional debate of man with nature, first represented by the mother, a debate on the relation between man and woman with respect to their respective differences.

Throughout the centuries, woman has lived in the shadow of man. Assigned to residing in the family home, the private property of the husband-father, she has served this husband-father as a maid, as a genetrice and a sexuate body through which, sheltered from the gaze of other men, he could pursue his differentiation from the mother-nature. The false dilemma between mother and whore was in fact played out above all within the family home, where man could continue to be confronted with his own natural origin. This confrontation required both the familiar context of infancy and the wife's submissive acceptance of the sexual clumsiness of the man, which could assume various aggressive forms. A tender and supposedly virginal maternal substitute, the spouse also had to show herself to be, at the appointed times, a valorous whore under the threat that her man, frustrated, would go elsewhere to prove himself. To pass from one role to the other was not an easy task for the woman, all the more so because no one had informed her of the means of bringing sexual desire to fruition, beginning with her own. Frustrated herself, she was also frustrating, and paralyzed by diverse forms of guilt that nothing would allow her to relativize: no civil or cultural identity could help her to put in perspective the tragedy, the suffering, the fatigue, and also the boredom that she experienced within the confines of the home. Procreation, necessary for her husband and for the state as proof of their power and guarantee of its perpetuation, seemed to justify everything else. That this procreation was the result of a behavior that was rather instinctively animal, if not worse, did not seem to pose any problem. Except that natural belonging should be confined within the private sphere without contaminating the functioning of the state. A compartmentalization between the private and the public spheres covered, and still covers, the unbelievable acts of violence toward half of humanity, a violence assuring, invisibly, the functioning of society itself and of its culture, including what is called democratic culture.

The movements of emancipation and liberation of women have denounced this inhumanity without always being able to discover how to remedy it. Which can reinforce the opinion that this feminine status is desired by woman herself.

It is true that the task which falls to women—and moreover to all of us—is to rethink the foundations of our culture and to analyze their partial and biased character before setting off again on a path toward individualization more in accordance with human identity.

It is above all through the constitution of our culture that the exclusion and oppression of women came about. The cultural elaboration of our natural belonging must be taken up again, particularly with regard to our sexuate belonging. Such a belonging is not a matter of sexuality in the strict sense, even if sexuality plays a decisive role, but of the manner in which our sexuate belonging determines the whole individual and establishes relations between individuals. Sexuate identity is a matter of bodily morphology, but also of the structuring of subjectivity. The relation to oneself, to the other, to the world does not obey the same imperatives for men and for women. Man is more interested in the object, in those similar to him who are often assimilated to the little-differentiated "one" of a member of the group, while woman is more interested in the subject, in a subject who is different, and prefers the relation between two to that with a group. The configuration privileged by the one or the other is dependent on their situation with regard to the mother and their attempt to emerge from an initial indifferentiation.

The obstacles to be overcome by the one and by the other are different. As is the manner in which, in the journey of each one, the relation to the same gender and to the other gender takes place. What fundamentally determines this relation to those who are the same as oneself and those who are different from oneself is the position with respect to the maternal origin. To remain between those who are the same as she can mean the risk of not winning one's autonomy for a feminine subject while, for a masculine subject, this represents an attempt to attain it. For the girl, the mother is the same as she: differing from the mother is realized through a relation with the other as man. For the boy, the mother is elusive in her difference because she is the one who gives birth. To emerge from this originary world is realized through a will to master, to dominate, and to re-create his origin—in particular through resorting to absolutes such as God, Truth, the Good, etc. The here and now has been deferred into a beyond without the relation to the other in the mother having been taken into consideration.

The Legacy of Antigone

Lacking a culture appropriate to her identity, woman has been subjected to those absolutes that were substituted for the maternal origin on the part of man. Which deprived her of the relation to herself, to her mother, but also of the possibility of cultivating a relational world that was her own. The most fundamental violence imposed on woman lies in this uprooting from her own world, to which the Greek origins of our culture bear witness, especially through the mythologies and tragedies of that epoch and their subsequent development. Sophocles' *Antigone* is one example of this cultural evolution that the thinkers and artists of our tradition have not stopped questioning.

The tragedy of *Antigone* presents the destructive and murderous events that inaugurated the establishment of the patriarchal world. It teaches us how, for the values of a more feminine world—respectful of life, of its generation, and of sexuate difference—those of patriarchy and phallocracy were substituted. These values have been imposed through the violence of arbitrary laws and discourses that aimed to cut the bonds with the preceding culture in order to establish a new power.

Antigone was sacrificed because she continued to observe the unwritten laws that governed a tradition called matriarchal. It was especially a matter of the duty to give a burial to the youngest son of her mother, the one who, after the eldest daughter, becomes the privileged inheritor under maternal law but has no right to inherit the father's powers or goods. King Creon, who embodies the figure imposing the new patriarchal reign, sentences Antigone to death for her fidelity to her own maternal origin and to the unwritten duties that correspond to it.

Antigone is enclosed alive in a tomb without being openly killed or buried. The king thus tries to absolve himself of all guilt of crime in the eyes of the city and the gods. He nonetheless deprives Antigone of life and love.

In fact, this episode that takes place at the advent of our tradition remains active throughout the unfolding of this tradition, assuming more or less ambiguous and decipherable forms. Hence the persistence of the myth and tragedy of Antigone across the centuries, as well as the enigma she continues to oppose to all the interpretations that have been attempted within our culture. Antigone invites us to not renounce the world that preceded this one—that is, to learn to coexist and to share in the respect of difference relative to our natural belonging and the values that it represents. A gesture that must happen first in the relation to our maternal origin in order to then be embodied between us as woman and man, women and men. It is only after having respected the values of the living world, passed on by her mother, that Antigone would have had the chance to share desire and love with an other, man, without denying her own identity and the values or ideals that were her own.

The tragedy of Sophocles tells us that Antigone was not able to attain or live such a stage in her life. And our History has not yet really allowed us to attain it. We thus have to acknowledge and overcome the dilemma of a choice between two worlds by building between us a culture of coexistence in difference, beginning with that of our sexuate identities, the one that represents the first and universal articulation between nature and culture.

NOTE

This essay was first published in French under the title "La démocratie ne peut se passer d'une culture de la différence" in "Libido: Sexes, genres et dominations," special issue, *Illusio* 4–5 (Autumn 2007): 9–20. Full permission for the English translation contained in this volume has been secured from the French publisher.

The Ecological Irigaray?

It could appear that the work of Luce Irigaray bears little relevance to environmental thought.[1] Irigaray is a feminist philosopher of sexual difference, after all, and the injustices that concern her are explicitly social and political. Most prominently, her work has sought to undermine the dominance of masculine culture by exposing the systematic exclusion of women from psychoanalytic theory and traditional Western philosophy; to discover positive forms of feminine subjectivity; and to imagine social and political relationships that advance beyond masculine monism and inaugurate a "culture of two subjects"—man and woman in their irreducible difference.[2] And yet, as we read "There Can Be No Democracy without a Culture of Difference" and other of Irigaray's later works—particularly *Sexes and Genealogies, Thinking the Difference,* and *I Love to You*—we cannot fail to notice the underlying presence of the natural. The social and political concerns that motivate these works may be more conspicuous, but what arguably distinguishes Irigaray from many other influential Continental feminist philosophers such as Beauvoir, Wittig, Kristeva, Cixous, and Butler is that she so often addresses her social and political concerns by appealing to nature— that which "precede[s] any definition or fabrication that tear [it] away from roots and origins that exist independently of humans' transforming activity."[3]

My aim here is to briefly explain how Irigaray's engagement with the natural makes her work a rich resource for environmental philosophers and ecocritics. While the environmental crisis itself has never been her focus, we may detect in her thought at least three veins of ecological attunement: (1) in the manner of an ecofeminist, Irigaray interprets the historical oppression of women as being bound up with the degradation of the earth; (2) in the manner of feminist ecocriticism, Irigaray's long-standing engagement with *Antigone* exposes and analyzes its interlinked representations of women and nature; and (3) Irigaray's proposal for creating a "positive becoming" of femininity is predicated upon her reinterpretation of both nature and its relation to culture.[4]

Irigaray's Ecofeminism

In the traditional nature-culture dichotomy, a primary object of critique both in ecofeminism and in much of Irigaray's later work, nature and culture exist as binary opposites, each defined as the negation of the other. Nature is devalued as the realm of the "uncultivated," of mere instinct, of passive materiality, and of the general mess of bodies and women. Culture, on the other hand, is positively valued as the realm in which, by means of our political, intellectual, and artistic achievements, we assert our mastery over nature and "differentiate [our]selves as human beings."[5] Recognizing both this historical subordination of nature to culture and also the historical identification of women with nature, most ecofeminists begin by arguing that, since this identification has been used to justify the oppression of women and nature, its interrogation is an essential part of any feminism or environmentalism.[6] Although Irigaray does not align herself with eco-feminism, her work shares its basic starting point. For her, the reciprocally reinforcing subordination of women and nature is obvious: it is quite simply a "failure of respect for nature" that lies at the root of patriarchal culture— the elaborate system of tradition, language, education, law, and politics by which men have dominated and determined women's bodies and so-cial roles.[7]

Irigaray's response to this failure of respect—to both reject the tradi-tional identification of women and nature and to propose a new relation between them—cuts a path between the contrasting but equally problematic strategies of radical ecofeminism and social constructionist feminism. Radi-cal ecofeminists such as Mary Daly, Susan Griffin, and Charlene Spretnak accept the traditional connection between women and nature but seek to overturn the masculine-culture/feminine-nature hierarchy by swapping the terms so that nature and women are revalued and lifted above culture and the masculine.[8] The trouble with such a strategy is that, in short, it fails to question the very dichotomy that has permitted the oppression of one side by the other and, moreover, fails to recognize that the idea of nature it revalues is itself a product of patriarchal culture.[9]

By contrast, social constructionist feminists such as Simone de Beau-voir, Monique Wittig, and Sherry Ortner, who are keenly aware that the historical ties between women and nature are a patriarchal construction, recommend that these ties be severed in order that women may reconstruct themselves within the realm of the cultural.[10] In *The Second Sex*, for exam-ple, Beauvoir argues that for both men and women the project of "affirming" our "subjective existence" consists in elevating ourselves above the passivity of our thing-like natural "immanence"—our "mere life"—and that women must not allow themselves to believe that their historical association with nature bars or exempts them from undertaking this task.[11] However, in accepting the notion that subjective becoming—the process of human self-definition—is a cultural project in express opposition to nature, Beauvoir and other social constructionists not only fail to question the nature-culture dichotomy (thereby committing the same error as the radical ecofeminists), but they also endorse the traditionally dominant side of the dichotomy, effectively proposing that women simply be relocated to the very position over and above nature (i.e., that of men) from which they have historically been oppressed.

For Irigaray, women's association with nature is not itself problematic; the problem is that women have been associated with a limited and oppressive interpretation of nature. It would therefore be unacceptable to embrace women's identification with nature in its conventional guise, as radical ecofeminists effectively propose, but it would also be unnecessary to cut all ties with nature, as the social constructionists propose. What is necessary, says Irigaray, is to "reinterpret the idea of nature."[12] As we shall see, her reinterpretation not only eliminates the binary opposition that allows for the subordination of nature to culture, but also opens the possibility for nature to serve as a "source of energy" for a subjective becoming that is proper to and positive for women.[13] We shall elaborate upon this reinterpretation shortly, but let us first discuss Irigaray's reading of *Antigone*, which reveals itself to be a piece of incipient ecocriticism and further demonstrates her ecofeminist affinities.

Irigaray's Ecocriticism

Irigaray's abiding and complex[14] interest in Sophocles' *Antigone* stems from her critique of Hegel's *Phenomenology of Spirit*, which invokes *Antigone* in its pivotal discussion of the family (§438–76). This interest, which she first expressed in *Speculum of the Other Woman*,[15] has become a source of controversy among scholars of her work,[16] but let it suffice for our purposes to briefly indicate how her later readings of *Antigone* trace and criticize its interrelated representations of femininity and nature.

In telling the story of the original "struggle to maintain feminine laws against an imperialist masculine power," says Irigaray, *Antigone* holds up a figure who is tragic but nonetheless demonstrates femininity's great potential for civility even in the face of the profound incivility of men's power struggles.[17] Before the action of the tragedy, Antigone's brother, Polyneices, led foreign forces against Thebes in an attempt to wrest power from his

older, patrilineally entitled brother, Eteocles. After the brothers' fated mutual killing in battle, however, their maternal uncle Creon inherited the
throne. In the principal episode of the myth, King Creon authorizes a proper
burial for Eteocles but, seeking to stabilize the city whose rule he did not
appear to fully deserve, he forbids the burial of the traitor Polyneices—in
defiance of the unwritten laws of the ancestral chthonic (earthly) gods.
When Antigone defies the edict and performs burial rites for Polyneices,
Creon orders her buried alive.

According to Irigaray, certain traditional interpretations of *Antigone* assume that Antigone's action is motivated by "suicidal pathos" or a will to
anarchy and then conclude that she represents an "eternal feminine" that is
"unable to surmount an excessive affectivity" and is incommensurate with
civil society.[18] Irigaray's own reading sets out to discredit these interpretations. What makes it a feminist ecocritical reading is that its defense of
Antigone emphasizes the interconnectedness of the oppression of femininity and nature sanctioned by Creon, who embodies the incipient patriarchal
culture. Finding his hold on power to be threatened by both women and the
old laws of the earthly gods, Creon commits a violence against Antigone the
woman that is at once a violence against the earth and our relation to it.
The work Creon sought to prevent Antigone from undertaking—returning
the body of the dead to its "earthly home"—is an expression of respect not
only for "maternal ancestry" (represented by Polyneices, the second son)
and "bodies borne by the mother" but also for the human connection to and
dependence upon the earth.[19] Antigone therefore does not represent an
irrational lover of death or a stubborn rebel against political order, as some
have suggested. On the contrary, in risking her life to ensure a proper burial
for Polyneices, she demonstrates an unflinching piety toward the laws of the
chthonic gods and enacts her insight that political order must be founded
upon rather than opposed to a prior earthly order. Irigaray's Antigone, then,
is a model for feminists and ecofeminists alike.

Rereading *Antigone* is no mere intellectual exercise for Irigaray. It is an
urgent political task. While the event the text represents—the violent transition from a matriarchal tribal society to a patriarchal civil society—"takes
place at the advent of our tradition," Irigaray's goal is to show us that this
event "remains active throughout the unfolding of this tradition."[20] To read
Antigone with Irigaray is to discover that, since our tradition is based upon
the patriarchal assumption that the stability of civil society requires the
sustained suppression of femininity, blood ties, and the ancient gods of the
earth, women and nature will continue to "relive Antigone's fate" so long as
we neglect to challenge the perpetuation of this assumption in contemporary political life.[21]

Returning to and Reinterpreting Nature

Given that women have traditionally been considered both inferior because of their proximity to nature and inferior *by* nature, many of Irigaray's interlocutors have prescribed the renunciation of nature, but Irigaray maintains that this very thing with which women's subordination is most closely associated is nevertheless also the source of their liberation. She calls for a "return to nature," insisting that "social justice has its roots in and takes its strength from nature."[22] The underlying injustice this return addresses is that, as she argues, our putatively neutral concept "human nature" has been revealed to be the product of "a culture constructed to respond to the requirements of . . . the masculine," a culture that masquerades as universal even while subordinating the feminine.[23] It is in order to disrupt the hegemony of the masculine "one," then, that Irigaray asserts sexual difference,[24] the notion that "the natural, aside from the diversity of its incarnations or ways of appearing, is at least two: male and female."[25]

Sexual difference implies a position for feminine subjectivity that cannot be determined by or in terms of the masculine economy. The appeal it makes to nature is intended to ground this position in "the real."[26] However, as we have seen, this does not mean that sexual difference refers to the nature with which femininity has been traditionally associated or to the differences that are conventionally assumed to obtain naturally between men and women. Having thus far "served" only as the material support for man's privileged becoming, woman "has yet to spread roots and bloom, . . . to be born to her own growth, her own subjectivity."[27] It is for this reason, says Irigaray, that sexual difference "has not yet had its chance to develop"; it is a real that has yet to be realized.[28] The return to nature required by the assertion of sexual difference is therefore a return to *thinking* about nature. Irigaray's hope is that this return will enable women to "discover a way to cultivate" a "natural belonging" that has yet to find expression.[29] Irigaray inverts Beauvoir's famous renunciation of nature accordingly: "It's not as Simone de Beauvoir said: one is not born, but rather becomes, a woman (through culture), but rather: I am born a woman, but I must still become this woman that I am by nature."[30]

Irigaray's allegiance to the natural commonly provokes charges of biological determinism, but her reinterpretation of nature reveals them to be misguided. As a type of essentialism, biological determinism is fundamentally conservative;[31] it holds that nature determines men and women to grow teleologically toward relatively fixed biological forms, that there exist an essential man and woman that individual men and women are destined to repeat. By contrast, Irigaray rethinks nature along the lines of Heidegger's pre-Socratic reinterpretation of the Aristotelian concept of *physis* (often translated as "nature"), that is, neither as a stock of static forms nor as passive material, but rather as a basic activity of self-emergence[32] and growth without any ultimate *telos,* or end.[33] "Nature does not repeat," says Irigaray, for "she grows, becomes, . . . [and] endlessly informs."[34] Irigaray does endorse a kind of natural determinism, but it is based upon her reinterpretation of nature as fundamentally unteleological, and, in contrast to biological determinism, it holds only that humans have naturally "given" modalities of becoming and that these modalities are naturally different for men and women.[35] The forms men and women may come to adopt are fluid in character—open to further transformation—and potentially infinite in number. Thus, the Irigarayan imperative—that we cultivate our natural belonging[36]—makes no reference to any biological essence, actual or projected. Rather, it calls us (men and women)[37] to discover the natural modalities of our sexed bodies and their styles of perception, and to take up these modalities as the very source of our subjective becoming, a dynamic process Irigaray compares to plant growth.[38] Just as a blossoming flower "comes forth" by "constantly moving between the appearance of its forms and the earth's resources," we, too, are called to come forth precisely from the energies flowing from our natural rootedness.[39]

As we can now see, Irigaray's reinterpretation of nature involves both a rejection of the binary opposition between nature and culture (which both radical ecofeminists and social constructionists retain as a premise) and also a proposal for a new nature-culture relation wherein culture is understood not as a break from or triumph over nature but rather as something continuous with and responsive to it. What makes this proposal ecologically germane is that it asks us to give up thinking of nature as what must be transcended in order for us to become independent and "cultivated" subjects, and to begin allowing the nature that manifests itself in us to spark and motivate our political, artistic, and intellectual life, to be the gift to which culture is a response rather than the plight from which it is the escape. For Irigaray, then, the cultural task of subjective becoming is simultaneously an ecological task.

Indeed, Irigaray's call for a return to nature leads her to make an argument for a sort of anthropocentric environmental ethic, as we see in "There Can Be No Democracy" and elsewhere. If our future lies in the cultivation of our natural belonging as opposed to our increasing technological mastery of the nature that exists both inside and outside our bodies, and if the natural world is the very "place of existence for living beings" without which we cannot become who we are "by nature," then nature must be "safeguarded", and "preserved in its present and future possibilities."[40]

It is a tribute to the interdisciplinary quality of Irigaray's thought that her feminist project is at once a contribution to ecocriticism and environmental philosophy. In her reading of *Antigone*, in her insistence that sexual difference has a natural basis, and in her radical revision of the nature-culture relation, she affirms nature as a power beyond our control but nonetheless conducive to our cultural being.

It may still trouble us that Irigaray does not supplement her account of the cultivation of our natural belonging with recommendations regarding the respectful cultivation of the natural world itself, and that she does not issue a call for radical nonanthropocentric ecological responsibility, but we cannot fault her for neglecting a topic she never claimed to be addressing. Moreover, if "what we do about ecology depends upon our *ideas* of the human-nature relationship," as Lynn White has argued, then Irigaray's work *already* contains a profound insight for environmental ethics.[41] In reconceiving nature as commensurate with and energizing for our cultural practices, Irigaray simultaneously advocates a mode of existence that would diminish or even preclude the tendency to widespread destruction that precipitated the development of ecocentric ethics in the first place.[42]

NOTES

1. Almost nothing has been written in this connection. Irigaray's work has apparently gone untapped by ecocritics, and, moreover, the two essays in environmental philosophy that invoke Irigaray do so only in a secondary manner (see Carol Bigwood's "Logos in the Eco of Our Feminine" and Sally Fischer's "Social Ecology in the Flesh," both in Cataldi and Hamrick, *Merleau-Ponty and Environmental Philosophy*).

2. Irigaray, *Key Writings*, viii.

3. Irigaray, *Sexes and Genealogies*, 129.

4. Irigaray, "There Can Be No Democracy," in this volume, 197–205.

5. Ibid., 199. Throughout this essay, Irigaray makes the controversial suggestion that the historical hierarchies of culture over nature and of men over women are attributable, at least in part, to the psychological development of the male infant, which, as a result of sexual difference, involves an especially traumatic separation from the mother (see esp. 203–4). In *Sexes and Genealogies*, it is suggested that the boy can cope with the trauma only by denying his original corporeal continuity with and dependence upon his mother and that it is this denial that leads him to adopt an attitude of superiority to women, the bodily, and nature (see 194–96).

6. For a clear explanation of how this "oppressive patriarchal conceptual framework" has been used to justify and maintain the mutual domination of nature and women, see Karen J. Warren's "The Power and the Promise," 20.

7. Irigaray, *Sexes and Genealogies*, 3.

8. See Charlene Spretnak's "Towards an Ecofeminist Spirituality"; Mary Daly's *Gyn/Ecology*; and Susan Griffin's *Woman and Nature*.

9. Irigaray, *Sexes and Genealogies*, 4.

10. See Simone de Beauvoir's *The Second Sex*; Sherry Ortner's "Is Female to Male"; and Monique Wittig's *The Straight Mind*. Although Judith Butler is perhaps the most recognizable contemporary social constructionist, I exclude her from this rough-and-ready list because her work is primarily descriptive. She argues that sex is always *already* constructed within generally oppressive cultural institutions and systems which are amenable to small-scale subversion, but which appear not to permit the construction or reconstruction of sex to be a free choice (see Butler's *Gender Trouble* and *Bodies That Matter*).

11. Beauvoir, *The Second Sex*, xxi, 97.

12. Irigaray, *Sexes and Genealogies*, 4.

13. Irigaray, *I Love to You*, 39.

14. As Luisa Muraro points out in "Female Genealogies," after Irigaray's 1988 essay "Civil Rights and Responsibilities for the Two Sexes" (included in *Thinking the Difference*), "Irigaray's interpretation of Antigone changes completely." Prior to 1988, Irigaray tended to interpret Antigone as a symbol of women's absence from culture, whereas she later tended to interpret Antigone as a tragic but uplifting defender of maternal genealogies and the earthly order.

15. Irigaray's primary discussions of Antigone can be found in *Speculum of the Other Woman* (214ff.), *Ethics of Sexual Difference* (91ff., 101ff.), *Sexes and Genealogies* (1ff., 110ff.), and *Thinking the Difference* (67ff.).

16. See, for example, Judith Butler's *Antigone's Claim*; Tina Chanter's *The Ethics of Eros*, 80–126; Elaine P. Miller's "The 'Paradoxical Displacement'"; Luisa Muraro's "Female Genealogies"; Kelly Oliver's "Antigone's Ghost"; and Margaret Whitford's *Luce Irigaray*, 118–21.

17. Irigaray, *Key Writings*, 198.

18. Irigaray, *Thinking the Difference*, 68; Irigaray, *Key Writings*, 198.

19. Irigaray, *Thinking the Difference*, 68.

20. Irigaray, "There Can Be No Democracy," 205.

21. Irigaray, *An Ethics of Sexual Difference*, 108.

22. Irigaray, *I Love to You*, 38; Irigaray, *Sexes and Genealogies*, 194.

23. Irigaray, "There Can Be No Democracy," 202 and 200.

24. This point—that sexual difference is conceived as a feminist strategy against patriarchal dominance and therefore does not aim to prescribe heterosexuality—mitigates concern about the strains of heterosexism many have detected in Irigaray's notion of sexual difference. However, the fact remains that this obviously controversial problem is not addressed in Irigaray's work.

25. Irigaray, *I Love to You*, 37.

26. See Irigaray, *Why Different*, 146–47: "I start . . . from a universal reality, sexual difference. . . . This reality of the two has always existed. But it was submitted to the imperatives of a logic of the one. . . . My procedure consists therefore in substituting, for a universal constructed out of only one part of reality, a universal which respects the totality of the real."

27. Irigaray, *Sexes and Genealogies*, 180.

28. Irigaray, *An Ethics of Sexual Difference*, 15.

29. Irigaray, "There Can Be No Democracy," 201.

30. Irigaray, *I Love to You*, 107.

31. See Elizabeth Grosz's *Space, Time and Perversion*, 47–49, for a lucid definition of essentialism and its cognates, including biological determinism, which Grosz calls "biologism."

32. Heidegger's interpretation of *physis* emphasizes that this self-emergence is always accompanied by an absencing or withdrawal (*Entzug*)—as, for example, with the blossom that withers away as the fruit emerges into presence—but this absencing does not appear to be crucial to Irigaray's project.

33. See Helen Fielding's "Questioning Nature." Fielding here explains how, in the *Forgetting of Air*, Irigaray both draws from Heidegger's view of *physis* and criticizes it, primarily for its neglect of sexual difference.

34. Irigaray, *Sexes and Genealogies*, 108.

35. Irigaray, "There Can Be No Democracy," 201, 199.

36. For an account of Irigaray's view of the objects of cultivation (e.g., bodies, living perception, and gender), see Karen Burke's "Masculine and Feminine Approaches to Nature."

37. Although this imperative is most often and most urgently addressed to women, it clearly applies to men as well. After all, the traditionally masculine definition of subjective becoming as a process of separation from nature lies at the very root of the problem that Irigaray is aiming to resolve. Irigaray herself suggests in "There Can Be No Democracy" that we "start off again . . . from the natural belonging of each one" (200).

38. Ibid.

39. Irigaray, *I Love to You*, 25.

40. Irigaray, "There Can Be No Democracy," 198.

41. White, "The Historical Roots," 1206.

42. Irigaray, "There Can Be No Democracy," 198.

5

MODELS FROM
PHYSICS & BIOLOGY

Cybernetics and
Social Systems Theory

Aldo Leopold's *A Sand County Almanac* opens with a walk in the hills of southwestern Wisconsin, in January, during a brief spell of thaw. The narrator follows the track of a skunk: "[It] leads straight across-country. . . . I follow, curious to deduce his state of mind and appetite. . . . In January one may follow a skunk track . . . with only an occasional and mild digression into other doings. . . . There is time not only to see who has done what, but to speculate why."[1]

The narrator thus resolves to shift his interest from the *facts* of nature (which, in his role as a scientist, he has been trained to observe) to the *purposes* which went into their making. The first chance to apply this different mode of observation offers itself up when the narrator encounters a field mouse:

> Why is he abroad in daylight? Probably because he feels grieved about the thaw. Today his maze of secret tunnels, laboriously chewed through the matted grass under the snow, are tunnels no more, but only paths exposed to public view and ridicule. Indeed the thawing sun has mocked the basic premises of the microtine economic system! The mouse is a sober citizen who knows that grass grows in order that mice may store it as underground haystacks, and that snow falls in order that mice may build subways from stack to stack: supply, demand, and transport all neatly organized.[2]

It requires little acumen on the reader's part to recognize the "microtine economic system" as an allegory of the kind of narrowly utilitarian relationship to the land which will be the chief target of Leopold's criticism in the *Almanac*—here exposed to the light of reason by the sun of his satirical prose. What complicates such a reading, however, is the fact that Leopold is writing not only as a satirist, but also as an ecologist: while the field mice are figurally humanized, they are also literally a part of the "wild nature" which

Leopold elsewhere sets in opposition to precisely that type of human behavior which the mice here serve to allegorize. If humans, as he charges, are
blind to their environment, the same is true of the field mice—and of most
other inhabitants of this landscape as well, as becomes apparent in the rest
of the section "January Thaw." The field mouse falls prey to a hawk whose
vision of his environment is no less myopic: "The rough-leg has no opinion
why grass grows, but he is well aware that snow melts in order that hawks
may again catch mice. . . . [T]o him a thaw means freedom from want and
fear."[3] The pattern is then reiterated by a rabbit and an owl. The only
creature that seems to defy such an analysis of its motives in terms of self-
interest is the narrator's guide, the skunk. It is with him that the section
concludes: "The skunk track leads on, showing no interest in possible food,
and no concern over the rompings or retributions of his neighbors. . . .
Finally the track enters a pile of driftwood, and does not emerge. I hear the
tinkle of dripping water among the logs, and I fancy the skunk hears it too. I
turn homeward, still wondering."[4] With this brief, imagined moment of
shared perception, Leopold subtly drives home the self-reflexive point of
"January Thaw": having contemplated the blindness of those other members
of the "land community," the narrator is confronted with the possibility of
his own blindness—a blindness that he, like them, would be unable to see.

Leopold died in the same year that the *Almanac* was published. He thus
did not live to think through the implications of the paradox which he had so
lucidly encapsulated in its opening chapter: that man is both "a part of"
nature and, at the same time and insofar as he is able to observe it, "apart"
from it[5]—a paradox which threatened to destabilize the very conceptual
foundation of the new ethics Leopold was expounding. Like Adam Smith's
market, the "land community" was assumed to function the way it did only
because its various members pursue their own self-interest blindly, their
conflicts ordered into a larger harmonious whole through the action of an
ecological equivalent of Smith's invisible hand—whose working is attested
to, in "January Thaw," by the neat way in which the respective blindnesses of
mouse and hawk complement each other. Yet man, in order to become a
member of this land community, would have to act unlike all its other
members by knowingly subordinating his interests to those of the whole—
thereby rendering moot the original definition of the land community as a
self-regulating system. Throughout the book, Leopold's narrative voice thus
oscillates between the hope for a secure vantage point from which humans
and their environment could be cognized and described as a totality, and the
belief that such aspirations are precisely what is wrong with humanity. In
one paragraph, the "land community" may thus appear as a scientific fact,

while in the next it is presented as something that will truly come into being only once humans learn to see it.

Cybernetics

Just as Leopold was finishing the *Almanac*, an interdisciplinary group of researchers had begun to work out a new conceptual framework to tackle problems of a very similar kind. In 1946, these researchers came together for a series of conferences entitled "Circular-Causal and Feedback Mechanisms in Biological and Social Systems" and now remembered, in honor of the organization which funded them, as the Macy Conferences. The members of this group came from a wide range of fields including medicine and physiology, mathematics, engineering, experimental physics, anthropology, economics, ecology, and zoology. The goal they pursued was sympathetic to Leopold's project: they, too, were looking for a way to bridge the gap between the humanities and the natural sciences, but whereas Leopold had been increasingly drawn toward the language of ethics and aesthetics, this group began by searching for new mathematical formalizations. One of their primary aims was to understand how complex systems are able to maintain their internal balance against fluctuations in their environment, and ultimately to find new scientific explanations for purposive behavior.

The belief that such explanations were now finally within reach rested on recent developments in the field of engineering, namely on the methodical exploration of the principle of feedback. The most popular example for mechanisms based on this principle is still the thermostat, which keeps a room's temperature constant by measuring its difference from the desired temperature and accordingly switching the heating system on or off; in other words, the output of the system (the room's temperature) is "fed back" into the system to regulate its subsequent operations. Similar homeostatic mechanisms were known to be at work in biological organisms, which also face the problem of maintaining certain variables (such as the sugar content of the blood or the osmotic pressure of bodily fluids) within bounds, or in ecosystems, where the numbers of predators and their prey would mutually control each other (as expressed in the Lotka-Volterra equations).[6] The properties of such a system could not be explained by breaking it down into its constituent parts—rather, it was the way in which these parts were interrelated, the organizational *patterns* which bound the components into a whole, which gave rise to "teleological" behavior. It was Norbert Wiener who coined the term *cybernetics* to designate the study of such self-regulating systems, and this nomenclature already indicated the larger hopes attached to the field: in classical Greek, a "kybernetes" is the pilot of a ship, and cybernetics was to enable scientists not only to "steer" the dynamics of complex systems of all kinds, but also to design machines that could steer themselves.[7]

Another one of the Macy group's paradigmatic objects of study was the nervous system. It was in this context that they encountered paradoxes logically analogous to those Leopold had run into with his land ethics and were forced to realize that the hope of "controlling" such systems had been overly optimistic. On the one hand, the nervous system was clearly amenable to a description in terms of circular causality and feedback loops. However, it turned out to be impossible to determine a direct correlation between external stimuli and the internal states of the system. Not only does the sensorium of living organisms rely on the principle of indifferent coding—that is, light, warmth, sound, and all other physical stimuli are all equally transfigured into electrochemical impulses;[8] most of the system's connections are not even to the sensory cells at all, but between the elements of the system (that is, the neurons). The nervous system can thus be considered as "closed" in terms of information, even as it is "open" in terms of energy: while it is nourished by the body, its internal states are not determined by the latter. The system computes new sensory input with its internal states in order to produce representations of the environment, but these representations cannot in any significant sense be said to have been *caused* by the environment—rather, they are a function of the system's earlier internal states. Most importantly, the nervous system can never compare its representations with objects in its environment, but only with *further* electric potentials as they appear within the system; in other words, it is utterly blind to everything in its environment that does not come in the form of an electric impulse.

Second-Order Cybernetics

The radical consequences of this model became apparent as soon as one took seriously the implication that the scientists who had generated this description of the nervous system had been able to do so only by virtue of their possessing nervous systems in the first place. In other words, they were not only "apart from," but also "a part of," the reality they were studying, and thus subject to precisely those limitations which they had described in their object of study. This clearly violated one of the basic precepts of scientific epistemology, namely, that "the properties of the observer must not enter into the descriptions of his observations."[9] The very idea of scientific objectivity had been founded on this principle of self-exemption, but in this context it was now exposed as a mystification. If cognizing systems are constituted like the nervous system, they can *only* refer to their environments by *simultaneously* referring to themselves; put differently, in the terms of the aprioric perfect familiar from Derridean deconstructivism: hetero-reference is *always already* auto-reference. The fact that such systems are radically closed off from their environments could no longer be seen as an obstacle to cognition; rather, this separation now had to be understood as the very condition of its possibility: the nervous system can "see" the world *only because* it is also blind to it. This realization required the reformulation of a number of concepts that had been central to the first wave of cybernetics. Information, for instance, could no longer be conceived as something that was present in the world "out there" and then transferred *into* the cognizing system; rather, it had to be seen as produced by distinctions that the system makes *internally*, by the act of selecting those elements of the environment which are relevant to its continuing self-reproduction. Consequently, communication could not be conceptualized as an "exchange" of information. When one person waves to another, what travels between them is not information, but a visual *signal*—which is "converted" into information only once the person waved to interprets it as an attempt to communicate (and the countless possibilities for misunderstanding make evident that the information which the wave is said to "carry" cannot possibly be intrinsic to it).

What all this amounted to was that the very idea of a singular "reality" or a total "environment" had to be given up. Environments and realities always come in the plural; as cognitive constructs, they are relative to an observer—indeed, they are *constituted* by the act of observation, which is necessarily blind to its own enabling conditions. Observing other observers within her environment, and observing that they cannot see what they cannot see, an observer can deduce that the same must be true for herself. She can thus shift her interest from the properties of the world as it is in itself ("*what* does the observer see?") to the properties of the observer who has brought it forth ("*how* does the observer see?"); she can proceed, as Heinz von Foerster was to put it, from the cybernetics of observed systems, that is, first-order cybernetics, to the cybernetics of observing systems, that is, second order-cybernetics[10]—and this, one may add, is the conceptual move implicit in the opening chapter of Leopold's *Almanac*. Such "second-order observations," however, cannot escape their own constitutive blindnesses: When Leopold's narrator observes the field mice and distinguishes between the environment as they see it and the environment as it "truly" is, he cannot at the same time determine whether the distinction he thus applies is *itself* "true" to the environment—or whether it subjects him to limitations analogous to those of the mice; he can only do so in *subsequent* observations, which again will be unable to see what they cannot see.

For the sake of convenience and with some justification in the chronology of their development, I have sketched out these ideas with the nervous system as my chief illustration. However, their range of application is much wider than that. Among the most significant developments which built on these insights was the work of the logician George Spencer Brown and of the biologists Humberto Maturana and Francisco Varela. In his book *Laws of Form*, published in 1969, Spencer Brown developed a "calculus of indications" which conceptualized observation as the act of drawing distinctions, and the latter as the formal basis for the logical description of all possible types of relationships. Drawing on Spencer Brown's new calculus, Maturana and Varela applied the principles of operational closure and self-organization to the workings of biological organisms, describing them as *autopoietic, that is, self-producing systems. Autopoietic systems close themselves off from their environment in order to maintain their own structure; they draw energy from their surroundings only in order to maintain the boundary that separates them from the environment. What occurs within this boundary is thus no longer determined by the chains of cause and effect that prevail outside, but by the previous states of the system itself, that is, by its history. Again, the properties of an autopoietic system cannot be explained by analyzing its components in isolation from the network of operations through which these components reproduce themselves. This process is circular, in that the system's structure is produced by its own operations, which are themselves conditioned by the structure. In the case of a cell, for example, enzymes are produced in order to metabolize nutrients, which are used to reproduce the DNA, which controls the production of enzymes in order to metabolize nutrients, and so forth. The only way in which the environment can directly determine the operations of such a system is by destroying it.

These were, of course, not the only developments that came out of early cybernetics. It also provided points of departure for new inquiries in numerous other fields such as ecology,[11] economics,[12] psychology,[13] physics,[14] as well as cognitive science, mathematics, and artificial intelligence.[15] While cybernetics had been launched as an interdisciplinary research agenda, it thus quickly turned into what can be called a metadiscipline, or as Ernst von Glasersfeld was to put it in the "Declaration of the American Society for Cybernetics" in 1981, "a way of thinking, not a collection of facts."

Niklas Luhmann's Theory of Social Systems

Rather than trying to sort out the many divergent paths which cybernetic thought has taken since the 1960s, I focus now on what is arguably the most sustained, provocative, and philosophically ambitious attempt to fully unfold the implications of second-order cybernetics and to synthesize the various strands of systems theory into a single, coherent theoretical architecture —namely the theory of social systems as it was developed by the German sociologist Niklas Luhmann. If Anglophone ecocritics have heard about Luhmann, it is most likely in connection with the single publication that he devoted explicitly to the subject of environmentalism, a book entitled *Ökologische Kommunikation* (*Ecological Communication*), which was published in 1986, in the heyday of Germany's green movement. The most immediate effect of this book was to turn the theory of social systems into a red rag for most environmentalists in Germany. Luhmann acknowledged the threat of ecological crisis, but he charged the movement with fearmongering and moral stridency. He answered the question which formed the subtitle of the volume—"Can modern society adapt itself to ecological dangers?"— largely in the negative. Yet Luhmann refused on principle to advance any comprehensive solutions, pronouncing as the goal of his inquiry not the remediation of environmental problems but the "avoidance of unnecessary excitement."[16] Lest these pronouncements seem willfully provocative, it will be necessary to consider them in the context of Luhmann's theory as a whole.

The basic building blocks of social systems theory are operationally closed, self-organizing, autopoietic systems such as they had been conceptualized by Maturana and Varela. However, Luhmann generalizes and radicalizes the concept. Not only biological organisms, but the individual consciousnesses which some of the latter "possess" *and* society as a whole can be described in these terms, although the operations through which they reproduce themselves do not involve biochemical components. Rather, they consist of meaningful events—mental events or "thought" in the case of consciousness, communication in the case of society.[17] What applies to biological systems also applies to psychic and social systems: their elements never occur as isolated phenomena, but only as links in a continuous sequence of similar events. As with the cell, the circular processes through which the elements of these systems reproduce themselves depend on a continuous "structural coupling" with an environment from which they are, however, also strictly separated. Structural coupling is thus the concept that takes the place of causality in the description of system/environment relations, and refers to the arrangement which allows a system to produce "resonance" with its specific environment. Consciousness cannot occur without a brain; if the brain dies, consciousness ceases. Yet neurological states can, as such, never "enter" consciousness but only "irritate" it. The same applies to society; it is structurally coupled with psychic systems,[18] but there is no transfer of patterns from consciousness into communication or vice versa (the same applies, mutatis mutandis, to psychic systems and their physical environments). Communication is therefore not, as early cybernetics would have it, the transmission of information from a sender to a receiver; it is an autopoietic process that determines by itself which parameters in the surrounding world are relevant to it, and becomes indifferent to the rest. It is this combination of closure and selective opening through which the system maintains itself as a system.

This is the basis for one of the most provocative claims of systems theory: humans are, Luhmann argues, not a part of society—rather, they constitute its environment. Furthermore, what we are accustomed to designate as a "human individual" is in fact not an "in-dividual" at all—it is not an indivisible unity, but rather a composite of several, structurally coupled systems which serve as each other's environment: psychic systems (consciousnesses) are the environment of social systems (communication), neurological systems (brains) are the environment of psychic systems, biological systems (i.e., human bodies) are the environment of neurological systems. Each of these systems is an "emergent" phenomenon, an explanation of which requires that we attend to the autopoietic process through which its components reproduce themselves. Accordingly, if we want to understand how society works, it is only of limited use to look at individual humans, bodies, or consciousnesses—rather, we have to examine the autopoiesis of communication.[19] Against this background, it should be apparent why Luhmann is skeptical with regard to the environmentalist project: humans are simply not in a position to impose their designs on society. They cannot "control" communication—communication can only change itself.

There is yet another serious obstacle to any attempt at social control. According to Luhmann, modern society is characterized by "functional differentiation," that is, it has evolved several distinct subsystems which perform specific social functions. Among these systems are law, politics, science, religion, and the economy. Each of these is an operationally closed, autopoietic system of communication in its own right, for which the other subsystems serve as intrasocial environments. These subsystems reproduce themselves by the use of specialized codes of communication—for example, legal/illegal for the law, true/false for science, payment/nonpayment for the economy—which they use to observe and distinguish themselves from the rest of society. "Communication" must not be confused with natural language—science, for example, would obviously be hard put if it had to rely only on language to establish the truth or falsity of a proposition, and mere words could hardly replace money. To increase the likelihood of successful communication, all of the function systems have therefore developed what Luhmann refers to as "symbolically generalized communication media," for example, money (for the economy), power (for politics), or jurisdiction (for the law). Each of the function systems creates its own reality, and none of them is in a position to control the operations of any of the others—there is no hierarchy between them, and they cannot be mapped onto each other: truth cannot buy you a sandwich, and a profitable crime is still a crime.[20]

The breakdown of the communist command economy is an obvious example for the problems that arise when the code of one system is forcefully imposed on that of another. Yet Luhmann is no Adam Smith: there is no invisible hand that would harmonize the actions of the function systems. As a mode of social organization, functional differentiation is not better or worse than any of the other modes of organization for which there are historical precedents.[21] Neither is Luhmann a traditional Darwinist: the fact that modern society is more complex than its predecessors by no means implies that it is better adapted to its environment—from a perspective within society (and, in terms of communication, there are no others), all we can say is that thus far, it has been able to continue its autopoiesis.

Not all communication takes place within the function systems—in most everyday conversations, for example, we do not distinguish whether what the other person says is legal or scientifically true; but that is also the reason why such conversations are so easily discontinued. As Luhmann puts it, the function systems "float on a sea of small-scale systems that are continuously newly built and then dissolved."[22] On the larger scale of social evolution, these ephemeral types of communication do not leave much of a trace. If a communication is to be of lasting consequence, it must use the code of one of the function systems. This is indeed the chief problem with which environmentalism has struggled, because the language it uses to describe both itself and its objects often does not meet this requirement. While it is quite possible to voice "mountain-like" thoughts[23] and to demand that society pay attention, it is naïve to expect that this will produce the desired consequences, as Aldo Leopold himself was fully aware. All of the different function systems have reacted to the attempts of the environmental movement to remodel society in accordance with ecological criteria. But they have done so on their own terms, namely by developing green subdiscourses which in effect subverted the movement's universalist aspirations: the system of politics reacted with environmentalist parties and the creation of new government agencies; the law with environmental legislation; the economy with organic food stores, "greenwashing," and carbon-credit systems; (Catholic) religion with declaring Francis of Assisi the patron saint of ecology; science with new environmental studies programs and, more recently, with the creation of a new subdiscipline of literary studies: ecocriticism. In each of these cases, the effects have been first and foremost on the respective function systems themselves—they have made a difference in communication, and only secondarily on the ecological environment.

Ecocriticism as Second-Order Observation

Now, what does all of this imply for ecocriticism? First of all, and most generally, it should be understood as a call to intellectual humility. This might sound somewhat surprising, coming from a thinker whose project was a "supertheory" aiming at universal applicability. Yet the crux of social systems theory and second-order cybernetics is that *all* observer positions come with a blind spot, and that it is precisely their blind spots which condition whatever purchase they have on the world. Luhmann was always quick to point out that social systems theory was itself nothing more than a theoretical option: it offers a vantage point from which old problems can appear in a new light (and without which some newer problems would perhaps not become visible at all). What it does *not* offer is an Archimedean point from which we could unhinge the social order—nor even the assurance that, though society may be beyond saving, at least we are not among the duped. As Hans-Georg Moeller writes, a "supertheory reflects on the fact that it and its validity are its own product—and is therefore absolutely contingent."[24] We need not do systems theory, and even if we do, we do not need to do it all the time. As a theory about society, social systems theory can produce a description of society that can claim to be scientifically true. But because it communicates within the function system of science, it cannot control what kind of resonance it will produce *outside* of that system. Therefore, it is not in a position to offer practical solutions for the ecological problems which society faces (although it is able to explain very well why those who have claimed to be able to do so have, by and large, fared so poorly). Systems theory does not deny that such practical solutions are necessary (and when Luhmann talks about the dangers facing modern society, ecological problems are always high on the list). It only denies that a theory, of whatever stripe, can be of much help in this respect. Social systems theory thus asks us to accommodate ourselves to the fact that what the environmental movement has been saying about nature applies just as much to society: we can never know it fully, and it is essentially beyond rational control.

Metaphorically speaking, one might therefore say that an engagement with systems theory can have the beneficial effect of a spasmolytic: It could help ecocriticism to accept its limitations as a necessary prerequisite for the production of a distinct kind of knowledge—in other words, to accept that what ecocritics do is read texts and write about them, not campaign for new environmental legislation or plug tailpipes. Only to the extent that ecocriticism is something other than the academic wing of the environmental movement can it render that movement a service which is perhaps more valuable than general consciousness-raising or the recruitment of new personnel. Rather than insist on the factuality of the ecological crisis (as environmentalists must), ecocritics might take seriously the question why the argument that the ecological crisis really is real has gained so remarkably little traction—and to ponder the possibility that where it did, the reasons for this might be found *within* society, and not in its environment (which also means: not in individual consciousnesses). Taking the position of a second-order observer, ecocriticism can examine how environmentalism (or another organization or social system) observes, which distinctions it uses in order to unfold the paradoxes these distinctions necessarily entail—it can try to see what environmentalism must lose from sight in order to see what it sees and to do what it does.

A glance back at Leopold's *A Sand County Almanac* may indicate how such an interpretive practice might proceed. The chief distinction the text employs is that between the "wild" and the "social," and it subordinates the latter term to the former—it is those qualities of the social which preserve a measure of wildness that are to be considered most valuable. However, the distinction reenters on *both* of its own sides: not only is there a "wild" side to the social, but the wild itself also displays social characteristics. What allows Leopold to nevertheless uphold the distinction and to use it in order to pass plausible judgments is the deployment of a set of tropes that is not only deeply embedded in the liberal tradition, but that was also part and parcel of the struggle against totalitarianism in which U.S. Americans at the time saw their country engaged. In the *Almanac,* the preservation of wild nature is the preservation of a space where the individual must take complete responsibility for its actions, and thus of a core repository of quintessentially American values. Human encroachments on wilderness, on the other hand, are consistently aligned with totalitarian ideology, as when modern farming is denounced as aiming at "a sort of Pax Germanica of the agricultural world."[25] A similar intertwining of "properly" ecological subject matter and concerns about social organization in a more general sense can be seen in many other key texts of the environmental movement.[26] From a perspective informed by social systems theory, such semantic parallels cannot be dismissed as merely ornamental—they are at the very heart of the matter, showing, as they are, that ecological communication is one of the modes in which society observes itself.

NOTES

1. Leopold, *Sand County Almanac*, 3–4.

2. Ibid., 4.

3. Ibid.

4. Ibid., 5.

5. Cf. Fritzell, "The Conflicts of Ecological Conscience," 139.

6. All these examples illustrate the principle of negative feedback, which was initially at the center of attention; the principle of positive feedback was explored only in the course of the 1950s.

7. The more immediate reference was, of course, to the "governor" of James Watt's original steam engine, the most consequential application of the principle of negative feedback in modern engineering.

8. As such, this was not a new discovery—it had already been made by the German physiologist Johannes Peter Müller in the middle of the nineteenth century.

9. von Foerster, "Cybernetics," 7.

10. Ibid., 8.

11. Central in this respect is the work of the brothers Howard T. Odum and Eugene P. Odum. For an overview, see Odum, *Systems Ecology*. James Lovelock's Gaia hypothesis and Lynn Margulis's work on the role of symbiosis in evolution are also strongly informed by systems theory (cf. Lovelock, *Gaia;* and Margulis, *Symbiotic Planet*).

12. Cf. Kenneth Boulding's *Evolutionary Economics*. It was also Boulding who had coined the catchphrase "Spaceship Earth" in 1965—a metaphor which neatly captures the view of earth as a closed system.

13. Most notably the research conducted at the Mental Research Institute at Palo Alto, the results of which were summarized in 1967 by Watzlawick, Beavin, and Jackson in *The Pragmatics of Human Communication;* the driving force behind much of this work was Gregory Bateson, *Steps to an Ecology of Mind.*

14. Most famously Ilya Prigogine's work on dissipative structures (cf. Prigogine and Stengers, *Order out of Chaos*).

15. Hofstadter's *Gödel, Escher, Bach* remains by far the most entertaining introduction to these developments.

16. Luhmann, *Ecological Communication*, xviii.

17. For a summary of Luhmann's account of meaning, which is heavily indebted to the phenomenology of Husserl, cf. Moeller, *Luhmann Explained*, 65–70.

18. And society is coupled *only* with psychic systems: "there can be no physical, chemical, or purely biological interferences with social communication" (Luhmann, *Einführung*, 123, my translation)—only events that have first passed through the "needle's ear" of consciousness can have effects on communication.

19. If these claims seem stark and counterintuitive, it is useful to recall what we know of humanity's evolutionary history. *Homo sapiens* as a biological species has been in existence for about 100,000 years; only in the last twentieth part of this time span has the evolution of larger social structures really taken off. If social evolution was determined by the biological properties of humans, this time-lag would present a considerable

conundrum; if we grant that society consists not of biological entities, but of communications, and that it therefore possesses a dynamic that is entirely its own, the incongruence between biological evolution and social evolution is a matter of course.

20. Wolfe, *Animal Rites,* 200.

21. The major other forms of social organization which Luhmann contrasts with functional differentiation are stratified differentiation (e.g., feudalism), segmentary differentiation (as in tribal societies), and center-periphery differentiation (as in many premodern empires); these forms are rarely found in "pure" forms, and in many regions of modern world society, functional differentiation is complemented by other modes of social organization.

22. Quoted in Moeller, *Luhmann Explained,* 30.

23. cf. Leopold, *Sand County Almanac,* 137ff.

24. Moeller, *Luhmann Explained,* 200.

25. Leopold, *Sand County Almanac,* 199.

26. For example, in Rachel Carson's *Silent Spring* or in the works of Edward Abbey and Gary Snyder. Cf. Bergthaller, *Populäre Ökologie.*

Ecocentric Postmodern Theory: Interrelations between Ecological, Quantum, and Postmodern Theories

The ecological turn has not only brought an integral awareness of the natural world into the field of literary studies, reorienting the humanities toward a more biocentric worldview, but has also drawn attention to the role of literature in influencing our knowledge of the world. According to Norman N. Holland: "Literature has power over us. At least it certainly *feels* that way when we are, as we say, 'absorbed' in a story or drama or poem."[1] The cognitive function accorded to literature is of fundamental importance for ecocritics, who expect of writers that they inscribe ecological viewpoints in their work. Scott Slovic's question, "How can literature and literary studies help us appreciate both local and global environmental concerns?"[2] recalls the earliest ecocritical inquiries into the possible effects of literary studies within the biotic processes, such as the memorable questions posed by Joseph W. Meeker, who asked if literature is "an activity which adapts us better to the world or one which estranges us from it."[3]

If literature and its study can in some sense help restore our connection to the earth, then its epistemological dimension becomes a core concern for ecocritical analysis. Literature is one of the most effective "signifying practices"[4] (producing and receiving experience), and conceptual frameworks (what we think and know about the world) find their best expression in it. Its influence upon our conceptions of ecological systems produces culture-specific discursive practices (acts of reading and writing the earth) that profoundly affect the state of human and nonhuman communities. Defining it as "an intellectual and emotional laboratory," Peter Swirski has argued that literature "contains the narrative and cognitive machinery for examining issues that challenged thinkers of yesterday, and will continue to challenge the thinkers of tomorrow." Indeed, as Swirski posits, literature in effect generates knowledge, because it involves inferences about the world which influence our perceptions: "like so many other things that human beings do naturally, universally, and transculturally, our aptitude for imagining other worlds is rooted in evolutionary adaptation."[5]

This leads straight to the effects of human knowledge on the natural environment, a subject on which Keith Wilde and Michael T. Caley have written in their interpretation of the Canadian philosopher Jerzy A. Wojciechowski's theory of the ecology of knowledge. According to Wojciechowski, humans are culturally and biologically transformed by knowledge. Our environments also undergo a deliberate transformation "transmitted through human minds whose interpretations are necessarily influenced by changes in the ambient world and the state of our species." Wilde and Caley contend that ecosystems and human knowledge "exist in complementary relationships." Knowledge, then, is the prime instrumental tool for the desired change from anthropocentrism to more holistic ecological thought in our biotic relations. "Humans create knowledge by acts of rational effort," the authors write, and "we use this knowledge to affect the world around us. In turn, the world acts back on us, motivating renewed acts of knowing. These actions employ and modify the body of knowledge, producing new impacts on the ambient world and consequently on the knower and her neighbors and progeny. Thus, humankind as knowers and thinkers, the ambient world and the body of knowledge are in an ecological relationship."[6]

The complementary relationship between knowledge and nature is best described by David Bohm, the chief proponent of the ecological paradigm in quantum theory. Relying on experimental evidence, Bohm avers that nature responds to human knowledge in a nearly synchronic manner. "What we are suggesting," he states, is "that only a view of knowledge as an integral part of the total flux of process may lead generally to a more harmonious and orderly approach to life as a whole." That is to say, nature responds to our mind-set, and consequent actions, in apparent physical manifestations. In order to explain more clearly how nature confirms our theories based on the present body of knowledge, Bohm offers a meaningful analogy in the first chapter of *Wholeness and the Implicate Order:* "experience with nature is very much like experience with human beings. If one approaches another man with a fixed "theory" about him as an "enemy" . . . he will respond similarly and thus one's "theory" will apparently be confirmed by experience. Similarly, nature will respond in accordance with the theory with which it is approached."[7]

Bohm warns us against falling "into the habit of seeing reality and acting toward it as if it were constituted of separately existent fragments corresponding to how it appears in our thought."[8] He clarifies his assertion further in his *Unfolding Meaning*, noting the destructive consequences of humanity's fragmentary view of life. "Now the same thing holds," he says, "in ecology. You divide the world into parts, but you find the division doesn't hold—that pollution occurs in one place and goes on to another, and problems created in one place spread out, and little things happening here and there all add up all over . . . that is fragmentation."[9] If we want to change today's climate of conflict in all areas of life, we must change our body of knowledge and restructure our discourses accordingly. Clearly, as Bohm also points out, "The challenge that faces humanity is unique . . . [and] a new kind of creative surge is needed to meet it. This has to include not just a new way of doing science but a new approach to society and even more, a new kind of consciousness."[10] This surge is already present in the ecological turn in the humanities. It has not, however, completely permeated our discursive formations, which are still confined within a whole set of misleading dichotomies.

Notably, the impact of anthropocentric discourses on our cultural and ideological standpoints, on public issues, and economic policies is everywhere to be found, with drastic consequences in the countless environmental problems surrounding us. The dualistic epistemologies and instrumentalist ideologies that regulate human practices have been unable to provide effective solutions for our pressing ecological as well as social problems. This social paradigm with its ideology of economic growth continues to have adverse effects on natural environments. Therefore, we need to replace it "with the ideology of ecological sustainability."[11] What inevitably follows is the question posed by Arne Naess: "how are the ecologically destructive, but firmly established ways of production and consumption . . . to be changed?" In answer, Naess makes a strong point with his proposal for changes that, according to him, "have to be from the inside *and* outside, all in one." For Naess, sustainable change in consciousness ("inside change") is inextricably linked with change in socioeconomic structures ("outside change"): "the necessity of efforts to change mentality is closely associated with the necessity of organized efforts for profound changes in the structure of society. These two kinds of efforts must be coordinated, not polarized against one another."[12] The solution to the problem of how such a goal can actually be realized lies in an ecologically grounded epistemic model capable of providing a foundation for discursive change. This demands a shift in our epistemological formulations concerning the complex interplay between human social systems and the ecosystems of the planet. In what follows I propose a postmodern ecocritical theory which paves the way toward this goal, and also offers a better understanding of literature's crucial role in human engagement with the environment, and our valuation and understanding of it.

The point here is to change the conceptual frameworks that have shaped our present way of thinking and are largely responsible for the ecological crisis. Ecocriticism holds such a promise, and can play a decisive role in our knowledge of the world. We need, however, an intellectual framework to formulate a consistent ecocritical theory that is not subject to arbitrary assumptions, or to correctness in any absolute sense, but can always be adjusted to new developments, supplying us with new epistemic models to represent the world. Then its practical and theoretical effects over a range of social disciplines will be more evident, and those of the new discourse formations to which it will lead. Such a framework is provided by a "reconstructive" postmodern theory, which can "effect a 'paradigm shift' of comparable significance to that associated with Copernicus."[13]

As Steven Best and Douglas Kellner ascertained in the 1990s, we have already witnessed "an epochal transformation," as "part of a major paradigm shift" that has influenced "multiple fields of knowledge." This is the postmodern paradigm that has distinctively bridged "the gulf between the 'two cultures' of science and the humanities," leading to a "cumulative" paradigm shift in many academic disciplines.[14] It is true that postmodernism has subverted traditional modes of thought by deconstructing, displacing, and demystifying "the logocentric, ethnocentric, phallocentric order of things,"[15] and articulated "a crisis about the legitimation of modern forms of knowledge" without proposing another essentialist form of knowledge.[16] This refusal to engage in essentialism has led to polemical debates around postmodernism, and rejection, especially in the ecocritical field.

Since then, however, an ecological reconceptualization of postmodernism has been under way. In its ecological turn, postmodernism has become a reconstructive theory,[17] and can thus offer prospects for the proposed discursive change as a possible solution to the planetary ecological crisis. Reconstructive postmodernism suggests that all knowledge is perspectival, and it supports cultural and biological diversity, in the sense, to quote J. Baird Callicott, of "unity and harmony in multiplicity." Significantly, as Callicott states, it rebuilds "from foundations constituted by the 'new physics' . . . and the 'new biology.' "[18] As such it provides a new conceptual framework that can close the ontological divide between nature and culture, and substitutes for the causal-realist model of reality a holistic and integrative model, from which more ecologically oriented webs of knowledge can be generated.

Postmodernism thus understood is "ecocentric" at its end, which I call "ecocentric postmodern theory," as it is characterized by interrelated ecological and quantum principles. The defining feature of this theory is the principle of interconnectedness. As Warwick Fox explains: "This is the idea that there is no firm ontological divide in the field of existence," and no "bifurcation in reality between the human and non-human realms. Rather all entities are constituted by their relationships."[19] Drawing upon the ecological implications of quantum physics, ecocentric postmodern theory stands in a reciprocal relation to the viewpoints effectuated by quantum theory. It generates the necessary epistemic model to accommodate the paradigm shift by providing a "fusion of horizons" in this connection. Its main persuasive force, therefore, comes from the holistic paradigm of quantum physics which, like postmodernism, has problematized "all our most basic conceptions of knowledge, truth, and reality."[20] The logic of quantum theory converges in significant ways with postmodern logic, and contributes to the formulation of a sustainable ecocritical thought which can appropriately address the multidimensional complexity of social and ecological reality.

The conjuncture of postmodern and quantum theories in the interpretation of the complex texture of reality is also suggested by postmodern theorists such as Baudrillard (*In the Shadow*), Kroker ("Baudrillard's Marx"), Deleuze and Guattari (*A Thousand Plateaus*), Hassan (*The Postmodern Turn*), and Lyotard (*The Differend*).[21] Undoubtedly quantum theories provide literary critics with theoretical models and concepts which afford "metaphorical insights into the literature of our period."[22] But connections to ecological perspectives have been largely ignored in their appropriation. The regulative idea of ecocentric postmodern theory, by contrast, is that of the "network" model of transdisciplinary research.[23] This model radically integrates scientific, ecological, and postmodern views in order to constitute a new cognitive paradigm.

Ecocentric postmodern theory is multiperspectival. It neither claims to set standards for absolute truths, nor does it fall into radical relativism. It embraces revisionary forms of knowledge by crossing the boundaries between various social and scientific disciplines. Therefore the assistance of a transdisciplinary theory is necessary to replace the anthropocentric epistemic model with an integrative one; one that is conjunctive, relational, holistic, and dialogic. Only a holistic approach, as Alan Marshall observes, "that integrates the various systems of a natural community, can hope to solve ecological and environmental problems."[24] The most rigorous formulations of this idea are found in quantum physics, which has predicated a new field of reality where everything is inextricably interconnected.

As the physicist John Archibald Wheeler announced: "useful as it is under every circumstance to say that the world exists 'out there' independent of us, that view can no longer be upheld. There is a strange sense in which this is a 'participatory universe.'"[25] Similarly Ilya Prigogine notes: "whatever we call reality, it is revealed to us only through an active construction in which we participate."[26] In quantum physics, this essential bond between human and nonhuman reality is called "quantum contextualism," where correlated nonlocal connections exist between apparently separate particles. Many physicists, foremost among them Werner Heisenberg, held that quantum theory irreversibly changed our view of reality. Although Heisenberg was convinced of the indeterminate nature of reality, in the sense that there are only probabilities, he did acknowledge the particles' nonlocal correlations and thus the interrelational nature of reality: "The world thus appears as a complicated tissue of events, in which connections of different kinds alternate or overlap or combine and thereby determine the texture of the whole."[27]

This process of connections can also be observed at the macrophysical level of reality,[28] which Richard Healey later described as having "irreducible dynamical properties" which are "its nonseparability and its holism." These two features of the process are distinct, and there "is an interesting relation between them."[29] This "interesting relation" has been defined by Niels Bohr, as "our positions as observers of that nature of which we are part ourselves."[30] Although Bohr's Copenhagen interpretation stands in marked contrast to the ontological interpretation most specifically known as the hidden-variable version of quantum theory devised by David Bohm, it, too, validates the interconnected nature of reality. Although the conceptual problems generated by the contending positions of the realists and antirealists in quantum theory have not been satisfactorily resolved,[31] it can be stated that the principle of interconnectedness is a key feature on which there seems to be a general agreement among physicists. In the words of d'Espagnant: "The world cannot consistently be described as essentially a collection of physical objects of finite size . . . which would each possess its own specific attributes, even if these attributes—size, location, velocity, and so forth—are only approximately determined, and even if the systems are allowed to interact through arbitrarily complex, long-range forces that decrease when distance increases."[32] "Overwhelmingly confirmed by experiment" as it is,[33] the new model of the "participatory universe" has certainly shattered the idea of a physical reality that is independent of ourselves, showing that the very nature of reality is characterized by wholeness. "The results of the measurements of two quantities," writes d'Espagnant, "are correlated in spite of the fact that the measurements take place in two regions of space that are arbitrarily far apart." And he goes on to state with certainty that the correlations between the subatomic particles defy the logic of cause-and-effect relationships, and no theory grounded in the causal-realist views of reality can account for this correlation. The experiments show, as d'Espagnant observes, "that the kind of physical reality whose regularities the principles of physics are expected to map" constitutes "a nonseparable whole, with properties quite different from those we are accustomed to attribute to any kind of reality."[34]

The nonlocal connections among the particles also formed the basis of Bohm and Hiley's observations. These particles are "strongly connected even when they are far apart," and "the measuring instrument and what is being observed interact in a well-defined way." Reality in its quantum states exhibits itself most clearly as an undivided whole. In Bohm and Hiley's words: "what actually happens is that the process of interaction reveals a property involving the whole context in an inseparable way—indeed it may be said that the *measuring apparatus* and that which is observed *participate irreducibly* in each other."[35] This insight possesses profound implications for our perception of nature and provides the most significant philosophical key to the nature of fundamental reality. This scientific dimension puts ecocentric postmodern theory in a strong position to describe our participatory role in our biotic relations.[36]

Its literary dimension is also particularly important as it can satisfactorily expand ecocriticism's scope, making it more inclusive, especially of postmodern fictions. The textual richness of a given literary text, or in Kate Rigby's words, "the formal qualities manifested by all texts,"[37] do not have to be excluded from ecocritical analyses. On this basis, in unfolding the holistic structure of ecological thought, postmodern fiction invites special ecocritical attention. It is a kind of fiction that is both "reflexively fictional,"[38] and decisively ecological. Compounding postmodern and ecological ideas, such as relationality, diversity, and multiplicity, it displays a multiperspectival approach to the real and the fictive. And it does so by conjoining literary realism with metafictional narrative strategies, creating an uneasy mingling of two seemingly incompatible narrative techniques.

This, however, serves an important purpose, which is to present the natural world both as a discursive construct and as an integral part of human experience. The challenge to realist notions of representation is maintained alongside an overt critique of radical textualism. That is why ecological postmodern fiction transcends "either/or" categories. Environmental awareness is there as well as the postmodern preoccupation with linguistic playfulness. In fact such fictions carry the signature of Bohm's notion of "a *new order* of creative surge," and often employ scientific principles in their ecologized metafictional narratives to contest the dualist conception of reality, and to instill environmental awareness in their readers even though their plots may not be primarily focused on ecological issues. The scientific dimension actually serves a discernible ecological purpose. The ecocritical reading of Jeanette Winterson's *Gut Symmetries* that follows provides an example of how ecocentric postmodern theory finds its best literary expression.

Focusing on the idea of a participatory universe from a postmodern perspective, *Gut Symmetries* conspicuously illustrates the views expressed so

far. It incorporates the ecological implications of quantum physics by exploring humanity's relationship to the entire universe on the metaphoric level
and plays with the symmetries of macro- and microphysical reality. Set at sea
on QE 2 and a smaller yacht, the action is based on a love triangle that
involves a young British physicist, Alice; a Princeton physicist, Jove; and his
poet wife, Stella, who narrate their intermingled relationships in chapters
titled after Tarot cards which reflect their identities. The stories of all three
characters, their family backgrounds, and different historical periods are
woven into a quantum quest for wholeness. The references to Paracelsus in
the opening pages, who believed that "the galaxa goes through the belly,"[39]
signal the text's engagement with the Grand Unified Theories in science and
life: "The Miracle of the One that the alchemists sought is not so very far
from the infant theory of hyperspace, where all the seeming dislocations and
separations of the atomic and sub-atomic worlds are unified into a cooperating whole" (2)

Later in the novel, this "whole" is revealed as a time-space continuum
where the distinctions between past, present, and future dissolve, which
Alice explains as a collapse into a wave function. In her account of her
father's death in this way, Alice states: "A wave function spreads indefi-
nitely. . . . Theoretically, it was always possible, though unlikely, to find my
father beyond the solar system, his clustered energies elsewhere. More obviously, my father seemed to be here, as you and I are here, but we too can be
measured as wave functions, unlimited by the boundaries of our bodies"
(161). Moreover, the repeated question of "What is it that you contain?" and
its answer, "The expanding universe in your gut" (2), forms the novel's
textualized representation of "Gut" (Grand Unified Theory) both as intuitive
knowledge that comes through the "gut," and also as a scientific model that
extends into the love story itself. That is why Winterson defines her story
through Alice as "a journey through the thinking gut" (13). Thus, by focusing
on life's unifying principle, Gut Symmetries calls attention to the importance
of constructing contextual versions of reality implicating ecocentric conceptions of the world.

To highlight this particular point, Winterson places the laws of quantum
physics in a complementary relationship with poetry, art, and mysticism.
Throughout the narrative, intertexts from physicists like Planck, Einstein,
Heisenberg, and Oppenheimer are interwoven with the ideas of alchemists
and mysticists, and with references to Greek myths, poets, painters and the
Kabbalah, in order to exhibit their interrelations, to present a dynamic
interaction of ideas, and to point to nature's undivided wholeness. The novel
becomes a perfect example of postmodern fiction's "pluralizing recourse" to
multiple discourses,[40] which blend to create multiple insights about what

Alice calls "the true nature of the world" (12). Like Stella and Jove, who struggle to define themselves in terms of the theoretical perspective of the new physics, Alice tries to adjust her life to the holistic vision she finds in quantum theory. "As a scientist I try to work toward certainties," she remarks. "As a human being I seem to be moving away from them. If I need any proof of the provisional nature of what is called the world I was beginning to find it" (27).

This exemplifies what Bohm calls humanity's "fragmentary self-world view,"[41] and the idea that reality corresponds to this view, which Alice underlines quite literally: "We reflect our reality" she says, and "our reality reflects us" (18). Winterson, however, also foregrounds the difficulty of applying holistic principles in the realm of human experience that is still underpinned by binary thought. Throughout the text, Alice struggles to resolve this problem. "I cannot see past my three-dimensional concept of reality," she declares, "bound as it is to good/bad, black/white, real/unreal, alive/dead" (208). The novel highlights this concern when it flaunts concepts of wholeness and fragmentation in a highly problematic integration. This creates a unique postmodern paradox similar to the paradoxes generated by quantum experiments: "Every quantum experiment has shown, again and again . . . that particles hold positions contradictory and simultaneous" (160). And it culminates in the problematic account of the Grand Unified Theory ("Gut") itself at the end of the novel.

Despite its deliberate problematization, "Gut" illustrates a holistic vision of reality, and operates as an index of truth that is both accepted as it underlines an implicit ecocentric outlook, and also rejected as its totalizing assumptions become problematic in the text's discursive field. Winterson uses the premises of "Gut" as the novel's central metaphor to emphasize the inseparability of existence, but she also subverts its implications as the only truthful metanarrative, reiterating the postmodern distrust of all totalizing masterly discourses, and echoing Bohm's views: "to take any physical theory as an absolute truth must tend to fix the general forms of thought in physics and thus to contribute to fragmentation."[42] As we have seen, Winterson calls attention to the provisional nature of all conceptual frameworks. Stella, for example, has learned from her Jewish upbringing to reject all fixed conceptualizations, "which are all and always provisional" (168). With this recognition she is able to perceive the world in terms of interconnections instead of fixed forms. Therefore, she sees symmetries instead of differences between herself and Alice, even though Alice has an affair with Jove.

Obviously the act of both addressing and subverting the truth claims enhances the postmodern paradox, "in an uneasy contradictory relationship of constant slippage." This slippage, which marks *Gut Symmetries*, opening it to "plural, contestatory elements without necessarily reducing or recuperating them,"[43] is expressed rather strikingly in terms of a dance metaphor by Stella:

> Is truth what we do not know?
>
> What we know does not satisfy us. What we know constantly reveals itself as partial. What we know, generation by generation, is discarded into new knowings. . . .
>
> Instead of a hoard of certainties . . . I can give up taxonomy and invite myself to the dance: the patterns, rhythms, multiplicities, paradoxes, shifts, currents, cross-currents, irregularities, irrationalities, geniuses, joints, pivots, worked over time, and through time, to find the lines of thought that still transmit. (82–83)

Winterson shows that contestatory relationships produce the illusion of separation. As Stella says: "What is the separateness of things when the current that flows to each is live? It is the livingness I want." Her relational vision is finally shared by Alice, while Jove remains unable to perceive it. He fails to understand what Alice realizes: "we and the sum of universe cannot be separated in the way of the old Cartesian dialectic of 'I' and 'world.' Observer and observed are part of the same process" (162). From this perspective, *Gut Symmetries* creates a fusion of horizons between what Jim Cheney calls "*Mind*scapes" and "*land*scapes,"[44] by invoking interrelations between knowledge and experience. Signifying the symmetries between mindscapes and landscapes, "Gut" seeks to unify the natural forces of "the strong, weak, and electromagnetic quanta" in a single theoretical framework (97). Thus all physical phenomena can be explained by an underlying interconnectedness.

Ecological meanings emerge from this standpoint: "The short and organised equations of physics are as beautiful and surprising as the natural forces they interpret," says Alice to emphasize our participatory relationship to nature: "Now more than ever . . . our place in the universe and the place of the universe in us, is proving to be one of active relationship" (97–98). In this way, the metaphor of Gut enacts the ecological vision embedded in quantum theories. The best example is again provided by Alice: "This is more than a scientist's credo. The separateness of our lives is a sham. Physics, mathematics, music, painting, my politics, my love for you, my work, the star-dust of my body, the spirit that impels it, clocks diurnal, time perpetual, the roll, rough, tender, swamping, liberating, breathing, moving, thinking nature, human nature and the cosmos are patterned together" (97). Such passages endorse the novel's ecocentric postmodern stance, and produce what Arne Naess calls "the relational total-field image" of life.[45]

Gut Symmetries also plays with the connections between language and knowledge as it crosses over from poetry to physics, fact to fiction, and from fragmentation to wholeness. Although in such border-crossings the postmodern challenge of referentiality is not altogether abandoned, the focus is kept on the interrelations of the fictional and the real, producing a postmodern blurring of boundaries. Already in the beginning the reader is prepared for it: "This is a true story. If it seems strange, ask yourself, 'What is not strange?' If it seems unlikely, ask yourself, 'What is likely?' " (9). The autobiography of Stella's immigrant father "that re-writes itself as fiction" provides another telling example: "The fictions that pass the thin walls of reality . . . assume a different kind of truth" 168). But when words become "weak signals into the outer space of each other" (25), as Alice claims, and when Stella announces them as "light things that change nothing . . . Nothing real only skill in the play" (31), the referential meaning of language is made highly suspect. Yet the novel also posits that the problematic relationship between the sign and its referent, if perceived in terms of symmetries, creates new possibilities in language. The word "symmetries" in the title invokes symmetries between art and science, heart and mind, love and reason, and human and the nonhuman realms, that exponentially manifest as "vibrations, relationships, possibilities" (207). *Gut Symmetries* concludes with the final awareness that all boundaries of fact/fiction, word/world, experience/theory, physics/poetry, and human/nonhuman are essentially fluid and provisional. Winterson's poetic statement in the prologue is effective in preparing the reader for this end. The deep ecological vision expressed here is the message of an ecocentric postmodern writer calling for a more integral awareness of our planet:

> It may be that here in our provisional world of dualities and oppositional pairs: black/white, good/evil, male/female, conscious/unconscious, Heaven/Hell, predatory/prey, we compulsively act out the drama of our beginning, when what was whole, halved, and seeks again its wholeness.
>
> Have pity on this small blue planet searching through time and space. (5)

NOTES

1. Holland, "The Power," 395.
2. Slovic, "Love Is Never Abstract," 18.
3. Meeker, *The Comedy*, 4.
4. Culler, *Literary Theory*, 43.
5. Swirski, *Of Literature*, 11, 6–7.
6. Wilde and Caley, "An Introduction," 47, 48, 46.
7. Bohm, *Wholeness*, 63, 6.
8. Ibid., 8.

9. Bohm, *Unfolding Meaning,* 28.

10. Bohm and Peat, *Science, Order,* 207.

11. Fox, "Deep Ecology," 155.

12. Naess, *Ecology, Community,* 87, 89, 91–92.

13. Fox, "Deep Ecology," 154.

14. Best and Kellner, *The Postmodern Turn,* viii, 253, 261.

15. Hassan, "Making Sense," 445.

16. Waugh, *Practising Postmodernism,* 54.

17. The term *reconstructive* (or *ecological*) postmodernism was coined by Charlene Spretnak, who argued that contrary to deconstructive postmodernism, reconstructive postmodernism "replaces groundlessness with groundedness" (*Resurgence,* 72).

18. Callicott, *Earth's Insights,* 185.

19. Fox, "Deep Ecology," 157.

20. Norris, "Quantum Nonlocality," 36.

21. This is not to deny the fact that although quantum theorists are mostly concerned with discontinuities of particles, probabilities, indeterminacy, chance, and uncertainty, all of which relate to the postmodern play of signifiers and textual discontinuity, their approach radically diverges from the logic of ecocentric postmodern theory.

22. Bohnenkamp, "Post-Einsteinian Physics," 20.

23. The "network model" was originated by Mary Hesse, who argues that academicians develop new theories upon a set of local beliefs at a given time, and apply old beliefs to new situations in building new theoretical knowledge. Although this is not exactly what the new reconstructive postmodern theory signifies, Hesse's approach partially corresponds to the way in which I formulate ecocentric postmodern theory.

24. Marshall, *Order from Chaos,* 140.

25. Wheeler quoted in Selleri, "Wave-Particle Duality," 297.

26. Prigogine and Stengers, *Order Out of Chaos,* 293.

27. Heisenberg, *Physics and Philosophy,* 7.

28. Many physicists are highly critical of applying quantum logic to macrophysical reality. For example, van Frassen cautions the scientific community to distinguish macrophysical objects from the subatomic ones whose indeterminate ontological status sparked off their numerous interpretations in the first place. Despite such objections, others like Alan Sokal argue that, "if the laws of physics, inferred from laboratory experiments, have no validity outside the laboratory, why on earth would anyone bother doing those experiments in the first place?" (Sokal and Bricmont, "Defence of a Modest Scientific Realism," 11).

29. Healey, *The Philosophy of Quantum Mechanics,* 143.

30. Bohr, *Essays,* 8.

31. The debate is about scientific realism and concerns the interpretation of the so-called hidden or unobservable particles as physical entities and processes. Scientific realism refers to the precise description of reality based on evidence. The antirealists, however, posit that the hidden variables are beyond any empirical data. David Bohm's ontological interpretation resolves this problematic issue by adopting the "logic of both" in the behavior of these entities (see David Bohm, *Causality and Chance*; Bas C. van

Frassen, *Quantum Mechanics*; Peter Holland, *The Quantum Theory of Motion*; James T. Cushing, *Quantum Mechanics*; and A. Matzkin, "Realism and Wavefunction").

32. d'Espagnant, *Conceptual Foundations*, 280.

33. Norris, "Quantum Nonlocality," 18.

34. d'Espagnant, *Conceptual Foundations*, 237, 239.

35. Bohm and Hiley, *The Undivided Universe*, 6.

36. If my references to quantum theory derive largely from the 1980s, this is not because the arguments put forward then fit in particularly well with ecocentric postmodern theory, but because they continue to constitute the foundations of ontological interpretations today and have not been superseded in subsequent debates.

37. Rigby, "Earth, World, Text," 437.

38. Hutcheon, *Politics*, 36.

39. Winterson, *Gut Symmetries*, 2, hereafter cited parenthetically.

40. Hutcheon, *Poetics*, 21.

41. Bohm, *Wholeness*, 3.

42. Ibid., 8.

43. Hutcheon, *Poetics*, 20, 21.

44. Cheney, "Postmodern Environmental Ethics," 87.

45. Naess, *Ecology, Community*, 3.

Affinity Studies and Open Systems: A Nonequilibrium, Ecocritical Reading of Goethe's *Faust*

Ecocriticism's contributions to the current rejection of dualistic thinking are noteworthy, particularly when this interdisciplinary field concentrates on hybridity and "relations" that preexist essences. In this mode, ecocriticism participates in a broader development of "affinity studies" that encompass the many efforts across the disciplines toward reconfiguring our "intra-actions" with the world in terms that avoid dichotomies and Newtonian linearity and that utilize instead nonlinear, nondualistic forms of "hybrid-ity." Hybrids, in Steve Hinchliffe's words, are "more or less durable bodies made up of similarly hybrid and impermanent relations. Things are, to use another commonly used term, configured, or drawn together, in order to become more or less stable forms. There are no pre-existing essences, only relations."[1] In affinity studies, in other words, human agency emerges as a complex entanglement of cultural and physical patterns, or as part of flows between "open systems." Nature and culture and other such divisions are replaced by hybrid forms with permeable boundaries. It is in light of affinity studies that I read Goethe's *Faust*, which may seem contradictory since the play is most frequently understood exactly as that against which I wish to argue here: as the ultimate vision of an individualistic (male, "European," "rational") mastermind who stands alone to alter and seek control over the world. In this essay, however, I explore how the play undermines such stan-dard interpretations with its triple-frames that contextualize Faust's choices within larger, cosmic, poetic, or theatrical situations, Mephistophelean in-fluence, and the play's (fluid) structure provided by the water imagery and flows. This is therefore a reinterpretation of *Faust* as a play questioning rather than exemplifying human control over nature-culture; it is a study of unleashed affinities hybridizing individual determination.

Ecocriticism presents a wide range of ideas relevant for affinity studies. Early ecocritics such as Patrick Murphy build on Merleau-Ponty's dialogics, emphasizing a dialogical process of "inter-animating relationships."[2] More recent strategies emphasize "multiplicities" rather than individual subjects. Eric Todd Smith suggests a move away from the "subject" as grandiose "agent." He notes, with significant relevance for *Faust:* "Perhaps, then, subjectivity should not be the goal. I suggest we drop the subject of the subject, and that of its defining opposite, the object, as the grand poles staking out existence. Let us think, rather, about multiple mediations and relationships, not marked out by membership in one of the two great camps of subject and object, but rather by specific embodiments, situations, and affinities."[3] Dana Phillips demonstrates how ecocriticism could benefit from postmodernism's rethinking of boundaries, and he also suggests a focus on hybrids: "I am persuaded that the truth of ecology must lie somewhere, if it lies anywhere at all, in nature-culture, a region where surprising monsters dwell. In order to adapt itself to the vagaries of nature-culture, ecocriticism needs to be more willing to hybridize than it has been: it needs to have a heart and a brain as well as arms and legs, and as many of each as possible, and it should not hesitate to borrow additional body parts here and there as the need arises."[4] Phillips's nature-culture, with its hybrid body parts, suggests a fluidity of boundaries or openness of systems much like I describe here with affinity studies. Most recently, Stacy Alaimo and Susan Hekman's volume *Material Feminisms* includes Karen Barad's discussion of how relations precede relata or phenomena ("In other words, relata do not preexist relations; rather, relata-within-phenomena emerge through specific intra-actions")[5] and Alaimo's discussion of "trans-corporeality" as "the time-space where human corporeality, in all its material fleshiness, is inseparable from 'nature' or 'environment.'"[6] Such emphases on relations, hybrids, and trans-corporality revealing the body's permeability to environment are typical of affinity studies.

In order to move into affinity studies via ecocriticism and *Faust,* I explore here an "open-systems" model for ecocriticism that builds on the continuum or open flow of inorganic matter, organisms, ecosystems, and cultural exchanges. In this system, there is no absolute separation between environment and organism; rather, every environment *makes* and *is made by* the organisms and flows composing it. This model for ecocriticism relates to the images described in Ilya Prigogine's open-system, nonequilibrium thermodynamics, and its shape is a spiraling flow of irreversible time: the image of a galaxy, hurricane, tornado, snail's twisting shell, or, perhaps appropriately, the water rushing down a flushing toilet. Prigogine's "new dialogue with nature" emphasizes the solar-energy driven flows among "open systems" (open boundaries exchanging energy, materials, information) including living beings, cultural structures, and ecologies.[7] It also suggests what

Peter Taylor terms "distributed agency" rather than a singular, monolithic causality. Distributed agency emerges within the interpersonal, cultural, and natural flows around it; that is, it is also "open" to other flows and influenced by affinities within them whether harmonious or not. An awareness of these flows requires, in Val Plumwood's words, overcoming our "illusory sense of autonomy" and "such monological and hegemonic forms of reason" that "misunderstand their own enabling conditions—the body, ecology and non-human nature."[8]

An affinity-studies model based on open systems and distributed agency recognizes the body, ecology, and nonhuman nature as "enabling conditions." Unlike the systems theory of Niklas Luhmann, which proposes a change from the "*unity* of the social whole as a smaller unity within a larger one (the world) to the difference of the system of society and environment," an open-systems model posits neither "unity" nor "difference" as its "theoretical point of departure."[9] Instead, it insists on hybridity, relations instead of essences, and the affinities of open systems. Luhmann's discussion relies upon the tension between open and closed systems: "The dynamics of complex autopoietic systems itself forms a recursively closed complex of operations, i.e., one that is geared toward self-reproduction and the continuation of its own autopoiesis. At the same time, the system becomes increasingly open, i.e., sensible to changing environmental conditions."[10] His emphasis is on the *internal communication* of social systems that perceive themselves as closed. In contrast, I suggest a model with greater emphasis on what we so often ignore: the porous boundaries and affinities of our bodies, minds, and cultures integrated with their environments in all forms. Robert E. Ulanowicz, in fact, describes organisms themselves as "super ecosystems," and notes, "In sum, the world is open, not deterministic or rigidly coupled."[11] Similarly, Richard C. Lewontin states, "Organisms, then, both make and are made by their environment."[12] It is not a unique characteristic of human beings to construct their world, but nor should we ignore the fact that we are also constructed by it. This "being constructed" includes the physical environment and our development within that environment as well as cultural systems. Lewontin's comments indicate an organism-environment continuum of sorts, one of affinities within open systems of exchange, reciprocal shaping, and distributed agency.

I explore *Faust* in terms of open systems and affinities, noting that the play portrays a "demigod" agent most often described as the "Übermensch," whose power derives, however, rather problematically from Mephistopheles and the witch's brew. Faust begins with the claim to be like the earth spirit's endless flows, or multidirectional "tides of living," then asserts that he is a unidirectional and violent waterfall, and finally has a massive dike built to contain the sea. In other words, he moves from claims about his own essence to a quest to control his surroundings through damming the water's tides and flows. Significantly, Faust's attempt to stop the flow concludes with his death. His dike thus becomes a metaphor for the Faustian consciousness that blindly sees its own agency but not its inevitable affinities and "enabling conditions," and thus believes that it can close the open systems of flow.

The model of open systems—as part of affinity studies—comes from the science of "nonequilibrium, open-system thermodynamics," a field that studies the complex systems like hurricanes, tornadoes, chemical reactions, life forms, and ecosystems that emerge as "dissipative structures" from the continuous influx of solar energy. Their boundaries are *not* impermeable and *not* at equilibrium. Prigogine, the 1977 Nobel laureate in chemistry for his work on nonequilibrium processes, writes: "Over the past several decades, a new science has been born, the *physics of nonequilibrium processes,* and has led to concepts such as *self-organization* and *dissipative structures,* which are widely used today in a large spectrum of disciplines, including cosmology, chemistry, and biology, as well as ecology and the social sciences."[13] Open-system thermodynamics are a recent corrective to the closed systems of traditional thermodynamics that reduce the study of energy patterns into a controllable, contained structure (the world as a one-quart container filled with gas—or, if you will, the Faustian delusion of control and closure), whose dynamics eventually reach equilibrium and maximum disorder.[14] Eric D. Schneider and Dorion Sagan summarize Prigogine's nonequilibrium, open-system thermodynamics as follows:

> It studies how energy flow works to bring about complex structures, struc-
> tures that cycle the fluids, gases, and liquids of which they're made, struc-
> tures that have a tendency to change and grow. Since you may recognize
> such structures—you are one of them!—as including life, the science in
> question can be described as the thermodynamics of life. But actually the sci-
> ence encompasses more than life. It extends to virtually all naturally occur-
> ring complex structures, from whirlpools to construction workers. Because
> the flow systems that seem sometimes to be self-organized or even miracu-
> lous are in fact *organized by the flows around them,* to which they are open
> and connected, another name for this science is open system ther-
> modynamics. Technically, open system thermodynamics has been known
> most often by the imposing name of "nonequilibrium thermodynamics"—
> because the systems of interest, the centers of flow, growth, and change, are
> not static, still or dead; *they are not in equilibrium.*[15]

The patterns of complexity—such as spiraling hurricanes, all life forms, ecosystems, and, Schneider and Sagan suggest, economic interactions including the flow between city and farm—emerge out of a gradient of difference (in temperature, pressure, chemistry, or quantity of resources, which move like heated molecules dissipating into the cool). As the gradient drives the rush of energy or materials, the system often leaps into new shapes of flow that more readily expend energy (thus following the second law of thermodynamics by increasing entropy) but thereby also *increase* complexity and even "self-organize"—express affinities—in perpetuating specific flows.

The mechanism for the emergence of the "dissipative structures" is simply the fluctuations in the flow. These inevitable fluctuations, whether very slight or large, can produce nondeterministic bifurcations (the unpredictable "leaps" into new orders of flow).[16] In the foreword to Prigogine's *Order Out of Chaos*, Alvin Toffler notes:

> In Prigoginian terms, all systems contain subsystems which are continually "fluctuating." At times, a single fluctuation or a combination of them may become so powerful, as a result of positive feedback, that it shatters the preexisting organization. At this revolutionary moment—the authors call it a "singular moment" or a "bifurcation point"—it is inherently impossible to determine in advance which direction change will take: whether the system will disintegrate into "chaos" or leap to a new, more differentiated, higher level of "order" or organization, which they call a "dissipative structure."[17]

The bifurcation, then, is the moment whose outcome cannot be predicted, and it is the leap into possible complexity which Prigogine terms "creativity" in nature such as the spiraling shapes of fractal images and weather systems. The systems emerge at the bifurcation and then, with continued gradient-driven flows, fluctuations, and positive feedback, can achieve another bifurcation and again leap into ever more powerful or complex systems—or collapse.

Prigogine summarizes the potential of this perspective: "We are observing the birth of a new scientific era. We are observing the birth of a science that is no longer limited to idealized and simplified situations but reflects the complexity of the real world, a science that views us and our creativity as part of a fundamental trend present at all levels of nature."[18] An open-systems model thus begins with the assumption that the human-nature interface is part of a *continuum* of complex, interrelated patterns rather than a question of (absolute) difference. It also suggests, however, that human culture emerges with its own distinctive patterns of creativity that both echo those of nature and that leap into other directions at the nondeterministic bifurcations—in Prigogine's words, the "intrinsic differentiation between different parts of the system."[19] Humanity's "intrinsic differentiation" and creativity take many forms, including the Faustian quest to conquer history, myth, and nature in order to "grasp" and control its enabling conditions.

Seeing the intrinsic differentiation via open systems whose enabling conditions cannot be controlled (Stuart Kauffman describes it biologically: "we cannot finitely prestate the configuration space of a biosphere")[20] should not, however, imply a grand-systems model disallowing cultural differences with another form of monolithic, "phallologocentric," or imperialistic Western thinking that perceives the world (and all its diverse cultures) in singular, universal, and hierarchical terms. Prigogine comments on the diversity of natural structures with terms he also applies to human cultures: "Our universe has a pluralistic, complex character."[21] The complex yet open aspects of the human/nature interface described by Prigogine are destabilizing, but it does not necessarily follow that there is no hope of altering systems. The overt Faustian lesson that we know all too well is, of course, that we can alter our world; the more subtle and significant lesson is that our alterations are part of multiple forces including nature and culture that alter us continually and that take on impressively diverse forms. As Kauffman puts it: "So organisms, niches, and search procedures jointly and self-consistently co-construct one another!"[22] There is, in other words, no dualism of "simple matter" versus "complex culture"; both nature and culture are complex and diverse, and both function within "co-constructing" exchanges. Prigogine provides here an exemplary type of affinity-studies thinking. Ira Livingston considers this turn toward relationality to be part of the economic development that moves from gold to paper money and then to "horizontally interaffiliated and outsourced networks" which occurs as "Newton's once comfortably hard and indivisible atoms, having already been shattered into bits and the bits into dancing probabilistic clouds, are further dematerialized into virtual 'spin networks' of pure relationality."[23] Agency takes on a new "spin" here in terms of affinity studies.

This is not the demise of individual agency, however. According to Prigogine, such a view still includes the unpredictable and powerful possibilities of the smallest participants or fluctuations to produce massive alterations:

> We know now that societies are immensely complex systems involving a potentially enormous number of bifurcations exemplified by the variety of cultures that have evolved in the relatively short span of human history. We know that such systems are highly sensitive to fluctuations. This leads both to hope and a threat: hope, since even small fluctuations may grow and change the overall structure. As a result, individual activity is not doomed to insignificance. On the other hand, this is also a threat, since in our universe the security of stable, permanent rules seems gone forever.[24]

In *Faust*, the hubris of individualistic agency explodes onstage with "small fluctuations" leaving massive wakes, even as it is simultaneously undermined by the many other affinities within the play. The "accomplishments" of Faust and Mephistopheles culminate with illusions of flooding and then with efforts to dam the sea, as if the world were merely the backdrop for their whims. One must contrast these bold acts with Goethe's frequently stated views and practices contextualizing our choices within "nature" and cultural trends. Goethe is famous for seeing human behavior in terms of patterns similar to those in nature. This has led to extensive discussion of his works, particularly *Faust*, in terms of complexity and chaos theory.[25] Additionally, Goethe (in)famously writes his literary texts as "open systems" of intertextuality woven from so many references and citations to other texts that much of the scholarship on Goethe simply clarifies the sources. The intertextuality of *Faust* is, one could say, itself a form of "distributed agency," with its typically Goethean composite of many texts, traditions, historical eras, and cultures that shape it and that are, in turn, shaped by Goethe's writing. Goethe himself called it a "collective effort."

Goethe scholars, in fact, readily assess parts of the play (which was composed over sixty years of Goethe's life) as being a "product" of his "Storm and Stress" period, or of the Enlightenment, or of his scientific works, his reaction to the French Revolution and the failed 1830 revolution, etc. Yet they are slower to see Faust the figure as a "product" of many forces instead of a Producer; they thereby perpetuate the Faustian myth of controlling agency. Faust's own delusions regarding his self-determined agency contrast similarly with the text's larger refusal to be isolated from its "enabling conditions." As John McCarthy notes, collective efforts (or distributed agency) can take on astonishing new forms through (Goethean) creativity.[26]

Turning to the question of agency, I ask in terms of affinity studies: Is Faust the powerfully active agent of modern subjectivity, or the hubristically individualistic man intoxicated by witch's brew and "drawn onwards" by multiple forces? Much of the scholarship answers with a clear emphasis on Faust's dominant agency, leading primarily to debates about whether it's a positive or negative force. Martin Swales, for example, describes Faust as the "modern man," leading a "way of life and form of subjectivity that is consistently expressive of modern culture." For Swales, Faust is "an intense individualist. He believes in the authority of his own experience, his own judgments, and is not beholden to received wisdom, to dogma, to shared institutional assumptions."[27] Géza von Molnár, similarly, claims that Faust "comes to see himself as a free agent among other free agents on free soil, that is to say on territory wrested from the control of nature and made into a free sphere of human intercourse."[28]

There are also notable analyses among those who directly criticize Faust's agency. For example, James van der Laan sees humanity's hubristic belief that we "agents" are in complete control via technology as likely leading to a world that is itself *controlled by technology*.[29] For Jochen Schmidt, Faust's grand error is to believe in the illusion of progress (ironically suggested by the final ascension) that is undermined by the play's final rejection of the "realm beyond" (*jenseits*), leaving only the senseless and destructive effects here in this realm.[30] Kate Rigby brings Goethe himself into the equation as one who may decry the horrible burning deaths of Philemon and Baucis, but also one who celebrates "man's gain of habitable land." Rigby's Goethe is "after all, the inheritor of a tradition from which he never entirely freed himself, whereby the appropriation and domination of the earth by humanity was in some sense preordained."[31] Jost Hermand, in contrast, defends Goethe by contrasting his "green world-piousness" with Faust's "false consciousness," rendered berserk by a "narcissistic and ego-maniacal drive towards destruction."[32] Indeed, Hermand criticizes the critics for their tendency to equate Goethe with Faust and to see them both as primarily positive, self-assertive agents. Hermand's deemphasis of striving agency with a turn to Goethe's science is fruitful, yet so is Rigby's concern that Goethe himself postulates a Promethean human agency that sees the world as material to be made into our own image. Combining these two views, the open-systems model of affinities reads Faust as a participant in systems that make and are made by their environments.

Goethe himself describes human agency as a "weave": "The weave of our lives and influences is made of various different threads, in that the necessary, the random, the involuntary and the purely desired—each with the most different form and each not often able to be differentiated—delimit each other."[33] Indeed, an emphasis on the weave in *Faust*—rather than individualistic agency—helps explains the brief scene in part 1: "Night, Open Field." As Faust and Mephistopheles rush to rescue Gretchen from prison and execution, they pass by mysterious figures in the dark. Faust asks "What are they weaving (*weben*) there around the raven-stone?"[34] It is Faust who poses the question about weaving, whereas Mephistopheles tries to deny any knowledge of the figures by claiming they're witches and shouting, "Away, Away!"[35] Mephistopheles avoids answering the question about these weaving women who appear like fates, for he is teaching Faust the illusion of self-directed agency. For Jane Brown, Mephistopheles teaches illusion because *Faust,* she claims, is about "the difficulty of knowing, about the ineffability of truth."[36] The illusion here, however, is more specific; it is the illusion of controlling the flow and determining both one's own fate and that of others. Gretchen's final moment damages Faust's illusion of power because she is "rescued" by a cosmic force, or by the Lord as the "voice from above." *Faust* portrays the illusions of those in the weave who see only their own unidirectional impetus.

Goethe is not coy with his idea that the weaving "flow" is significant. Faust's conjuring begins with the earth spirit which describes itself as

> An endless flow
> A changeful plaiting,
> Fiery begetting,
> Thus at Time's scurrying loom I weave and warp
> And broider at the Godhead's living garb.[37]

The earth spirit weaves, the "fates" or witches weave, and even Mephistopheles tries to weave with illusions; this is Faust's realm where the many flows interact with the ripples of his own influence. Taylor's theory of "distributed agency" formulates such a "weave," stating that we need

> metaphors and concepts that *do not rely on the dynamic unity and coherency of agents.* And to the extent that such patterns of thought persist because of their resonance with actions in the material and social world, we need different experiences. Or, better, we need to highlight submerged experience of ourselves as *"object-like" or "distributed," that is, as agents dependent on other people and many, diverse resources beyond the boundaries of our physical and mental selves.* After all, the primary experience of becoming an autonomous subject is not "raw" experience, let alone uniform and universal experience . . . but experience mediated through particular social discourse.[38]

Distributed agency—a typical concept in affinity studies—implies that our "human environment" is composed of, and influenced by, other human beings, and "diverse resources beyond the boundaries of our physical and mental selves."[39] For Taylor, this deemphasis of individual self-determination allows for individual agency, but one that is influenced by, and produces effects through, "intersecting processes" of different agents.[40] *Faust,* the play, enacts "distributed agency" in its overall "weave" but also with the weighty implications of its frame of three prefatory texts ("Dedication," "Prelude in the Theater," and "Prologue in Heaven"), which provide multiple inconsonant impulses—or, perhaps, inescapable influences on the figures and action—coming from the poet, the director, the merry person, as well as from the Job-like gamble made between the Lord and Mephistopheles (which provides a relevant context for Faust's own gamble). This excessive framing serves to accentuate the plethora of perspectives and influences on the action, and also the fact that this is a play where Faust is a fluid point in a matrix rather than the central will. He acts within multiple larger (and open) frameworks: that is, his movements are "organized by the flows around them."[41]

Faust fails to see the flows around him except as something to "grasp" like nature's "breasts":

> How, boundless Nature, seize you in my clasp?
> You breasts where, all life's sources twain,
> Both heaven and earth are pressed,
>
> . . . .
>
> You brim, you quench, yet I must thirst in vain?[42]

Failing to emulate the earth spirit and unable to grasp nature's "breasts," Faust instead drinks the witch's brew, seduces and impregnates Gretchen, and then dances with witches, all the while thinking of himself as a destructive "waterfall" in part 1. The immediate link to part 2 occurs when Faust wakes up in the "charming landscape" of act 1, the site where he observes a waterfall and the resulting rainbow:

> So, sun in back, my eye too weak to scan it,
> I rather follow, with entrancement growing,
> The cataract that cleaves the jagged granite,
> From fall to fall, in thousand leaps, outthrowing
> A score of thousand streams in its revolving.[43]

The rainbow's significance has been thoroughly debated, yet it is the "waterfall" and its crashing streams that are Faust's motif in the next four acts. In fact, acts 2–5 all deploy influential female water spirits or nymphs. At the end of act 2, the sirens lure Homunculus to make his final leap into the ocean. Once he has leaped, their chorus celebrates it with such passion that the entire cosmos joins the song. Act 3's depiction of Helena, Faust, and Euphorion is framed by Helena's chorus of women who convince Helena to join Faust, and then decide at the end of the act to stay in the realm above and become water nymphs rather than return with her to the underworld. These nymphs proclaim the various powers they shall hold, via growing fruits, water's crashing thunder, water cycling through the land, the trees, and the air, and, finally, the grapes that become Dionysian wines. They are water as agency. In act 4, in fact, it is the water spirits who help Mephistopheles create the illusion of a flood that defeats the enemy emperor's soldiers. This flood is another "waterfall," one sent by the "Undines" of the Great Mountain Lake. Mephistopheles notes that this is an amusing illusion: "I can see nothing of these watery lies, / The spell bewilders only human eyes, / I am amused by the bizarre affair."[44] From the desire for control to the illusion of control: that is the Faustian trajectory.

It is also act 4 where Faust declares his desire to harness the water's power by damming the ocean, since he is annoyed by its lack of "purpose":

> On the high sea my eye was lately dwelling,
> It surged, in towers self upon self upwelling.
> Then it subsided and poured forth its breakers
> To storm the mainland's broad and shallow acres.
>
> . . . .
>
> There wave on wave imbued with power has heaved,
> But to withdraw—and nothing is achieved;
> Which drives me near to desperate distress!
> Such elemental might unharnessed, purposeless![45]

With the damming of the sea in act 5, we have the culmination of Faustian efforts. It is at the moment of deluded technological control over the flow, just as Faust exalts in rapture over the "future land" (funded by piracy and colonization), that he collapses into death. The dike itself appears real, not an illusion as was the military waterfall; the illusion here is that Faust can control the water. Mephistopheles says in an aside:

> For us alone you are at pains
> With all your dikes and moles; a revel
> For Neptune, the old water-devil,
> Is all you spread, if you but knew.
> You lose, whatever your reliance—
> The elements are sworn to our alliance,
> In ruin issues all you do.[46]

Even Mephistopheles' final glee over Faust's defeat, however, is misled, as he himself is distracted in the end by the burning roses and angelic backsides. The dam represents the grandiose belief in agency that can contain the sea's flows. Faust is the "waterfall" smashing others even while being pummeled by the tumultuous flows of open systems.

As part of affinity studies, an ecocritical model of open systems looks at flows, boundaries, and agency; it asks how the human/nature interface is portrayed in terms of open or closed boundaries and/or in terms of individual, cultural, or open and distributed agency. *Faust* reveals how powerful the illusion of unidirectional control is—it reinforces, in fact, the control we and all organisms have in "environment-making." But it also suggests—despite what Faust himself believes and despite what much of the critical scholarship asserts—that environments or cosmic forces, if you will, simultaneously *make us* in multidirectional flows and that control is often an illusion.

Goethe's *Faust* begins with a bargain between the Lord and Mephistopheles, a framing strategy that overtly insists that forces are at work driving
Faust far more than he realizes, and the play ends with Faust being drawn
passively and inertly as voices sing a request to the "Holy Virgin, Mother,
Queen, / Goddess, pour Thy mercies."[47] Somewhere in between the Lord's
pact and the eternal feminine's act of drawing him onward, we find Faust
with his "agency" as the possibility of nondeterministic fluctuation, his
Mephistophelean gifts, and his acceptance of unidirectional illusions. It is in
this in-between that affinity studies place us, as agents individually and yet
also as part of distributed agency, as enacting relations rather than essences.
Goethe's *Faust* shares with affinity studies a move instead toward perspectives of relationality. Attractive though relationality may sound in this context, it also presents us often being drawn *involuntarily* onward. *Faust,* the
play, successfully portrays the provocative in-between of hybridity as part of
affinities, even as its "heroic" figure becomes a caricature of monstrously
devouring power with multiple origins far beyond his perception.

NOTES

1. Hinchliffe, *Geographies,* 53.

2. Murphy, *Literature, Nature, and Other,* 35.

3. E. T. Smith, "Dropping the Subject," 35.

4. Phillips, *Truth of Ecology,* 39.

5. Barad, "Posthumanist Performativity," 133.

6. Alaimo, "Trans-Corporeal Feminisms," 238.

7. Prigogine writes in *Order Out of Chaos:* "We now know that far from equilibrium,
new types of structures may originate spontaneously. In far-from equilibrium conditions
we may have transformation from disorder, from thermal chaos, into order. New dynamic states of matter may originate, states that reflect the *interaction of a given system
with its surroundings*" (12, emphasis added).

8. Taylor, "Distributed Agency," 313; Plumwood, *Environmental Culture,* 9, 16–17.

9. Luhmann, *Ecological Communication,* 6–7.

10. Ibid., 13.

11. Ulanowicz, *Ecology,* 147. Ulanowicz describes here an open-systems, nonequilibrium study of ecology.

12. Lewontin, "Gene, Organism and Environment," 66.

13. Prigogine, *The End of Certainty,* 3.

14. Prigogine comments: "In the classical view, the second law expressed the increase of molecular disorder; as expressed by Boltzmann, thermodynamic equilibrium
corresponds to the state of maximum 'probability'" (*From Being to Becoming,* xii).

15. Schneider and Sagan, *Into the Cool,* xii, emphasis added.

16. Prigogine and Grégoire Nicolis describe this as follows: "But beyond a critical
value . . . the effect of fluctuations or small external perturbations is no longer damped.
The system acts like an amplifier, moves away from the reference state, and evolves to a

new regime. . . . This is the phenomenon of *bifurcation*" (Nicolis and Prigogine, *Exploring Complexity,* 72).

17. Toffler, foreword, xv.

18. Prigogine, *The End of Certainty,* 7.

19. Nicolis and Prigogine, *Exploring Complexity,* 74.

20. Kauffman, *Investigations,* x.

21. Prigogine, *Order Out of Chaos,* 9.

22. Kauffman, *Investigations,* 20.

23. Livingston, *Between Science and Literature,* 153.

24. Prigogine, *Order Out of Chaos,* 312–13.

25. See especially the discussions in McCarthy, *Remapping Reality;* Rowland, *Goethe;* and van der Laan, "Faust and Textual Chaos."

26. See McCarthy's *Remapping Reality.*

27. Swales, "The Character," 42.

28. von Molnar, "Hidden in Plain View," 64.

29. See van der Laan, "Faust the Technological Mastermind," 12.

30. See especially Schmidt's chapter "Fortschritt als Zerstörungswerk der Moderne."

31. Rigby, *Topographies,* 211.

32. Hermand, *Im Wettlauf,* 48, my translation.

33. Goethe, *Sprüche in Prosa,* 373, #6.20.1, my translation.

34. In some cases, the translation is mine for reasons of clarity. Here, for example, the quotation is from the Frankfurt edition of *Faust: Texte,* 4399.

35. Goethe, *Faust,* 4404.

36. Brown, *Faust,* 50.

37. Goethe, *Faust,* 505–9.

38. Taylor, "Distributed Agency," 313, emphasis added.

39. Ibid.

40. Ibid., 327.

41. Schneider and Sagan, *Into the Cool,* xii.

42. Goethe, *Faust,* 456–59.

43. Ibid., 4715–19.

44. Ibid., 10734–36.

45. Ibid., 10198–219.

46. Ibid., 11544–50.

47. Ibid., 12101–3.

Blake, Deleuze, and the Emergence of Ecological Consciousness

Gilles Deleuze (often in collaboration with Félix Guattari) sought to move analytic philosophy and theoretical psychoanalysis beyond "abstraction" and toward a "transcendental empiricism" already present in earlier philosophic work. This remarkable combination of traditionalism and innovation describes a state elusively beyond any linguistic epistemology—yet resident in any experiential event—and offers a method to capture individual experience of "pure immanence."[1] The emphasis Deleuze placed on event and experience stimulated the energetic analysis of their interrelations by Alain Badiou, turning philosophy away from cognitive mapping through Kantian categorical imperatives and re/turning it to the world. Rereading "the role of rhythm and sensation in Kant's philosophy"[2] and adopting a position equally grounded in "the Substance of Spinoza['s]" pantheistic model of life,[3] this return also required "a radical break with the demands of the self," a rejection of Enlightenment dualism, for pure immanence can only be an experiential event when "consciousness becomes a fact . . . when a subject is produced at the same time as its object."[4]

Under such conditions, consciousness as "fact" flows into a "domain of pure intensities," whose existential topography "is composed of intensive and differential dimensions . . . in a continual state of flux and transformation."[5] Within this terrain, "identities are lost."[6] This territory of infinite possibilities requires a paradoxical individual act of deterritorialization "to subvert [the] standard . . . gridded territory of conventions, codes, labels and markers."[7] This space exists at the event-horizon where subject-object relations break down, which vibrates "with the creative potential of endless evolutions and innovations."[8] Contemporary physical terms populate the preceding remarks because the unique demands made on theory by ecocritical discourse require interdisciplinarity, since such criticism emerges from what Freya Matthews terms an "ecological self" and what Danah Zohar terms a "quantum self."[9] The motive for ecological discourse emerges from a con/fusion of consciousness and cosmos as an "assemblage," another Deleuzian concept brought to bear on ecocritical problems, where "each thing gets defined by what it connects to and where it leads."[10]

Like Deleuze's thinking, Matthews's argument extends from Spinoza to the new physics, and the thrust of Zohar's argument returns sensate experience to the construction of reality. Both, I argue, attempt to articulate a philosophy capable of achieving what John Keats termed "negative capability" as its primary perceptual mode—the ability to rest in "uncertainties."[11] Blake's description of this perceptual location occurs in his poem *Milton:* "There is a Moment in each Day that Satan cannot find / Nor can his Watch Fiends find it, but the Industrious find / The Moment & it multiply. & when it once is found / It renovates every Moment of the Day if right placed."[12] Blake often associated "Satan" with the "Spectre [as] the Reasoning Power in Man,"[13] and these "Watch Fiends" are both perceptual and temporal. The renovation of the "Moment," the eternal and infinite spacetime of the imagination itself,[14] creates rippling waves of potential transformation, whose panpsychic fibers form, in Deleuzian language, deterritorializing "lines of flight" that "defuse" "into a single harmonious wave."[15] This experiential assemblage will be termed "ecological consciousness" hereafter.

This ecological view is necessarily positioned in a zone of interaction between micro- and macro-events defined by principles of "interconnectedness and non-localizability of particles and . . . their inherent dynamism," as well as the "less radical principle of indeterminism."[16] However, this state can be experienced only by the willed sacrifice of self-consciousness. The problem confronting any act of ecological engagement, then, can be found closer than one might imagine, in self-consciousness itself. As Deleuze argues, "'the self' is only a fiction or artifice," and Zohar makes the same observation, noting that, from within the new physics, such a self "is just a chimera."[17] Ecological acts rest upon a preceding mental event, resulting in the emergence of ecological consciousness. This event is perhaps best defined as an experience of intersubjectivity, a state of heightened awareness of implication within a broader field of interconnected forces. Yet, for such events to achieve the "endless evolutions and innovations" posited by Deleuze, the state itself cannot be disconnected from the body of experience.[18]

Deleuze and Guattari advocate such a mode of consciousness in *A Thousand Plateaus,* which offered the concepts most fruitfully applied to an ecological criticism predicated on movement beyond a rigidly defined self:[19] "A fiber stretches from a human to an animal, from a human or animal to molecules, from molecules to particles, and so on to the imperceptible. Every fiber is a Universe fiber. A fiber strung across borderlines constitutes a line of flight or a deterritorialization."[20] These fibrous elements form an ontological string theory stretching across the boundaries of self and alterity. Indeed, within their descriptions, elements drawn from chaos theory, high-energy physics, and quantum cosmology prevail, since such forms involve dynamic processes brought into mutual illumination as a method by which to enter a schizoanalytic position required for the emergence of ecological consciousness.

Quantum events unfold through interactions of subatomic particles in the brain, yet quantum dynamics teaches that nonlocalized particles often oscillate in harmony, even if separated by light-years, and simultaneously emerge in discrete acts of observation.[21] This model thereby provides the vehicle for energetic flights across the boundaries between the human and the more-than-human. The immanent physical field envisioned by Deleuze beyond the event-horizon of "selfhood" as Blake and Matthews define it "is a continuous multiplicity of varying relations that stand as the condition for . . . the fractured I and dissolved self."[22] Beyond the territorial border of the self-conscious, mentality and materiality merge to shape the singularity of Deleuze's transcendental empiricism as experiential event. This act of mutual illumination manifests "a more fluid self, changing and evolving at every moment"[23] that participates in "a continuous dancing and vibrating motion whose rhythmic patterns are determined by the molecules, atomic and nuclear configurations."[24] As Steve Baker proposes, the "concept of becoming-animal" offers a method or "form of inhabiting which is also a kind of unselfing."[25]

The continuum of "becoming"[26] charted in these central chapters identifies "zones of indeterminacy" and "fractal voids" revealed by "affective interference patterns" manifesting interactive energies.[27] Situated on binary boundaries erected by Western Enlightenment thought, this dynamic zone creates conditions for "a life-space to open," a space where "life or the environment [rather than] the living being [is] the primary unit of biological study."[28] The dilemma remains the ability to represent or reproduce the renovation of thought in the field of culture, and thereby broaden the experience of the *chaosmos* that Deleuze and Guattari evoke, giving rise to ecological consciousness.

Arkady Plotnitsky speaks directly to the difficulty of writing from within this perspective, for "the processes responsible for the creation or annihilation of forms, for their birth and disappearance, or for the speed of both, may not be representable or even conceivable by any means available to us."[29] If any mode of representation can model this type of interactive and mutual determination, poetry perhaps offers the most promise. The condensed nature of verse is governed by metrical oscillations capable of interaction with both the human and more-than-human through the semiotic fibers strung across borderlines that therein constitute lines of flight or of deterritorialization. The poetic environment of William Blake offers a particularly rich zone within which to explore such possibilities, since his work unfolds through a composite form of word and design, yielding the broadest range of semiotic expression of the "new axiom . . . that situations are infinite and that human life is infinite."[30]

Blake's poetry moves beyond the deadening effects that Enlightenment thought and its technological by-products exerted on the more-than-human world by recognizing the culpability of self-consciousness in those practices. Blake's stance critiques systems emblemized as "satanic mills" increasingly dispersed throughout the countryside. His visionary practices analyze those systems and conditions recently dismantled by Deleuze, and I have elsewhere assessed the psychological conditions underwriting the emergence of ecological consciousness and the subsequent transformative impact this visionary physics exerts on "everything that lives."[31] However, the earlier books of illuminated prophecy bring into view the struggles of a visionary poet attempting to represent that which is unrepresentable at the event-horizon of active perception. Blake strives to articulate the inherent dynamism of those principles of "interconnectedness," "non-localizability" and "indeterminacy" promoted by Deleuze as the base for "transcendental empiricism." Here already, as for Deleuze, "everyday use of expressions as a means of relating one's self to others emerges . . . as a solution to the problem left by Descartes."[32]

Blake's "The Book of Thel" and *Songs of Innocence and of Experience* present a textual fusion of word and design situated on the borderlines between visual and verbal representation. Blake musters the broadest range of semiotic expression to articulate the elusive elegance of an emergent ecological consciousness connected by dynamic dialogic exchanges extending to and from all that exists beyond the self. While the term "biosemiosis" has only recently gained broad currency, it speaks rather cogently to Blake's aesthetics, since Blake shares its vision of "a synthesis of biology and semiotics" and shares its attempt to recognize "that organic sign action, codes and processes of interpretation are fundamental components of a living world."[33] Indeed, the poetic interrogation of imaginative and interactive semiotic relations across the subject-object divide actually dominates the early canon. However, the dramatization of deterritorialization itself occurs less often and adopts a form of "panpsychism," a philosophic move that asserts "a truly nondualistic view of matter that implicates the mentalistic in the material."[34] In the final plates of *Jerusalem*, Blake achieves the apotheosis of his biosemiotic panpsychism even as he recognizes the "unrepresentable" nature of a singular event of mind, the awakening of awareness at the position of the other through a process built upon sequential acts of becoming animal, becoming woman, and becoming other.[35]

"The Book of Thel" dramatizes the resistance of self-consciousness to "unselfing" itself and apprehending that "everything that lives is Holy." The work reflects Blake's initial attempt to represent the more-than-human world's spectrum of semiosis, although as Kevin Hutchings suggests, the attempt is rendered extremely problematic by the mediation of Thel herself, whose contracted vision mimics "an oppressive discourse of androcentric instrumentalism."[36] The message expresses a generic truth repressed by Thel's enclosure within oppressive self-consciousness. Nonetheless, when elements of a signifying nature speak to Thel, the principles asserted clearly intersect the Deleuzian position, with alterity conceived as discrete "centers of vibrations, each in itself and every one in relation to all the others." "This is why they all resonate rather than cohere or correspond with each other,"[37] and why poetic representation functions as the best way to model such vibrations.

As the poem opens, Thel laments the fading state of individual existence, and in response various elements of nature gently yet consistently assert the countervalue "not only [of] a *living* world [but] a world *to be lived* in."[38] The Lilly rejoices in a life transfused with "all the others," primarily because this vision of life requires, rather than obviates, the participation of the body to achieve spiritual ends:

> I am visited from heaven and he that smiles on all
> Walks in the valley. And each morn over me spreads his hands
> Saying rejoice thou humble grass, thou new-born lilly flower,
> Thou gentle maid of silent valleys, and of modest brooks;
> For thou shalt be clothed in light, and fed with morning manna;
> Till summers heat melts thee beside the fountains and the springs
> To flourish in eternal vales: then why should Thel complain?[39]

Unconvinced by this argument, Thel subsequently questions a cloud about her lack of "use" in such a natural economy, although she betrays her own argument by acknowledging that she will only "be at death the food of worms." The cloud adopts her own argument, suggesting "How great thy use. How great thy blessing; everything that lives, / Lives not alone, nor for itself," and the clod of clay makes a similar assertion: "we live not for ourselves."[40]

The dispersed life of cyclical recurrence, promoted here by the Lilly, cloud, and Matron Clay along the vector of cyclic temporality, provides a biomechanical form of eternal life as active becoming rather than passive being. Deleuze, as well, specifically proposes this location for the thought-event to experience his transcendental empiricism, although he pushes beyond his Nietzschean source in describing analogous forms of eternal recurrence: "the world of the eternal return is a world of differences, an intensive world, which presupposes neither the One nor the Same, but whose edifice is built both on the tomb of the one God and on the ruins of the identical self. The eternal return is itself the only unity of this world."[41]

As the poem closes, Thel is invited to pursue a deterritorializing line of flight that rejects self-consciousness in favor of a consciousness of "absolute immanence" beyond, yet Thel greets this budding awareness with horror and rejects it, finding life a sphere of brute blindness, since the *jouissance* of this state is predicated on the ability of "the Ear [to] be closed to its own destruction."[42] Here Blake's language intersects a more recent view articulated by Freya Matthews: "To represent the world as brute and blind requires that we ourselves assume an attitude of bruteness and blindness. We must march through the world unseeing and unfeeling, *turning away from the poetic order that unfurls about us, closing our ears to the inexhaustible eloquence of things, trampling underfoot the exuberant infinity of tendrils reaching around us.*"[43]

Blake's "Book of Thel" dramatizes an incipient yet finally failed act of deterritorialization, a poetic closing that leaves Thel reenclosed in her preliminary self-conscious state, the primary impediment for her realization of ecological consciousness. This last state requires a shift in perspective from the poetic exploration of "what it is to be *us*" to the vastly different and more difficult examination of "what it is to be *living*."[44] In a number of poems collected in *Songs of Innocence and of Experience*, Blake grapples with precisely this issue by retaining the biosemiotic dimension of his imaginative dialogue with externality while expanding beyond the point of engagement in a particular human subject position.

Blake's best-known work encodes his theory of contraries as a dynamic element to forge connections between the psychological development of individuals situated within cultural processes and the temporal development of the human within natural processes. As Blake proposes in *The Marriage of Heaven and Hell*, "Without Contraries is no progression,"[45] and the contraries bridge hardened territories of identities. Blake's awareness of the ecological crisis in his own day emerges in the radically different background to his respective frontispieces for *Innocence* and *Experience*.[46] In the first, a dense forest stands behind a flock of grazing sheep, and the human figures are framed by the design, whereas in the second, the forest has been clear-cut. The difference in designs traces, in Terry Gifford's view, a passage beyond an accessible pastoral world, which has given way to the "satanic mills" of cultural production.[47]

Hutchings's extended ecocritical reading of Blake's *Songs* focuses on lyrics like "The Echoing Green," a poem of innocence presenting a cosmos where "human and non-human beings coexist in a spirit of harmonious mutual interchange,"[48] although the visual field privileges the human.[49] The visual field itself often provides a mode of "contra-diction," and the expansive presence of biosemiotic paths of communication comes into view particularly well in "Laughing Song."

The head design depicts a dinner table where human figures sit and drink in apparent celebration, creating an expectation that the laughing will result from human conversation, but the actual words suggest that laughing emerges from a "semiosphere, a sphere constituted by meaningful communications":[50]

> When the green woods laugh, with the voice of joy
> And the dimpling stream runs laughing by,
> When the air does laugh with our merry wit,
> And the green hills laugh with the noise of it.[51]

Blake's poem prioritizes communications that issue forth from a semiosphere of natural signs (woods, streams, air, and hills), and the visionary poet here rhythmically moves in vacillating iambs toward a solution sought by Deleuzian strategies in the seemingly simple "concept of *expression*" by which "substance expresses itself in attributes."[52] However, in "Laughing Song," the priority of the more-than-human drives the poem toward a concluding interpellation for collective communication across normally species-bound modes of interchange: "Come live & be merry and join with me, / To sing the sweet chorus of Ha, Ha, He."[53] Blake locates the sound of laughter within both the human and more-than-human, and the rhythmically unruly ex/pression of joy (Ha, Ha, He) forms the "transcendental yet empirical" bridge of embodiment leading to an experience of "pure immanence."

Within the poetic and pictorial, method and theme form transformative semiotic fibers connecting rhythmic oscillations of the human body and the material body of the cosmos. Poetic expression is a biosemiotic act, what Badiou might term an invitation to the event, and its dynamic reception unleashes rhythmic waves of energy enfolded within its body capable of moving self-consciousness through a panpsychic experience toward an altered state of becoming other as a prelude to the formation of ecological consciousness. The one becomes many beyond this border, the first step in a process of "becoming," as Deleuze and Guattari recognize, and their description in *A Thousand Plateaus* provides a philosophical form of textual concerns at play in Blake's early poetic dialogues: "Multiplicities, thresholds, becomings are intersected, traversed, and brought into co-existence, like the vibrations of different sounds, the sound of a bird, a rainstorm, a thunderbolt, a child's cry, that are brought together in the immanence of a moment, becoming single sound, so that the singularity of each vibration becomes imperceptible even as this imperceptibility is just what is heard."[54]

At this early phase of his career, Blake clearly moved toward "becoming-animal" as a necessary stage in the maturation of consciousness, and when one steps into the poetic realm of *Experience,* this move occurs with immediate force. Following the frontispiece design, the bardic voice pleads, "O Earth O Earth return! / Arise from out the dewy grass," and begs the Earth to "Turn away no more."[55] Highlighting this concern for the increasing absence of voice from the semiosphere, the next poem offers "Earth's Answer," which images a planetary process of oppression resulting from patriarchal control, an anticipation of ecofeminist concerns. The following poem, "The Clod & the Pebble," returns to the dialogic mode, but to one that unfolds outside human communication. Clearly, the burden of human entry into the state of experience is borne by both humanity and the more-than-human world, and Blake attempts to provide a voice and thereby recover active biosemiotic relations in a stunning group of poems, including "The Sick Rose," "The Fly," "The Tyger," "Ah! Sun-Flower," and "The Lilly." This sequence comes to a crescendo with "The Garden of Love" and "The Poison Tree," where cultural control denigrates natural systems and processes.

While *Songs of Experience* pursues an intensive form of "becoming-animal," Blake's *Visions of the Daughters of Albion* adopts a compelling poetic form of "becoming-woman." This already began to emerge in "The Book of Thel," but *Visions* positions its hero, Oothoon, in another boundary space between the blustering rapist Bromion and the tortured/torturing Theotormon:

> Now thou maist marry Bromion's harlot, and protect the child
> Of Bromions rage, that Oothoon shall put forth in nine moons time.
> Then storms rent Theotormons limbs; he rolld his waves around.
> And folded his black jealous waters round the adulterate pair
> Bound back to back in Bromions caves terror and meekness dwell.[56]

Bromion's rage reduces Oothoon to her use value, an implied critique of the overly simplistic arguments previously offered by the Blakean semiosphere in "Thel," and becomes embodied as rape and a desire to sire a child. The enraged subject writes its message (psychological [isolated] phallocentrism/ Bromion) upon a living medium (woman's body/Oothoon), directed toward another subject (patriarchal [collective] phallocentrism/Theotormon) to generate jealousy. Oothoon becomes the contested field without subjectivity upon which is enacted male ex/pression. This structural analysis of the "wrongs of woman" dramatizes a well-known and long-critiqued symptom of patriarchal phallocentrism: the woman (Oothoon) as object is exchanged between men (Bromion/Theotormon) to reify masculine power and satisfy male-centered desire.[57]

Blake converts Oothoon's location at/as the interactive zone where male desires compete for supremacy into a subject position with discursive power, yet the danger inherent in "Thel" remains, since in Blake, as well as Deleuze, "becoming-woman is, after all, the creation of woman by men."[58] This feminist critique of Deleuze resonates with Blake's poetic mimicry of the female voice, yet what other option does a visionary poet or philosopher have but to attempt "an exponential expansion of a body's repertory of responses" through "thought-as-imagination" that "actualizes some thing new"?[59] In this way, the mental event of transcendental experience occurs by maintaining empirical attachment through the body, the very transcendental empiricism toward which Deleuze gestures.

Blake's modeling of psychological states intersects the threads of prior argument, since the lamentation uttered with terrific power by Oothoon symbolically adopts natural analogies of living: "I cry arise O Theotormon for the village dog / Barks at the breaking day. The nightingale has done lamenting. / The lark does rustle in the ripe corn, and the Eagle returns." As well, her argument progresses through an interrogative mode whose queries juxtapose the human and more-than-human: "With what sense is that the chicken shuns the ravenous hawk? / With what sense does the tame pigeon measure out the expanse? / With what sense does the bee form cells?" Oothoon's highest rhetorical moment concludes the work and articulates a counter-ethos to that represented by masculine presence in the poem:

> I cry, Love! Love! Love! happy happy Love! Free as the mountain wind!
> Can that be Love, that drinks another as a sponge drinks water?
> That clouds with jealousy his nights, with weepings all the day:
> To spin a web of age around him. Grey and hoary! Dark!
> Till his eyes sicken at the fruit that hangs before his sight.
> Such is self-love that envies all![60]

For Oothoon, love as learned across the body of the poem and as written on her body is best represented as a chaotically beautiful and fluidly free natural process ("mountain wind"), one incorporating complex vortical movement operating through principles of chance, uncertainty and indeterminacy.

Blake images both the antithetical state ("self-love" rather than hate) and its activities through recourse to the more-than-human realm (self-love

= sponge; selfish acts = webs that capture and fruits that rot). In Oothoon's concluding appeal for re/cognition of the biosemiotics that span the divides of species, Blake weaves together all the available semiotic fibers to represent a panpsychic mental event embraced by a character and experienced in textual reception:

> Does the sun walk in glorious raiment on the secret floor
> Where the cold miser spreads his gold? Or does the bright cloud drop
> On his stone threshold? Does his eye behold the beam that brings
> Expansion to the eye of pity? Or will he bind himself
> Beside the ox to thy hard furrow? Does not that mild beam blot
> The bat, the owl, the glowing tyger, and the king of night.
> The sea fowl takes the wintry blast. For a cov'ring to her limbs:
> And the wild snake, the pestilence to adorn him with gems and gold.
> And trees, & birds. & beasts. & men. Behold their eternal joy.
> Arise you little glancing wings, and sing your infant joy!
> Arise and drink your bliss, for everything that lives is holy![61]

The evocative play of light leads from an enclosed miserly human chamber to a descriptive catalogue of animality, and finally extends to "everything that lives." Biosemiotic and semiospheric conditions within the poem evolve into an "ecocosm"[62]—a cosmological state of interconnection generating joy as the boundary condition for living without adopting an anthropomorphic principle—through the emergent event of awakening into ecological consciousness. While Thel's line of deterritorialized flight fails, Oothoon's nomadic journey succeeds. There is even a minimal historical impact encoded in the work, when "the Daughters of Albion hear her woes and eccho back her sighs."[63]

Blake's early works struggle "with the concept of *expression*" and continually seek to create conditions where "substance expresses itself in attributes," a Blakean mode of "becoming animal" observed in "Thel." In *Visions*, the process of "becoming woman" through Oothoon cultivates inner revolution and brings into view a semiospheric ecocosm teeming with difference and radiating *jouissance* as its steady state. This description of Blakean textual dynamics sounds remarkably close to the Deleuzian reading of Nietzsche: "Liberation, joy, creation. That is what the affirmation of difference, the embrace of the eternal return, amounts to. Not sadness, resentment, pangs of conscience, or self-denial, but their opposite."[64] Oothoon embodies this state to the highest degree possible in Blake's initial attempts to find a voice for alterity, and he employs the poetic mechanism of becoming woman across the remainder of the poetic canon. For example, the crescendo of Blake's final poetic work *Jerusalem* manifests analogous semiotic threads and represents Blake's most energetic attempt to describe the farther shores of alterity through a decidedly heterological idiom which is rather schizoanalytic in its effects.

When Freya Matthews evokes a masterpiece of Blake's illuminated canon, she does so to highlight his opposition to the "dehumanizing and desocializing effects of the new scientific worldview." Yet she equally points to the play of the rhythmic ("the inimitable cadences of Blake"), something briefly analyzed in my essay "Blake's Deep Ecology."[65] The critical extension of Deleuze's philosophic assemblage beyond the shared affinities with German Romanticism to specific figures in English Romanticism has occurred only recently,[66] yet much common ground has emerged, for Blake's epics thematize *and* characterize fragmentation and reintegration, order collapsing into chaos and subsequently rising into unity. The epics collectively critique transcendence, as Peter Otto argues, through a reconceptualization of the apocalypse as singular event in the mind-body complex. Given the complexity of its semiotic composite form, the plot of Blake's *Jerusalem* can be described in surprisingly straightforward terms that foreground its ecological connections to Deleuze, as Hutchings's exemplary analysis makes abundantly clear: "Jerusalem's central action recounts the simple tale of Albion's withdrawal from dynamic relationality, his fall into solipsism, and his ultimate renovation as a fully integrated, resocialized human being." The simplicity of Hutchings's presentation of narrative events in *Jerusalem* accords well with Blake's description of his "Sublime Allegory," his unique form of schizoanalytic poetics "address'd to the Intellectual powers [which] . . . is altogether hidden from the Corporeal Understanding."[67]

This sublime allegory demands decoding through continuous hermeneutic acts to perceive the warp and woof of interwoven aesthetic production, historical conditions, narrative strategies, mythic archetypes, and psychological states. As the poem draws to a close, Blake overcomes the unrepresentable nature of mental events through self-emptying, with the textual spectrum of semiosis itself pressed into schizoanalytic service, where "the subject of discourse & every Word & Every Character / Was Human according to the Expansion or Contraction, the Translucence or / Opakeness of Nervous fibers." Psychological conditions for reception and textual conditions break free in closing tropes of interconnectedness:

> All Human Forms identified even Tree Metal Earth & Stone, all
> Human Forms identified, living going forth & returning wearied
> Into the Planetary lives of Years Months Days & Hours reposing
> And then Awaking into his Bosom in the Life of Immortality.
> And I heard the Name of their Emanations they are named Jerusalem[68]

Human apprehension crosses the event-horizon of selfhood, aided by liberated expression, restoring the free play of imagination that connects essential and dynamic contraries vibrating with rhythmic life at the position of alterity, by cultivating the ability to expand and contract into a "Life of Immortality" defined by radical forms of embodied liberty that unite the human and more-than-human as "all."

The sequence of "becomings" inaugurated in Blake's earlier poetry comes to fruition in this final textual space. This successful deterritorializing act, empowered by a willed act of self-annihilation, allows entry to the event of ecological consciousness. Blake bundles "elements of thought" in his sublime allegory, which "form the cohesion and consistency" and "then crystallize into the creation of something that is thought, or a poem with 'unity of impression'" found only beyond thinking itself.[69] In Blakean schizoanalysis, like that presented by Deleuze and Guattari, "mankind [must] strip itself of *all* anthropomorphic and anthropological armoring, all myth and tragedy, and all existentialism, in order to perceive what is nonhuman in man, his will and his forces, his transformations and mutations."[70] This is a process for poets and philosophers alike predicated on the necessary "unselfing" that allows "a *unified* view of life by integrating life's biological, cognitive and social dimensions."[71]

NOTES

1. Deleuze, *Pure Immanence,* 25, 30.

2. Mitchell, "Transcendental," 1.

3. Sellars, "The Point of View," 2–3. Badiou attempts to map a similar state in *Being and Event,* where "an infinite positive state of fidelity is generic" (338) and arrives at a position quite close to both Deleuze and Blake, for entry into the "generic" state of truth beyond Badiou's "super subject" and Blake's "spectre" creates "a rupture" that reveals "that situations are infinite and that human life is infinite" (Badiou, *Infinite Thought,* 131, 137).

4. Badiou, "Of Life" 195; Deleuze, *Pure Immanence,* 26.

5. Marks, introduction to "Deleuze and Science," 15.

6. Deleuze, *Desert Islands,* 122.

7. Bogue, "The Minor," 111–12.

8. Kearns, "Chaos and Control," 67.

9. Matthews, *The Ecological Self,* 117–63; Zohar, *Quantum Self,* 162–70.

10. Broglio, *Technologies,* 91. As subsequent discussion will make clear, "to achieve Deleuzean difference, identity must be dissolved" (Baulch, "Repetition, Representation, and Revolution," 5).

11. Keats, *Complete Poems and Selected Letters,* 492.

12. Blake, *Complete Poetry and Prose,* 136. Subsequent citations of this work refer to page, plate, and line (e.g., for this reference, Blake, 136:35.42–45).

13. Ibid., 142:40.34.

14. Lussier, "Blake's Vortex," 266–75.

15. Sellars, "The Point of View," 2.

16. Matthews, *Ecological Self*, 51.

17. Deleuze, *Pure Immanence*, 12; Zohar, *Quantum Self*, 110. See also my "Inner Revolution/Self-Annihilation: Blake's Milton, Buddhism, and Ecocriticism," 39–57.

18. Morton, *Ecology without Nature*, 104, 106–7.

19. Two applications of this approach can be found in Steve Baker's "What Does Becoming-Animal Look Like?" 67–98; and Mark Halsey's "Environmental Visions," 33–64.

20. Deleuze and Guattari, *A Thousand Plateaus*, 249.

21. Zohar, *Quantum Self*, 76–91.

22. Blake, 108: 14.30; Matthews, *Ecological Self*, 107–9; J. Williams, "Science and Dialectics," 112.

23. Zohar, *Quantum Self*, 124.

24. Matthews, *Ecological Self*, 54.

25. Baker, "Becoming-Animal," 78.

26. Deleuze and Guattari, *A Thousand Plateaus*, 238.

27. Massumi, *User's Guide to Capitalism and Schizophrenia*, 100.

28. Ibid., 101; May, *Gilles Deleuze*, 87.

29. Plotnitsky, "Chaosmologies," 41.

30. Badiou, *Infinite Thought*, 137.

31. Blake, 45. My analyses are found, respectively, in "Blake's Vortex," 263–91; and "Blake's Deep Ecology," 393–408.

32. Bell, *Philosophy at the Edge of Chaos*, 188.

33. Emmeche, paper presented at "Nature Matters" conference, Toronto, 25–28 October 2007. The movement's evolutionary approach is well displayed in the diverse essays collected in *Biosemiotics: The New Biological Synthesis* by Marcello Barbieri.

34. Matthews, *For Love of Matter*, 27. In Romantic Europe, especially in its German form, "panpsychism continued to play a prominent role," leading to the view of Herder and Goethe that "humans were unified deeply with nature, physical forces were seen as manifestations of a single underlying force, and mechanism was soundly rejected" (Skrbina, *Panpsychism in the West*, 112, 115).

35. This dimension of the schizoanalytic work of Deleuze and Guattari has been most deployed in criticism questioning the relationship of the human and more-than-human, as in Cary Wolfe's arguments, founded upon this view, that mimetic acts often become "the enemy rather than the agent of a relationship of *becoming* between humanity and animality" (xv). Along this same line of argument, Steve Baker's critique of "imitation" shares Wolfe's concerns, since "it is Deleuze and Guattari who have made this question so difficult for the postmodern artist" ("Sloughing," 157).

36. Blake, 45; Hutchings, *Imagining Nature*, 18.

37. Deleuze, quoted in Duffy, "The Difference between Science and Philosophy," 119.

38. May, *Gilles Deleuze*, 116.

39. Blake, 4:1.19–25.

40. Blake, 5:3.23; 5:3.27–28; 5:4.10.

41. Deleuze, *Desert Islands*, 123.

42. Deleuze, *Pure Immanence*, 26; Blake, 6:6.1 & 6.11.

43. Matthews, *Reinhabiting Reality*, 15, emphasis added.

44. May, *Gilles Deleuze*, 25.

45. Blake, *The Marriage of Heaven and Hell*, in *The Complete Poetry and Prose of William Blake*, 34:3.6.

46. Bindman, *William Blake*, 44, 70.

47. Gifford, *Pastoral*, 134–35.

48. Hutchings, *Imagining Nature*, 213.

49. Bindman, *William Blake*, 48–49.

50. Harries-Jones, "Introducing Biosemiotics," 3.

51. Blake, 11:14.1–4.

52. Deleuze, *Desert Islands*, 36.

53. Blake, 11:15.11–12.

54. Sotirin, "Becoming-Woman," 102.

55. Blake, 18:30.11, 16.

56. Blake, *Visions*, 46:2.1–5.

57. See Luce Irigaray's "Women on the Market" and "Commodities among Themselves," in *This Sex That Is Not One*, 170–97.

58. Sotirin, "Becoming-Woman," 104.

59. Massumi, *User's Guide to Capitalism and Schizophrenia*, 100–101.

60. Blake, *Visions*, 47:2.23–25; Blake, 47:3.2–4; 50:7.16–22.

61. Blake, 51:7.30–8.10.

62. Matthews, *Ecological Self*, 147.

63. Blake, 51:8.12.

64. May, *Gilles Deleuze*, 36, 69.

65. Matthews, *Ecological Self*, 42; Lussier, "Blake's Deep Ecology," 405–8.

66. The essays gathered by Ron Broglio in *Romanticism and the New Deleuze* (2008) forge connections with Blake, Shelley, and Wordsworth, while the most provocative recent study was done by Justin Clemens, who connects the indeterminate nature of Romanticism to a broad range of contemporary theory.

67. Otto, *Blake's Critique*, 1–35; Hutchings, *Imagining Nature*, 156; Blake, 730.

68. Blake, 258:98.35–7; 258–59:99.1–5.

69. Bell, *Philosophy at the Edge of Chaos*, 154.

70. Deleuze and Guattari, *Anti-Oedipus*, xx.

71. Kearns, "Chaos and Control," quoting Capra, 66.

The Biosemiotic Turn: Abduction, or, the Nature of Creative Reason in Nature and Culture

In this essay I explore an ecocritical theory of cultural, and thus also literary, creativity from a biosemiotic point of view. While what follows might be thought broadly to fall within what is sometimes called the "post" humanities, in fact biosemiotics is a thoroughly interdisciplinary proto-discipline; it seeks not only to change how humanists think about culture, the arts, and the biological sciences but also to change how scientists and social scientists think about biological science and the arts and humanities.

Essentially, the biosemiotic "project" first fully self-identified a quarter century ago consists in an elaboration, by biologists, psychologists, anthropologists, philosophers, semioticians and, more recently, the odd cultural and literary critic, of the observation that *all* life—from the cell all the way up to us—is characterized by communication, or semiosis. This insight, which places humans back in nature as part of a richly communicative global web teeming with meanings and purposes, and which makes human culture, and thus technology, evolutionary and natural, should be of particular interest to ecocritics.

I begin with a brief summary of what biosemiotics is, and then focus on my main topic here, which is the nature of personal and cultural creativity— particularly as overtly manifest in aesthetic work. Two things, closely related, are central to my discussion. One is Charles Sanders Peirce's idea of abduction/retroduction as the logic of creative thinking in all spheres. The second is the idea, found in Peirce's related conception of "the play of musement," that *Non knowing frames the ability to know.*[1] As I hope will become clear, this involves a semiotic and biosemiotic turn concerning both the nature of reasoning and reason in nature. Intuitive "abductive" knowing —knowing but not knowing quite how you know, not being able to offer normal inductive or deductive causal relations, depending on belief and on the significance of *semiotic* causal relations—forms the subject of my brief discussion of A. S. Byatt's *Angels and Insects,* and more extended discussion of Ian McEwan's *Black Dogs,* toward the end of this essay. Since the late 1980s, English novelists have shown increasing interest in the question of what constitutes "knowledge" in both the arts and the sciences, and in whether there is really a great difference between these two supposedly different systems of knowledge and belief. Since *Black Dogs* is centered around the modern estrangement of these two ways of understanding the world, and in particular around the question of signs, meanings, and causality, it offers a particularly rich object for biosemiotic meditation.

"The play of musement" is Peirce's account of the condition most conducive to that form of creative reasoning which he named abduction (and sometimes retroduction).[2] Although Peirce's discussions of abduction were concerned only with the logic of creative thought in humans, his idea of abduction can be very fruitfully developed within the biosemiotic understandings which have subsequently grown from his own semiotic philosophy. I will suggest some of the ways in which recent work in epigenetics ("evo devo," or evolutionary developmental biology), and systems biology more broadly, allows us to begin to see the evolutionary continuity between the expression of communicative forms and patterns in nature, and those we are familiar with in culture and in aesthetic expressions.

The Development of Biosemiotics

A very full and thorough account of the development of biosemiotics can be found in Donald Favareau's "The Evolutionary History of Biosemiotics."[3] Here, I offer a much briefer account before moving on to some of the implications from an ecocritical point of view. The seeds of biosemiotics are to be found in the semiotic philosophy of the American scientist and philosopher Charles Sanders Peirce (1839–1914). For Peirce, "the universe is perfused with signs,"[4] and all living things—from the humblest forms of single-cell life upward—are engaged in sign relations.[5] I think it must be clear that all biological systems are relational—that is, informational— systems. But, for Peirce (as for many others), biological systems are never simply mechanical. What goes on *inside* an organism, and *between* an organism and its environment (the two processes being intimately connected), always involves what, for lack of a better word, we must call interpretations —however minimal. In purely physical systems, we can talk cybernetically of positive (excitatory) and negative (dampening) feedback; but, in living things, such feedback is always subject to "understanding" and "interpretation"—however sometimes primitive. Thus we cannot talk simply about "information" (which applies to abiotic cybernetic systems also), but can, and where biotic systems are concerned, must properly speak about communication as semiosis. This led Peirce to the view that "mind" and "ideas" are not properties of humans alone, but are immanent in all living things. Since nothing comes from nothing—all evolutionary life is an elaboration of antecedent forms—this seems an inevitable conclusion.

Quite separately from Peirce, the German-Estonian biologist Jakob von Uexküll (1864–1944) reached similar conclusions concerning the semiotic nature of life.[6] All organisms, von Uexküll argued, live in *Umwelten* which are *signifying* environments characterized by semiotic loops (von Uexküll's *Funktionskreis*, or functional cycle) flowing ceaselessly between the *Umwelten* (semiotic environments) and *Innenwelten* (semiotic "inner worlds") of creatures: each making each in a ceaseless living ecological process. This has subsequently led to the observation that the biosphere is also the semiosphere.[7] What a creature (as instance of a species) recognizes, or knows (and compares), are the signs in its environment which are necessary to its survival (and, thus, to its species' survival). And, of course, this applies to humans too; but our environments (*Umwelten*) are both natural *and* cultural.

In his detailed account of von Uexküll, Kalevi Kull places von Uexküll in a lineage going both back through scholars such as Goethe, Geoffroy Saint-Hilaire, and Karl Ernst von Baer, and also forward to those such as Konrad Lorenz, Brian Goodwin, René Thom, Robert Rosen, Arne Naess, and Stuart Kauffman—not to mention Martin Heidegger, Ernst Cassirer, Ortega y Gasset, Gilles Deleuze, Rainer Maria Rilke, Thomas Mann, Peter Høeg, and Giorgio Agamben, all of whom were influenced by his work.[8] Also influenced by von Uexküll, the biologist Ludwig von Bertalanffy (1901–1972) developed general systems theory, a form of proto-biocybernetics which emphasized holism over reductionism and organism over mechanism. General systems theory is a forerunner of what is now more usually called systems biology, and I shall return to this later. The semiotician Thomas A. Sebeok (1920–2001) synthesized the ideas of Peirce, von Uexküll, Gregory Bateson, and others, including insights offered by general systems theory and cybernetics, and thereby formulated the beginnings (in 1984 in a special issue of the journal *Semiotica*)[9] of the interdiscipline now known as biosemiotics.

This brings us to the biosemiotic present and to a model of evolutionary systems characterized by stratification and emergence in communicative systems: levels, or layers, of relative stability are always pregnant *in potentia* with the emergence of new adaptive forms in response to environmental pressures. Each "layer" is, over time, increasingly rich in communication, or semiosis. Thus, one of the best known of the present generation of biosemioticians, the molecular biologist Jesper Hoffmeyer, speaks of evolution as the evolution of ever-greater extents of both semiotic richness and "semiotic freedom."[10]

The important thing to remember—and Neil Shubin's work demonstrates this well—is that all these layers, or concentric nested semiotic systems, remain contained and active within us. At the end of *Your Inner Fish*, Shubin writes: "Looking back through billions of years of change, everything innovative or apparently unique in the history of life is really just old stuff that has been recycled, recombined, repurposed, or otherwise modified for new uses. This is the story of every part of us, from our sense organs to our heads, indeed our entire body plan."[11] Improvisation is the key to both natural and cultural creative evolution. It is a central part of my biosemiotic argument that culture is emergent in nature, and mind is emergent in body/environment. The patterns which are emergently evolved and established in the one, are rearticulated, worked over, remodeled, repurposed, recombined and emergently evolved in the other. Body plans and patterns thus become mind plans and patterns. In humans, these (bio)semiotic mind plans and patterns inform all our life in signs, including aesthetics and ethics.

Peirce's Logic (Abduction/Retroduction)

In order to think in a little more detail about how creative recursivity (the ceaseless cycle of feedback and change between creatures and environments) might work in humans, I now turn to Peirce. Peirce had a particular interest in the philosophy of logic. He was especially exercised by the limitations surrounding the question of logical inferences. Logicians, he noted, normally confine the latter to deductive inference and inductive inference alone. But these, he repeatedly pointed out, gave no account of the generation of hypotheses (i.e., creative thought) in the first place: "Abduction is the process of forming an explanatory hypothesis. It is the only logical operation which introduces any new idea; for induction does nothing but determine a value, and deduction merely evolves the necessary consequences of a pure hypothesis. Deduction proves that something must be; Induction shows that something actually is operative; Abduction merely suggests that something may be."[12] In order to explain the generation of ideas in the first place, as well as the gaps and failures in deductive and inductive inferential procedures which are, in fact, routinely supplied by hunches and informed guesses on the part of scientists and artists alike, Peirce suggested this third type of logical inference that he called "abduction." It is the strange—obscure and dark—semiotic process whereby signs are read, and interpreted, often without ever necessarily having reached consciousness at all.

Abduction is essentially a sort of intuitive "following your nose" by which the well-informed mind (i.e., the *Umwelt*-alert mind), allowing itself to fall into what Peirce called "the play of musement,"[13] is able to gain access to unconscious or preconscious (or what Michael Polanyi—another scientist and philosopher—called "tacit") antecedent knowledges.[14]

Abductions and Art

Abductions are intuitive—that is, sensed. They are, as Paul Ricoeur says of metaphor, "the fusion of "sense" and "sensa," understood . . . as an iconic unfurling of sense in imagery." Ricoeur continues: "the power of metaphor would be to break an old categorization in order to establish new logical frontiers on the ruins of their forerunners" and "Metaphor . . . presents in an open fashion, by means of a conflict between identity and difference, the process that, in a covert manner, generates semantic grids by fusion of differences into identity."[15] We can add that the similarity which establishes the identity of species and genera is, at the same time, the source of evolution in both organisms and languages. Such abductive "carryings over" are produced by "the play of musement." This is human creativity: the intuitive openness and reaching after signs; the search for new likenesses; the attempt to step back from old enframings in order to see freshly into the life of things; the attempt to see repetition in difference, and difference in repetition, which brings signs and ideas previously held apart into a new productive union which, in turn, sets off the pursuit of implications some of which, like children or seeds, will reproduce while others do not. As Percy Bysshe Shelley noted,[16] such creative play cannot be called forth to order. It is entirely resistant to the precision and ordering of modern techno-rational life, and depends, as Peirce knew, upon the noninstrumental and passionately interested following of hints and hunches, and upon having faith in processes which are beyond our will, half beyond our knowing, and which also seem to have a life of their own within us. Abductions are informed guesses; they are based on intuition and belief.

When Wordsworth, in book 3 of *The Prelude*, talks of his poetry as making "breathings for incommunicable powers" which "lie far hidden from the reach of words," and when Lawrence, in "The Novel and the Feelings," talks of reeducating ourselves by "listening in to the voices of the honourable beasts that call in the dark paths of the veins of our body . . . to the lowing of the innermost beasts, the feelings, that roam in the forest of the blood, from the feet of God within the red, dark heart," they are both intimating these deeply embodied biosemiotic resources of human knowing in non-knowing.[17]

The Depth of Metaphor

"Metaphor lies deeper in our languages and our thought processes than we might wish to recognise. There is very little that we can say of great human significance without metaphor. This is obviously true of poetry and other literary forms. It is also true of scientific language."[18] In *The Music of Life: Biology Beyond Genes*, the systems biologist Denis Noble wants to explain why the gene-centric reductionist and deterministic view developed in sociobiology in the 1970s and renamed as evolutionary psychology in the 1980s and 1990s is inadequate. He goes to some lengths to explain the complexity of the relationship between the information encoded in DNA and the ways in which it is "read off" and "interpreted" (his terms, and *not* metaphors as logocentrically understood) by proteins in the cellular manufacture of living things. DNA code (the encodement of information for the future in genes or gene sequences) is simply inert. As with a never read book, on its own, DNA cannot cause anything to happen. It is only when it is read off by proteins in the cell (which interpret its potential meanings in different ways according to time, to higher-level processes and purposes, and to environmental inputs both internal and external to the organism) that its potential meanings (in the building activities of proteins) become activated. The "meanings" of genes, in other words, lie in what proteins make of and from them in particular contexts. As Noble writes:

> The DNA code of a gene is nonsense (just a sequence of CGAT bases) until it is interpreted functionally, first by the cell/protein machinery that initiates and controls transcription and post-transcriptional modifications, and then by the systems-level interaction between proteins that generate higher-level function. A gene can do nothing without this interpretation by the system.
>
> On its own, the stretch of DNA code for a gene is like a word without the semantic frame of its language. The system provides the semantic frame and gives the gene its functionality, its meaning.[19]

Indeed, Noble likens the actions of proteins interpreting DNA sequences to the human activity of creation via metaphor:

> Genetic and cultural forms of evolution share this messiness, or, to use a less derogatory term, inventiveness. For it is through a complicated series of bodges that nature has arrived at the huge diversity of life as we know it. Tangled intricacy is the mother of nature's invention. The idea of metaphor is important here, too. On that basis, we can say that, as the genome has developed, nature has switched from one metaphor to another. It has plun-

dered the treasure chest of old DNA modules to form new combinations and to give old genes new functions.[20]

Such semiotic expressions belong to life from its earliest beginnings.[21] We might say that we, the creatures who make in metaphor in human minds and words, are ourselves first made in bodies which are swarms of nature's metaphors.

The Human Grasp of the World

If biosemiotic thought is to be helpful in the thinking of cultural poiesis, this must consist not only in thinking the nature in culture and the culture in nature, but also in thinking this flow of mind—which belongs to all living entities in the form of their semiotic responsiveness to their *Umwelten*—in terms of human consciousness and language and the evolutionary strata which subtend it.

Abductive belief, human-animal mind, belongs to the scientist as much as to the artist. The capacity to *think* our being phenomenologically, as relational body-mind-environment, cannot lie in a science only of objects, or of subjects "objectively" understood; no such "science" (as the word is currently understood) exists or could exist. Subjectivity is not made of symbolic mental representations in a brain (which could be transposed into other kinds of symbolic logic—in a computer, for example), but is a semiotic relational process in which "mind" is the embodied grasping of an afforded world. The human grasp of the world is essentially aesthetic (from the Greek *aisthanesthai*, to perceive). It derives from percepts (that is, from enworlded bodies) by which we *are* the reaching out into world, into alterity, which discovers itself in this encounter.

The human fascination with art is a fascination with the particular kind of poiesis in which we are required to reflect upon the mystery of human meaning-making itself. Thus art, and especially art in language, remains the place of our best hopes of self-understanding. When A. S. Byatt, in the twinned novellas of *Angels and Insects*, offers us two contrasted ways of grasping the world (via Darwinian science in *Morpho Eugenia*, and via poetry and mediumship in *The Conjugial Angel*) she is not implying (as the modern world seems to do) that we must choose between them—the one modern, scientific, and *true*, the other fraudulent and deluded. Rather, she is indicating, very clearly (for William Adamson, the Darwinist, is equally a willfully deluded Son of Adam) that there are different orders of truth. What can appear as outdated—allegorical interpretation in *Morpho Eugenia*; mediumship and the power of ghosts in *The Conjugial Angel*—remains causally efficacious in both novellas. Reality, in both stories, is always mediated in the telling of it, and by the willing and reaching for worlds which characterize both fictional protagonists and the writer, as medium, herself.

Similarly, in Ian McEwan's *Black Dogs,* we are not allowed to settle with Bernard Tremaine's scientific account against June Tremaine's spiritual one. We see too clearly the gods which failed, and the long line of puritanical revolutionaries who hacked and burned their way to salvation. When ex-Communist Bernard, referring to Isaiah Berlin on the fatal quality of utopias, says, "If I know for certain how to bring humanity to peace, justice, happiness, boundless creativity, what price can be too high? To make this omelette there might be no limit to the eggs I might need to break,"[22] we hear Brecht's only partial *mea culpa* in the poem "To Posterity": "Alas we / Who wished to lay the foundations of kindness / Could not ourselves be kind." And while still hanging on to the truth of scientific method, Bernard does acknowledge that, even in the "well-designed experiment," "our desires permeate our perceptions."[23] The possibility of truth in June's revelation in the encounter with the black dogs on the way to St Maurice de Navacelles in 1946 is not undone by Bernard's science. Indeed, in the narrative structure, it is Bernard's science, his pause to consider a caravan of caterpillars on the pathway and his leaving June to walk ahead alone without him, which makes the latter's animal encounter and experience of transcendence possible.

Encountering ourselves as semiotic animals, more susceptible than we know to a world perfused with signs, we encounter mind in all its reverberations in the world. This, surely, is the care, the non-naïve responsiveness to world, that ecocritical perspectives have set out to find. In *Black Dogs,* Bernard's scientific pause on the pathway down the Gorge de Vis, his own wonder at the purposeful procession of tiny life before him, reminds us both of the ant nests in *Morpho Eugenia,* and also of the other processions of desire and perception which *Black Dogs* and *Angels and Insects* both set out to allegorize. The "scientific pause" of modern "objective" science may still find its way, later down the path, to the essentially semiotic nature of all natural and cultural revelations of meanings, layered and emergent over time, and to always mysterious purposes.

All literature is, of course, always about its own moment. If *Black Dogs* is about spiritual beliefs versus scientific ones, both of them, finally, as belief systems, as ways of being in the world and as different ways of accounting truth, it is also very much of its own "postmodern" moment in being concerned about signs and, indeed, about what *counts* as a sign. Cast as a story about revelation and how we "read" the world—whether "rationally" as science and as "scientific" Marxian ideology on Bernard's part, or "irrationally" and spiritually on June's—the narrator, Jeremy, typifies nihilistic modern consciousness in never letting himself (and hence the reader) quite

settle into the supposed certainties of either. Bernard, in Berlin in 1989 as
the Wall is falling, is saved from attack by Nazi thugs by a young woman who
looks uncannily like June in her youth; she looks like the June whom Bernard says he searches for in the faces of crowds after her death.[24] Jeremy
wonders if this could be a "message" from June beyond the grave (how else
would such a thing be done?), but for Bernard it is simply, "Quite a coincidence, I suppose."[25] Rational, scientific, Bernard cannot pay attention to, is
not interested in, indeed is "impatient" with, the hints, guesses and improvisations of creative abductive life. Yet this, both Peirce and Michael
Polanyi claim, is the way that all art, all science, all evolutionary life itself,
makes its journey into the future—primarily not as conscious reason but as
guess and intuition, improvisation and belief. For June, in contrast, not only
the human world but, perhaps more importantly, the natural world *speaks*.
For her, the encounter with the black dogs in the Gorge de Vis in the
summer of 1946 is a feeling and a message which cannot be simply rationally
interpreted. Farther down the path than Bernard, June experiences the
savage black dogs let wild by departed Nazis as the immediacy of living
metaphor. This is not metaphor tamed as a figure of speech, but the real wild
incarnation of life's extraordinary patterning itself.

The Causse de Larzac, with its dolmens associated with fertility earth-
goddess worship, is a holy place. It is fitting that June, pregnant with the narrator's wife-to-be, should have her revelatory experience of spiritual power
and connectedness in such a place and wrapped in an ovoid of "coloured
invisible light."[26] Here, Bernard's rationality, a belief system just as much as
June's, but with harsher this-worldly consequences for the human imagination, is also the "spirit hound" enemy. June's intuitions—her feelings of fear
approaching the Gorge de Vis, and of rightness afterward about following
the shepherd, and in buying his bergerie above St. Privat, as with the narrator's encounter with darkness and the scorpion in the bergerie in 1989—are
not based in "scientific" mechanical causality but on chance associations,
improvisations, and ideas as *semiotic causality*.[27] Are they less *meaningful* for
all that? This is, in fact, precisely how biological evolution (and "meaning-
making") proceeds.[28]

In the bergerie in 1989, in the novel's other most fear-gripped passage, it
is Jeremy's sense of the presence of dead June, his feeling of his skin as an
acute "organ of perception,"[29] which prevents him from touching the unseen
scorpion on the fuse box cupboard handle. And if June's "coloured invisible
light" in the Gorge de Vis in 1946 reminds us of an inversion of Milton's
description of Satan's Hell (as "darkness visible") in *Paradise Lost*,[30] Jeremy's
June-haunted one in the bergerie in 1989 does too. In absolute darkness
seeking the fuse box cupboard to turn on the light, he describes the cupboard

as a patch of darkness visible: "Even in this darkness it showed as a blacker patch ahead of me."[31]

These signs (are they signs?) are the stuff of Carl Gustav Jung's "synchronicity,"[32] and are the nonmechanical causally related signs, also, of the serendipitous discovery which drives so much real creative thought in science and art.[33] Such "chance" connections of "knowing in not knowing" and semiotic causation are also, of course, the conjuring with words and their iconic associations, and the making of these into new signs, by which the literary text, itself, is made. It is in literature that we are still reminded, in our own disenchanted modern time, of the conjuring power of signs in the making of worlds. The word "poiesis" derives from the ancient Greek ποιέω, to make or create. We read literature well when we are alert to such magical "makings." And this perhaps accounts, too, for literature's evolutionary power and survival; it reminds us, in a prosaic world where such things are too easily forgotten, of the etymological connection between "grimoire" (a book of spells) and "grammar," and of the generative magic, the pregnancy, of signs. In *Black Dogs,* the linguistic signs take us back to the nonlinguistic world not only through the iconic signs upon which all metaphor is based, but because they remind us that the natural world of embodied human intuitions and of biosemiotic nature—the black dogs, the scorpion—might also be living signs perfused with meanings too.

In the long dusk of the modern and postmodern day, we begin to rediscover what the world of mythic premodernity knew long before: that not only humans, but *all* nature, "speaks."[34] The "linguistic turn" and the "postmodern" focus on signs (via Saussurean semiology) were not entirely wrong except that they stopped, anthropocentrically, at the human word and world alone. The biosemiotic turn will, hopefully, take us beyond that limitation into the "more-than-human world"[35] where we understand not only that the natural world is perfused with signs, meanings and purposes which are material and which evolve, but also that it is in the human use of signs in poetic language, wherever it is found, that this mythic understanding has often best been preserved.

Black Dogs plots a story of orphaned humanity (Jeremy is an orphan in search of some new Adam and Eve—Bernard and June—as first parents "Before the fall")[36] in which June's vision is, in the end, more compelling than Bernard's. It is June's abductive guess about the meaning of the black dogs—that they *do* mean—and Jeremy's final agreement, that they are real signs of a mythic monstrosity within modern reason which will return again to haunt us, which close the novel. The implication—that myth is already a form of enlightenment, and that Enlightenment reason produces mythic monstrosities—belongs, of course, to Adorno and Horkheimer's *Dialectic of*

Enlightenment. Black Dogs, which pits June's intuitive, mythic vision of cultural *and* natural signs and meanings against Bernard's rationalist vision of both nature's and culture's disenchanted purposelessness,[37] might well be seen as a novelistic meditation on Adorno and Horkheimer's central thesis. Moving *beyond* the latter must mean grasping a wider sense of "reason" and "meaning" as inhering not only in myth, and then in modernity, but also, finally, in nature itself. As theoretical biology begins to understand that semiosis has a natural, as well as a cultural, history, we can perhaps begin to glimpse some new light in which all are understood as living semiotic *processes* and *relations* in life's organic evolution on earth.

In his narratorial preamble, Jeremy notes that he married into "a divided family."[38] *Black Dogs* tries to narrate the causes of that relational breakdown. That this should hang on Bernard's and June's divergent understandings, their "readings," of signs and sign relations is appropriate in the postmodern dusk. Jeremy, himself, concludes that *relation* ("love") is the only redemptive power:

> It will not do to argue that rational thought and spiritual insight are separate domains and that opposition between them is falsely conceived. Bernard and June often talked to me about ideas that could never sit side by side. Bernard, for example, was certain that there was no direction, no patterning in human affairs or fates other than that which was imposed by human minds. June could not accept this; life had a purpose and it was in our interests to open ourselves to it. Nor will it do to suggest that both these views are correct. To believe everything, to make no choices, amounts to much the same thing, to my mind, as believing in nothing at all. I am uncertain whether our civilisation at this turn of the millennium is cursed by too much or too little belief, whether people like Bernard and June cause the trouble, or people like me. But I would be false to my own experience if I did not declare my belief in the possibility of love transforming and redeeming a life.[39]

Relations break down when we are shut off in different stories. Bernard's and June's stories are the unbridgeable stories of modernity in which the Cartesian sundering has divided what counts as knowledge itself. In understanding that semiosis and meaning-making belongs to all living things, perhaps the biosemiotic turn will prove itself part of a wider movement toward reuniting what has too long been held apart.

NOTES

    1. Clarke, *Posthuman Metamorphosis,* 71, original emphasis.

    2. Peirce, "Neglected Argument," 436.

    3. Favareau, "The Evolutionary History of Biosemiotics," 1–67.

4. Peirce, "The Basis of Pragmaticism in the Normative Sciences," 394.

5. In Peirce's semiotic, these sign relations are triadic and phenomenologically grounded in organistic experience of the world, not dyadic and purely relational as in the anthropocentric semiology of F. de Saussure (see Merrell, "Charles Sanders Peirce's Concept of the Sign").

6. For an extremely detailed account of J. von Uexküll's work, including biography and full bibliography, see Kull, "Jacob von Uexküll: An Introduction."

7. Kull, "On Semiosis, Umwelt, and Semiosphere"; Kull, Emmeche, and Favareau, "Biosemiotic Questions."

8. Kull, "Jacob von Uexküll."

9. Anderson et al., "A Semiotic Perspective."

10. Hoffmeyer, Signs of Meaning.

11. Shubin, Your Inner Fish, 201.

12. Peirce, "The Nature of Meaning," 216.

13. Peirce, "Neglected Argument."

14. Polanyi, Tacit Dimension.

15. Ricoeur, Rule of Metaphor, 250, 233, 234.

16. "Poetry is not like reasoning, a power to be exerted according to the determination of the will. A man cannot say, 'I will compose poetry.' The greatest poet even cannot say it; for the mind in creation is as a fading coal, which some invisible influence, like an inconstant wind, awakens to transitory brightness; this power arises from within, like the colour of a flower which fades and changes as it is developed, and the conscious portions of our natures are unprophetic either of its approach or its departure. Could this influence be durable in its original purity and force, it is impossible to predict the greatness of the results; but when composition begins, inspiration is already on the decline" (Shelley, A Defence of Poetry, 1821; first published 1840)

17. Wordsworth, The Prelude, 63; Lawrence, "Novel and the Feelings," 205.

18. Noble, Music of Life, 141.

19. Ibid., 21.

20. Ibid., 103–4.

21. Hoffmeyer, Biosemiotics, 32.

22. McEwan, Black Dogs, 88.

23. Ibid., 89.

24. Ibid., 83.

25. Ibid., 100.

26. Ibid., 150.

27. Hoffmeyer, Biosemiotics, 64.

28. Neuman, Reviving the Living.

29. McEwan, Black Dogs, 115.

30. Milton, Paradise Lost, bk. 1:l.63, 48.

31. McEwan, Black Dogs, 114–5.

32. Jung, Synchronicity.

33. Boden, Creative Mind.

34. Kane, The Wisdom of the Mythtellers.

35. Abram, *Spell of the Sensuous.*

36. McEwan, *Black Dogs,* 45.

37. Ibid., 20.

38. Ibid.

39. Ibid.

Bibliography

Abbey, Edward. *The Monkey Wrench Gang.* 1975. New York: Harper Perennial, 2000.

Abel, Darrel. "A Key to the House of Usher." *University of Toronto Quarterly* 18 (1949): 176–85.

Abram, David. "Merleau-Ponty and the Voice of the Earth." *Environmental Ethics* 10 (1988): 101–20.

———. *The Spell of the Sensuous: Perception and Language in a More-Than-Human World.* New York: Vintage, 1997.

Adorno, Theodor. *Aesthetic Theory.* Translated and edited by Robert Hullot-Kentor. London: Athlone Press, 1997.

———. *History and Freedom: Lectures 1964–1965.* Edited by Rolf Tiedemann. London: Wiley, 2006.

———. *Negative Dialectics.* Translated by E. B. Ashton. London: Routledge, 1973.

Aichele, George. "Reading Beyond Meaning." *Postmodern Culture* 3, no. 3 (May 1993). Project MUSE. Monash University Library, Clayton, Vic. http://muse.jhu.edu/.

———. *Sign, Text, Scripture: Semiotics and the Bible.* Sheffield: Sheffield Academic Press, 1997.

Alaimo, Stacy. "Trans-Corporeal Feminisms and the Ethical Space of Nature." In *Material Feminisms,* edited by Alaimo and Susan Hekman, 237–64. Bloomington: Indiana University Press, 2008.

Althusser, Louis. *Lenin and Philosophy and Other Essays.* Translated by Ben Brewster. New York: Monthly Review, 2001.

———. *On Ideology.* London: Verso, 2008.

Anderson, Myrdene, John Deely, Martin Krampen, Joseph Ransdell, Thomas A. Sebeok, and Thure von Uexküll. "A Semiotic Perspective on the Sciences: Steps toward a New Paradigm." *Semiotica* 52, no. 1 (1984): 7–47.

Arendt, Hannah. "Introduction: Walter Benjamin, 1892–1940." In Walter Benjamin, *Illuminations: Essays and Reflections*, edited by Arendt, 1–55. New York: Schocken Books, 1968.

Armbruster, Karla, and Kathleen R. Wallace, eds. *Beyond Nature Writing: Expanding the Boundaries of Eco-Criticism.* Charlottesville and London: University Press of Virginia, 2001.

Assmann, Aleida. *Erinnerungsräume: Formen und Wandlungen des kulturellen Gedächtnisses* (Realms of Memory: Forms and Transformations of Cultural Memory). 1999. 4th ed. Munich: Beck, 2009.

Assmann, Jan. *Das kulturelle Gedächtnis: Schrift, Erinnerung und politische Identität in frühen Hochkulturen* (Cultural Memory: Writing, Memory and Political Identity in Early Advanced Civilizations). 1992. 6th ed. Munich: Beck, 2007.

———. *Religion and Cultural Memory.* Translated by Rodney Livingston. Stanford: Stanford University Press, 2006.

Atterton, Peter, and Matthew Calarco, eds. *Animal Philosophy: Ethics and Identity.* London and New York: Continuum, 2007.

Auden, W. H. *Selected Poems.* Edited by Edward Medelson. New York: Vintage, 1989.

Austin, Mary. *The Land of Little Rain.* 1903. New York: Penguin, 1997.

Ayers, David. "Materialism and the Book." *Poetics Today* 24, no. 4 (2003): 759–80.

Badiou, Alain. *Being and Event.* Translated by Oliver Feltham. London: Continuum, 2005.

———. *Infinite Thought.* Translated by Oliver Feltham and Justin Clemens. London: Continuum, 2005.

———. "Of Life as a Name of Being, or Deleuze's Vitalist Ontology." *Pli: The Warwick Journal of Philosophy* 10 (2000): 191–99.

Baker, Steve. "Sloughing the Human." In *Zoontologies: The Question of the Animal,* edited by Cary Wolfe, 147–64. Minneapolis: University of Minnesota Press, 2003.

———. "What Does Becoming-Animal Look Like?" In *Representing Animals,* edited by Nigel Rothfels, 67–88. Bloomington: Indiana University Press, 2002.

Bakhtin, Mikhail Mikhailovich. *Art and Answerability: Early Philosophical Essays.* Edited by Michael Holquist and Vadim Liapunov. Translated by Liapunov. Austin: University of Texas Press, 1990.

———. *The Dialogic Imagination: Four Essays.* Edited by Michael Holquist. Translated by Caryl Emerson and Holquist. Austin: University of Texas Press, 1981.

———. *Problems of Dostoevsky's Poetics.* Edited and translated by Caryl Emerson. Minneapolis: University of Minnesota Press, 1984.

———. *Rabelais and His World.* Translated by Hélène Iswolsky. 1968. Bloomington: Indiana University Press, 1984.

———. *Toward a Philosophy of the Act.* Edited by Vladim Liapunov and Michael Holquist. Translated by Liapunov. Austin: University of Texas Press, 1993.

Barad, Karen. *Meeting the Universe Halfway: Quantum Physics and the Entanglement of Matter and Meaning.* Durham: Duke University Press, 2007.

————. "Posthumanist Performativity: Toward an Understanding of How Matter Comes to Matter." In *Material Feminisms*, edited by Stacy Alaimo and Susan Hekman, 120–54. Bloomington: Indiana University Press, 2008.

Barbieri, Marcello, ed. *Biosemiotics: The New Biological Synthesis*. Amsterdam: Springer Verlag, 2006.

Barnes, John, and Brian McFarlane, eds. *Cross-Country: A Book of Australian Verse*. Sydney: Heinemann, 1984.

Barnes, Julian. *England, England*. New York: Vintage, 2000.

Bataille, Georges. *Theory of Religion*. Translated by Robert Hurley. Cambridge: MIT Press, 1992.

Bate, Jonathan. "Living with the Weather." *Studies in Romanticism* 55, no. 3 (1996): 431–48.

————. *Romantic Ecology: Wordsworth and the Environmental Tradition*. London and New York: Routledge, 1991.

————. *The Song of the Earth*. London: Picador, 2000.

Bateson, Gregory. *Steps to an Ecology of Mind*. New York: Ballantine, 1972.

Baudrillard, Jean. *In the Shadow of Silent Majorities*. New York: Semiotext(e), 1983.

Bauer, Walter. *A Greek-English Lexicon of the New Testament and Other Early Christian Literature*. 2nd ed. Translated, revised, and augmented by William F. Arndt, F. Wilbur Gingrich, and Frederick W. Danker. Chicago: University of Chicago Press, 1979.

Baulch, David. "Repetition, Representation, and Revolution: Deleuze and Blake's *America*." In *Romanticism and the New Deleuze*, edited by Ron Broglio. Romantic Circles Praxis Series no. 20 (January 2008). www.rc.umd.edu/praxis/deleuze/index./html.

Bell, Jeffrey A. *Philosophy at the Edge of Chaos: Gilles Deleuze and the Philosophy of Difference*. Toronto: University of Toronto Press, 2006.

Bell, Michael. *D. H. Lawrence: Language and Being*. Cambridge: Cambridge University Press, 1991.

Benjamin, Walter. *Berlin Childhood around 1900*. Translated by Howard Eiland. Cambridge: Belknap Press of Harvard University Press, 2006.

————. *Charles Baudelaire: A Lyric Poet in the Era of High Capitalism*. Translated by Harry Zohn. London: New Left Books, 1969.

————. *Das Passagen-Werk (The Arcades Project)*. Translated and edited by Howard Eiland and Kevin McLaughlin. Cambridge: Belknap Press of Harvard University Press, 1999.

————. "On Some Motifs in Baudelaire." In *Illuminations: Essays and Reflections*, edited by Hannah Arendt, 155–200. New York: Schocken Books, 1968.

————. "Theses on the Philosophy of History." In *Illuminations: Essays and Reflections*, edited by Hannah Arendt, 252–64. New York: Schocken Books, 1968.

————. "Über Sprache überhaupt und die Sprache des Menschen" (On Language in

General and the Language of Man). In *Gesammelte Schriften*, vol. 2, pt. 1, edited by Rolf Tiedemann, 140–57. Frankfurt am Main: Suhrkamp, 1977.

———. "Unpacking My Library." In *Illuminations: Essays and Reflections*, edited by Hannah Arendt, 59–67. New York: Schocken Books, 1968.

Bennett, Michael. "Anti-Pastoralism, Frederick Douglass and the Nature of Slavery." In *Beyond Nature Writing: Expanding the Boundaries of Eco-Criticism*, edited by Karla Armbruster and Kathleen R. Wallace, 195–210. Charlottesville and London: University Press of Virginia, 2001.

Benthall, Jonathan, ed. *Ecology: The Shaping Enquiry*. London: Longman, 1972.

Bergthaller, Hannes. *Populäre Ökologie zu Literatur und Geschichte der modernen Umweltbewegung in den USA*. Frankfurt am Main: Peter Lang, 2007.

Berry, Wendell. "The Regional Motive." In *A Continuous Harmony: Essays Cultural and Agricultural*, 63–70. New York: Harcourt Brace Jovanovich, 1972.

———. *The Unsettling of America: Essays Cultural and Agricultural*. 1977. Rev. ed. San Francisco: Sierra Club Books, 2004.

Best, Steven, and Douglas Kellner. *The Postmodern Turn*. New York: Guilford Press, 1997.

"Bible Paper." *Encyclopaedia Britannica*. 2009. Encyclopaedia Britannica Online. www.britannica.com/EBchecked/topic/64466/Bible-paper.

Bindman, David, ed. *William Blake: The Complete Illuminated Books*. London: Thames and Hudson, 2000.

Black, Michael. *D. H. Lawrence. The Early Philosophical Work*. Cambridge: Cambridge University Press, 1992.

Blake, William. *The Complete Poetry and Prose of William Blake*. Edited by David V. Erdman. Garden City, N.Y.: Anchor Books/Doubleday, 1982.

Bleich, David. "The Materiality of Reading." *New Literary History* 37 (2006): 607–29.

Bloch, Ernst. *The Principle of Hope*. Translated by N. Plaice, S. Plaice, and P. Knight. Cambridge: Harvard University Press, 1995.

Bloom, Harold, and Lionel Trilling. *Romantic Poetry and Prose*. Oxford: Oxford University Press, 1973.

Boden, Margaret A. *The Creative Mind: Myths and Mechanisms*. London: Weidenfeld and Nicolson, 1990.

Bogue, Ronald. "The Minor." In *Gilles Deleuze: Key Concepts*, edited by Charles J. Stivale, 110–20. Montreal: McGill-Queen's University Press, 2005.

Bohm, David. *Causality and Chance in Modern Physics*. London: Routledge, 1957.

———. *Unfolding Meaning: A Weekend of Dialogue with David Bohm*. 1985. New York: Ark Paperbacks, 1987.

———. *Wholeness and the Implicate Order*. 1980. New York: Routledge, 1995.

Bohm, David, and B. J. Hiley. *The Undivided Universe: An Ontological Interpretation of Quantum Theory*. London: Routledge, 1993.

Bohm, David, and F. David Peat. *Science, Order and Creativity.* London: Routledge, 1989.

Böhme, Gernot. "An Aesthetic Theory of Nature: An Interim Report." *Thesis Eleven* 32 (1992): 90–102.

———. *Aisthetik: Vorlesungen über Ästhetik als allgemeine Warhnehmungslehre.* Munich: Fink, 2001.

———. *Anmutungen: Über das Atmosphärische* (Impressions: On the Atmospheric). Ostfildern: Edition Tertium, 1998.

———. *Atmosphäre: Essays zur neuen Ästhetik* (Atmosphere: Essays on the New Aesthetics). Frankfurt am Main: Suhrkamp, 1995.

———. "Atmosphere as the Fundamental Concept of a New Aesthetics." *Thesis Eleven* 36 (1993): 113–26.

———. "Contribution to the Critique of the Aesthetic Economy." *Thesis Eleven* 73 (May 2003): 71–82.

———. "Der Raum des Gedichts" (The Space of the Poem). In *Raum für Sprache—Raum für Literatur* (Space for Language—Space for Literature), edited by Brigitte Labs-Ehlert, 94–111. Detmold: Literaturbüro Ostwestfalen-Lippe, 2001.

———. *Die Natur vor uns: Naturphilosophie in pragmatischer Hinsicht* (Nature before Us: Philosophy of Nature from a Pragmatic Perspective). Kusterdingen: Die Graue Edition, 2002.

———. "Driven by the Interest in Reasonable Conditions." *Thesis Eleven* 81 (May 2005): 80–90.

———. *Ethics in Context: The Art of Dealing with Serious Questions.* 1997 (German original). Translated by E. Jephcott. Cambridge: Polity, 2001.

———. *Für eine ökologische Naturästhetik* (Toward an Ecological Aesthetics of Nature). Frankfurt am Main: Suhrkamp, 1989.

———. *Leibsein als Aufgabe: Leibphilosophie in pragmatischer Hinsicht* (The Task of Bodily Existence: Philosophy of the Body from a Pragmatic Perspective). Kusterdingen: Die Graue Edition, 2003.

———. "Mir läuft ein Schauer übern ganzen Leib"—das Wetter, die Witterungslehre und die Sprache der Gefühle" (A Shiver Is Passing over My Whole Body—The Weather, Meteorology and the Language of Feeling). *Goethe-Jahrbuch* 124 (2007): 133–41.

———. *Natürlich Natur: Natur im Zeitalter ihrer technischen Reproduzierbarkeit* (Naturally Nature: Nature in the Age of Its Technical Reproducibility). Frankfurt am Main: Suhrkamp, 1992.

———. "The Space of Bodily Presence and Space as a Medium of Representation." In *Transforming Spaces. The Topological Turn in Technology Studies,* edited by Mikael Hård, Andreas Lösch, and Dirk Verdicchio (2003). www.ifs.tu-darmstadt.de/gradkoll/Publikationen/transformingspaces.html.

Böhme, Gernot, and Hartmut Böhme. *Feuer, Wasser, Erde, Luft: Eine Kulturge-schichte der Elemente* (Fire, Water, Earth, Air: A Cultural History of the Elements). Munich: Beck, 1996.

Böhme, Gernot, and E. Schramm, eds. *Soziale Naturwissenschaft: Wege zu einer Erweiterung der Ökologie* (Social Natural Science: Paths toward an Expansion of Ecology). Frankfurt am Main: Fischer 1985.

Böhme, Hartmut. "Aussichten einer ästhetischen Theorie der Natur" (Prospects for an Aesthetic Theory of Nature). In *Wahrnehmung von Gegenwart*, edited by Jörg Huber, 31–55. Basel: Stroemfeld, 1992.

——. "Germanistik in der Herausforderung durch den technischen und ökolo-gischen Wandel" (German Literary Studies and the Challenge of Technical and Ecological Change). In *Germanistik in der Mediengesellschaft*, edited by Ludwig Jäger and Bernd Switalla, 63–77. Munich: Fink, 1994.

——. *Natur und Subjekt* (Nature and Subject). Frankfurt am Main: Suhrkamp, 1988.

Bohnenkamp, Dennis. "Post-Einsteinian Physics and Literature: Toward a New Poetics." *Mosaic* 22 (1989): 19–30.

Bohr, Niels. *Essays 1958–1962 on Atomic Physics and Human Knowledge.* London: Wiley, 1963.

Boulding, Kenneth E. *Evolutionary Economics.* Beverly Hills, Calif.: Sage, 1981.

Boyarin, Daniel. "A Question of Theory or Experimentality?" *Semeia* 86 (1999): 223–25.

Braudel, Fernand. *The Structures of Everyday Life: The Limits of the Possible.* London: Collins, 1981.

Braun, Volker. *Bodenloser Satz* (Groundless Sentence). Frankfurt am Main: Suhr-kamp, 1990. (First published in *Sinn und Form* 41, no. 6 [1989]: 1235–46.)

Brawley, Robert L. *Text to Text Pours Forth Speech: Voices of Scripture in Luke-Acts.* Bloomington: Indiana University Press, 1995.

Broglio, Ron, ed. *Romanticism and the New Deleuze.* Romantic Circles Praxis Series (January 2008). www.rc.umd.edu/praxis/deleuze/index./html.

——. *Technologies of the Picturesque: British Art, Poetry, and Instruments, 1750–1830.* Lewisburg: Bucknell University Press, 2008.

Brown, Jane K. *Faust: Theater of the World.* New York: Twayne, 1992.

Brunner, John. *The Sheep Look Up.* 1972. Dallas: Benbella Books, 2003.

Buck-Morss, Susan. *The Dialectics of Seeing: Walter Benjamin and the Arcades Proj-ect.* Cambridge: MIT Press, 1989.

——. "The Flâneur, the Sandwichman and the Whore: The Politics of Loitering." In *Walter Benjamin and the Arcades Project*, edited by Beatrice Hanssen, 33–65. London: Continuum, 2006.

Buell, Lawrence. "The Ecocritical Insurgency." In "Ecocriticism," special issue, *New Literary History* 30, no. 3 (1999): 699–712.

Burke, Karen. "Masculine and Feminine Approaches to Nature." In *Luce Irigaray: Teaching*, edited by Luce Irigaray and Mary Green, 189–200. London: Continuum, 2008.

Burroughs, John. *Birch Browsings: A John Burroughs Reader*. Edited by Bill McKibben. New York: Penguin, 1992.

Butler, Judith. *Antigone's Claim*. New York: Columbia University Press, 2002.

———. *Bodies That Matter*. New York: Routledge, 1993.

———. *Gender Trouble*. New York: Routledge, 1990.

Byatt, A. S. *Angels and Insects*. London: Vintage, 1995.

Callicott, J. Baird. *Earth's Insights: A Multicultural Survey of Ecological Ethics from the Mediterranean Basin to the Australian Outback*. Berkeley and Los Angeles: University of California Press, 1994.

Campbell, Colin. *The Romantic Ethic and the Spirit of Modern Capitalism*. Oxford: Blackwell, 1987.

———. "Understanding Traditional and Modern Patterns of Consumption in Eighteenth-Century England: A Character-Action Approach." In *Consumption and the World of Goods*, edited by John Brewer and Roy Porter, 40–57. London: Routledge, 1993,

Campbell, SueEllen. "The Land and Language of Desire: Where Deep Ecology and Post-structuralism Meet." In *Ecocriticism Reader*, edited by Cheryll Glotfelty and Harold Fromm, 124–36.

Capra, Fritjof, and Charlene Spretnak. *Green Politics*. London: Hutchinson, 1984.

Carson, Rachel. *Silent Spring*. 1962. New York: Mariner, 2002.

Castellina, Luciana. "Why Red Must Be Green Too." In *Socialism on the Eve of the Twenty-First Century*, edited by Miloš Nicolić, 43–57. London: Verso, 1985.

Cataldi, Suzanne L., and William S. Hamrick, eds. *Merleau-Ponty and Environmental Philosophy: Dwelling on the Landscapes of Thought*. Albany: State University of New York Press, 2007.

Chanter, Tina. *The Ethics of Eros*. New York: Routledge, 1995.

Cheney, Jim. "Postmodern Environmental Ethics: Ethics as Bioregional Narrative." In *Environmental Ethics: Divergence and Convergence*, edited by Susan J. Armstrong and Richard G. Butler, 86–95. New York: McGraw Hill, 1993.

Chisholm, Dianne. *Queer Constellations: Subcultural Space in the Wake of the City*. Minneapolis: University of Minnesota Press, 2005.

Clarke, Bruce. "The Flow of Energy through a System": Getting Started with Systems in the Whole Earth Catalog." In *The Whole Earth, Parts Thereof*. UC Davis, 8 May 2006. www.faculty.english.ttu.edu/clarke/essays/systemswec.htm.

———. *Posthuman Metamorphosis: Narrative and Systems*. New York: Fordham University Press, 2008.

Clemens, Justin. *The Romanticism of Contemporary Theory: Institutions, Aesthetics, Nihilism*. Aldershot: Ashgate, 2003.

Coleridge, Samuel Taylor. *Coleridge's Poetry and Prose*. Edited by Nicholas Halmi, Paul Magnuson, and Raimona Modiano. New York: Norton, 2004.

Commoner, Barry. *The Closing Circle: Nature, Man, and Technology*. New York: Knopf, 1972.

Coupe, Laurence, ed. *The Green Studies Reader: From Romanticism to Ecocriticism*. London and New York: Routledge, 2000.

Crichton, Michael. *State of Fear*. New York: HarperCollins, 2004.

Culler, Jonathan. *Literary Theory: A Very Short Introduction*. Oxford: Oxford University Press, 1997.

Curkpatrick, Stephen. "Parable Metonymy and Luke's Kerygmatic Framing." *Journal for the Study of the New Testament* 25, no. 3 (2003): 289–307.

Cushing, James T. *Quantum Mechanics: Historical Contingency and the Copenhagen Hegemony*. Chicago: University of Chicago Press, 1994.

Daly, Mary. *Gyn/Ecology*. Boston: Beacon Press, 1978.

Dawkins, Richard. *The Ancestor's Tale: A Pilgrimage to the Dawn of Life*. London: Phoenix, 2005.

———. *The Selfish Gene*. Oxford: Oxford University Press, 1976.

de Beauvoir, Simone. *The Second Sex*. Edited and translated by H. M. Parshley. New York: Vintage, 1952.

Deleuze, Gilles. *Desert Islands and Other Texts, 1953–74*. Translated by Michael Taomina. Edited by David Lapoujade. Paris: Semiotext(e), 2004.

———. *Pure Immanence: Essays on a Life*. Translated by Anne Boyman. New York: Zone Books, 2005.

Deleuze, Gilles, and Félix Guattari. *Anti-Oedipus: Capitalism and Schizophrenia*. Translated by Robert Hurley, Mark Seem, and Helen R. Lane. Minneapolis: University of Minnesota Press, 1983.

———. *A Thousand Plateaus: Capitalism and Schizophrenia*. Translated by Brian Massumi. Minneapolis: University of Minnesota Press, 1987.

Derrida, Jacques. "The Animal That Therefore I Am (More to Follow)." Translated by David Wills. *Critical Inquiry* 28 (2002): 369–418.

———. *The Animal That Therefore I Am*. Edited by Marie-Louise Mallet. Translated by David Wills. New York: Fordham University Press, 2008.

———. "*Geschlecht II:* Heidegger's Hand." Translated by John P. Leavey Jr. In *Deconstruction and Philosophy: The Texts of Jacques Derrida*, edited by John Sallis, 161–96. Chicago: University of Chicago Press, 1987.

———. "Hostipitality." In *Acts of Religion*, edited, translated, and introduced by Gil Anidjar, 356–420. London and New York: Routledge, 2002.

Descartes, René. "Discourse on the Method of Rightly Conducting Reason and Seeking the Truth in the Sciences" (1637). In *Descartes—Key Philosophical*

Writings, translated by E. S. Haldane and G. R. T. Ross, 71–122. Hertfordshire: Wordsworth Editions, 1997.

———. *The Philosophical Works of Descartes.* Vol. 1. Translated by Elizabeth S. Haldane and G. R. T. Ross. Cambridge: Cambridge University Press, 1911.

d'Espagnant, Bernard. *Conceptual Foundations of Quantum Mechanics.* 1971. New York: Addison-Wesley Press, 1976.

Dickens, Peter. *Reconstructing Nature: Alienation, Emancipation and the Division of Labour.* New York: Routledge, 1996.

Diringer, David. *The Book before Printing: Ancient, Medieval and Oriental.* New York: Dover, 1982.

Dodd, C. H. *The Parables of the Kingdom.* New York: Scribners, 1961.

Dorrian, Mark. "The Way the World Sees London: Thoughts on a Millennial Urban Spectacle." In *Architecture between Spectacle and Use,* edited by Anthony Vidler, 41–57. Williamstown: Sterling and Francine Clark Art Institute; New Haven: Yale University Press, 2008.

Duffy, Simon. "The Difference between Science and Philosophy: The Spinoza-Boyle Controversy Revisited." In "Deleuze and Science," edited by John Marks, 115–38, special issue, *Paragraph: A Journal of Modern Critical Theory.* Eastbourne: Edinburgh University Press, 2006.

Eagleton, Terry. *After Theory.* London: Penguin, 2004.

———. *The Ideology of the Aesthetic.* Oxford: Blackwell, 1990.

———. "The Marxist Rabbi." In *The Ideology of the Aesthetic,* 316–40. Oxford: Blackwell, 1990.

———, ed. *Raymond Williams: Critical Perspectives.* Cambridge, U.K.: Polity Press, 1989.

Eiland, Howard. "Translator's Foreword." In Walter Benjamin, *Berlin Childhood around 1900,* translated by Eiland, vii–xvi. Cambridge: Belknap Press of Harvard University Press, 2006.

Eldridge, John, and Lizzie Eldridge. *Raymond Williams: Making Connections.* London and New York: Routledge, 1994.

Elias, Norbert. *The Civilising Process: Sociogenetic and Psychogenetic Investigations.* 1939. Oxford: Blackwell, 2000.

———. *The Court Society.* New York: Pantheon, 1983.

———. *Involvement and Detachment.* Oxford: Blackwell, 1987.

———. *The Society of Individuals.* New York: Continuum, 2001.

———. *The Symbol Theory.* Edited and transcription by Richard Kilminster. London: Sage, 1991.

———. *Time: An Essay.* Oxford: Blackwell, 1994.

Ellis, David, ed. *D. H. Lawrence's Women in Love: A Casebook.* Oxford: Oxford University Press, 2006.

Elvey, Anne. *An Ecological Feminist Reading of the Gospel of Luke: A Gestational Paradigm.* Lewiston: Edwin Mellen Press, 2005.

Emerson, Ralph Waldo. "Civilization" (1870). In *The Works of Ralph Waldo Emerson*, vol. 3, *Society and Solitude: Letters and Social Aims Addresses*, edited by George Sampson, 11–19. London: Bell and Sons, 1906.

——. *The Early Lectures of Ralph Waldo Emerson, 1833–1842*. 3 vols. Cambridge: Harvard University Press, 1959–72.

——. *Essays and Lectures*. Edited by Joel Porte. New York: Library of America, 1983.

Emmeche, Claus. Paper presented at "Nature Matters" conference, Toronto, 25–28 October 2007.

Erll, Astrid. *Kollektives Gedächtnis und Erinnerungskulturen: Eine Einführung* (Collective Memory and Memory Cultures: An Introduction). Stuttgart and Weimar: Metzler, 2005.

Erll, Astrid, and Ansgar Nünning, eds. *Cultural Memory Studies: An International and Interdisciplinary Handbook*. Berlin and New York: de Gruyter, 2008.

——. "Where Literature and Memory Meet: Towards a Systematic Approach to the Concepts of Memory Used in Literary Studies." In *Literature, Literary History, and Cultural Memory* (REAL: Yearbook of Research in English and American Literature 21), edited by Herbert Grabes, 262–94. Tübingen: Gunter Narr, 2005.

Favareau, Donald. "The Evolutionary History of Biosemiotics." In *Introduction to Biosemiotics: The New Biological Synthesis*, edited by Marcello Barbieri, 1–67. Dordrecht: Springer, 2008.

Fernández-Armesto, Felipe. *So You Think You're Human?: A Brief History of Humankind*. Oxford and New York: Oxford University Press, 2004.

Fetterley, Judith. *The Resisting Reader: A Feminist Approach to American Fiction*. Bloomington: Indiana University Press, 1978.

Fielding, Helen. "Questioning Nature: Irigaray, Heidegger, and the Potentiality of Matter." *Continental Philosophy Review* 36, no. 1 (2003): 1–26.

Finke, Peter. "Die Evolutionäre Kulturökologie: Hintergründe, Prinzipien und Perspektiven einer neuen Theorie der Kultur" (Evolutionary Cultural Ecology: Background, Principles, and Perspectives for a New Theory of Culture). *Anglia* 124, no. 1 (2006): 175–217.

Forsyth, Tim. *Critical Political Ecology: The Politics of Environmental Science*. London: Routledge, 2003.

Fox, Warwick. "Deep Ecology: A New Philosophy of Our Time." In *Philosophical Dialogues: Arne Naess and the Progress of Ecophilosophy*, edited by Nina Witoszek and Andrew Brennan, 153–65. New York: Rowman and Littlefield, 1999.

Friends of the Earth briefing sheet. "The Environmental Consequences of Pulp and Paper Manufacture." www.foe.co.uk/pubsinfo/briefings/html/19971215 150024.html.

Fritzell, Peter. "The Conflicts of Ecological Conscience." In *Companion to "A Sand County Almanac": Interpretive and Critical Essays,* edited by J. Baird Callicott, 128–56. Madison: University of Wisconsin Press, 1987.

Gamble, Harry Y. "Bible and Book." In *In the Beginning: Bibles before the Year 1000,* edited by Michelle Brown, 15–35. Washington, D.C.: Freer Gallery of Art and Arthur M. Sackler Gallery, Smithsonian Institution, 2006.

Garrard, Greg. *Ecocriticism.* London and New York: Routledge, 2004.

Gebhard, Gunther, Oliver Geisler, and Steffen Schröter, eds. *Heimat: Konturen und Konjunkturen eines umstrittenen Konzepts* (Heimat: Dimensions and Fortunes of a Controversial Concept). Bielefeld: transcript, 2007.

Gersdorf, Catrin, and Sylvia Mayer, eds. *Nature in Literary and Cultural Studies: Transatlantic Conversations on Ecocriticism.* Amsterdam and New York: Rodopi, 2006.

Gifford, Terry. *Pastoral.* London: Routledge, 1999.

Gillan, Garth. "In the Folds of the Flesh." In *The Horizons of the Flesh: Critical Perspectives on the Thought of Merleau-Ponty,* edited by Gillan, 1–77. Carbondale: Southern Illinois University Press, 1973.

Gilroy, Paul. "Melancholia or Conviviality: The Politics of Belonging in Britain." *Soundings* 29 (2004): 35–46.

Glasersfeld, Ernst. "Declaration of the American Society for Cybernetics." *American Society for Cybernetics Newsletter.* 1981. www.univie.ac.at/constructivism/ EvG/papers/065.pdf.

Glotfelty, Cheryll. "Introduction: Literary Studies in an Age of Environmental Crisis." In *The Ecocriticism Reader: Landmarks in Literary Ecology,* edited by Glotfelty and Harold Fromm, xv–xxxvii. Athens: University of Georgia Press, 1996.

Glotfelty, Cheryll, and Harold Fromm, eds. *The Ecocriticism Peader: Landmarks in Literary Ecology.* Athens: University of Georgia Press, 1996.

Goethe, Johann Wolfgang. *Faust: A Tragedy.* Translated by Walter Arndt. New York: Norton, 2001.

———. *Faust. Texte.* In *Johann Wolfgang Goethe: Sämtliche Werke,* vol. 7, pt. 1. Frankfurt am Main: Klassiker, 1994.

———. *Sprüche in Prosa.* In *Johann Wolfgang Goethe. Sämtliche Werke,* vol. 13. Frankfurt am Main: Klassiker, 1993.

Goodbody, Axel. *Nature, Technology and Cultural Change in Twentieth-Century German Literature: The Challenge of Ecocriticism.* Basingstoke: Palgrave Macmillan, 2007.

Goudsblom, Johan, and Stephen Mennell, eds. *Norbert Elias on Civilization, Power, and Knowledge: Selected Writings.* Chicago: University of Chicago Press, 1998.

Graham, William A. *Beyond the Written Word: Oral Aspects of Scripture in the History of Religion.* Cambridge: Cambridge University Press, 1987.

Grass, Günter. *The Rat (Die Rättin)*. Translated by Ralph Manheim. San Diego: Harvest Books, 1989.

Griffin, Susan. *Woman and Nature*. New York: Harper and Row, 1978.

Grosz, Elizabeth. *Jacques Lacan: A Feminist Introduction*. St. Leonards, New South Wales: Allen and Unwin, 1990.

———. *Sexual Subversion: Three French Feminists*. St. Leonards, New South Wales: Allen and Unwin, 1989.

———. *Space, Time and Perversion*. New York: Routledge, 1995.

———. *Volatile Bodies: Toward a Corporeal Feminism*. St. Leonards, New South Wales: Allen and Unwin, 1994.

Gunster, Shane. " 'You Belong Outside': Advertising, Nature and the SUV." *Ethics and the Environment* 9, no. 2 (2004): 4–32.

Habel, Norman C. "Introducing the Earth Bible." In *Readings from the Perspective of Earth*, edited by Habel, 25–37. The Earth Bible 1. Sheffield: Sheffield Academic Press, 2000.

———. Review of *An Ecological Feminist Reading of the Gospel of Luke: A Gestational Paradigm*, by Anne Elvey. *Australian Religion Studies Review* 21, no. 1 (2008): 116–17.

Halbwachs, Maurice. *On Collective Memory*. Edited and translated by Lewis A. Coser. Chicago: Chicago University Press, 1992.

Halsey, Mark. "Environmental Visions: Deleuze and the Modalities of Nature." *Ethics and the Environment* 9, no. 2 (Fall/Winter 2004): 33–64.

Handke, Peter. *Repetition*. Translated by Ralph Manheim. New York: Farrar, Straus and Giroux, 1988; Frankfurt am Main: Suhrkamp, 1986. (German original *Die Wiederholung*.)

Hanssen, Beatrice, ed. *Walter Benjamin and the Arcades Project*. London: Continuum, 2006.

Haraway, Donna. *Modest Witness@second Millennium.FemaleMan© Meets Onco Mouse™: Feminism and Technoscience*. New York and London: Routledge, 1997.

———. "Situated Knowledges: The Science Question in Feminism and the Privilege of Partial Perspective." In *Simians, Cyborgs, and Women: The Reinvention of Nature*, 183–201. New York: Routledge, 1991.

Harries-Jones, Peter. "Introducing Biosemiotics." Unpublished conference paper.

Hartman, Geoffrey. *The Fate of Reading*. Chicago: Chicago University Press, 1975.

Hassan, Ihab. "Making Sense: The Trials of Postmodern Discourse." *New Literary History: A Journal of Theory and Interpretation* 18, no. 2 (1987): 437–59.

———. *The Postmodern Turn: Essays in Postmodern Theory and Culture*. Columbus: Ohio State University Press, 1987.

Healey, Richard. *The Philosophy of Quantum Mechanics: An Interactive Interpretation*. 1989. Cambridge: Cambridge University Press, 1991.

Heidegger, Martin. *Basic Writings.* Translated and edited by David Farrell Krell. New York: HarperCollins, 1993.

———. *Being and Time.* Translated by John Macquarrie and Edward Robinson. Oxford: Basil Blackwell, 1990.

———. "Conversation on a Country Path about Thinking." In *Discourse on Thinking,* translated by John M. Anderson and E. Hans Freund. New York: Harper and Row, 1966.

———. *Introduction to Metaphysics.* Translated by Gregory Fried and Richard Polt. London: Yale University Press, 2000.

———. "Language." In *Poetry, Language, Thought,* translated by Albert Hofstadter, 187–210. New York: Harper and Row, 1971.

———. "The Origin of the Work of Art." In *Poetry, Language, Thought,* translated by Albert Hofstadter, 15–87. New York: Harper and Row, 1971.

———. *Pathmarks.* Translated and edited by William McNeill. Cambridge: Cambridge University Press, 1998.

———. "Supplement." In *Metaphysical Foundations of Logic,* translated by M. Heim, 221. Bloomington: Indiana University Press, 1984.

———. *What Is Called Thinking?* Translated by J. Glenn Gray and Fred Wieck and with introduction by J. Glenn Gray. New York: Harper and Row, 1968. (Originally *Was Heisst Denken?* in 1954.)

Heise, Ursula K. *Sense of Place and Sense of Planet: The Environmental Imagination of the Global.* Oxford: Oxford University Press, 2008.

Heisenberg, Werner. *Physics and Philosophy: The Revolution in Modern Science.* New York: Harper Torchbooks, 1958.

Heraclitus. "On the Universe." In *Hippocrates,* vol. 4, Loeb Classical Library 150, translated by W. H. S. Jones. Cambridge: Harvard University Press, 2005.

Hermand, Jost. *Im Wettlauf mit der Zeit: Anstöße zu einer ökologiebewußten Ästhetik* (Racing with Time: Impulses for an Ecologically Conscious Aesthetics). Berlin: Sigma Bohn, 1991.

Hesse, Mary. *Revolutions and Reconstructions in the Philosophy of Science.* Bloomington: Indiana University Press, 1980.

Hinchliffe, Steve. *Geographies of Nature: Societies, Environments, Ecologies.* Los Angeles: Sage, 2007.

Hoffman, Michael. "The House of Usher and Negative Romanticism." *Studies in Romanticism* 4 (1965): 158–68.

Hoffmeyer, Jesper. *Biosemiotics: An Examination into the Signs of Life and the Life of Signs.* Scranton and London: University of Scranton Press, 2008.

———. *Signs of Meaning in the Universe.* Bloomington: Indiana University Press, 1996.

Hofstadter, Douglas. *Gödel, Escher, Bach.* New York: Basic Books, 1979.

Holland, Norman N. "The Power(?) of Literature: A Neuropsychological View." *New Literary History* 35, no. 3 (Summer 2004): 395–410.

Holland, Peter. *The Quantum Theory of Motion: An Account of the de Broglie-Bohm Causal Interpretation of Quantum Mechanics*. Cambridge: Cambridge University Press, 1993.

Hopkins, Gerard Manley. "God's Grandeur." In *Poems of Gerard Manley Hopkins*, edited by W. H. Gardner and N. H. MacKenzie. London, Oxford, and New York: Routledge, 1970.

Hurtado, Larry W. *The Earliest Christian Artifacts: Manuscripts and Christian Origins*. Grand Rapids: Eerdmans, 2006.

Hutcheon, Linda. *A Poetics of Postmodernism: History, Theory, Fiction*. 1988. London: Routledge, 1990.

——. *The Politics of Postmodernism*. 1989. New York: Routledge, 1991.

Hutchings, Kevin. *Imagining Nature: Blake's Environmental Poetics*. Montreal and Ithaca: McGill-Queen's University Press, 2002.

Inglis, Fred. *Raymond Williams*. London and New York: Routledge, 1995.

Irigaray, Luce. "A Chance to Live." In *Thinking the Difference: For a Peaceful Revolution*, translated by Karin Montin, 3–35. New York: Routledge, 1994.

——. *An Ethics of Sexual Difference*. Translated by Carolyn Burke and Gillian C. Gill. Ithaca: Cornell University Press, 1993.

——. *I Love to You*. Translated by Alison Martin. New York: Routledge, 1996.

——. *Key Writings*. New York: Continuum, 2004.

——. *Sexes and Genealogies*. Translated by Gillian C. Gill. New York: Columbia University Press, 1993.

——. *Thinking the Difference*. Translated by Karin Montin. New York: Routledge, 1994.

——. *This Sex Which Is Not One*. Translated by Catherine Porter. Ithaca: Cornell University Press, 1985.

——. *Why Different? A Culture of Two Subjects*. Translated by Camille Collins and Sylvere Lotringer. New York: Semiotext(e), 1999.

Iser, Wolfgang. *The Fictive and the Imaginary: Charting Literary Anthropology*. Baltimore: Johns Hopkins University Press, 1993.

——. "Towards a Literary Anthropology." In *The Future of Literary Theory*, edited by Ralph Cohen. 208–28. New York: Routledge, 1989.

Jablonka, Eva, and Marion J. Lamb. *Evolution in Four Dimensions: Genetic, Epigenetic, Behavioural and Symbolic Variation in the History of Life*. Cambridge: MIT Press, 2005.

Jung, Carl Gustav. *Synchronicity: An Acausal Connecting Principle*. Translated by R. F. C. Hull. London: Routledge and Kegan Paul, 1972.

Kane, Paul. "Woful Shepherds: Anti-Pastoral in Australian Poetry." In *Imagining Australia: Literature and Culture in the New World*, edited by Judith Ryan and Chris Wallace-Crabbe, 269–84. Cambridge: Harvard University Press, 2004.

Kane, Sean. *The Wisdom of the Mythtellers.* Peterborough, Ontario: Broadview, 1994.

Kauffman, Stuart. *Investigations.* Oxford: Oxford University Press, 2000.

Kearns, Matthew. "Chaos and Control: Nanotechnology and the Politics of Emergence." In "Deleuze and Science," edited by John Marks, 57–80, special issue, *Paragraph: A Journal of Modern Critical Theory.* Eastbourne: Edinburgh University Press, 2006.

Keats, John. *Complete Poems and Selected Letters of John Keats.* Edited by Edward Hirsch. New York: Modern Library, 2001.

Kelber, Werner H. "Oral Tradition in Bible and New Testament Studies." *Oral Tradition* 18, no. 1 (2003): 40–42.

Keller, Catherine. *Face of the Deep: A Theology of Becoming.* London: Routledge, 2003.

Kilminster, Richard. "From Distance to Detachment: Knowledge and Self-Knowledge in Elias' Theory of Involvement and Detachment." In *The Sociology of Norbert Elias,* edited by S. Quilley and S. Loyal, 25–41. Cambridge: Cambridge University Press, 2004.

Kort, Wesley A. *"Take Read": Scripture, Textuality, and Cultural Practice.* University Park: Pennsylvania State University Press, 1996.

Kristeva, Julia. "From One Identity to an Other." In *The Portable Kristeva,* updated ed., edited by Kelly Oliver, 93–115. New York: Columbia University Press, 2002.

———. "Reading the Bible." In *New Maladies of the Soul,* 115–26. New York: Columbia University Press, 1995.

———. *Revolution in Poetic Language.* Translated by Margaret Waller. New York: Columbia University Press, 1984.

———. "The System and the Speaking Subject." In *The Kristeva Reader,* edited by Toril Moi, 24–33. Oxford: Blackwell, 1986.

———. "Word, Dialogue and Novel." In *The Kristeva Reader,* edited by Toril Moi, 34–61. Oxford: Blackwell, 1986.

Kroker, A. "Baudrillard's Marx." *Theory, Culture and Society* 2, no. 3 (1985): 69–84.

Kull, Kalevi. "Jacob von Uexküll: An Introduction." *Semiotica* 134, no. 1 (2001): 1–59.

———. "On Semiosis, Umwelt, and Semiosphere." *Semiotica* 120, no. 3 (1998): 299–310. www.zbi.ee/~kalevi/jesphohp.htm.

Kull, Kalevi, Claus Emmeche, and Donald Favareau. "Biosemiotic Questions." *Biosemiotics* 1, no. 1 (March 2008): 41–55. *www.zbi.ee/~kalevi/KullEmmeche Favareau08.pdf.*

Lakoff, George, and Mark Johnson. *Philosophy in the Flesh.* New York: Basic Books, 1999.

Langer, Monika. "Nietzsche, Heidegger, and Merleau-Ponty: Some of Their Con-
    tributions and Limitations for "Environmentalism." In *Ecophenomenology:
    Back to the Earth Itself,* edited by Charles S. Brown and Ted Toadvine, 103–20.
    Albany: State University of New York Press.
Latour, Bruno. *Aramis or the Love of Technology.* Translated by Catherine Porter.
    Cambridge: Harvard University Press, 1996.
———. *Pandora's Hope: Essays on the Reality of Science Studies.* Cambridge: Harvard
    University Press, 1999.
———. *The Pasteurization of France.* Translated by Alan Sheridan and John Law.
    Cambridge: Harvard University Press, 1988.
———. *The Politics of Nature: How to Bring the Sciences into Democracy.* Translated by
    Catherine Porter. Cambridge: Harvard University Press, 2004.
———. *Reassembling the Social: An Introduction to Actor-Network Theory.* Oxford:
    Oxford University Press, 2007.
———. *Science in Action: How to Follow Scientists and Engineers through Society.*
    Cambridge: Harvard University Press, 1987.
———. *War of the Worlds: What about Peace?* Translated by Charlotte Bigg. Chicago:
    Prickly Paradigm Press, 2002.
———. *We Have Never Been Modern.* Translated by Catherine Porter. Cambridge:
    Harvard University Press, 1993.
———. "Why Has Critique Run out of Steam?: From Matters of Fact to Matters of
    Concern." *Critical Inquiry* 30, no. 2 (Winter 2004).
Latour, Bruno, and Steve Woolgar. *Laboratory Life: The Construction of Scientific
    Facts.* Princeton: Princeton University Press, 1979.
Lawrence, D. H. *The Cambridge Edition of the Works of D. H. Lawrence: Introductions
    and Reviews.* Edited by N. H. Reeve and John Worthen. Cambridge: Cam-
    bridge University Press, 2005.
———. "The Novel and the Feelings." In *Study of Thomas Hardy and Other Essays.* In
    Cambridge Edition of the Works of D. H. Lawrence, edited by B. Steele. Cam-
    bridge: Cambridge University Press, 1985.
———. *The Rainbow.* Ware: Wordsworth Editions, 2001.
———. *The Selected Letters of D.H. Lawrence.* Edited by James T. Boulton. Cam-
    bridge: Cambridge University Press, 1996.
———. *Women in Love.* London: Penguin, 1995.
Le Guin, Ursula K. *Buffalo Gals and Other Animal Presences.* New York: Penguin,
    1987.
Leakey, Richard. *The Sixth Extinction: Biodiversity and Its Survival.* London: Weiden-
    feld and Nicolson, 1996.
Lee, Debbie. "Yellow Fever and the Slave Trade: Coleridge's 'The Rime of the
    Ancient Mariner.'" *ELH* 65, no. 3 (1998): 675–700.

Leopold, Aldo. *A Sand County Almanac.* 1949. New York: Ballantine, 1966.

Letwin, Oliver. "Conducting Politics as if Beauty Matters." Speech to the Centre for Social Justice, 6 June 2005.

Levinas, Emmanuel. *Existence and Existents.* Translated by Alphonso Lingis. Pittsburgh: Duquesne University Press, 2003.

———. *Otherwise Than Being: Or Beyond Essence.* Translated by Alphonso Lingis. Pittsburgh: Duquesne University Press, 1998.

———. *Totality and Infinity: An Essay on Exteriority.* Translated by Alphonso Lingis. Pittsburgh: Duquesne University Press, 1969.

Lewontin, Richard. "Gene, Organism and Environment." In *Cycles of Contingency: Developmental Systems and Evolution,* edited by Susan Oyama, Paul E. Griffiths, and Russell D. Gray, 59–66. Cambridge: MIT Press, 2001.

———. *The Triple Helix: Gene, Organism, and Environment.* Cambridge: Harvard University Press, 2000.

Lingis, Alphonso. "Animal Body, Inhuman Face." In *Zoontologies: The Question of the Animal,* edited by Cary Wolfe, 165–82. Minneapolis: University of Minnesota Press, 2003.

Livingston, Ira. *Between Science and Literature: An Introduction to Autopoetics.* Urbana: University of Illinois Press, 2006.

Lovelock, James. *Gaia.* London: Oxford University Press, 1979.

———. *The Revenge of Gaia: Earth's Climate Crisis and the Fate of Humanity.* New York: Basic Books, 2007.

Luhmann, Niklas. *Ecological Communication.* 1986. Translated by John Bednarz Jr. Chicago: University of Chicago Press, 1989.

———. *Einführung in die Systemtheorie* (Introduction to Systems Theory). Edited by Dirk Baecker. Heidelberg: Carl Auer, 2004.

Lussier, Mark. "Blake's Deep Ecology." *Studies in Romanticism* 35, no. 3 (1996): 393–408.

———. "Blake's Vortex: The Quantum Tunnel in Blake's *Milton.*" *Nineteenth-Century Contexts* 18 (1994): 263–91.

———. "Inner Revolution/Self-Annihilation: Blake's *Milton,* Buddhism, and Ecocriticism." *Literature and Religion* 40, no. 1 (Spring 2008): 39–57.

Lyotard, Jean-François. *The Differend: Phases in Dispute.* Minneapolis: University of Minnesota Press, 1988.

Maran, Timo. "Where Do Your Borders Lie?: Reflections on the Semiotic Ethics of Nature." In *Nature in Literary and Cultural Studies: Transatlantic Conversations on Ecocriticism,* edited by Catrin Gersdorf and Sylvia Mayer, 455–76. Amsterdam: Rodopi, 2006.

Margulis, Lynn. *Symbiosis in Cell Evolution.* San Francisco: Freeman, 1979.

———. *Symbiotic Planet: A New View of Evolution.* New York: Basic Books, 1998.

Margulis, Lynn, and Dorion Sagan. *Microcosmos*. New York: Simon and Schuster, 1986.

Marks, John, ed. "Deleuze and Science." Special issue, *Paragraph: A Journal of Modern Critical Theory*. Eastbourne: Edinburgh University Press, 2006.

——. Introduction to "Deleuze and Science," edited by John Marks, 1–18. Special issue, *Paragraph: A Journal of Modern Critical Theory*. Eastbourne: Edinburgh University Press, 2006.

Marshall, Alan. *Order from Chaos and the Economy-Ecology Analogy*. Edited by Arno Bammé, Günter Getzinger, and Bernhard Wieser. Yearbook 2001 of the Institute for Advanced Studies on Science, Technology and Society. Munich: Profil, 2001.

Marshall, I. Howard. *The Gospel of Luke: A Commentary on the Greek Text*. New International Greek Testament Commentary. Grand Rapids: Eerdmans, 1978.

Massumi, Brian. *A User's Guide to Capitalism and Schizophrenia: Deviations from Deleuze and Guattari*. Cambridge: MIT Press, 1992.

Matthews, Freya. *The Ecological Self*. Savage, Md.: Barnes and Noble Books, 1991.

——. *For Love of Matter: A Contemporary Panpsychism*. Albany: State University of New York Press, 2003.

——. *Reinhabiting Reality: Towards a Recovery of Culture*. Albany: State University of New York Press, 2005.

Maturana, Humberto R., and Francisco J. Varela. 1980. *Autopoiesis and Cognition: The Realization of the Living*. Cambridge: MIT Press, 1986.

Matzkin, A. "Realism and Wavefunction." *European Journal of Physics* 23 (2002): 285–94.

May, Todd. *Gilles Deleuze: An Introduction*. Cambridge: Cambridge University Press, 2005.

Mazis, Glen. *Humans, Animals, Machines: Blurring Boundaries*. Albany: State University of New York Press, 2008.

McCance, Dawne. "*L'écriture limite*: Kristeva's Postmodern Feminist Ethics." *Hypatia* 11, no. 2 (Spring 1996): 141–60.

McCarthy, John. *Remapping Reality: Chaos and Creativity in Science and Literature (Goethe—Nietzsche—Grass)*. Amsterdam: Rodopi, 2006.

McEwan, Ian. *Black Dogs*. London: Vintage, 1988.

McGahern, John. *Amongst Women*. London: Faber, 1990.

——. *The Dark*. London: Faber, 1965.

McGann, Jerome. *The Beauty of Inflections, Literary Investigations in Historical Method and Theory*. Oxford: Clarendon, 1985.

Meeker, Joseph. *The Comedy of Survival: Studies in Literary Ecology*. New York: Charles Scribner's Sons, 1974.

Mellor, Mary. *Feminism and Ecology*. Cambridge: Polity Press, 1997.

Mennell, Stephen. *Norbert Elias: Civilization and the Human Self Image*. Oxford: Blackwell, 1989.

Merleau-Ponty, Maurice. *Consciousness and the Acquisition of Language*. Translated by Hugh J. Silverman. Evanston: Northwestern University Press, 1973. (Originally *La conscience et l'acquisition du language*, 1964.)

———. *Nature: Course Notes from the Collège de France*. Translated by Robert Vallier. Compiled and with notes by Doninique Séglard. Evanston: Northwestern University Press, 2003. (Originally *La nature*, 1994.)

———. *Phenomenology of Perception*. Translated by Colin Smith. London: Routledge, 1962. (Originally *Phénoménologie de la perception*, 1945.)

———. *The Structure of Behavior*. Translated by Alden L. Fisher. Pittsburgh: Duquesne University Press, 2002. (Originally *La structure de comportement*, 1990.)

———. *The Visible and the Invisible*. Translated by Alphonso Lingis. Edited by Claude Lefort. Evanston: Northwestern University Press, 1968. (Originally *Le visible et l'invisible*, 1979.)

Merrell, Floyd. "Charles Sanders Peirce's Concept of the Sign." In *The Routledge Companion to Semiotics and Linguistics*, edited by P. Cobley, 28–39. London and New York: Routledge, 2001.

Miller, Elaine P. "The 'Paradoxical Displacement': Beauvoir and Irigaray on Hegel's Antigone." *Journal of Speculative Philosophy* 14, no. 2 (2000): 121–37.

Milton, John. *Paradise Lost and Paradise Regained*. Edited by C. Ricks. New York and Scarborough Ontario: Signet, 1968.

Mitchell, Robert. "The Transcendental: Deleuze, P. B. Shelley, and the Freedom of Immobility." In *Romanticism and the New Deleuze*, edited by Ron Broglio. Romantic Circles Praxis Series no. 22 (January 2008). www.rc.umd.edu/praxis/deleuze/index./html.

Moeller, Hans-Georg. *Luhmann Explained: From Souls to Systems*. Chicago: Open Court, 2006.

Moi, Toril. *Sexual/Textual Politics: Feminist Literary Theory*. London: Routledge, 1985.

Montgomery, Robert E. *The Visionary D. H. Lawrence: Beyond Philosophy and Art*. Cambridge: Cambridge University Press, 1994.

Moore, Stephen D. "Illuminating the Gospels without the Benefit of Colour: A Plea for Concrete Criticism." *Journal of the American Academy of Religion* 60, no. 2 (Summer 1992): 257–79.

Morton, Timothy. *The Ecological Thought*. Cambridge and London: Harvard University Press, 2010.

———. *Ecology without Nature: Rethinking Environmental Aesthetics*. Cambridge: Harvard University Press, 2007.

Muir, John. *The Mountains of California*. 1894. New York: Penguin, 1985.

Müller, Timo. "Formen kulturökologischen Erzählens von Dickens bis Ishiguro" (Forms of Cultural-Ecological Narrating from Dickens to Ishiguro). In *Kulturökologie und Literatur: Beiträge zu einem transdisziplinären Paradigma der Literaturwissenschaft*, edited by Hubert Zapf, 59–74. Heidelberg: Winter, 2008.

———. "'The Poet's Voice': Dialogicity and Cultural Regeneration in Faulkner's *Absalom, Absalom!*" *Anglia* 126, no. 3 (2008): 503–19.

Muraro, Luisa. "Female Genealogies." In *Engaging with Irigaray*, edited by Carolyn Burke, Naomi Schor, and Maraget Whitford, 317–34. New York: Columbia University Press, 1994.

Murphy, Patrick. *Farther Afield in the Study of Nature-Oriented Literature*. Charlottesville: University of Virginia Press, 2000.

———. *Literature, Nature, and Other: Ecofeminist Critiques*. Albany: State University of New York Press, 1995.

Naess, Arne. *Ecology, Community and Lifestyle*. 1989. Translated and edited by David Rothenberg. Cambridge: Cambridge University Press, 1992.

Nancy, Jean-Luc. *Listening*. Translated by Charlotte Mandell. New York: Fordham University Press, 2007.

Neuman, Yair. *Reviving the Living: Meaning Making in Living Systems*. London: Elsevier, 2008.

Neumeyer, Harald. "Historische und literarische Anthropologie" (Historical and Literary Anthropology). In *Konzepte der Kulturwissenschaften*, edited by Ansgar Nünning and Vera Nünning, 108–31. Stuttgart: Metzler, 2003.

Newton, Tim. *Nature and Sociology*. New York: Routledge, 2007.

Nicholsen, Shierry Weber. *The Love of Nature and the End of the World*. Cambridge: MIT Press, 2002.

Nicolis, Grégoire, and Ilya Prigogine. *Exploring Complexity*. New York: Freeman, 1989.

Noble, Denis. *The Music of Life: Biology beyond Genes*. Oxford: Oxford University Press, 2006.

Nora, Pierre. "Between Memory and History: *Les Lieux de Mémoire*." In "Memory and Counter-Memory," special issue, *Representations* 26 (Spring 1989). (French original published as the introduction to the first volume of *Les lieux de mémoire*.)

———. "From *Lieux de mémoire* to *Realms of Memory*." In *Conflicts and Divisions* (1996), xv–xxiv, vol. 1 of *Realms of Memory: Rethinking the French Past*, under the direction of Nora, English-language edition, 3 vols., edited by Lawrence D. Kritzman, translated by Arthur Goldhammer. New York and Chichester: Columbia University Press, 1996–98.

———, ed. *Les lieux de mémoire*. 7 vols. Paris: Gallimard, 1984–92.

Norris, Christopher. "Quantum Nonlocality and the Challenge to Scientific Realism." *Foundations of Science* 5, no. 1 (March 2000): 3–45.

Nutu, Ela. *Incarnate Word, Inscribed Flesh: John's Prologue and the Postmodern.* Sheffield: Sheffield Phoenix Press, 2007.

O'Connor, Alan. *Raymond Williams: Writing, Culture, Politics.* Oxford and New York: Blackwell, 1989.

Odum, Howard T. *Systems Ecology.* New York: Wiley, 1983.

Oliver, Kelly. "Antigone's Ghost: Undoing Hegel's *Phenomenology of Spirit.*" *Hypatia* 11, no. 1 (1996): 67–90.

———. *Reading Kristeva: Unraveling the Double-Bind.* Bloomington: Indiana University Press, 1993.

Ong, Walter J. *Orality and Literacy.* London: Routledge, 2002.

Ortner, Sherry. "Is Female to Male as Nature Is to Culture?" In *Women, Culture, and Society,* edited by Michelle Zimbalist Rosaldo and Leslie Lamphere, 67–88. Stanford: Stanford University Press, 1974.

Otto, Peter. *Blake's Critique of Transcendence: Love, Jealousy, and the Sublime in "The Four Zoas."* Oxford: Oxford University Press, 2000.

Oxford English Dictionary. dictionary.oed.com.

Paracelsus, Theophrastus. "Von den natürlichen Dingen" (Of the Natural Things). In *Werke,* vol. 1., edited by Will-Erich Peuckert, 297–319. Basel: Schwabe, 1965.

Parham, John. "The Poverty of Ecocritical Theory: E. P. Thompson and the British Perspective." In "Earthographies: Ecocriticism and Culture," edited by Wendy Wheeler and Hugh Dunkerley, special issue, *New Formations* 64 (Spring 2008): 25–36.

Pattel-Gray, Anne. "Dreaming: An Aboriginal Interpretation of the Bible." In *Text & Experience: Towards a Cultural Exegesis of the Bible,* edited by Daniel L. Smith-Christopher, 247–59. Sheffield: Sheffield Academic Press, 1995.

Pattie, Thomas S. "The Creation of the Great Codices." In *The Bible as Book: The Manuscript Tradition,* edited by John L. Sharpe III and Kimberly Van Kampen, 61–72. London: British Library, 1998.

Payne, Michael. *Reading Theory: An Introduction to Lacan, Derrida, and Kristeva.* Oxford: Blackwell, 1993.

Peirce, Charles Sanders. "The Basis of Pragmaticism in the Normative Sciences." In *The Essential Peirce: Selected Philosophical Writings,* vol. 2, *1893–1913,* edited by the Peirce Edition Project, 371–97. Bloomington and Indianapolis: Indiana University Press, 1998.

———. "The Nature of Meaning." In *The Essential Peirce: Selected Philosophical Writings,* vol. 2, *1893–1913,* edited by the Peirce Edition Project, 208–25. Bloomington and Indianapolis: Indiana University Press, 1998.

———. "A Neglected Argument for the Reality of God." In *The Essential Peirce: Selected Philosophical Writings*, vol. 2, *1893–1913*, edited by the Peirce Edition Project, 434–50. Bloomington and Indianapolis: Indiana University Press, 1998.

Phillips, Dana. *The Truth of Ecology: Nature, Culture and Literature in America.* Oxford and New York: Oxford University Press, 2003.

Pliny the Elder. *Natural History: A Selection.* Translated by John F. Healy. London: Penguin, 1991.

Plotnitsky, Arkady. "Chaosmologies: Quantum Field Theory, Chaos and Thought in Deleuze and Guattari's *What Is Philosophy?*" In "Deleuze and Science," edited by John Marks, 40–56, special issue, *Paragraph: A Journal of Modern Critical Theory.* Eastbourne: Edinburgh University Press, 2006.

Plumwood, Val. *Environmental Culture: The Ecological Crisis of Reason.* New York: Routledge, 2006.

———. "Nature, Self, and Gender: Feminism, Environmental Philosophy, and the Critique of Rationalism." In *Ecological Feminist Philosophies*, edited by Karen Warren, 155–180. Bloomington: University of Indiana Press, 1996.

Poe, Edgar Allan. "The Fall of the House of Usher." In *Selected Tales*, 76–95. London: Penguin, 1994.

Polanyi, Michael. *The Tacit Dimension.* London: Routledge and Kegan Paul, 1967.

Prigogine, Ilya. *The End of Certainty: Time, Chaos, and the New Laws of Nature.* New York: The Free Press, 1997.

———. *From Being to Becoming.* San Francisco: Freeman, 1980.

Prigogine, Ilya, and Isabelle Stengers. *Order Out of Chaos.* Toronto: Bantam, 1984.

Ricoeur, Paul. *The Rule of Metaphor: The Creation of Meaning in Language.* Translated by R. Czerny with K. McLaughlin and J. Costello. London and New York: Routledge, 2003.

Rigby, Catherine [Kate]. "Beyond the Frame: Art, Ecology and the Aesthetics of Nature." *Thesis Eleven* 32 (1992): 114–28.

———. "Earth, World, Text: On the (Im)possibility of Ecopoiesis." *New Literary History* 35, no. 3 (2004): 427–42.

———. *Topographies of the Sacred: The Poetics of Place in European Romanticism.* Charlottesville: University of Virginia Press, 2004.

———. "Tuning in to Spirit of Place." In *Changing Places: Re-imagining Australia*, edited by John Cameron, 107–15. Double Bay: Longueville Books, 2003.

———. "Writing after Nature." *Australian Humanities Review* 39–40 (2006). www.australianhumanitiesreview.org/archive/Issue-September-2006/rigby.html.

Rigney, Ann. "Plenitude, Scarcity and the Circulation of Cultural Memory." *Journal of European Studies* 35, no. 1 (2005): 11–28.

Robbins, Vernon. "Historical, Rhetorical, Literary, Linguistic, Cultural, and Artistic Intertextuality—A Response." *Semeia* 80 (1997): 291–303.

Ronell, Avital. *The Telephone Book: Technology, Schizophrenia, Electric Speech.* Lincoln: University of Nebraska Press, 1989.

Rose, Steven. *Lifelines: Biology, Freedom, Determinism.* London: Penguin, 1997.

Rouse, Joseph. "Merleau-Ponty's Existential Conception of Science." In *The Cambridge Companion to Merleau-Ponty,* edited by Taylor Carmen and Mark B. N. Hansen, 265–90. New York: Cambridge University Press, 2005.

Rowland, Herbert, ed. *Goethe, Chaos, and Complexity.* Amsterdam: Rodopi, 2001.

Ryle, Martin. *Ecology and Socialism.* London: Hutchinson Radius, 1988.

———. *Journeys in Ireland: Literary Travelers, Rural Landscapes, Cultural Relations.* Aldershot: Ashgate, 1999.

———. "The Past, the Future and the Golden Age: Some Contemporary Versions of Pastoral." In *The Politics and Pleasures of Consuming Differently,* edited by Kate Soper, Martin Ryle, and Lyn Thomas. London: Palgrave, 2009.

———. "Place, Time and Perspective in John McGahern's Fiction." *Irish Studies in Europe* 2 (2009).

Sandilands, Catriona. "A Flâneur in the Forest?: Strolling Point Pelee with Walter Benjamin." *TOPIA: Canadian Journal of Cultural Studies* 3 (2000): 37–57.

Schacter, Daniel. *Searching for Memory: The Brain, the Mind, and the Past.* New York: Basic Books, 1996.

Schama, Simon. *Landscape and Memory.* London: Harper Perennial, 1996.

Schellmann, Joseph. *Joseph Beuys: The Multiples.* Munich: Edition Schellmann, 1997.

Schlaeger, Jürgen. "Cultural Poetics or Literary Anthropology?" In *Aesthetics and Contemporary Discourse,* REAL 10, edited by Herbert Grabes, 65–80. Tübingen: Narr, 1994.

Schmidt, Jochen. *Goethes Faust: Erster und Zweiter Teil: Grundlagen—Werk—Wirkung* (Goethe's Faust: Part I and II: Background—Texts—Reception). Munich: Beck, 1999.

Schneider, Eric D., and Dorion Sagan. *Into the Cool: Energy Flow, Thermodynamics, and Life.* Chicago: University of Chicago Press, 2005.

Scott, Nathan. *Negative Capability.* New Haven: Yale University Press, 1969.

Sellars, John. "The Point of View of the Cosmos: Deleuze, Romanticism, Stoicism." *Pli: The Warwick Journal of Philosophy* 8 (1999): 1–24.

Selleri, F. "Wave-Particle Duality: Recent Proposals for the Detection of Empty Waves." In *Quantum Theory and Pictures of Reality: Foundations, Interpretations, and New Aspects,* edited by Wolfram Schommers, 297–32. Berlin: Springer, 1989.

Shakespeare, William. *The Complete Works.* Edited by Peter Alexander. London and Glasgow: Collins, 1951.

Shelley, Percy Bysshe. *The Complete Works of Shelley.* Edited by Roger Ingpen and Walter E. Peck. New York: Gordion, 1965.

———. *A Defence of Poetry and Other Essays.* Project Gutenberg, EBook #5428 (April 2004). www.gutenberg.org/etext/5428.

Shklovsky, Victor. "Art as Technique." In *The Critical Tradition: Classic Texts and Contemporary Trends,* edited by David H. Richter, 717–26. 2nd ed. Boston: Bedford/St. Martin's, 1998.

Shubin, Neil. *Your Inner Fish: A Journey into the 3.5-Billion-Year History of the Human Body.* London: Allen Lane, 2008.

Siebert, Charles. *Wickerby: An Urban Pastoral.* New York: Crown, 1997.

Skrbina, David. *Panpsychism in the West.* Cambridge: MIT Press, 2005.

Slovic, Scott. "Love Is Never Abstract: Bioregionalism, Narrative Discourse and the Value of Nature." *Watershed: Environment and Culture* 2, no. 1 (Spring/Summer 2005): 16–23.

Smith, Eric Todd. "Dropping the Subject: Reflections on the Motives for an Ecological Criticism." In *Reading the Earth: New Directions in the Study of Literature and the Environment,* edited by Michael P. Branch, Rochelle Johnson, Daniel Patterson, and Scott Slovic, 29–39. Moscow: University of Idaho Press, 1998.

Smith, Mick. "Lost for Words?: Gadamer and Benjamin on the Nature of Language and the 'Language' of Nature." *Environmental Values* 10, no. 1 (2001): 59–75.

Snyder, Gary. "For All" (1983). In *No Nature: New and Selected Poems,* 308. New York: Pantheon Books, 1993.

———. *The Practice of the Wild.* San Francisco: North Point, 1990.

Sokal, Alan, and Jean Bricmont. "Defense of a Modest Scientific Realism." 1–25. Talk given by Alan Sokal at the Bielefeld-ZiF conference "Welt und Wissen—Monde et Savoir—World and Knowledge," June 18, 2001. www.physics.nyu.edu/faculty/sokal/bielefeld_finalrev.pdf.

Soper, Kate. "Alternative Hedonism, Cultural Theory and the Role of Aesthetic Revisioning." *Cultural Studies* 22 (2008): 567–87.

———. "The Fulfilments of Post-Consumerism and the Politics of Renewal." In *Feelbad Britain: How to Make It Better,* edited by Pat Devine, Andrew Pearmain and David Purdy, 130–41. London: Lawrence and Wishart 2009.

———. "Nature and Culture, the Mythic Register." In *Becoming Human,* edited by Paul Sheehan. Westport, Ct. and London: Praeger, 2003.

———. "The Other Pleasures of Post-Consumerism." *Soundings* 35 (2007): 31–40.

———. "Re-thinking the "Good Life": The Citizenship Dimension of Consumer Disaffection with Consumerism." *Journal of Consumer Culture* 7, no. 2 (2007): 205–29.

———. *What Is Nature?: Culture, Politics and the Non-Human.* Oxford and New York: Blackwell, 1995.

Soper, Kate, Martin Ryle, and Lyn Thomas, eds. *The Politics and Pleasures of Consuming Differently.* London: Palgrave, 2009.

Sotirin, Patty. "Becoming-woman." In *Gilles Deleuze: Key Concepts*, edited by Charles J Stivale, 98–109. Montreal: McGill-Queen's University Press, 2005.

Spencer Brown, George. *Laws of Form*. London: Allen and Unwin, 1969.

Spretnak, Charlene. "Towards an Ecofeminist Spirituality." In *Healing the Wounds: The Promise of Ecofeminism*, edited by Judith Plant, 127–32. Philadelphia: New Society Publishers, 1989.

———. *Resurgence of the Real: Body, Nature and Place in the Hypermodern World*. New York: Routledge, 1999.

Starhawk. *The Fifth Sacred Thing*. New York: Bantam, 1993.

Stephenson, Neal. *Zodiac*. 1988. New York: Bantam, 2003.

Stivale, Charles J., ed. *Gilles Deleuze: Key Concepts*. Montreal: McGill-Queen's University Press, 2005.

Swales, Martin. "The Character and Characterization of Faust." In *A Companion to Goethe's "Faust" Parts I and II*, edited by Paul Bishop, 28–55. New York: Camden, 2006.

Swirski, Peter. *Of Literature and Knowledge: Explorations in Narrative Thought Experiments, Evolution and Game Theory*. London: Routledge, 2007.

Taylor, Peter. "Distributed Agency within Intersecting Ecological, Social, and Scientific Processes." In *Cycles of Contingency: Developmental Systems and Evolution*, edited by Susan Oyama, Paul E. Griffiths, and Russell D. Gray, 313–32. Cambridge: MIT Press, 2001.

Thoreau, Henry David. *Excursions*. Edited by Joseph J. Moldenhauer. Princeton: Princeton University Press, 2007.

———. *The Maine Woods*. Edited by Joseph J. Moldenhauer. Princeton: Princeton University Press, 1972.

———. *Walden*. Edited by J. Lyndon Shanley. Princeton: Princeton University Press, 1971.

———. *The Writings of Henry David Thoreau: Journal*. Edited by John C. Broderick et al. 7 vols. to date. Princeton: Princeton University Press, 1981 .

Tiedemann, Rolf. "Dialectics at a Standstill." Translated by Gary Smith and André Lefevere. In Walter Benjamin, *Das Passagen-Werk (The Arcades Project)*, translated and edited by Howard Eiland and Kevin McLaughlin, 929–45. Cambridge: Belknap Press of Harvard University Press, 1999.

Toadvine, Ted. "The Primacy of Desire and its Ecological Consequences." In *Ecophenomenology: Back to the Earth Itself*, edited by Charles S. Brown and Toadvine, 139–53. Albany: State University Press of New York, 2003.

Toffler, Alvin. Foreword to Prigogine and Stengers, *Order Out of Chaos: Man's New Dialogue with Nature*, xi–xxvi.

Ulanowicz, Robert E. *Ecology, the Ascendent Perspective*. New York: Columbia University Press, 1997.

van der Laan, James. "Faust and Textual Chaos." In *Goethe, Chaos and Complexity,* edited by Herbert Rowland, 105–15. Amsterdam: Rodopi, 2001.

———. "Faust the Technological Mastermind." *Bulletin of Science, Technology & Society* 21, no. 1 (2001): 7–13.

———. *Seeking Meaning for Goethe's "Faust."* London: Continuum, 2007.

van Frassen, Bas C. *Quantum Mechanics: An Empiricist View.* Oxford: Clarendon Press, 1991.

Vološinov, V. N. *Freudianism: A Critical Sketch.* Translated by I. R. Titunik. Edited by Titunik and Neal H. Bruss. 1976. Bloomington: Indiana University Press, 1987.

———. *Marxism and the Philosophy of Language.* Translated by Ladislav Matejka and I. R. Titunik. Cambridge: Harvard University Press, 1986.

von Bormann, Alexander. *Die Erde will ein freies Geleit: Deutsche Naturlyrik aus sechs Jahrhunderten* (The Earth Seeks Safe-Conduct: German Nature Poetry from Six Centuries). Stuttgart: Reclam 1987.

von Foerster, Heinz. "Cybernetics of Cybernetics." In *Communication and Control in Society,* edited by Klaus Krippendorff, 5–8. New York: Gordon and Breach, 1979.

von Molnár, Géza. "Hidden in Plain View: Another Look at Goethe's *Faust.*" *Goethe Yearbook* 11 (2002): 33–76.

von Uexküll, Jakob. "The Theory of Meaning." Translated by B. Stone and H. Weiner. Special issue, *Semiotica,* edited by Thure von Uexküll, 42 (1982): 42–85.

Wainwright, Elaine M. *Shall We Look for Another?: A Feminist Rereading of the Matthean Jesus.* Maryknoll: Orbis Books, 1998.

Wallace, Jeff, Rod Jones, and Sophie Nield, eds. *Raymond Williams Now: Knowledge, Limits and the Future.* Basingstoke and London: Macmillan, 1997.

Walls, Laura Dassow. "Romancing the Real: Thoreau's Technology of Inscription." In *A Historical Guide to Henry David Thoreau,* edited by William E. Cain, 123–51. New York: Oxford University Press, 2000.

Warren, Karen J. "The Power and the Promise of Ecological Feminism." In *Ecological Feminist Philosophies,* edited by Karen J. Warren, 19–41. Bloomington: Indiana University Press, 1996.

Watzlawick, Paul, Janet Beavin, and Don Jackson. *Pragmatics of Human Communication: A Study of Interactional Patterns, Pathologies and Paradoxes.* New York: Norton, 1967.

Waugh, Patricia. *Practising Postmodernism/Reading Modernism.* London: Edward Arnold, 1992.

Welty, Eudora. *The Collected Stories of Eudora Welty.* New York: Harcourt, 1980.

Werber, Bernard. *Empire of the Ants (Le jour des fourmis).* Translated by Margaret Rocques. New York: Bantam, 1998.

Westling, Louise. "Darwin in Arcadia: The Human Animal Dance from Gilgamesh to Virginia Woolf." *Anglia* 124 (2006): 11–43.

———. "Virginia Woolf and the Flesh of the World." *New Literary History* 30 (1999): 855–75.

White, Lynn, Jr. "The Historical Roots of Our Ecologic Crisis." *Science* 155 (1967): 1203–7.

Whitford, Margaret. *Luce Irigaray: Philosophy in the Feminine.* London: Routledge, 1991.

Wilde, Keith, and Michael T. Caley. "An Introduction to Jerzy A. Wojciechowski's Theory of The Ecology of Knowledge." *Trumpeter* 20, no. 1 (2004): 44–63.

Williams, James. "Science and Dialectics in the Philosophies of Deleuze, Bachelard and DeLanda." In "Deleuze and Science," edited by John Marks, 98–114, special issue, *Paragraph: A Journal of Modern Critical Theory.* Eastbourne: Edinburgh University Press, 2006.

Williams, Linda. "Modernity and the Other Body: The Human contract with Mute Animality." In *The Future of Flesh: A Cultural Survey of the Body,* edited by Z. Detsi-Diamante, K. Kitsi-Mitakou, and E. Yiannopoulo, 221–39. New York: Palgrave, 2009.

Williams, Raymond. "Base and Superstructure in Marxist Cultural Theory." *New Left Review* 82 (1973): 3–16.

———. "Beyond Actually Existing Socialism." Review of Rudolph Bahro, *The Alternative in Eastern Europe. New Left Review* (1980): 3–19. Reprinted in Williams, *Problems in Materialism and Culture.* London, Verso, 1980.

———. *Border Country.* London: Chatto and Windus, 1960.

———. *The Country and the City.* 1973. London: Hogarth, 1993.

———. "Culture Is Ordinary." In *Conviction,* edited by Norman Mackenzie. London: McGibbon and Kee, 1958. Reprinted in *Border Country: Raymond Williams in Adult Education,* edited by John McIlroy and Sallie Westwood, 89–102. Leicester: National Institute for Adult Continuing Education, 1993.

———. *Democracy and Parliament.* London: Socialist Society, 1982.

———. "Ideas of Nature." *Times Literary Supplement* 4 December 1970.

———. *Marxism and Literature.* London and New York: Oxford University Press, 1977.

———. *People of the Black Mountains.* 2 vols. London: Chatto and Windus, 1989 and 1990.

———. *Politics and Letters: Interviews with New Left Review.* London: New Left Books, 1979.

———. "The Politics of Nuclear Disarmament." In *Exterminism and Cold War,* edited by New Left Review, 65–85. London: New Left Books, 1982.

———. *Problems in Materialism and Culture.* London, Verso: 1980.

———. "The Red and the Green." Review of Rudolf Bahro, *Socialism and Survival. London Review of Books* 5, no. 2 (February 1983): 3.

——. "Response to the Debate." In *The Forward March of Labour Halted?* edited by Martin Jacques and Francis Mulhern, 142–52. London: Verso, 1981.

——. Review of Alva Myrdal, *The Dynamics of European Nuclear Disarmament.* *Guardian,* 13 August 1981, 12.

——. *Socialism and Ecology.* London: SERA, undated [1982].

——. "Socialists and Coalitionists." In *The Future of the Left,* edited by James Curran, 182–94. Cambridge: Polity Press and New Socialist, 1984.

——. "Towards Many Socialisms." In *Socialism on the Eve of the Twenty-first Century,* edited by Miloš Nicolić, 294–311. London: Verso, 1985.

——. *Towards 2000.* London: Chatto and Windus, 1985.

Williams, Tess. "Carnival in Space and Time: Shared Metaphors of Change in 'Post Neo-Darwinian' Evolutionary Theory and Feminist Science Fiction." Ph.D. diss., University of Western Australia, 2008.

Winterson, Jeanette. *Gut Symmetries.* 1997. London: Granta Books, 1998.

Winthrop-Young, Geoffrey. Interview by Rudolf Maresch. "Die Zeit der Kulturkriege ist vorbei: Über Schaumschläger und Beamte, den Import europäischer Theorie und ihr Irrelevant-Werden in Europa" (The Era of Cultural Wars Is Over: On Hot-Air Merchants, Civil Servants, the Import of European Theory, and Its Becoming Irrelevant in Europe). *Telepolis,* 23 April, 2006. www.heise .de/tp/r4/artikel/22/22430/1.html.

Wittig, Monique. *The Straight Mind and Other Essays.* Boston: Beacon Press, 1992.

Wohlfarth, Irving. "Et Cetera? The Historian as Chiffonier." In *Walter Benjamin and the Arcades Project,* edited by Beatrice Hanssen, 12–32. London: Continuum, 2006.

Wolfe, Cary. *Animal Rites: American Culture, the Discourse of Species, and Posthumanist Theory.* Chicago: University of Chicago Press, 2003.

——. Introduction to *Zoontologies: The Question of the Animal,* edited by Wolfe, ix– xxiii. Minneapolis: University of Minnesota Press, 2003.

——, ed. *Zoontologies: The Question of the Animal.* Minneapolis: University of Minnesota Press, 2003.

Woolf, Virginia. *Between the Acts.* New York: Harcourt, 1941.

Wordsworth, William. *The Fourteen-Book Prelude.* Edited by W. J. B. Owen. Ithaca: Cornell University Press, 1985.

——. *The Prelude; or, Growth of a Poet's Mind.* New York: D. Appleton and Co., 1850. *http://books.google.co.uk/books?id=a-skopU3lxMC.*

——. *Selected Poems of William Wordsworth.* Edited by Roger Sharrock. London: Heinemann, 1958.

World Bank Environment and Social Development Sector, East Asia and Pacific Region. *Faiths and the Environment: World Bank Support 2000–05.* Washington: International Bank for Reconstruction and Development, 2006.

Wright, Judith. *Collected Poems.* Sydney: Angus and Robertson, 1994.

Yamashita, Karen Tei. *Through the Arc of the Rain Forest.* Minneapolis: Coffee House Press, 1990.

———. *Tropic of Orange.* Minneapolis: Coffee House Press, 1997.

Yates, Frances A. *The Art of Memory.* London: Routledge and Kegan Paul, 1966.

Young, Julian. *Heidegger's Philosophy of Art.* Cambridge: Cambridge University Press, 2001.

Zapf, Hubert. "Literary Ecology and the Ethics of Texts." *New Literary History* 39, no. 4 (2008): 847–68.

———. *Literatur als kulturelle Ökologie: Zur kulturellen Funktion imaginativer Texte an Beispielen des amerikanischen Romans* (Literature as Cultural Ecology: On the Cultural Function of Imaginative Texts, with Examples from the American Novel). Tübingen: Niemeyer, 2002.

Žižek, Slavoj. *In Defense of Lost Causes.* London and New York: Verso, 2008.

Zohar, Danah. *The Quantum Self: Human Nature and Consciousness Defined by the New Physics.* New York: Quill / William Morrow, 1990.

Contributors

HANNES BERGTHALLER is Associate Professor in the Department of Foreign Languages and Literatures at National Chung Hsing University in Taichung, Taiwan. He is the author of *Populäre Ökologie* (2007), a discussion of the literature and cultural history of the U.S. environmental movement, and coeditor of *Addressing Modernity*, a volume on Niklas Luhmann's social systems theory and American studies (together with Carsten Schinko). His other publications include essays on the work of Rachel Carson, Toni Morrison, Dr. Seuss, Walt Whitman, among other subjects. He is a founding member and the current Vice President of the European Association for the Study of Literature, Culture and the Environment (EASLCE).

CHRISTOPHER COHOON is currently an Invited Researcher at Université Paris-Sorbonne (Paris IV) and a doctoral candidate in philosophy at SUNY Stony Brook in New York, where he is writing a dissertation on Emmanuel Levinas and ecophenomenology.

ANNE ELVEY is an Adjunct Research Fellow in the Centre for Comparative Literature and Cultural Studies at Monash University, an Honorary Research Associate with the Melbourne College of Divinity, and an Associate Research Fellow of Trinity College Theological School. Her publications include *An Ecological Feminist Reading of the Gospel of Luke: A Gestational Paradigm* (2005) and two poetry chapbooks, *Stolen Heath* (2009) and *Claimed by Country* (2010). Her current research focuses on the materiality of the text. She is the convenor of a Melbourne-based ecological spirituality and theology research group and the 2011 President of the Fellowship for Biblical Studies, Victoria.

AXEL GOODBODY is Professor of German and European Culture at the University of Bath. He has published in German and English on twentieth-century German literature and film in its social and political context, and on ecocritical theory. A past President of the European Association for the Study of Literature,

Culture, and Environment (EASLCE), he is editor of the Rodopi book series "Nature, Literature and Culture," and associate editor of the online journal of European ecocriticism *Ecozon@*.

LUCE IRIGARAY is a leading philosopher of the twentieth and twenty-first centuries. She is the Director of Research at the Centre National de Recherche Scientifique in France. In addition to holding a Ph.D. in philosophy—*Speculum of the Other Woman* (French original 1974) was first presented as a doctoral thesis on the position of woman in the history of philosophy—she is trained in linguistics, philology, psychology, and psychoanalysis. Her work focuses on the elaboration of a culture of human subjectivity as sexuate, something she approaches through different disciplines: philosophical, scientific, political, and also poetic. Such an undertaking implies a cultural deconstruction aiming toward a return to our natural origin with a view to its cultivation and sharing, from the most intimate to the most global and universal level. She is the author of more than thirty books, including *An Ethics of Sexual Difference* (1985), *I Love to You* (1992), *To Be Two* (1997), *Between East and West* (1999), *The Way of Love* (2002), and *Sharing the World* (2008). Her work has been translated into many languages.

MARK LUSSIER is Professor of English at Arizona State University. He is the author of *Romantic Dynamics: The Poetics of Physicality* and *Blake, Lacan, and the Critique of Culture* (2010), and a coeditor of *Engaged Romanticism: Romanticism as Praxis* (2008). His essays on William Blake have appeared in numerous collections and journals.

TIMOTHY MORTON is Professor of English (Literature and the Environment) at the University of California, Davis. He is the author of seven books, including *The Ecological Thought* (2010) and *Ecology without Nature* (2007), and more than sixty essays on literature, ecology, philosophy, and food.

TIMO MÜLLER is Assistant Professor of English at the University of Augsburg, Germany. His main research interests are modernism and literary theory. He has published articles on Faulkner, Joyce, and ecocriticism, as well as a full-length study, *The Self as Object in Modernist Fiction: James, Joyce, Hemingway* (2010).

PATRICK D. MURPHY is Professor of English at the University of Central Florida, where he teaches nature-oriented courses on literary works and cultural studies issues ranging from nature poetry to science fiction, and from books on hurricanes to climate-change texts and websites. Founder of the journal *ISLE: Interdisciplinary Studies in Literature and Environment* in 1993, he played a leading role in theorizing ecocriticism in the early years of the movement. His publications include *Ecocritical Explorations in Literary and Cultural Studies* (2009), *Farther Afield in the Study of Nature-Oriented Literature* (2000), and *Literature, Nature, and Other: Ecofeminist Critiques* (1995).

TREVOR NORRIS is Senior Lecturer in English at London Metropolitan University. His research focuses on literary modernism and modernist aesthetics. He is currently writing a study of the correspondences between the novels and critical writings of D. H. Lawrence and the thought of Martin Heidegger.

SERPIL OPPERMANN is Professor of English at Hacettepe University in Ankara, Turkey. She is the author of a book in Turkish, *Postmodern Theory of History: Historiography, New Historicism and the Novel* (1999; 2006), and of articles on postmodernism, literary theory, ecophilosophy, and ecocriticism. Currently she is working on theorizing material-discursive practices in ecocritical thought, and coediting a book on feminist ecocriticism with Simon Estok and Greta Gaard. Her new book project with Serenella Iovino and Scott Slovic concerns material ecocriticism.

KATE RIGBY, FAHA, is Associate Professor of Comparative Literature and Cultural Studies at Monash University. Her research ranges across German studies and European philosophy, literature and religion, and culture and ecology. Her most recent book, *Topographies of the Sacred* (2004), is an ecocritical study of European Romantic-era philosophies and aesthetics of nature and place. She is a coeditor of the journal *Philosophy Activism Nature*, and was the founding President of the Association for the Study of Literature and Environment (Australia–New Zealand).

MARTIN RYLE is a Reader in English at the University of Sussex. Within a broad interest in twentieth-century and contemporary fiction, he has engaged especially with novels that represent, criticize, and suggest alternatives to globalized consumer culture. His recent publications discuss Michel Houellebecq, John McGahern, Ali Smith, Kazuo Ishiguro, and others. His *Counter-Consumerism and Its Pleasures*, coedited with Kate Soper and Lyn Thomas (2008), offers a general rethinking of the relations between work, consumption, happiness, and sustainability.

CATRIONA (CATE) SANDILANDS is Professor and the Canada Research Chair in the Faculty of Environmental Studies at York University. Her current work concerns the role of literature and criticism in the formation of an environmental public culture, a project that has brought her into conversation with authors as diverse as Hannah Arendt, Cormac McCarthy, and Jane Rule. She also maintains a strong interest in the intersections between queer theory and environmental politics.

KATE SOPER is Emeritus Professor of Philosophy at London Metropolitan University and Visiting Professor at Brighton University. She has published widely on environmental philosophy, aesthetics of nature, and cultural theory. Her books include *What Is Nature?: Culture, Politics and the Non-Human* (1995) and (with Martin Ryle) *To Relish the Sublime? Culture and Self-Realisation in Postmodern Times* (2002). She has recently completed a research project on "alternative hedonism," and is a coeditor of *Citizenship and Consumption* (2008) and *The Politics and Pleasures of Consuming Differently* (2009).

HEATHER I. SULLIVAN is Associate Professor of German and Chair of the interdisciplinary minor in comparative literature at Trinity University in San Antonio. Her current research is on Goethe, ecocriticism, and science. She is the author of *The Intercontextuality of Self and Nature in Ludwig Tieck's Early Works* (1997). Her essays have appeared in the *Goethe Yearbook, Monatshefte, Interdisciplinary Studies in Literature and the Environment, Studies in Eighteenth-Century Culture,* the *European Romantic Review, Bulletin of Science, Technology, and Society,* and *1650–1850: Ideas, Aesthetics, and Inquiries in the Early Modern Era.*

LAURA DASSOW WALLS is John H. Bennett Jr. Chair of Southern Letters at the University of South Carolina. She has published widely on Thoreau (*Seeing New Worlds,* 1995), Emerson (*Emerson's Life in Science,* 2003), and related figures. She coedited the *Oxford Handbook of Transcendentalism* (2010) and is the editor of *The Concord Saunterer: A Journal of Thoreau Studies.* Her most recent book, *Passage to Cosmos: Alexander von Humboldt and the Shaping of America* (2009), won the OAH's Merle Curti Award for best book in intellectual history and the MLA's James Russell Lowell Prize for the best book in literary studies.

LOUISE WESTLING is Professor of English and Environmental Studies at the University of Oregon. Her research has migrated from a focus on landscape imagery in American literature to ecocritical theory and critical animal studies. Key publications are *Sacred Groves and Ravaged Gardens: The Fiction of Eudora Welty, Carson McCullers, and Flannery O'Connor* (1985) and *The Green Breast of the New World: Landscape, Gender, and American Literature* (1996). At present she is completing a book on Merleau-Ponty, animal studies, and language.

WENDY WHEELER is Professor of English at London Metropolitan University. She is the author of *A New Modernity? Change in Science, Literature and Politics* (1999), *The Whole Creature: Complexity, Biosemiotics and the Evolution of Culture* (2006), and many essays on biological systems theory and biosemiotics. She is the coeditor (with Jeremy Gilbert) of *New Formations: A Journal of Culture/Theory/Politics,* and sits on the editorial board of *Green Letters,* the journal of ASLE-U.K.

LINDA WILLIAMS is Associate Professor of Art History and Critical Theory at RMIT University in Melbourne, Australia, where she leads a research cluster on art and the environment. She has published widely on visual culture, and on transdisciplinary approaches to cultural and social histories of the *longue durée* and ecocritique—especially in response to human-animal relations. Her recent research also investigates cultural history in relation to the history and philosophy of science.

Index

Lightning Source UK Ltd.
Milton Keynes UK
UKOW04f1100020714

234424UK00001B/11/P